TALES OF AN ECOTOURIST

TALES OF AN
ECOTOURIST

WHAT TRAVEL TO WILD PLACES CAN TEACH US ABOUT CLIMATE CHANGE

MIKE GUNTER JR.

excelsior editions

STATE UNIVERSITY OF NEW YORK PRESS

Published by State University of New York Press, Albany

© 2018 State University of New York

Excelsior Editions is an imprint of State University of New York Press

For information, contact State University of New York Press, Albany, NY
www.sunypress.edu

Production, Ryan Morris
Marketing, Kate R. Seburyamo

Library of Congress Cataloging-in-Publication Data

Names: Gunter, Michael M., 1969- author.
Title: Tales of an ecotourist : what travel to wild places can teach us about climate change / Mike Gunter, Jr.
Description: Excelsior editions. | Albany : State University of New York Press, 2018. | Includes bibliographical references and index.
Identifiers: LCCN 2016051106 (print) | LCCN 2017016471 (ebook) | ISBN 9781438466804 (e-book) | ISBN 9781438466798 (hardcover : alk. paper) | ISBN 9781438466781 (pbk. : alk. paper)
Subjects: LCSH: Ecotourism. | Tourism—Environmental aspects. | Climatic changes. | Global environmental change. | Gunter, Michael M., 1969—Travel.
Classification: LCC G156.5.E26 (ebook) | LCC G156.5.E26 G86 2017 (print) | DDC 304.2/5--dc23
LC record available at https://lccn.loc.gov/2016051106

10 9 8 7 6 5 4 3 2 1

Dedicated to JUDY AND MICHAEL GUNTER for all the sacrifices you made in helping create a better world for your children. May our larger society mimic your dedication to younger generations, continually reminding itself that we do not inherit the Earth from our ancestors, but rather, in the words of Wendell Berry and others, we borrow it from our children.

CONTENTS

ACKNOWLEDGMENTS

SPANNING SEVEN CONTINENTS and over a dozen years, this project was a long time coming—with many individuals to thank. Nowhere near all of them can be noted here, but a number deserve special mention. Pulitzer Prize–winning author E. O. Wilson graciously reviewed and endorsed my first book, *Building the Next Ark*, and more pointedly, provided validation for this project during a brief conversation at the 2005 Jackson Hole Wildlife Film Festival. Our discussion on the potential for ecotourism in addressing daunting aspects of developing-world poverty continued to resonate over the years, even as other research projects and teaching commitments commanded my attention. Three additional renowned environmentalists I hosted here at Rollins provided further motivation through their work and more extended conversations. Larry Schweiger, president and CEO of the National Wildlife Federation; Mark Plotkin, president of the Amazon Conservation Team; and Bill Meadows, former president of The Wilderness Society, each offered valuable insight and encouragement.

In many ways, though, none of this would have been possible but for a mix of other individuals much earlier in my life. In camping trips throughout middle Tennessee, scout leader Norm Dukes instilled in me an appreciation for the natural world from an early age, while Jack Sallee taught me not only American history but, quite honestly, both the art and science of becoming a student. More specifically, in terms of the art of writing, Ken Bain cultivated my early work at Vanderbilt University, and Charles Denning, my editor in yet another life at the Cookeville *Herald-Citizen*, showed patience in developing a green, in many shades of the term, reporter.

In academia, I also benefited much from the wisdom of my mentors at the University of Kentucky, Ernie Yanarella and Karen Mingst, both of whom showed similar patience and offered endless encouragement during my graduate student career. Special thanks also to my mentor-colleague Craig Warkentin, now a professor at SUNY Oswego, who graciously advised me during the initial stages of academia, and the late Christopher C. Joyner of Georgetown University, who took time over a number of years to share his expertise, ranging from the Antarctic Treaty System to his time with the experience-driven Semester at Sea program. And most notably, I forever owe a debt to my father, Michael Gunter, a world-renowned academic in Kurdish studies, for providing a window into the life of academia at such an early age, and igniting my initial intellectual curiosity as well as my love for learning more about the world through travel.

At Rollins College, I've been fortunate to work with a number of supportive colleagues and administrators over the last seventeen years. Three deans were particularly instrumental in funding different stages of this work, and for that I am deeply grateful to Roger Casey, Laurie Joyner, and Jennifer Cavenaugh. Many thanks also to my colleagues in the departments of Environmental Studies and Political Science, especially Tom Lairson for pushing me to continue to expand as a scholar and Barry Allen for introducing me to Costa Rica and highlighting its ecotourism mecca, Monteverde. Thanks also to Bobby Davis, Bob Moore, Julian Chambliss, Bruce Stephenson, Sally Lairson, Ed Royce, Socky O'Sullivan, Gary Williams, Ed Cohen, Deb Wellman, Dan Chong, Lee Lines, Lauren Bradley, Jonathan Miller, Susan Montgomery, Yusheng Yao, Alexander Boguslawski, Patricia Tomé, Keith Wittingham, Doug Little, Gail Sinclair, Micki Meyer, Julia Maskivker, Karim Rahemtulla, Mark Anderson, and Josh Almond for sharing their knowledge over the years. Their continuing advice and friendship is greatly valued.

Special thanks also to the many unnamed professionals around the globe who dedicate their lives daily to poverty alleviation and environmental activism, not to mention the scientists themselves who study climate change. Having participated in its 2015 workshop in Miami, thanks to Meredith Hein and Mary Conway Dato-on, Al Gore's Climate Reality Project deserves emphasis for their inspiration and annual training of citizen activists around the globe. Distinguished Professor of Atmospheric Science and director of the Earth System Science Center at Pennsylvania State University Michael Mann generously shared his famous hockey-stick graph, while Ralph Keeling, professor at Scripps Institution of Oceanography and director of the Scripps

CO_2 Program, the measurement program behind the Keeling curve, similarly shared the Mauna Loa Observatory graph.

More pointedly, in connection with my travels in Ecuador and the Galápagos Islands, I must thank native Galápagos naturalist and park guide Bitinia Espinoza; the entire crew of the Lammer Law; Roger Casey, for developing our expedition and sharing his wide breadth of travel experience; former director of environmental programs at the Associated Colleges of the South Elizabeth MacNabb, for facilitating partial funding; my faculty colleagues on the trip, particularly Rachel Simmons and Dana Hargrove, for sharing their masterful artistic journals; and the staff of the Charles Darwin Foundation, Galápagos National Park, and Cerro Blanco Protected Forest outside Guayaquil.

From Australia and the Great Barrier Reef I am indebted to Matt Curnock, research projects officer in ecosystem sciences at the Australian Tropical Science and Innovation Precinct at James Cook University; Samantha Stone-Jovicich, research scientist and anthropologist also with the Australian Tropical Science and Innovation Precinct; Chris Briggs, former director of tourism and recreation at the Great Barrier Reef Marine Park Authority; Paul Marshall, former lead scientist from the Australia-Caribbean Collaboration on Climate Change and Coral Reefs at the Great Barrier Reef Marine Park Authority; Julie Traweek, project manager for the Sea Turtle Foundation; Jeremy Goldberg, doctoral student at James Cook University; Doug Baird, environment and compliance director for Quicksilver in Cairns; Gareth Phillips, marine biologist at Reef Teach in Cairns; Sonia Batley, information services project officer at the Great Barrier Reef Marine Park Authority; Rhonda Banks, cartographer at the Spatial Data Centre for the Great Barrier Reef Marine Park Authority; Laurie Murphy, associate professor of business at James Cook University; Sue Lim, science communicator at Australian Institute of Marine Science in Cape Ferguson; Ross McLennan, operator manager for Hidden Valley Cabins outside of Townsville; Patricia O'Callaghan, general manager of tourism and events for Townsville Enterprise; Col McKenzie, executive director of the Association of Marine Park Tourism Operators; Sigrid Eve Pope, marine biologist and guide with Frankland Islands Cruise and Dive; Rick Braley, marine biologist and environmental activist with Aquasearch; Wendy Tubman, coordinator of the North Queensland Conservation Council; the staff of Sunlover Reef Cruises in Cairns, Calypso Reef Cruises out of Port

Douglas, and Frankland Islands Cruise and Dive; as well as my colleagues Denise Cummings, Giselda Beaudin, and Mike Rainaldi at Rollins for their valued advice and financial support.

From South Africa's Hluhluwe-iMfolozi individuals of note include Dave Druce, park ecologist and project director; Abednig Mkhwanazi, my Zulu language teacher and research technician; dozens of rangers who patrol the park daily, especially Bheki, Njbula, Jacob, Johan, Biella, Mandella, Mealla, Mpuma, and Jericho, for sharing their time and wisdom with me; the congenial and irreplaceable south camp manager Cameron as well as assistant camp manager Caiphus Khumalo and our cook Studla; Dennis Wood, design studio manager at Ezemvelo KZN Wildlife; Mary Ellen Rowe, expedition coordinator from Earthwatch; Alix Morris, senior science writer at Earthwatch; and the entire staff of KwaZulu-Natal Wildlife Parks as well as iSimangaliso Wetland Park within the St. Lucia Estuary.

From the Peruvian Amazon and Tambopata Research Center I wish to thank zoologist and former TRC director Donald Brightsmith (now with Schubot Exotic Bird Health Center at Texas A&M University); the most generous and polite tent-mate one could ever envision, Berwyn Roberts; fellow Earthwatch travelers and macaw nest observation coconspirators Ellen Wang, Brenda Oswald, Carol Colip, and the late Jim Devaney; our Infierno community guides Reuben Paiva and Cesar; Earthwatch volunteer and photographer Jeff Wilson; the entire staff of Posada Amazonas and Tambopata Research Center; Rainforest Expeditions and Earthwatch expedition coordinator Tina Woolston; and Tambopata photographer Jeff Cremer. Special thanks also to the Ese'eja native community within the community of Infierno for sharing their home.

From Antarctica, this work was only possible thanks to Lapataia Bay Expeditions and expedition leader Kara Weller; marine biologist Anjali Pande; ornithologist David Drummond; historian Shane Murphy; geologist Wolfgang Bluemel; zodiac drivers and naturalists Vladimir Seliverstov, Alex Preston, and Julian Onyszezuk as well as the officers and entire crew of the now sadly lost-at-sea *M/V Lyubov Orlova*; and several park guides in Tierra del Fuego National Park outside Ushuaia. Special thanks also to a Cornell Distinguished Faculty award for making this particular journey financially possible, and to my artist colleague Rachel Simmons for the vision to create a once-in-a-lifetime opportunity.

At SUNY Press, thanks to Michael Rinella for first taking on this project, Ryan Morris, Aimee Harrison, Daniel Otis, and Rafael Chaiken for their deft guidance during the production process, Kate Seburyamo as a stellar promotions manager, and the entire team within SUNY as instrumental in crafting the more polished final product before you. Similarly, two anonymous reviewers deserve my gratitude for their thoughtful input and making this work all the stronger with their suggestions. I also wish to thank deeply my former literary agent Lisa Hagan, whose faith in this project never wavered, and my administrative assistants here at Rollins, Nakia Gater, Alison Reeve, and Austa Weaver, who helped keep me on track with other teaching and administrative responsibilities throughout the research and writing of this book.

Thanks also to my family and extended family and friends for their support over the years, including my Thursday night YMCA basketball buddies, who provided weekly chiding and commentary on the progress of this project. Of special note, my parents, Judy and Michael Gunter, have sacrificed much for their children and continue to model a delightfully infectious passion for life, from locales both near and far. My hope is that you see this work as an extension of all your love and support. And finally, warm hugs and kisses to my confidant, best friend, and expert traveling partner Linda as well as our three lovely children, Ansleigh, Malachi, and Emerson, who are fast becoming travel experts in their own right. You each paradoxically postponed yet simultaneously sped up this project in your own special way. For that, and much, much more, I will always be grateful.

Winter Park, FL
January 2017

INTRODUCTION
Seeing the World Anew

> You cannot solve a problem from the same consciousness
> that created it. You must learn to see the world anew.
>
> —Albert Einstein

TRAVELING WITH YOUR CHILDREN should be mandatory in the parenting handbook—the longer and farther, the better. Yet Americans, even those without kids, spend on average only thirteen paid vacation days a year, according to the World Tourism Organization. That's not very good. Canadians spend twenty-six days. Brazilians enjoy thirty-four. The French thirty-seven. And Italians play for forty-two.[1] Indeed, according to a May 2013 report by the Center for Economic and Policy Research in Washington, D.C., the United States is alone among twenty-one advanced economies worldwide in failing to guarantee *any* paid vacation time or holidays for its workers.

Yes, but we are much more productive, you say.

Not necessarily true. According to the Organization for Economic Cooperation and Development, Belgium, Norway, Ireland, and Luxembourg all placed ahead of the United States in 2012 in terms of GDP per hour worked.[2] In short, the American workplace might not be a carbon copy of the inefficiency parodied on TV sitcoms such as *The Office*, but there is a bit of fact in their fiction.

You already know this deep down. There is a line of diminishing returns when it comes to worker productivity. You need breaks. You actually perform better when you take breaks from work. It's healthier–and more productive.

1

But I digress. This is *not* a book about taking time off from work, at least not for the sake of workplace productivity. There is another rationale at its heart: travel makes us wiser. We learn best from experiences that are meaningful, directed, and allow for reflection afterward.

Two and a half centuries ago, French philosopher Jean-Jacques Rousseau championed experience as the preferred method to fully develop knowledge.[3] Pioneering twentieth-century American educator John Dewey built on this legacy, suggesting that traditional, authoritarian education was misdirected in its emphasis on delivering knowledge from an all-knowing lectern and needed to better utilize direct student experiences.[4] He argued that students build their knowledge around prior experiences, and his work paved the way for the active learning, service learning, and environmental or outdoor education of today.

When you consider it, people understand this intuitively from their early childhood experiences, from learning how to read or to ride a bike. Name-dropping famous philosophers such as Dewey and Rousseau isn't necessary. We already know experiential education drives our understanding of the world around us.

You have your own experiences to draw on here. Recall the first sights, smells, and sounds of a metropolis such as New York City. Or if you had the good fortune to visit a foreign land as a youngster, remember when you heard that thick, unknown accent for the first time and attempted to process it through background context and body language. Recall the wonderment when you got your first glimpse of a famous landmark you'd read about— or tasted an exotic dish you were nervous about sampling. You might not have realized it then, but you were utilizing what arguably is our species' greatest strength, its intellectual curiosity. You were learning for the pure joy of it.

There is an important and underappreciated corollary to travel as well. It's simply healthy to spend some quality family time together. It is somewhat ironic that it happens on the road instead of at home. Without all the distractions of the next sports practice, play date, television show, computer task, and video game, though, it's amazing how much you actually talk with your kids. Furthermore, it's not necessarily where you travel that is important; it's simply *that* you travel. You've heard the quip before: treasure not the destination but the journey. Travel teaches you something about yourself, and your family grows from it.

Over the years, travel with our families has become a rite of passage of sorts, or perhaps more accurately, a stint of hazing, particularly when traveling with little ones. To be honest, although few of us go to the extremes of Chevy Chase and the Griswold family vacations, travel with children is not easy. Accidents happen. Precious baby blankets get lost. Tempers flare. Nothing goes perfectly.

But then again, it's not as hard as people think, either. Yes, more is unknown on the road. You may not know where the next nap will be, whether the next meal will include everyone's preferred food groups, or even if you will make the bus-to-boat transfer in time. But that happens at home sometimes, too, at least figuratively, if not literally.

The only real difference, then, is the amount of stress you let build because you are outside your comfort zone—and the fact that you don't have your usual stuff around you. This can be particularly disconcerting for those of us with young children. We've been socialized, dare I say brainwashed through Madison Avenue marketing, to think of all sorts of baby equipment extras as necessities. A simple trip to the beach can seem like moving an army, even as our society paradoxically worships convenience. The truth is, kids really don't need all those accessories, the containers and kits, toys and tidbits. They really just need you—and your attention.

Now in the interest of full disclosure, I'm not the best with little ones, particularly those under twelve months. You could say that, until they start walking and talking and acting more like real humans than some alien form of poo-making, sleep-depriving distraction, I struggle. But I'm fortunate in that my wife is really good with them, so I have a master to learn from— or at least pick up a few tips from.

That said, we have traveled together, long distance, with all three of our children, even when they were quite young, as seen here in Figure I.1 during my daughter's first trip to Australia. Despite the occasional hardships, I can honestly say it was good for them—and us. Travel teaches us to get by with less, both in travel itself and in life more generally. You simply don't need all that stuff you think you need. In the immortal words of British economist and noted 1970s environmental author E. F. Schumacher, small is beautiful.[5] Too much clutter takes attention away from what is really important. In this case, it distracts us from truly learning about the world— and learning about ourselves.

So whether it is you alone or the entire family flock, get out and see the world. Too many Americans don't. In fact, nearly two out of three Americans aren't even *eligible* to travel outside our country, according to data extrapolated from the U.S. State Department.[6]

If you're one of the 65 percent of Americans without a passport, maybe you'd prefer to start slowly. Think domestic. Further, merging general travel with an environmental theme, our national parks are a great place to start, particularly those already feeling the effects of climate change. Take Glacier National Park, for example. In 1850, at the end of the Little Ice Age, it held as many as 150 glaciers. Today there are only 26.[7] By 2030, maybe even 2020, there probably won't be any.[8] Better see them now.

Then, once you have a couple domestic trips under your belt, move beyond our borders. Venice is sinking at the rate of up to two millimeters (0.08 inches) per year, according to a 2012 report by the Scripps Institution of Oceanography at the University of California, San Diego.[9] St. Marks Cathedral literally acquires pools of water every summer. Trust me; I've seen it. It's a wonderful place to take meandering walks or magical gondola rides, where a feast for the eyes and taste buds lies around every corner.

Go before it's gone, too. And when you do, think about why this is happening.

That brings us to the other focus of this book, climate change. Some might scoff at the idea that you can travel to see climate change. They'd probably also point out that your travels are part of the problem, actually causing the changes we seek to avoid.

Of course, to a certain degree, they are right, on both counts. No matter how responsibly we

1.1   Have purple, fuzzy suitcase, will travel.

travel, greenhouse gas emissions are created (more on that in a bit). And any events we directly witness, such as hurricanes and tornadoes or even floods and droughts, are more accurately described as weather, not climate (more on that in the Galápagos chapters).

It is only over extended periods of time, when *patterns* of hurricanes, floods, droughts, and tornadoes develop, that we can speak of climate change. I am not actually going to see sea levels rise in Venice or corals turn white on the Great Barrier Reef, then. What I'm really curious about, and encourage you to witness as well, are the ramifications of climate change. Even better, traveling with your children underscores the generational issues at stake here. Climate change will affect our children much more than it affects us.

Braving thirty-foot waves in crossing from Ushuaia, Argentina, to the Antarctic Peninsula is not about checking the seventh continent off your list or seeing Adélie penguins in their natural habitat—although, admittedly, that is an amazing experience. More importantly, trips like this help us learn how ecosystems are responding to a warming climate, one that we pass on to our children, for better or worse.

Widely considered a bellwether of climate change, Adélie penguins are one of two penguin species (out of seventeen total) that are restricted to the cold, white, and historically dry continent. But these ten- to twelve-pound flightless birds, standing one-and-a-half to two-and-a-half feet high, need more than a rocky beach to build their cozy pebble nests, which they do with remarkable persistence, I might add.

They also need to eat. As such, they live only where there is sea ice to support their fishing requirements.

As the Antarctic Peninsula warmed an incredible 10.8 degrees Fahrenheit this past half-century, though, both these basic needs have been compromised. For one, there is less sea ice from which to launch their required fishing expeditions. For another, there is less nesting habitat as warmer temperatures bring a higher water-vapor concentration in the air and, thus, more snowfall. This snowfall covers the rocky slopes the Adélie would otherwise return to each spring, which, incidentally, favors surging gentoo penguin colonies that have the admirable ability to adapt more quickly, particularly given that they do not require sea ice to fish. Over the last thirty-odd years, in contrast, Adélie colonies northeast of the Ross Sea have collapsed, falling nearly 90 percent.[10]

But the deeper you dig, both figuratively and literally, the more you find that climate change is never that simple. According to an international team of experts led by the University of Minnesota Polar Geospatial Center, Adélie penguins are doing very well in southern Antarctica, migrating in record numbers to the southern Ross Sea. Here, using a combination of aerial photography since 1958, and modern satellite imagery more recently, researchers found an 84 percent increase in Adélie populations on Beaufort Island, as formerly unsuitable nesting habitat lost some of its cover of snow and ice.[11] The catch here is these gains are expected to be temporary, with climate models predicting that the rest of the Antarctic continent will begin to mimic the temperature increases seen on the peninsula over the last fifty years. Initial nesting gains then would be cancelled out as the sea ice required for Adélie fishing expeditions eventually melts as well.

Experiences along Australia's Great Barrier Reef tell a similar story, where climate change is best understood as a series of complex onion-like layers you must continue to peel away. Snorkeling along the pristine outer Moore Reef, on a calm day with good water clarity, you see an entirely new underwater world. It is said that director James Cameron used the Great Barrier Reef for inspiration in creating the vivid animation for his otherworldly film *Avatar*. That isn't really a surprise given the burst of color on the reef, but the diversity of aquatic life is still jaw-dropping. Most importantly, between gulps of salt water while struggling with your snorkel, you could easily forget that, in the midst of this immediate beauty, the Great Barrier Reef and reefs across the globe have already faced mass coral bleaching events[12] in 1998, 2002, and 2016.[13] Record sustained summer sea surface temperatures are widely suspected to be the lead culprit (bleaching events at the Great Barrier Reef in 2008 and 2011 were due to an influx of fresh water, also tied to climate change), as temperature increases of only one to two degrees Celsius above average spur coral bleaching.

Corals bleach when the algae-protozoan known as zooxanthellae that feed coral polyps oxygen and give them their extraordinary colors abandon ship. In turn, this shuts down the coral feeding grounds for a diverse array of fish, and the bleached coral becomes colonized by green algae instead.

In contrast to its highly diverse predecessor, a ghostly ecosystem with limited types of inhabitants emerges. In 1998 approximately 42 percent of the Great Barrier Reef was hit with mass coral bleaching. Later, in early 2002, the bleaching was even worse, in both scale and severity, with roughly 54 percent bleaching to some extent and nearly twice as many offshore reefs bleaching compared to 1998 (41 percent compared to 21 percent), according to a study by the Australian Institute of Marine Science.[14]

But not all coral are equally prone to bleaching. Faster-growing coral such as plate and branching coral are most likely to suffer. And other phenomena, such as cyclones and voracious crown-of-thorn starfish, can be even more destructive, although admittedly these threats to coral reefs are tied to climate change as well (as will be described in subsequent chapters).

The point is, you cannot always believe what you see when it comes to climate change. First impressions can be misleading. Everything might appear to be fine, as on my Moore Reef visit in mid-August 2013, when in fact the reef was dealing with serious challenges with positive (in a negative way) feedback loops that threaten even a semblance of normalcy.

This is precisely why we need to know more.

When it comes to learning about climate change around the world, and our role in it, the timing could not be more crucial, for our sake and our children's. "Human beings are now carrying out a large scale geophysical experiment of a kind that could not have happened in the past nor be reproduced in the future," as oceanographer Roger Revelle and chemist Hans E. Suess warned over a half-century ago.[15]

According to a noted 2013 study examining a whopping 11,944 abstracts of peer-reviewed journal articles from 1991 to 2011, of those expressing a position on anthropogenic climate change, 97.1 percent endorsed the consensus position, that climate is changing because of us.[16] Yet, the general public is woefully ignorant when it comes to this complex phenomenon. Only 38 percent of Americans believe there is scientific consensus, for example, on global warming, according to a May/June 2012 survey by the Chicago Council on Foreign Affairs, and similarly a mid-March 2013 poll by the Pew Research Center found only 42 percent think "the Earth is warming due mostly to human activity."

Admittedly, question wording, shifting between phrasing such as "climate change" and "global warming," as well as current events themselves shape our numbers significantly from year to year, even month to month or week to week. An early March 2016 Gallup poll, for instance, found a slightly more comforting (in terms of representing awareness) number of 64 percent of Americans "worry about global warming."[17]

Still, all told, public concern vacillates considerably when it comes to acknowledging the threat of climate change, ranging between 50 percent and 72 percent over the last twenty years according to Gallup. This helps explain why, despite its significance and the overwhelming consensus within the scientific community, climate change remains politically problematic, particularly in the United States.

Two schools of thought exist when it comes to addressing climate change, conceptualized as top-down or bottom-up approaches. Phrased more precisely, climate change governance takes either an international-institution approach building from the top as seen through efforts within the United Nations,[18] or a nonstate approach building from the bottom. In the latter, a mix of state (think not country but Florida) and local officials, nongovernmental organizations, and for-profit enterprises lead the way.

Much of the recent literature suggests that bottom-up approaches hold more promise. At least until the Paris Agreement in December 2015, the top-down model appeared dead in the water. In late 2009, for example, the 15th Conference of Parties to the U.N. Climate Change Conference in Copenhagen all but rang the funeral bells. Paris provides much needed resuscitation, with renewed hope that particularly the United States and China will lead internationally in climate governance efforts. As will be explored later in chapters on Antarctica and the politicization of climate change, though, the United Nations route is only part of the path needed. It may also be merely more complementary than critical.

But we are getting a little ahead of ourselves here. This book targets not the macro but the micro level in explaining why climate change is so poorly understood by the general public. It examines why people, at least significant subsets of them, don't care about climate change or think it requires action.

In part, overarching flaws within twentieth- and now twenty-first-century environmentalism are to blame here. During the latter twentieth century, environmentalism evolved to be too much of a special interest in the United States, often pitting one group of interests against another. Former California governor Arnold Schwarzenegger, aka "the Carbon Terminator," perhaps best explained this handicap as one bogged down in negatives, fixated on what could *not* be done and what people could *not* enjoy. As Schwarzenegger tells it, environmentalists were acting like prohibitionists at a fraternity party.

Environmental authors such as Michael Schellenberger and Ted Nordhaus echo this sentiment with a policy-oriented twist, arguing that environmentalists must avoid characterization as special interests and instead purposefully link ecological arguments to other compelling policy issues, such as health care and job creation.[19] Environmentalism needs to return to its interdisciplinary roots and articulate the bigger picture. Obsession with concrete victories on limited policy matters did more harm than good, this perspective asserts, and postponed calls for revolutionary change.

A more holistic approach is indeed needed, recognizing that the environment is not separate but, in fact, literally part of us. We all lose when our environment is damaged. Everyone has a compelling interest in preserving it, whatever one's political beliefs.

This bipartisanship is worth emphasizing. In fact, if anything, despite its label as a liberal agenda item, climate change is inherently a conservative issue. Let's face it. Conservatism, by definition, focuses on minimizing rapid change and conserving resources.

This is true of many environmental issues, which historically, for much of the twentieth century, were nonpartisan, championed by members from both sides of the aisle. The Clean Air Act of 1970 offers an ideal illustration. Acting with the idea that technology can reduce pollution and, thus, improve the quality of the air we breathe, this historical legislation was signed into law by a Republican president, Richard Nixon, and later strengthened in 1990 under another Republican, President George H.W. Bush.

Along these theoretical lines, respected environmental historian William Cronon points out the pitfalls of creating a false dualism between civilization and nature.[20] Ignoring ecological interdependence creates dangerous patterns of neglect, even outright self-destructive behavior such as the U.S. Navy's program to dispose of decommissioned ships by sinking them. Known as Sinkex, the Navy destroyed unwanted ships such as the massive USS *America* aircraft carrier in 2005 several hundred miles off the coast of Norfolk, Virginia, and gained some welcome target practice in the process. Unfortunately, the USS *America*, like most ships in the program, wasn't exactly empty. It had more than 500 pounds of polychlorinated biphenyls (PCBs) on board.

And PCBs are not the type of passenger you want to let loose. Banned in the United States in 1979, PCBs are persistent toxic chemicals that bio-accumulate when moving up through the food chain. That means by the time we eat the fish that ate the fish that was exposed to the PCBs, it is even more dangerous than before, perhaps deadly. Asbestos, lead, mercury, and other harmful substances are also typically found in the wiring, insulation materials, keels, and felt gaskets of these decommissioned ships, so it's essentially a toxic cocktail settling to the ocean seabed after each exercise. Maybe we should rethink this practice.

That's what the late American forester and noted environmental author Aldo Leopold would argue. As outlined in his seminal work, *A Sand County Almanac*, when we neglect his "land ethic" and stop "thinking like a mountain," problems inevitably develop.[21] When we fail to recognize the necessary role of predators as well as prey, disaster can strike. For instance: wolves are a necessary part of the ecosystem and perform important tasks, such as keeping the deer population in check, which in turn shapes all sorts of vegetation growth, including the aspen trees they favor when feeding along riverbanks. Eventually, overpopulation among the deer may spur disease and death, and perhaps a crash in their population, too.

Again, you have to think big picture. The wolves are part of the environment, not separate from it. As the most feared predator of all, we must think of ourselves in the same manner. We are part of the environment, not separate from it.

This was the powerful message marine biologist Rachel Carson brought in 1962 with her passionate, groundbreaking work, *Silent Spring*.[22] Not an argument against pesticides, but rather against their indiscriminate use, *Silent Spring* explained why we needed to be worried about pesticides for very selfish reasons. Her emphasis was on human health. She argued we were only hurting ourselves by ignorantly relying on only partially understood chemicals.

My narrative builds on the work of such renowned environmental authors and outlines a decidedly different approach to addressing climate change, the most challenging policy problem our society faces today—scientifically, economically, culturally, socially, and politically. Indeed, climate change is arguably an issue larger than anything we've ever faced before, from World War I and World War II as well as the Cold War of the twentieth century to international terrorism now in the twenty-first.

I'm not alone in this assessment. Take, for example, Anthony Giddens, former director of the London School of Economics. He asserts that climate change is unlike any global challenge we have ever faced. With its unique scale and time horizon, Giddens believes climate change is in fact *the* most challenging social problem of the modern era.[23] Despite this significance, however, the average American, as mentioned above, has little comprehension of this complex issue beyond possibly connecting it to disasters such as Hurricane Sandy in 2012 or Hurricane Katrina in 2005. Climate change happens somewhere else, to someone else, in faraway places.

While only partially accurate, thanks to a variety of factors we will explore, this faulty perception prevails in the public mind. Visiting places where climate change is a daily reality helps us develop a more complete understanding, and climate change impacts become more tangible, more real, and take on more urgency. In short, climate change becomes better understood. Experience breaks through these walls of misunderstanding.

Recall here our earlier Gallup figures on American public concern with climate change, namely ranging between 50 percent and 72 percent over the last twenty years. As troublesome as these numbers might be, what is of even more concern is the increasing polarization of American public opinion on climate change. In a study spanning a decade of Gallup Poll data from 2001 to 2010, researchers Aaron McCright and Riley Dunlap found a "sizable political divide between liberals/Democrats and conservatives/Republicans" exists within the American public, one that has grown "substantially" over the last decade.[24] Equally if not more alarming, this divide grew even as more information on climate change became available and individuals claimed increasing personal knowledge about climate change.

How can that be?

For one, some of the information the public consumes is highly misleading, rooted not in peer-reviewed studies but those sponsored by the fossil fuel industry. Further, in an effort to appear neutral, a number of media outlets "balance" their reporting on the peer-reviewed consensus surrounding human-caused climate change with these highly questionable contrarian works, in effect equating the two schools. This occurs despite the fact, as noted earlier, that 97 percent of climate experts fall into the camp concerned about human-induced climate change,[25] a number that older television commercial afwicionados will note is even better than the four out of five dentists who recommend Trident gum.

An even more nuanced answer, though, highlights how this is about more than simply getting information to people, erroneous or not. For all its praise, Al Gore's award-winning film explaining climate change, *An Inconvenient Truth*, didn't change people's perception. It enhanced their existing opinions, even as the former vice president shared the 2007 Nobel Prize with the Intergovernmental Panel on Climate Change for his work.

In fact, when it comes to climate change, adding more conventionally distributed information alone might actually exacerbate the current partisan divide, as research shows individuals process their understanding based on values, ideology, and experiences. Turning again to McCright and Dunlap, we find that political orientation actually serves as a critical moderating effect here, depending on whether individuals get their news from National Public Radio, MSNBC, and the *New York Times* or conservative talk radio, FOX News, and the *Wall Street Journal*.

What is required, then, is far more than simply providing information. Context must be presented as well. Values and ideology, it seems, would only be influenced by changes in *experience*. Ecotourism does just that, providing valuable experience that might well shape values and ideology—and shift opinion on climate change.

I.2 Among the misty clouds in Peru's Machu Picchu.

Ecotourism not only transports travelers to such exotic, faraway places as Peru's famed ruins of Machu Picchu seen here in Figure I.2; it helps them understand how their activities back home significantly affect such places.

But what exactly is ecotourism?[26] Is it a mix of camping and hiking? Does it include nature photography and bird or whale watching? What about botanical study? Do river rafting, canoeing, and fishing count? How about mountain climbing? Or going on safari, or hunting?

It turns out, the answer here depends on who you ask, and not everyone even uses the same language. The Washington, D.C.–based environmental think tank Worldwatch Institute, for example, outlines seven related categories of tourism used in the industry. This complicates matters all the more, with terms such as *adventure tourism, geotourism, mass tourism, nature-based tourism, pro-poor tourism, responsible tourism,* and *sustainable tourism*. Fortunately, ecotourism is emerging as not only the term with the most cachet within the industry, but the one with the most meaning within academia. The International Ecotourism Society offers a concise definition, popular within industry circles and academia alike: "Responsible travel to natural areas that conserves the environment and improves the welfare of local people."

The key here is that ecotourism can be any type of outdoor activity involving travel as long as it both minimizes environmental impact and empowers the local population, not only putting money directly into local pockets but potentially financing larger environmental protection initiatives in the community.[27] Some elements in the tourist industry, of course, claim to be ecotouristic but really aren't. They merely adopt practices that save them money. Better labeled as "ecotourism lite" or "greenwashing," they seek to exploit the popularity of green design and practices, and to save some "green" of their own.

Full-fledged ecotourism does simultaneously address, at least in part, three key issues:

- Financial need in poorer parts of the world, particularly the Global South
- The need to protect the ecology of these poor parts of the world— so past mistakes made from the Global North are not replicated
- Increasing global awareness about these issues—that is, connecting local issues to global understanding

As one of the top five export earners in over 150 countries, according to the International Ecotourism Society,[28] tourism at large offers remarkable potential to link conservation interests to economic development. When the developed world participates, in turn, its people better understand climate change and the dangers it presents. This emphasis on the developed world is critical. It opens the eyes of those outside the Global South, demonstrating how their own daily lives connect to the places they visit.

As a final caveat, ecotourism also faces the danger of being a victim of success as well as failure. Special places can become so popular that they struggle with too many visitors. This has been an issue for over a century with some parts of our national park system such as Yellowstone National Park.[29] Furthermore, like any successful enterprise, popular ecotourist destinations have incentives to expand. This temptation, combined with the attention of outside operators seeking to enter the market and replicate the successes of initial offerings, can place dangerous, possibly irreversible population pressures on fragile ecological situations. And as doors open to the wider world, other social influences often arrive, from drugs and alcohol to prostitution and crime.

What follows, then, is a series of engaging travel tales from five high-profile ecotourist destinations around the globe. Each story acknowledges important overlaps but at the same time emphasizes one of the five key obstacles to understanding climate change and acting on it: scientific, economic, cultural, social, and political considerations.

To most, the scientific and economic obstacles are the most obvious considerations here, and they are addressed in the first two sets of chapters, on the Galápagos Islands and the Great Barrier Reef, respectively.[30]

Beginning with the sexual tribulations of the last of his kind, an individual of a subspecies of Galápagos tortoise named Lonesome George, we trace the steps of Charles Darwin and his ship, HMS *Beagle*. Drawing key distinctions between climate and weather, this tale explores climate modeling, positive feedback loops, scientific probability, and scientific uncertainty.

The next chapters on the Great Barrier Reef follow this scientific lead, discussing what causes coral bleaching as well as endemism and the supercontinent of Gondwana from which Australia spawned. It quickly moves to an economic focus centered around tourism and both commercial and recreational fishing along the reef.

The third tale explores the African continent's oldest park, South Africa's Hluhluwe-iMfolozi, and revolves around two-and-a-half weeks working for scientists conducting wildlife population studies. Hluhluwe-iMfolozi is the park that saved the southern white rhino from extinction and world-renowned for its game population and park management. Indeed, every white rhino today traces its heritage genetically to this flagship park in KwaZulu-Natal. Now the park is attempting to replicate that success with the black rhino. Utilizing metaphors from Nelson Mandela to the *Wizard of Oz*, these chapters emphasize cultural considerations and highlight tensions between long- and short-term interests in our society. The merits of preparation and insurance are reinforced while crossing paths with lions, elephants, rhinoceros, and Cape buffalo, four of the "big five" most dangerous animals to encounter on foot within the red continent.

A two-week stint studying macaws in the Peruvian Amazon at Tambopata Research Station serves as the focal point for the fourth adventure, particularly its examination of social dimensions as illustrated by the partnership between Rainforest Expeditions and the local Infierno community to run three Amazonian lodges in this remote region. This story offers analogies of climate change to the civil rights movement, combining the eloquent idealism of Martin Luther King, Jr., with the pragmatic self-interest of employment needs. Scholars such as Martha Honey assign an economic value to these majestic macaws of roughly $4,700 per free-flying bird.[31] Further exploration of the nongovernmental organization Earthwatch, which funds scientific research at Tambopata (and Hluhluwe-iMfolozi too), also highlights this set of chapters. This is appropriate as the stated goal of Earthwatch is not only to fund research and reduce costs by supplying volunteers to help gather scientific data, but also to improve general public awareness of their various projects by turning volunteers into apostles trumpeting the value of the project once they return to their home communities.

Our final tale is perhaps both the most imposing and controversial of all. It combines the Antarctic Peninsula with political considerations. Here I outline the 1959 Antarctic Treaty System, critiquing its flaws and strengths, before comparing it to the United Nations Convention on Climate Change, which came into force in early 2005. Throughout this adventure, as I battle seasickness along the infamous Drake Passage, these chapters question philosophically what it means to be an ecotourist. Not everything that says it is ecotourism really is. As noted earlier, money must find its way into the hands of local stakeholders, and the ecological footprint must be significantly minimized. Indeed, when it comes to remote, fragile destinations such as Antarctica, earning the ecotourist label is darn difficult, if not impossible.

The truth is, trade-offs shape all our decisions in life: from drinking tap water or draft beer instead of bottled water or bottled beer to riding bicycles or walking to work versus driving conventional internal combustion automobiles. Individuals must weigh benefits against costs, daily. Everything we do has ecological impact. How we minimize it is what matters. On the seventh, most remote continent, nothing could be more important.

In conclusion, this work offers two concise recommendations in a call for direct investment in our future: we must enthusiastically embrace political power while simultaneously avoiding narrow, overly technical policy battles. Initiatives such as Costa Rica's green-leaf certification program follow just such a blueprint, integrating the true interdisciplinary nature of environmental issues while welcoming the political power of the consumer and economic marketplace.

To have a fighting chance in the United States, though, we must build better awareness of the dangers of climate change. Such a revolution is unlikely unless individuals themselves return to a childhood of sorts. Borrowing from the Einstein quote that began this introduction, we need a new consciousness to tackle the complex problems of climate change. Old ways of thinking are insufficient. We must cultivate new experiences. Like children, we must learn to see the world anew.

WHAT'S UP, DOC?

The Galápagos Islands and Scientific Obstacles to Understanding Climate Change

When we try to pick out anything by itself,
we find it hitched to everything else in the Universe.

—American naturalist and author John Muir,
My First Summer in the Sierra, 1911

chapter one

CARTOONISH BEGINNINGS

ARE YOU A BUGS BUNNY FAN? Come on, you have to admit it. That disarmingly clever bunny, even though a bit of a bully at times, has a certain impish charm. He's one of the most popular and recognizable figures in the world. A classic, down-to-earth trickster, Bugs is refined, old-world cultured, and simultaneously earthy, exuding new-world initiative, willing to defy any rule to achieve his desired results. To many, Bugs would personify the American can-do spirit. A few years back, a piece on National Public Radio made that very claim.[1] Seriously, do you admit to a secret crush on that rascally rabbit?

Believe it or not, this is the initial question I ask first-year college students in my introduction to international relations course. I do this in part to get their attention, jolting them awake to the possibility that they walked in on the wrong class, perhaps a postmodern English course on deconstructing humor—or maybe something a little less stuffy, along the lines of American studies and film or the history of comics and cartoons. Another reason I do this is my deep-seated belief in the power of a well-drawn cartoon. In a spin on the old adage that a picture is worth a thousand words, cartoons can pack quite a punch in a tightly constricted space. I ask my students about Bugs in an effort to achieve the same effect. I draw them a mental image right off the bat, something for them to manipulate with what I say next.

Further, despite the mixed messages sent by Bugs Bunny's gravity-defying Looney Tunes colleagues Road Runner and Wile E. Coyote, cartoons can be highly effective representations of reality. Deftly drawn cartoons, from the silly to the serious, employ humor to great purpose, applying the tried-and-true formula: tragedy plus time equals comedy. Comedy, in turn, like mathematics, is a language that transcends cultures.

I mean, who doesn't like Bugs Bunny with his irrepressible wit, thick New York accent, and flippant catch phrase, "What's up, Doc?" He has his own star on the Hollywood Walk of Fame for gosh sakes.

There are three other reasons I ask a question one might expect more in preschool than in college. They are really important—and, ironically, underscore how preschool programs often understand learning better than higher-education programs.

In part, I ask such an odd, seemingly unrelated question in a course on international relations because I want students to engage in experiential learning. I want them to relate the big ideas we discuss in our academic course to their own individual, nonacademic experiences, even if that means drawing analogies to pop culture consumed many, many years ago.

Another reason I ask this Bugs Bunny question is to set up a follow-up query about a specific Looney Tunes episode. I know you've seen it. It's the one set in 1492, where Bugs Bunny sails the Atlantic, initially as the lucky mascot to Christopher Columbus. When his fortune changes, though, after weeks with no land in sight, he becomes the target of Columbus's increasingly exasperated crew. Our rascally rabbit empties his usual bag of tricks, of course, to successfully hold these sailors at bay while keeping the chuckles coming.

Yet, in this 1951-released short, the indelible image for me is Bugs and Chris, as Bugs calls him, sharing a meal in the captain's mess. I suppose some of my memory revolves around the word association of *mess* and *meal*. After all, we all know children enjoy experiencing mealtime with more than just their sense of taste; they love to test the texture and temperature of their food—all over themselves. Further, as a bit of a disclaimer, I personally love any meal, messy or not. So, right off the bat, there are two good reasons for me to remember it alone.

A third factor, though, is the kicker for me. It's the imagery of how Bugs and Chris eat. There's a long, rectangular table with one wooden bowl that shifts from end to end as rolling waves tip the boat from side to side. I distinctly remember this. I also recall the two having a conversation between each spoonful as the bowl slides from one end of the table to the other. Looking back, I thought they were arguing about the shape of the Earth, but that wasn't exactly right. My memory there seems to have faded a bit over the years, hopefully not a harbinger of things to come.

Their conversation, instead, was about striking land the next day. The argument about the shape of the Earth came earlier. Bugs Bunny, after all, would never be considered a flat-Earth follower. He pops up literally at the beginning of the cartoon, baseball and glove in hand, in defense of Christopher Columbus, attempting to help him prove the Earth is round in his argument with the king of Spain.

It is here that I make my initial political point to the class, my leap to international relations theory. Columbus was not trying to discover America, of course. He had no idea it was there. His goal was to find a quicker, cheaper route to the East Indies—by sailing west. Unlike many in his day, Columbus thought the Earth was round, that he could get to the East by sailing west. His map, his mental model about the shape of world, was different. The Bugs Bunny cartoon "Hare We Go" highlights the power of maps as well as models and theories more generally, calling attention to the fact that they are not merely ideas about how the world works. They are also representations of power itself, establishing parameters for what we debate. Inherently political, models and theories determine what options are available, thus shaping the distribution of resources.

Models are tremendous assets to our society. They make our world more understandable, from the molecular level to global phenomena like climate change. Yet models, by definition, are also oversimplifications of how the world really works. They are imperfect representations complete with their own inherent biases.

Take for example the age old Mercator projection, a map of the world first developed by the Flemish cartographer Gerardus Mercator in 1569. It's an extremely useful map for navigation, accurately displaying direction and distance. On the other hand, this map is also greatly flawed, enlarging the favored Northern Hemisphere to such an extent that Greenland and Africa are shown as essentially the same size, when in reality Africa is roughly fourteen times as big as Greenland. In fact, regions along the equator all appear smaller than they should, especially relative to Europe, and the equator itself does not appear until two-thirds of the way down the map. That means the southern half of the world receives only one-third the space.

Again, recall the context. Constructed by a European in an age of imperialism, its driving purpose was to facilitate efficient navigation, trade, and conquest.

First introduced by Arno Peters in 1974, the Peters projection corrects for these errors, appropriately drawing the equator across the middle of the map and displaying the correct proportion of each landmass. Immediately, this map draws attention to the developed countries of the South where three-quarters of the world's population lives. With that action, though, it greatly distorts the shape and position of each landmass, rendering it virtually useless for navigation.

Herein lies the real peril of making and using models, what we refer to in the field of international relations as theory construction and application. One must always remember that some distortion is inevitable when simplifying the complex, whether within the field of cartography—or computer models of climate change.

Maps, models, and theories, by definition, are imperfect representations of the larger world. They focus on certain components while neglecting others. As world-renowned climatologist and, until he retired in 2013, the leading climate modeler for the National Ocean and Atmospheric Association (NOAA) James Hansen notes, "models are valuable, but only when used with knowledge of their capabilities and limitations."

So while climate models have evolved with remarkable accuracy over the last three decades, keep in mind they remain a work in progress—and always will be. You might say they mimic both their makers and their targets in that respect, continually adapting and adjusting to their surroundings.

Within this margin of error, though, one more crucial point deserves emphasis. Natural causes cannot explain the rate of change underway today. We are the main causal agent. We are the ones driving climate change.

That does not discount additional fascinating forces at work. Over tens of thousands of years, these were important, too, driving past ice ages and interglacial cycles. Indeed, thanks to a Serbian scientist named Milutin Milanković, we have identified the connection between climate and the Earth's orbital motions.[2] In particular, the Earth's orbit changes in three basic respects. The axis spin wobbles slowly, or precesses, through a 26,000-year cycle. The angular tilt of this rotation axis, the obliquity, varies from 22 degrees to about 24.5 over a 41,000-year period. And perhaps most familiar to the majority of us, the shape of the Earth's orbit around the sun is not a circle, but rather an ellipse, which varies roughly every 100,000 years.

None of these, however, can explain the current climate shift underway.

The term *climate change* first appeared in scientific publication in 1956 in the journal *Tellus*,[3] with the term *global warming* following, by most accounts, two decades later.[4] It was not until the summer of 1988, though, in well-publicized hearings before the Senate Energy and Natural Resources Committee, that climate change broke into the public consciousness.[5] Hansen, in particular, drew attention for stating with 99 percent certainty that the documented warming trend was not natural, and a graph accompanying his testimony forecast three possibilities for this continued warming in the twenty-first century.[6]

Back then it was called "global warming" and thought of as a future threat. Today we emphasize not only the future but also the here and now. Like college students with credit card debt compounding with each missed payment, our actions today, or perhaps more accurately our inaction to ending dependence on fossil fuels that drive business as usual, greatly influences the climate threats for tomorrow.

Another key item to note here is one of semantics. While some in the popular media continue to use the term "global warming" regardless of their political persuasion, that phrasing is also a favorite whipping boy of those predisposed to ignore the advancing scientific research, especially when winter storms such as those in 2014–2015 continually dropped more than a foot of snow on the Northeast, one even topping three feet in some locations. Climatologists, on the other hand, have come to prefer the term "climate change" to "global warming," particularly because it shifts our attention to how temperature changes affect water vapor in the atmosphere and the resulting precipitation patterns over long periods of time.

Indeed, we now know that, over a period of decades instead of mere months or years, climate change in the twenty-first century does mean a warmer world overall. This will continue to initiate the melting of ice, from the tropics (in glaciers at high elevations) to the poles and, thus, higher sea levels across the globe, particularly as Antarctica and Greenland melt more each year. In fact, sea level is now rising more than three centimeters a decade worldwide, double the rate of the twentieth century. Further, in this warmer world, climate change also means much more powerful storms, increasingly violent weather regardless of the season (which, by the way, is another issue, as seasons become progressively less defined).

Perhaps one of the least-known aspects of climate change among the general public, this timing of the seasons is visibly shifting. Since World War II, for example, butterfly territories have moved northward in Europe by thirty to sixty miles, according to scientists Camille Parmesan and Gary Yohe. Ruling out habitat destruction, these scientists find a shift toward the pole of approximately four miles per decade, with spring events such as egg laying and tree flowering shifting to 2.3 days earlier per decade.[7] Over time, the consequences of this shift will be felt more and more.

Nothing illustrates this better than the Intergovernmental Panel on Climate Change (IPCC). Created in 1988 by the World Meteorological Organization and the United Nations Environment Program, the IPCC consists of around two thousand scientists from over a hundred countries. Cowinner of the Nobel Peace Prize in 2007 along with former Vice President Al Gore, it is the largest, most rigorous peer-reviewed scientific collaboration in history. Noted climatologist Michael Mann sums up their status simply as "the gold standard for evaluating scientific understanding of climate change."[8] Every five to seven years, since 1990, the IPCC publishes a three-volume work on climate change. The first volume, known as Working Group 1, focuses on the science of climate change. The second, Working Group 2, concentrates on projected impacts. The third, Working Group 3, addresses the potential for mitigation.

Roughly a dozen scientific experts in their respective subdisciplines serve as the lead authors for each chapter in a report, with fifty or more additional contributing authors. Each working group also develops a summary for policymakers of findings accessible to a general audience. This is what most people see referenced in the mainstream media, the exact wording determined after extensive discussion in a final plenary meeting; for example, the synthesis report of the Fifth Assessment Report (AR5) was released from Copenhagen in October 2014.[9]

Following the watershed year of 1988, with the establishment of the IPCC and the aforementioned congressional hearings in the United States, one might argue that the next major political climate-change landmark came in 1995 when the IPCC, in the decidedly conservative language of science, stated that a "discernible human influence" on our climate exists. This is not to say the years between 1988 and 1995 were devoid of politics surrounding climate change. Far from it. Climatologists became more and more convinced of warming trends during these years, and fossil-fuel interests shifted their attention from merely suppressing the release of scientific studies to outright attacks on the messengers that delivered them. After 1995, furthermore, these tactics morphed into full-fledged strategies, as addressed later in this book in the fifth set of chapters on Antarctica and the politics of climate change.

Perhaps not by coincidence, my own work in the field of environmental politics began at roughly that time two decades ago, although I did not focus on climate change till late summer of 2004. As I put the finishing touches on my first book on environmental groups and their species-protection efforts, I was hunting for a new project. Research projects tend to develop more slowly when teaching at a liberal arts college. Time is devoted first and foremost to interactions with students and continual class preparation. Despite that handicap of sorts, you might also argue there are more opportunities to experiment outside our standard academic disciplinary silos than at a typical research institution. Professors at smaller schools, provided they have the time, are more likely to refresh and revise their research agenda periodically as a result, particularly if it relates to the classroom.

In any case, I jumped quickly late that summer of 2004 when our energetic dean presented a unique opportunity to visit the Galápagos Islands after the upcoming academic year. In preparation, beginning in January 2005, my colleagues and I went back to school that spring semester as not only professors but also students, taking turns leading weekly seminars for each other about the Galápagos Islands and Ecuador, all tailored to the grand finale of the trip itself in May.

Departure day started smoothly enough. Meeting in a campus parking lot early that morning, sixteen of us drove a rental van from Winter Park to Miami International Airport, saving a bit on the airfare as academic cheapskates everywhere are wont to do. The four extra hours actually went by surprisingly quickly and served an added benefit of allowing the group to coalesce in ways only tightly constricted seating arrangements can encourage. In short, picture your typical summer family vacation drive with all the anticipation of the final destination, and then add to that a group of individuals who love to really, really talk.

That all changed when we boarded our flight to Guayaquil and fatigue started to set in. The first rule of travel, at least in my book, is to have fun. I guess it's my version of carpe diem. Seize the day. Live life for each precious moment. But even as you do that, always remember there will be complications. That's where my second rule of travel enters the fray. Expect the unexpected. Nothing will ever go precisely as planned. Eventually, no matter how meticulous your plans, you will need to improvise . . . . or simply wait.

The latter is what was in store for us. As our bags were loaded onto the plane, the tow rig damaged our plane's landing gear. For the next hour, airport personnel attempted to fix the damage, but eventually we were instructed to change planes. It turned out that was problematic too as we boarded before our baggage and then, with shift changes and tight departure schedules, we literally could not find anyone to load our baggage. After another four hours waiting on the tarmac, our flight finally departed. Arriving in the port city of Guayaquil at 3:30 A.M. the next day, hours behind schedule, we did not actually check into our lodging for that night, the simple but efficient Hotel Doral, until the painfully late hour of 5 A.M.

We'd adjusted our schedule smartly to see the high-elevation capital city of Quito at 9,350 feet above sea level[10] (particularly in comparison to our near-sea-level start in Florida) on our return trip, thus postponing potential altitude sickness until then, but no one could have foreseen the extensive five-hour-plus airplane delay. In an ironic twist of my initial argument in this chapter that art imitates life, with cartoons representing reality, at least to some degree, you might say my adventure to the Galápagos was off to its own cartoonish start.

Expect the unexpected.

The following day was devoted to sightseeing, including an evening on the Malecon, a lovely mile-and-a-half boardwalk along the western shore of the Guayas River populated with historical monuments, museums, gardens, fountains, restaurants, and bars. Kurt Vonnegut's novel *Galápagos* starts here as the main characters gather for the "Nature Cruise of the Century" amid a global economic crisis, and I resisted the brief urge to draw analogies to my own voyage the next morning, that life would not imitate art once again on this trip.[11]

Actually it did, but not in the apocalyptic manner that Vonnegut relays. Natural selection, as in Vonnegut's page-turning work, would take center stage. My photographs and mental images would last a lifetime, and hopefully they now take larger form here. That said, unlike with Vonnegut's characters, my own trip from mainland Ecuador to the Galápagos Islands, what *National Geographic* labels as one of the top ten wildest places on Earth, went largely as scheduled.

1.1 The Galápagos Islands.
   Source: Wikimedia Commons via 2002 NASA satellite photo.

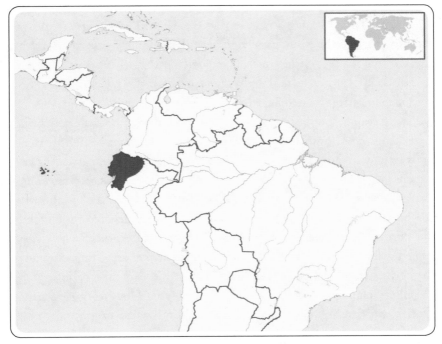

1.2 Ecuador and South America. Source: Wikimedia Commons.

The Galápagos Islands, as noted in Figures 1.1 and 1.2, are a group of thirteen major islands (those larger than four square miles) plus six smaller ones, and more than a hundred islets. Over the next eight days we'd land on nine of the islands and snorkel offshore on a tenth. I'd be practicing what I preached in my classroom back in Florida, living and breathing experiential learning. And I'd be doing it in one of the most ideal environmental settings one could imagine, the "origin of all my views" according to the one of the most famous names on the planet and originator of the theory of natural selection, Charles Darwin.[12] Heck, even a gaggle of academic tourists like ourselves would feel like biologists in that context, and we had the added bonus of actually having one in our midst.

The Galápagos Islands, officially named the Archipelago de Colón since 1892, rest on a geological conveyor belt, gradually moving southeast one to two inches a year. Beginning with volcanic eruptions some twenty million years ago on the western edge of the Nazca plate, lava flows finally broke the surface of the Pacific Ocean about three to five million years ago to form the Galápagos Islands.

The islands on the east side are older, with the younger ones to the west. Isabela, the largest island, straddles the equator with a seahorse shape, the result of six volcanoes merging together approximately one million years ago, making it a relative teenager in geologic time. Five of the six volcanoes on Isabela are still active, adding to the teenager analogy as one of the most volcanically active places on earth.

Interestingly, despite its equatorial location, the Humboldt current brings cold ocean waters to the islands, and it is these cold waters, which are richer in oxygen and plankton, that foster the diversity of life here, particularly the famous marine and bird diversity. The currents of the Galápagos, which rotate clockwise in the warmer north and counterclockwise in the cooler south, also add an air of mystery to accompany the intriguing diversity of the islands. For part of the year, they are enshrouded in a cloak of mist, which helps explain why Spanish explorers first referred to them as Las Islas Encantadas, the bewitched or enchanted islands.

The Galápagos Islands are famed as a living laboratory of unusual species, which exist nowhere else on Earth, and whose origin most likely stems from ancestors on the mainland six hundred miles to the east. Swept out to sea millions of years ago, perhaps during a flash flood, the hardiest among them survived on rafts of vegetation before striking this volcanic patch of land.[13] Most introductions to the Galápagos highlight the first historical account of March 10, 1535, when stormy weather blew a Roman Catholic bishop off course during his voyage from Panama to Peru. Fewer recite Tomás de Berlanga's succinct one-line quote about his surroundings in a letter back to his Spanish king, "It looked like God had caused it to rain stones."

That sentiment, though, summed up the prevailing attitude about the Galápagos for many years to come. The Spanish government never attempted to colonize the islands, and failed to even investigate them for nearly two centuries, mindful that the single biggest limitation of the entire chain was its lack of fresh water. Such limitations, of course, provided unique opportunities for a number of other creatures, many of which, like the marine iguana, are found nowhere else on earth. As seen in Figure 1.3, though, this harsh and unforgiving environment can take its toll.

Despite that history, the Galápagos owe their popular name to the Spanish, which they received in the early 1570s. Another noted Flemish cartographer, Abraham Ortelius, first published maps in Europe identifying the islands by this name based on the Castilian term for the distinguishing characteristic of their giant tortoises, their carapace or shell, which resembled the front piece of a riding saddle.

Averaging over a hundred years in lifespan, Galápagos tortoises are the longest-lived of all vertebrates, with one in captivity once lasting 152 years. Still, when first viewed, it is their size that garners your immediate attention. Along with the giants of Seychelles, they are the world's largest tortoises, with some impressive specimens registering five feet in length. Males can reach 550 pounds, and females average 250. The Galápagos tortoise underscores that, while

1.3 Marine iguana skeleton on Santiago.

mammals tend toward dwarfism on islands, reptiles decidedly favor the opposite, gigantism.

Don't pinch yourself if the face in Figure 1.4 looks oddly familiar. Legend has it one Galápagos tortoise, Winston from the San Diego zoo, served as inspiration and face model for the main character in Steven Spielberg's 1982 classic, *E. T.* A zoo volunteer even claims that Winston still receives gratitude packages from Spielberg on occasion.

The next set of characters to influence the Galápagos were a motley crew of buccaneers, a legacy manifested in several respects, including endangering of the islands' namesake tortoises and leading to a noted 1729 map of the archipelago in which islands were named for British nobles as well as officials who favored these pirates. Intriguingly, these swashbucklers had a continually shifting status, sometimes considered to be admired adventurers and at other times notorious thieves, depending on their usefulness to the powers that be.

Their presence grew more commonplace when Spain conquered first Mexico in 1519 and then Peru in 1532. An enormous amount of gold and silver was extracted from the fallen Incan empire in the aftermath. By the seventeenth century, English, French and Dutch pirates were essentially waging a war against Spain, periodically raiding Spanish galleons along the coast. France and England, furthermore, engaged in heated competition as maritime powers at the time, targeted precious metals from the Americas, and buccaneers were handy assistants, often literally working with official commissions.

Much of this activity centered in the Caribbean, of

1.4 Galápagos tortoise at Charles Darwin Research Station.

course, but as competition grew, some pirates moved closer to the sources of booty in the Pacific. The Galápagos and harbors such as James Bay in Santiago became a convenient hideaway and restocking point. Giant tortoises were a prime target for this restocking, because they have slow metabolisms and vast internal water storage in their bladders, enabling them to survive as long as a year without eating or drinking—and thus providing a valuable source of fresh meat for the pirates and other seafarers.

By the early nineteenth century, whaling replaced pirating as the leading human influence in the Galápagos—and tortoise fortunes took an even worse turn. With its confluence of ocean currents, the Galápagos waters were, and remain, an ideal feeding and breeding ground for large baleen whales such as fins, sperms, and humpbacks. Seeking valuable oil fuel extracted by cooking fresh blubber, an array of Europeans found their way to the Galápagos as well. The oil rush continued for fifty years, essentially until discovery of commercial quantities of petroleum.

During this period, like their brethren from the sea, the Galápagos giant tortoises faced slaughter of unprecedented proportions. Whaling crews remained at sea for months, sometimes years, with no refrigeration to preserve fresh meat or produce. Tortoise meat was a welcome alternative to salt pork and biscuits. While some 100,000 prospered among the islands at the beginning of the whaling era in 1780, only about 15,000 to 20,000 exist today.

Ecuador took possession of the Galápagos as this oil rush was still underway in 1832, but the first time people stayed on the islands for a substantial time was nearly a century later, although Darwin witnessed a small penal colony on Floreana in 1835.

World War II forever changed this equation. Just four days after the Japanese bombed Pearl Harbor, U.S. troops occupied the islands in an effort to protect the Panama Canal. By most accounts, Ecuador begrudgingly rented the islands situated just above Santa Cruz to the U.S. military, which subsequently began constructing an air force base on the island of Baltra in February 1942. The Americans eventually stationed one thousand personnel on the island, dynamited a mile-long landing strip, and constructed some two hundred wooden buildings, including a beer garden, chapel, cinema, mess hall, and bowling alley. As substantial as this impact was, though, the events it set in motion were even more significant.

The American presence created a new source of income for settlers on Santa Cruz, and its population expanded with this newfound opportunity. Today, as tourism continues to grow, according to the Ecuadorian National Census of 2010, the residential population in the Galápagos totals over 25,000 across five islands, although people are officially restricted to 3 percent of the total land area of the islands.[14]

As we shall elaborate later, more in this case is decidedly not better, and these increasing numbers of people fundamentally threaten the islands with the clearing of primordial forests, uncontrolled hunting, and the introduction of domesticated animals as well as invasive species. In recognition of this detrimental growth, in a desperate attempt to curtail populations doubling every decade or so, the 1998 Special Law for Galápagos includes an amendment to Ecuador's national constitution authorizing restrictions on domestic immigration to the islands. Permanent residency was restricted to three categories: those born in the Galápagos, those who lived there five or more years before the law, and the spouses or children of residents. Other features of the Special Law were limits on local fishing, widening of protection boundaries, establishing quarantine systems for nonindigenous species, and general education of islanders about conservation of resources.

Mainlanders come to the islands largely for one reason: money can be made from tourists. Tourism, then, is driving population increases. It is part of the problem. In a refrain that will be often repeated in my travels, ecotourism, by definition, brings its own set of special challenges.

Following World War II, tourism in the Galápagos slowly picked up where the American GIs had left off, bringing not only more damage from the tourists themselves but inspiring Ecuadorians to relocate to the Galápagos to profit off those tourists, requiring additional infrastructure for both tourists and domestic immigrants. The first large tourist boat arrived in the mid-1960s, and the industry has been growing ever since. Now more than eighty vessels from a range of travel companies regularly ply its waters, with peak season from mid-November to January and roughly 180,000 tourists spending $120 million a year.

National and international environmental interests foresaw this rise and scrambled to prepare for the onslaught. In 1959, on the hundredth anniversary of the publication of Charles Darwin's seminal *The Origin of Species*, and with funding from the United Nations Educational, Scientific and Cultural Organization (UNESCO), World Wildlife Fund (WWF), the New York Zoological Society, and the United States government, 97 percent of the Galápagos was declared a national park. Only the land was protected at this point, though, and even with that so-called protection, invasive species ran roughshod, figuratively if not literally, throughout.[15]

With their destruction of natural habitat, feral goats, descendants of earlier generations left behind by sailors and fishermen to hunt for replenishing supplies, pose arguably the greatest threat to the islands. Other invasive species are problematic too, but the goat quickly became a prime target for conservationists. Native flora expert Duncan Porter sums up the general sentiment with the stern assessment that, "The only good goat on Galápagos, is a dead goat."[16] More on that in a bit.

In 1978, UNESCO proclaimed the Galápagos a World Heritage Site, and, by 1986, Ecuador was ready to expand the Galápagos protection efforts to declare a marine reserve within its perimeter out to five miles offshore. Like paper parks throughout Latin America, though, enforcement was lacking as fishermen continued extracting everything they could get their hands on.

A surprisingly inconspicuous species arose as a major galvanizing force at this point. Sea cucumbers cover the ocean floor by the millions in the Galápagos, living in relatively shallow waters and inching harmlessly along the ocean floor. Most closely related to starfish and sea urchins, they belong to a group of animals called *echinoderms*. These headless, tubular slugs don't just look like oversized worms, they act like them too. Sucking up muck and spreading nutrients like an earthworm aerating soil, sea cucumbers perform a valuable function for many other ocean species.

It turns out that people value the sea cucumber too. Bedrooms from Tokyo to Beijing and beyond treasure them as an aphrodisiac, and that lucrative market offers premium prices. In the late 1980s, decreasing supplies along South America's west coast combined with increasing demand among a number of Asian societies to push the price of these dog poop–sized creatures still higher and higher. Discovery of commercial quantities[17] in the Galápagos in the early 1990s set off a new round of conflicts as this decided economic incentive quickly divided local settler interests from international conservationists even further.

It should also be noted that removing the sea cucumbers themselves was not the only negative aspect of these fishermen's transgressions. How they did it mattered. Freshly picked sea cucumbers must be processed with large pots of boiling water. To fuel those cooking fires, fishermen chopped down mangrove after mangrove, and then left behind their trash and human waste when they were ready to move on.

Following the park service bust of an illegal fishermen camp on Fernandina in which an amazing thirty million sea cucumbers were confiscated, President Rodrigo Borja Cervallos announced a total ban on their harvesting in June 1992. Fishermen were forced underground, and pirate camps, particularly on Isabela, continued to plunder the species. Antagonism between park officials and fishermen grew so great that several dozen *pepineros*, as the sea cucumber fishermen are called, even blockaded the entrance to the Charles Darwin Research station in early January 1995. That scary, three-day standoff highlighted their demand to reopen the fisheries after a failed three-month experimental permit season beginning in June 1994 was cut short.

Finally, in 1997 fishermen, tourist, and protection interests all sat down to discuss proposed enlargements to the boundaries up to ninety miles. These negotiations appeared doomed to failure until a compromise of forty miles emerged after extensive pressure from UNESCO on the Ecuadorian government. Today only tourism and local fisheries are allowed in this area, and the Galápagos are the second-largest marine reserve in the world, second only to the second stop on our itinerary, Australia's Great Barrier Reef.

Enforcement is by no means perfect, but it is greatly improved over the last twenty years. An array of actors found common ground thanks to the fundamental ecological principle of interdependence. This is not just a lesson for the Galápagos Islands. It's one we must apply to global climate change as well. Our world is intricately hitched together, as noted American naturalist and author John Muir famously articulated. It's a concept now deeply ingrained within environmentalism. We do not act in a vacuum. Our actions today shape our options tomorrow. Everything is connected.

chapter two

FROM MAPS TO MODELING

THERE ARE TWO SEASONS IN THE GALÁPAGOS, wet and warm and dry and less warm. Half the year the islands are bathed in warm waters from the north, half the year they receive cool waters from the south. Despite its location along the equator, then, the archipelago does not have a typical equatorial climate. Temperature differences vary as much as ten degrees. If not for its alternating currents, in fact, the islands would not have seasons at all, nor would they harbor their breathtaking diversity of flora and fauna.

The hot season, from December to May, brings high humidity and occasional tropical showers. Average air temperatures are in the eighties. Water temperatures range between seventy and eighty degrees. This combines with calmer seas, with visibility typically sixty to eighty feet, to make it the most comfortable time for snorkeling.

In May and June, the dry season saunters in as southern trade winds usher north the colder Humboldt current, and for half the year, the aforementioned layer of mysterious mist envelops the island skies. While typically hot and sunny in their own right, these days are cooler and windier than earlier in the year, which also means sea swells sometimes make it challenging to land on shore. Until November, sea temperatures range between sixty-five and seventy-five degrees and visibility drops to thirty to fifty feet.

That said, there really is not a bad time to visit the Galápagos Islands. Green turtles lay their eggs in January. Humpback whales begin to arrive in June. July through late September is peak seabird-viewing time, and November is your best bet to play with sea lion pups. Giant tortoise eggs hatch in December. I could go on and on. The point is: each month has its highlights.[1]

Our group arrives at the end of the warm season in May, after our spring semester of teaching obligations finishes, and avoiding the busiest times of the year in the Galápagos from December to January and July to August.

That's certainly a plus any time you travel, and it's magnified on island settings such as these. Go when the crowds do not.

Despite a late start, wildlife tourism is tightly controlled in the Galápagos today. Tourists must be accompanied by a local guide and are restricted to forty-eight approved sites (research scientists are allowed in additional areas), tiny pockets of the national park with designated landing spots and marked trails protecting vegetation and wildlife. Groups are kept small, but popular areas easily become congested. The way to avoid such crowds is to forgo a leisurely breakfast and venture ashore early. Early landings on the islands also offer the best light for photographers (although late afternoons have beautiful lighting as well), and are the best time to see peak animal activity.

With the significant distances involved and minimal hotel options, the most practical and popular way to explore the islands is aboard live-in boats that serve as both transportation and lodging. More than eighty vessels are licensed to operate within the archipelago, each making different stops during the day and cruising between the islands mostly at night. Most go ashore twice a day, hitting approximately ten different islands.

That's nearly the itinerary we have before us for the next eight days, nine islands with multiple landings each day. Our vessel is the *Lammer Law*, a boat run by Iguana Tours and captained by Bolívar Vélez. It's a motor sailing trimaran, which means it has three hulls, including a main hull and two smaller outrigger hulls connected with lateral beams.

It's an impressive boat. Some ninety-three feet long and equipped with both sails and motor, it holds sixteen passengers in eight double cabins, each 125 square feet, as well as a crew of seven plus our naturalist guide, Bitinia Espinoza. It's the perfect combination of big and small, large enough to provide security on the wide-open seas but petite enough to make you feel at home.

In short order, I do just that. In the middle of the trimaran is a spacious, homey lounge with a small but amply supplied (and used) combination bar and library. It is also where we will have many of our daily briefings from Bitinia. While I'm hard pressed to pick a favorite spot on the *Lammer Law* over the next week, this one is right up there, at least after my meds kick in. You see, like most traditional bars, and libraries for that matter, this one does not have windows. It's not the best place to hang out, then, if you have seasickness, a discovery I make later the next evening.

After boarding, we stow our airline- and tourist industry-dictated twenty-two kilos (roughly 48.5 pounds) of luggage and set out to explore the rest of our temporary home. On top, a nondescript sun deck with a handful of lounge chairs boasts panoramic views. The site quickly becomes a group favorite for sundowners at sunset as we speed out to our next destination late each afternoon. The back deck is another favorite gathering spot, especially because it's the scene of scrumptious meals and twice-daily snacks amply served up by Wilmer the chef. A handful of us will also congregate here regularly for intense late-afternoon competition over the card game created for children of all ages, Uno.

First up that afternoon, as we round the island of San Cristóbal, is Kicker Rock, a massive volcanic tower split in two and profusely splotched white with bird guano. Jutting five hundred feet from the surface of the sea like a giant shark fin, Kicker Rock is one of those iconic images of the Galápagos, and when calm seas allow it, tourists like us love to bounce echoes off its walls as they pass between its two sides. We take turns eagerly hopping into a *panga*, a small, outboard-powered boat open to the elements. Commonly used for fishing, these become our main method of transfer from the *Lammer Law* to each island for the next eight days. Sometimes called Zodiacs, they are built to hold twelve, but Americans' reputation for size precedes us, and our guide Bitinia delicately keeps an eye on each transfer while setting our limit at eight.

We awake to day two offshore from Genovesa Island in a lovely lagoon of pale blue water. Our morning destination is the aptly named Darwin Bay Beach; it has white coral sand and a handful of sunbathing sea lions. As amazing as they are, and they truly are amazing, the real draw here is the birds. In fact, the birding is so good here that the nickname for Genovesa is Bird Island.

Now I'm never going to be considered a bird aficionado. I've never quite understood those who are. In fact, I've been a little leery of hanging out with more than a dozen feathered flyers at one time ever since my wife suggested we watch Alfred Hitchcock's famous 1963 horror film. But even an easily alarmed novice like me appreciates a bird mecca like this. Set in a submerged caldera, Genovesa certainly lives up to its nickname, boasting the highest breeding density of boobies in the islands and hosting all three species of boobies found in the Galápagos.

Mixing Madison Avenue advertising with Broadway showmanship, the color markings on boobies are prime examples of sexual selection at work. To many, the blue-footed booby takes center stage in this group. With its elaborate eight-hour mating dance, the show is not exactly fast, but it is dramatic. The blue-footed booby patiently paces through his routine of sky pointing, beak whistling, and blue foot raising—the higher, the better, all the while waiting for a response from its mate.

Not to be outdone in pageantry of sexual selection is the impressive frigatebird. There are five varieties of frigatebirds, or man-o'-wars as they are also known. Two, the great frigatebird and the magnificent frigatebird, are native to the Galápagos but not endemic, meaning they are found elsewhere as well.

Frigatebirds spend almost all their time at sea, but cannot swim and rarely land on water as they lack the oil gland necessary to waterproof their feathers. With their small bodies but large wings, they fly hundreds of miles at a stretch. Still more fascinating, at least to me, is the origin of their other commonly used name, "man-o'-war."

It's not a nod to the pirate-ship past of the Galápagos, or a reference to their flight mimicking the speed and agility of those infamous ships, although the birds, too, can change direction quickly, thanks to their forked tails. Each of those explanations would make perfect sense, but there is another equally appropriate rationale for their name: their piracy tactics. These birds are kleptoparasites, attacking and harassing other seabirds in flight until they drop their catch. The frigatebird then swoops down to snag the meal in midair, before it hits the water. Now that's impressive.

From a distance I think I catch a couple of such dives near a cliff along the edge of Darwin Bay Beach, but I cannot be certain. What I can attest to unequivocally, because you simply cannot miss it, is a crowd pleaser of a different sort, their mating display.

When the mood is right, the male fills his wrinkled gular sac, what we might equate to a throat, into what looks literally like a ridiculously large red balloon such as that partially displayed in Figure 2.1. Perched precariously below his sharp, curved beak, when fully inflated, this red gular sac can literally obscure the bird's head. It's simultaneously magnificent and comical. And, paradoxically, it's also practical. You see, this ridiculous red balloon plays a crucial role in frigatebird reproduction. Females judge their male counterparts based on who has, well, the biggest balloon. Seriously.

Getting back to boobies, though, three species are found on Genovesa, from the largest, the Nazca booby,[2] to the smallest and most common, the blue-footed, to the one in between, the red-footed. The origin of the first part of each name is fairly obvious, but the genesis of the name "booby" itself is less clear. The best guess suggests derivation from the Spanish term *bobo*, or clown, a reference to the habit of these types of birds landing on ships at sea and how easily they could be approached when doing so.

In any case, all are keen at catching fish. With torpedo-like bodies, they dive from sixty to one hundred yards above the surface, applying stereovision once underwater to follow fish.

But in a common Galápagos refrain, why exactly are there three types of boobies?

Turns out the answer lies in a key axiom of ecology, that closely related species in the same region must occupy different niches. The three boobies in the Galápagos follow this rule. While of similar but slightly different sizes, they feed and nest in distinctly different fashions. Blue-footed boobies fish close to shore, red-footed boobies fish far out to sea, and Nazca boobies occupy the space in between. Blue-footed boobies nest on low rocks near the shore. Nazca boobies nest on higher cliffs. Red-footed boobies nest in trees on the more isolated islands.

2.1 Showing off on Genovesa.

When it comes to the red- and blue-footed boobies, furthermore, their colors are prime examples of sexual selection and are tied directly to their food sources, carotenoid pigments from their fresh-fish diet. Blue feet, for example, vividly illustrate the health of a blue-footed booby. Their foot brightness decreases when they are deprived of food for forty-eight hours, meaning foot color is an accurate and quick indicator of an individual's current nourishment levels. That helps explain the aforementioned eight-hour mating dance, during which the male flaunts his blue feet repeatedly in an effort to impress his potential mate. Periodically presenting treasured nest materials with head and bill sky-pointing while keeping its wings and tail raised, the blue-footed booby definitely knows how to call attention to his assets, as seen on Española in Figure 2.2.[3]

Of course, sexual selection was not Charles Darwin's main claim to fame. That was secondary to natural selection, in both his mind and his legacy. Parts of this story are well known, others less so. Indeed, the tale of the *Beagle*'s five-year voyage around the globe is filled with remarkable adventures, and only in its fourth year on September 17, 1835, does Darwin finally reach the Galápagos for his famous five-week stay.

Darwin joined the crew at age twenty-two as an unpaid gentleman's companion to the captain, who was worried about the loneliness of command and guided by social mores that restricted his conversations with crew members lower in life's station. The ship's previous captain had committed suicide, and this time around the *Beagle* would traverse some of the same desolate waters off the coast of South America as its previous voyage.

2.2 May I have this dance?

Indeed, the chief mission for Captain Fitzroy was to survey the continent of South America and uncover safe new sea routes through the eerie smoke of Tierra del Fuego. The Galápagos were to be a minor part of the itinerary, and the initial landing party in the Galápagos, like many before and after it, was primarily sent out to seek giant tortoises for meat and soup.

Interestingly, before the *Beagle* even set sail, Darwin almost missed his life-changing assignment. He was not the first choice of the Cambridge circle seeking a naturalist on the boat. In a series of twists of fate, however, the other candidates declined, and Darwin quite literally had nothing better to do.

A former medical student, he was pursuing a proper liberal arts education at Cambridge to prepare him for a career in the ministry, an occupation with more of a social than a religious function in the Anglican clergy of the time. Darwin was attracted to it as his interest in nature was considered a suitable hobby for clergy. After receiving approval from his father, the voyage was to be a last hurrah of sorts for Darwin the student, before returning home to become a country parson. Darwin was much more interested in beetles than scripture, though, and the Galápagos dramatically reinforced those natural interests, forever changing Darwin's legacy as the founder of evolutionary theory.

In the popular imagination, Darwin's famous finches, closely related to sparrows, were instrumental in uncovering that "mystery of mysteries" on the origin of species. One can readily grasp why this might be the case because they represent an intriguing array of species. One feasts on green leaves, something birds simply are "not supposed to do," as writer Jonathan Weiner relates in his 1995 Pulitzer Prize–winning work, *The Beak of the Finch*.[4] Another, from the remote islands of Wolf and Darwin, the vampire finch, draws blood to drink from the tails and wings of boobies. The carpenter finch uses a wooden stick as a tool to dig larvae out of stumps, much as chimpanzees use twigs as fishing rods to remove termites for tasting. Others hop onto the backs of iguanas and feast on ticks. There is even a vegetarian species that strips the bark off twigs for nourishment. Still another, the cactus finch, not only nests in cacti, but eats and drinks from their flowers while pollinating them.

Darwin's finches, specifically their beaks as noted in Figure 2.3, have become universal symbols of evolution, like the massive eyebrows and distinctive beard of Darwin himself. In short, a finch beak is to evolution what Newton's apple is to gravity. Nevertheless, University of California at Berkeley

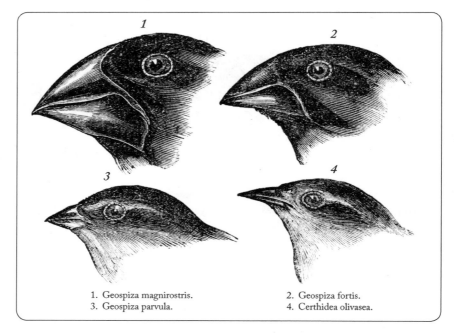

1. Geospiza magnirostris.   2. Geospiza fortis.
3. Geospiza parvula.   4. Certhidea olivasea.

2.3 Darwin's finches. Source: The Complete Works of Charles Darwin Online.

historian Frank J. Sulloway suggests that Darwin did not think the finches were all that important, perhaps being misdirected by their stunning diversity. In his argument, Sulloway points to the fact that Darwin never mentioned them in his final draft of *Origin* as evidence.

Instead, Darwin begins that seminal work with pigeons and spends considerable time on them. Twice as many pages are devoted to pigeons and pigeon breeding as analogies to natural selection than to any Galápagos species. In fact, the Galápagos is only mentioned six times in the entire work, all at the end. Even when addressing the Galápagos, Sulloway argues, finches played second fiddle in Darwin's mind. More notable to him was the mockingbird, which unlike the finches,[5] he took the time to label.

The real inspiration to Darwin actually came a few years after returning home from the Galápagos when, in the fall of 1838, he read Thomas Malthus's *An Essay on the Principle of Population*. Malthus suggested checks on human population arose naturally through famine, epidemics, and war, dictating only the fittest survived. Darwin then applied this logic to plants and animals, contending, in effect, that death was a creative entity. The Galápagos subsequently emerged as an ideal laboratory to observe this process and the "origin of all my views."

As he shared his specimens and wrote a series of publications on barnacles, coral reefs, volcanic islands, and South American geology, Darwin became an increasingly prominent Victorian gentleman scientist. What made him known among the general public most of all, though, was his popular journal of the *Beagle's* voyage, a collection of eco-adventure tales if you will, published in two stages in 1839 and 1845.[6] Following the second volume, Darwin kept his theory of natural selection essentially to himself for over a decade, only publicly announcing his grand theory in 1858 when field naturalist Alfred Russell Wallace appeared poised to beat him to the punch.

Funny how some things never change, no matter what era or arena. Competitive pressure brings out the best in people—or the worst.

Speaking of pressure bringing out the worst in someone, I'm not feeling so well later that night. After a beautiful morning on Darwin Bay and equally impressive afternoon hiking up Prince Philip's Steps through a colony of both Nazca and red-footed boobies in the thin Palo Santo Forest, I'm in for some unpleasant gastronomical pressure that night. Our night sails unfurl, and we have some distance to our next destination of Fernandina. The seas are not exactly rough, but they pack enough punch to put me on the canvas extra early that night.

This same drowsy haze surrounds our understanding of climate change. But it shouldn't.

French mathematician and physicist Joseph Fourier proposed the idea of a greenhouse effect in 1824. British physicist John Tyndall was the first to prove it with measurement in 1859. And Sweden's Svante Arrhenius helped outline the basic chemistry and physics, publishing a famous 1896 paper in *Philosophical Magazine and Journal of Science*, which recognized that industrialization would lead to climate change.[7] Arrhenius determined that a doubling of carbon dioxide would increase average global temperatures between nine and eleven degrees, a figure that, amazingly, approximates the "most sophisticated climate models in operation today."[8] Interestingly, Arrhenius viewed this development positively, believing it would increase agricultural productivity. He was also off a bit on his timing, thinking the oceans would serve as such a reliable sponge that the buildup would take as long as three thousand years to double in the atmosphere.

So how much was he off? I suppose the cheeky answer is to say we are about to find out.

The real reason I bring this up, though, is to underscore the degree to which uncertainty continues to drive discussion on climate change. Yes, we know the climate is changing. Yes, we know it is changing in part because of the greenhouse gases such as carbon dioxide that we are adding to the atmosphere. And yes, we know this translates into all sorts of expensive, perhaps life-altering, complications for us, from flooding, to droughts, to sea-level rise, to increased intensity in storms.[9]

In spite of all that we do know, however, uncertainty remains. Literally, that means we could be overestimating the direness of our situation—or we could be underestimating it. I'm afraid the latter is more likely than the former. As Ken Caldeira, researcher at Carnegie Institution Department of Global Ecology at Stanford, asserts, "If anything, the history of climate modeling has been one of conservatism and underestimating the impacts of climate change." When wrong, climate models almost always underestimate the scale and pace of the problem.[10]

How bad will it really be? What actions will we take? Will we take them soon enough to make a difference? Needless to say, there are a lot of variables in this mix. Probably the most fundamental of them all is simply public awareness, or more harshly, ignorance. You see, changes in temperature from year to year can easily mask what is really transpiring with climate to the untrained eye. An arctic chill in the air this week doesn't mean climate change with warming temperatures is not still underway. Weather is not climate, but the layman can easily confuse the two and, as a result, struggle with distinguishing signals from noise, particularly if examining a limited time horizon.[11]

Much of what we know, first and foremost, is gleaned from paleoclimate records, hundreds of thousands of years of data from nearly two-mile-deep ice cores drilled in central Greenland and Antarctica. Differences in summer and winter snow allow scientists to tell where one year ends and the next begins. Then, from these samples, climatologists analyze the isotopic composition of the ice, determining the temperature when the layer formed. These records show a steady two-century rise that coincides with the Industrial Revolution, and the carbon isotopes point to the burning of fossil fuels as the source.[12]

Combined with modern temperature data, including data from the National Oceanic and Atmospheric Administration and NASA showing that 2016 surpassed 2015 as the hottest year on record,[13] these then create an even sharper image of the changes underway in our atmosphere. A young chemist named Charles David Keeling captured one of the best-known graphics here when he was able to convince the United States Weather Bureau to use his technique for monitoring carbon dioxide in 1958 at 11,000 feet above sea level on the Hawaiian slope of Mauna Loa. Measurements taken every four hours are now maintained and updated by the Scripps Institution of Oceanography. What they show is a distinctive saw-tooth curve, fluctuating over the course of each year, as seen in Figure 2.4 below. Carbon dioxide levels fall to a minimum in the summer as the trees of the Northern Hemisphere suck up more carbon dioxide, but then rise in the winter when those trees are dormant.[14]

In 1959, Keeling's first full year, he measured carbon dioxide at 316 parts per million (0.0316 percent of molecules in the air). In 1960 he recorded 317 parts per million. By 1970 it had reached 325. In 1990 it was 354. In January 2017 it was 406.95 ppm. This rise is unmistakable and stands

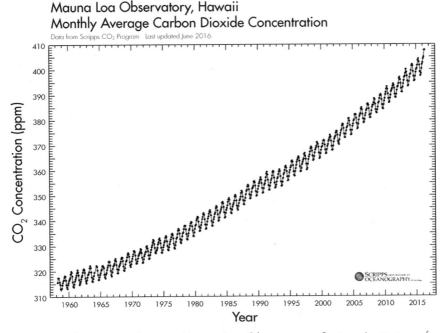

2.4 The Keeling curve. Source: Mauna Loa Observatory, Scripps Institution of Oceanography, Scripps CO2 Program.

in stark contrast to the 280 parts per million constant for the 10,000 years before the Industrial Revolution. By around 2030, extrapolated from current trends, we should hit 450, according to noted climatologist and Penn State professor Michael Mann.[15] That means another degree Celsius in warming and a total of two degrees compared to preindustrial levels. To avoid such a rise, we would need 80 percent reductions relative to 1990 levels in less than a decade. Others, such as NASA's James Hansen believe 450 ppm is too dangerous and suggest 350 ppm should be the real goal.

Combining measurement in real time with reconstruction of the paleo-climatic record, MIT atmospheric scientist Kerry Emanuel asserts that climate modeling is "perhaps the most complex endeavor ever undertaken by mankind."[16] As he explains, the typical model consists of millions of lines of computer instruction. It includes the flow of the oceans, condensation and precipitation of water inside clouds, as well as transport of heat, water, and atmospheric constituents by turbulent convection currents. It also considers the transfer of solar and terrestrial radiation through the atmosphere as well as its partial absorption and reflection by the surface, clouds, and atmosphere itself. That's pretty heavy stuff.

Given this context, one may rightly question the application of the sage advice of fourteenth-century logician and Franciscan friar William of Ockham. Occam's razor, as it has come to be known, recommends "entities should not be replicated unnecessarily." In practice, as applied from Isaac Newton to Albert Einstein to Stephen Hawking, this means choose the simplest explanation possible. Perhaps it goes without saying, but I'll say it anyway. When it comes to climate modeling, that's easier said than done.

As evidence, let's take a closer look at someone who knows the ins and outs of climate modeling intimately. On the corner of Broadway and West 112th Street in New York City, four blocks south of the main entrance to Columbia University and just above Tom's Restaurant of TV's *Seinfeld* fame, lie the offices of NASA's Goddard Institute for Space Studies. Led by James Hansen from 1981 to 2013, the institute's research initially emphasized a broad array of global change, but today it focuses on making climate forecasts. Algorithms that explain atmospheric behavior are their particular specialty.

While the Goddard Institute global circulation models (GCMs) focus on the atmosphere, others concentrate on oceans, vegetation, clouds, or ice sheets. Regardless of focus, two types of equations are applied in every model.

The first are fundamental physical principles, such as the conservation of energy and the law of gravity. The second are known as "parameterizations," patterns we can observe but only partially understand. Again, here rises the ugly head of uncertainty.

Hansen is often referenced as the godfather of climate modeling, but legendary basketball coach John Wooden might be a better analogy. Hansen has never left a horse's head in anyone's bed to emphasize a point, but he has delivered championship results consistently, year after year. His research at Goddard emphasized the broad study of global change, an interdisciplinary initiative addressing natural and man-made changes on various time scales. These included one-time "forcings" such as volcanic explosions, seasonal effects such as El Niño, and finally the millennia of ice ages. The GCM his group made famous, called ModelE, contributed to several IPCC Assessment Reports, including the two most recent in 2007 and 2014.

Of a couple dozen global circulation models across the globe, roughly fifteen major ones are recognized in operation today. Each divides the world into a series of boxes, fifty miles horizontally and a few hundred vertically. That translates into 3,312 boxes to cover the surface of the Earth, a pattern repeated twenty times upward through the atmosphere. Each box represents an area of four degrees latitude by five degrees longitude. Time is measured in discrete, half-hour intervals. A single run of a Goddard model, even on a supercomputer, typically takes a month. The initial Goddard model took almost seven years to finish.

Such complexity is not our only obstacle, however. In thinking back to our discussion about Bugs Bunny, maps, and theories, climate-change modeling is also problematic because it is not complicated enough. Like every model, it's an imperfect representation of the way the world works. Modeling takes shortcuts as many critical processes develop on much smaller geographic scales. Cumulus clouds, for example, are key agents in transferring heat and water, but, typically no more than a few miles across; they cannot be integrated into models with fifty-mile long blocks.

Despite the challenges, climate-change models have come a long way in a short time. One graph, in particular, stands out, the hockey-stick graph. An easy-to-understand image that quickly became an icon, it was first produced by Penn State professor Michael Mann and colleagues

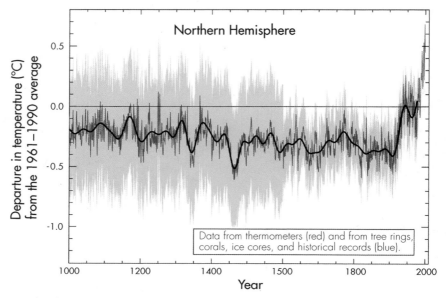

2.5 The hockey-stick graph.
   Source: Albritton, Daniel L., et al. "Summary for Policymakers." *Climate
   Change 2001: The Scientific Basis*. Contribution of Working Group I to the
   Third Assessment Report of the Intergovernmental Panel on Climate Change.
   Eds. J. T. Houghton, Y. Ding, D. J. Griggs, et al. Cambridge, UK: Cambridge
   University Press, 2001, pp. 1–20.

in 1998 and covered six hundred years of temperature data over the entire
Northern Hemisphere, where most of the climate data exists.[17] With a 1999
follow-up article extending the time covered to a millennium, Mann et al.
were able to illustrate changes in the Earth's temperature back to 1000 CE.
Mann subsequently became the lead author on one of the IPCC's third
assessment reports, and the hockey stick was featured in its 2001 "Summary
for Policymakers."

   The graph is fuzzy for most of the nine hundred years, represented by the
so-called stick that reflects the extent to which ice cores, corals, and tree ring
data are proxies, and thus, imperfect thermometers. Tree rings are the most
widespread of these, and they come with noted limitations. For one, their use
restricts measurement to the continental regions where trees grow, leaving out
the polar regions as well as much of the water-covered Southern Hemisphere.
For another, tropical trees typically do not exhibit annual growth rings, so that
leaves tropical regions underrepresented. And finally, another issue is what

scientists label a clear "divergence problem" in ring density at higher altitudes, beginning in 1960 with an unexpected decline in tree growth, despite continued warming temperatures, perhaps due to pollution.[18]

Toward the end of our time graph, the twentieth-century "blade" of the hockey stick illustrates the more precise measurements of temperature through direct observation, without the need for proxy data. This was further magnified when the original draft reconstruction of climate temperatures, which ended in 1980, was updated with current observational data per recommendation of an anonymous reviewer. Since its initial publication in *Geophysical Research Letters*, Michael Mann's famous graph, as seen in Figure 2.5, has appeared in everything from numerous academic journals to Al Gore's *An Inconvenient Truth*.[19]

chapter three

QUEASINESS AND UNCERTAINTY

ON AVERAGE, Americans emit roughly sixteen tons of carbon each year. For visual reference, picture three large adult male African elephants. Multiply them times our population, and in 2013, the United States emitted around 5.38 billion tons, according to the Energy Information Administration.[1]

And we are not even the worst offender anymore, with China surpassing us in annual emissions in late 2006.[2] According to the Global Carbon Project, nearly forty billion tons were released worldwide into the atmosphere in 2013, only a 2.1 percent increase over 2012 but a staggering 61 percent more than the 1990 baseline year for the Kyoto Protocol.[3]

What's worse, the carbon emitted today lasts a long, long time. Most climate-change assessments neglect this fact, or almost casually note that carbon dioxide lingers in the atmosphere, like a bad dinner guest, much longer than it should. Typically, the reference number here is over a century, but University of Chicago oceanographer David Archer disagrees with that estimate. He asserts, "The lifetime of fossil fuel CO_2 in the atmosphere is a few centuries, plus 25 percent that lasts essentially forever."[4]

All that is a bit unsettling. The natural reaction, some might argue, is to shut down when confronted with numbers like these. You don't want to know how bad it really is. Ignorance is bliss. And indeed, for many, climate change is truly overwhelming. That might be yet another reason why it's so hard to grasp—because we just don't want to.

At the moment, though, I'm fighting a different battle—with an unsettled stomach. I'm attempting to dine with my colleagues on the back deck of the *Lammer Law* for our second dinner of the trip. Last night was a delicious feast and, in hobbit-like fashion, I've never been one to miss a meal. But my stomach now recommends otherwise.

If you've never had motion sickness, you are a lucky soul. Those who have know what I mean when I say you just want to die. It's not an exaggeration. I never could have made this journey in the early nineteenth century with Darwin, or if I somehow did, no one would have wanted to make it with me. It would not have been pretty. Without modern medicine, it would have taken me weeks to get my sea legs, and, by that point, there probably wouldn't be much of me—or my mates—left.

The culprit here is the inner ear, or, technically, the combination of your eyes, inner ear, and sensory nerves instrumental in helping keep your balance. More precisely, it is their failure to agree on whether your body is in motion or not. For example, when in the cabin of a moving ship, your inner ear can detect movement from the waves, even as your eyes fail to record any motion. These mixed messages are sent to the brain, and motion sickness results.

As with any illness, prevention is your best bet. Once symptoms start, motion sickness is hard to stop. Relief really only comes when the motion itself stops, but you can minimize queasiness by sitting or lying where the least movement takes place.

Like a good Boy Scout, this is something for which I've come prepared—I think. I've always tried to keep my over-the-counter medicinal intake to a minimum. It's not something I've extensively researched, just a hunch that I'd rather dance with the devil I know than the one I don't—the potential side effects from pharmaceuticals. I rarely introduce even aspirin and cough medicine to my body.

In graduate school, of all places, I consciously weaned myself off caffeinated sodas and caffeine more generally. Not sure what possessed me to attempt that, especially considering some of the dry material we had to read the first couple years. But I've been healthier for it, and it means that even a hot chocolate does the trick of a strong coffee nowadays. Of course, payback comes the next day with the inevitable piercing caffeine headache.

With this perhaps odd pharmaceutical philosophy in mind, my pathetic level of preparation for motion sickness extends only to constriction wristbands, terry-cloth bands with plastic lumps roughly the height of a couple shirt buttons stuck together. These constriction bands supposedly apply acupressure, utilizing the same principles acupuncture has applied over thousands of years in China. The idea is my life force or *qi* flows along channels known as "meridians" in the body, and special acupressure points lie along these meridians.

Hogwash. Wish I'd looked a little more into this before the trip instead of after, or at the bare minimum done a test run. When it comes to my so-called meridians, at least, these things are useless. The end result: I sadly spend dinner on the top deck desperately attempting to hold lunch down while orienting my innards, and inner ear, according to the equatorial night sky.

By the end of the dinner, I've been successful on the first part but not much so with the latter. In short, I need help, and fortunately there is a savior in our midst. An economics colleague comes to my rescue with something called a "transdermal patch," in essence a circular bandage loaded with meds that you stick behind your ear. Medicated with 1.5 mg of scopolamine, it lasts for three days. Side effects include eyes that are more sensitive to sunlight, and the need to minimize your alcohol intake, but by the next morning, my nausea and dizziness are gone.

Wish I could say the same about uncertainty on climate change. Part of the problem here is not just the public's lack of understanding when it comes to the science of climate change. It's the public's lack of understanding on science. According to the California Academy of Sciences, a majority of the U.S. public is unable to pass even the most basic scientific literacy test.[5]

Think that's bad? It gets even worse when you consider simply how scientists conduct their research and publish it. As the National Science Foundation reports, two-thirds of Americans do not clearly understand the scientific process.[6] The typically slow peer review process is designed to facilitate a healthy skepticism with each new study, to breed continual objective criticism, but the lay public too often confuses this with disagreement and confusion within scientific ranks. In short, the scientific method comes off as wishy-washy. An ill-informed public simply does not understand the difference between probability confidence measures and street lingo "uncertainty." Scientists mean statistical deviation around a mean whereas the general public interprets the term to mean that scientists just don't know. And as we shall see shortly, this becomes more problematic when confusing the difference between weather and climate.

Day three, though, is a new day filled with new hope, for uncertain stomachs and uncertainty on climate change science. We enjoy an early-morning snorkel in a cove off the northwest tip of Isabela, that younger, teenage island that formed about one million years ago as six volcanoes broke the surface and joined together.

Among other attributes, Isabela is noted as one of the two breeding locales for the Galápagos penguin, which is the only penguin to venture north of the equator, albeit just barely. It is found mostly in the westernmost islands of the Galápagos where cooler currents keep water temperatures low. I definitely feel the chill on this snorkel, but frolicking with sea-lion pups such as this one in Figure 3.1 as we straddle the equator is definitely worth it. Sea lions, distinguishable from fur seals to the less initiated like

3.1 A playful sea lion is part of the welcoming party at Fernandina.

me by their external ear flaps, are warm-blooded mammals, which means they give birth to live young that suckle milk. They breathe air but prefer water to the land, and, perhaps most notable of all, are amazing swimmers—and surfers. Seriously, these dudes love to surf.

After the obligatory mid-morning snack, or second breakfast for the hobbits among us, we are off to our next island stop. Fernandina is the youngest of the main islands of the archipelago, so young that it is literally still in the midst of its birth.

As we get ready to disembark, there is a bit of confusion in the air about whether we will actually land. Causing the confusion is something else in the air—volcanic ash. As the westernmost main island in the archipelago, Fernandina sits directly above the Galápagos hot spot, making it the most active of the islands in terms of volcanic eruptions. There have been at least twenty-five historical eruptions documented on Fernandina in the last two hundred or so years. One of these occurred the week prior to our departure from Orlando, and as we reach its shore today it's still erupting—and will continue for the next five days.[7] Fortunately, with the volcano on the opposite side of the island and prevailing wind patterns deemed safe, we are allowed to proceed on schedule. It's high tide, though, so we are in for a wet landing on the northeast side of the island at Punta Espinoza, a site itself that was tectonically uplifted in 1975.

To land on Fernandina is to transport back to an earlier time. Lacing up my boots and ascending the inland trail, an almost otherworldly landscape unfolds. Two of the three basalt lava types lay before us, and a genuinely prehistoric aura permeates the path ahead. As one of those esoteric facts that my middle child loves, it's the remains of lava that shot up in molten red rivers from the depths of the Earth, where it can reach temperatures seven to ten times hotter than boiling water. We are walking on an older, dried lava flow, a small portion of which is set aside by the national park in an effort to minimize our footprint.

Known by their Hawaiian names, *aa* is a lava with a stony, rough surface sharp enough to penetrate the highest-grade combat boot, whereas *pahoehoe* is smooth with an unbroken, billowy surface. Each is captivating, but I can't seem to take my eyes off the undulating rolls of *pahoehoe*. It extends

3.2 Pioneer species.

3.3 Marine iguanas on alert.

uninterrupted for great stretches until we come to a rise in the trail where my biologist colleague points out a plant, conspicuous because it is one of the few to be found here on this basalt outcrop, a lava cactus as seen in Figure 3.2. Growing where no other plants can survive, it serves as a pioneer species, meaning it creates soil from the lava and enables other species to later take hold.

Coming around a bend in the trail, we then gradually descend back to the shoreline where a decidedly different species has taken hold, by the hundreds if not thousands. They are Darwin's "imps of darkness," marine iguanas. Found nowhere else in the world, there may be as many as 300,000 across the Galápagos, and Fernandina hosts one of the largest colonies. Today, as on most days, they are lounging about on the rocky shores in an effort to raise their body temperature before bravely launching themselves back into the cold sea in search of nourishment. These marine iguanas, the only sea-going lizards in the world, are essentially vegetarian[8] and forage for green algae encrusted on rocks at depths of six to sixty feet in the cold waters offshore before returning to land to digest their meal, essentially cooking it in their stomach, like these in Figure 3.3.

Their preference for land rather than water fascinated Darwin. He speculated that they evolved from land iguanas after he repeatedly tossed them into the ocean and found that they always returned to land. What is most intriguing to me, though, is the coping mechanism they have developed to expel excess salt from their dragon-like bodies. Special glands allow them to spray it fifty centimeters out of their nostrils in dramatic fashion. Extremely territorial, they use this adaptation to warn those that venture too close to their sunning space.

But to get back to our theme of uncertainty. A confused public not only trips on its own two feet when it comes to understanding science. An active disinformation campaign, one heavily bankrolled by the fossil fuel industry, obfuscates as well. Such corporate maleficence is nothing new—there are examples from the manufacture of paint, toys, furniture, and an array of plastic products, to name just a few.[9] As satirized in the 2005 Hollywood film, *Thank You for Smoking*, significant financial interests motivate this thinking. In the climate-change arena, the strategy evolved from first arguing that climate change was not happening, to then contending that it was negligible, and finally asserting that it was beneficial and merely a natural phenomenon.

Award-winning journalist Ross Gelbspan highlighted the "drumbeat of doubt" during President George W. Bush's administrations with a memo political consultant Frank Luntz wrote to the Republican Party in November 2002. In a section of that memo entitled "Winning the Global Warming Debate," Luntz suggested that voters still failed to see the scientific consensus on climate change but warned, "Should the public come to believe that the scientific issues are settled, their views about global warming will change accordingly. Therefore you need to continue to make the lack of scientific certainty a primary issue."

Something called the Oregon Petition is a prime example of putting this advice to work. Widely cited as evidence of scientific uncertainty, this April 1998 document states in part:

> There is no convincing scientific evidence that human release of carbon dioxide, methane, or other greenhouse gases is causing or will, in the foreseeable future, cause catastrophic heating of the Earth's atmosphere and disruption of the Earth's climate.

Moreover, there is substantial scientific evidence that increases in atmospheric carbon dioxide produce many beneficial effects upon the natural plant and animal environments of the Earth.[10]

Of the 31,487 signatures boasted of by the Oregon Institute of Science and Medicine that organized this petition, however, only one-third were PhDs—and none were climatologists. Indeed, an analysis conducted by *Scientific American* found that the list included the likes of Geri Halliwell of the Spice Girls and fictional characters such as B. J. Hunnicutt from the television series *M.A.S.H.*

In keeping with this pattern of misdirection, a research paper that mimicked the style of the prestigious journal of the Academy, *Proceedings of the National Academy*, accompanied the petition along with a cover letter from noted climate skeptic Fred Seitz, who served as president of the National Academy of Science thirty years earlier, from 1962 to 1969. Together, they sent the false impression the work came from the academy itself. Indeed, the opposite was true, and the academy felt compelled to release a press release stating the project "was a deliberate attempt to mislead scientists" and "not based on a review of the science of global climate change, nor were its signers experts in the field of climate science."

Despite this climate of deception, and even with the largest player, ExxonMobil, remaining obstinate, some shifts within the oil industry are underway. British Petroleum was the first major oil company to at least acknowledge the stakes in 1997 when CEO John Browne announced BP's initials now stood for Beyond Petroleum and reflected planned reductions in greenhouse gases with a transition to renewable energy. Royal Dutch/Shell followed this lead in 2001, announcing that half its energy would be either renewable or natural gas by 2020.

Natural gas, by the way, per unit of energy, burns more cleanly by emitting two-thirds the carbon of oil and half that of coal. These improvements are quickly lost, though, if methane (eighty-six times more potent than carbon dioxide) from natural gas escapes into the atmosphere unburned. Alarmingly, research over the last several years by Cornell biogeochemist and ecosystem scientist Robert Howarth suggests this is indeed happening at much higher rates than originally thought, meaning both shale gas and conventional natural gas may actually have a larger greenhouse gas footprint than either coal or oil.[11]

In any case, years of denial by fossil fuel interests certainly took their toll on the truth that we are causing climate change with all of these emissions. As any propaganda artist knows, if people hear a lie repeated often enough, they come to actually believe it, particularly when it is dressed up in official clothing and touches on raw political nerves regarding government intrusiveness. As noted in our introduction, for example, the American public falsely believes no scientific consensus exists on climate change. With states such as my native Tennessee passing a law a few years back allowing climate change skepticism to be taught in schools, that confusion may continue to fester.[12]

Now, admittedly, scientists share a little of the blame here. Climate-gate with the alleged manipulation of data by scholars at the University of East Anglia is one example. While in reality the "crisis" turned out to be little more than a weak choice of wording in a series of email exchanges illegally retrieved by global warming deniers, the general pattern of scientists being poorly prepared for prime-time public relations remains. Let's face it, unless your job is selling, it's hard to be good at both your job and at selling what you do at your job. Precious few have it, that "it" factor. Furthermore, some who do probably rely on their charisma a little too much, taking away valuable time from the day-to-day work in the trenches that rarely receives headlines.

In short, like most academics, many scientists struggle relaying their message to a wider audience without the crutches of their disciplinary-specific jargon. It's rare to find the eloquent Rachel Carson or passionate Carl Sagan who writes or speaks as well as they conduct their research, although two we've briefly mentioned might qualify: climatologists James Hansen and Michael Mann.

Further muddying the waters, all too often, the U.S. press plays the role of unwitting accomplice when it comes to a misinformed and downright confused American public. As journalist Ross Gelbspan asserts, reporters are rewarded disproportionately for political reporting.[13] This combines with the mantra of journalistic balance to encourage uncritical pieces that integrate the disinformation campaigns of the fossil fuel industry directly into a story in an effort to appear fair and unbiased. Ticking off a list of additional handicaps, Gelbspan emphasizes reporters' lack of scientific experience, lack of time to cover an issue in depth, the conservative language of science, the outright laziness of reporters, and the finances of the news-media boardroom, which dictate staff cutbacks and the determination that stories on celebrities and self-help simply sell better.

Despite such imposing obstacles, a blueprint for overcoming these odds exists. It's found in the shift in public opinion in the United States regarding cigarettes at the end of the twentieth century, which not coincidentally exposed the very playbook climate deniers themselves adapted from the tobacco industry. Coverage of the science on tobacco addiction and its health damage "profoundly changed the nation's smoking habits," according to Gelbspan.[14] The hope is that media coverage of greenhouse gases could have the same impact on consumption of fossil fuels.

Of course, that's not exactly comparing apples and oranges. You might say it's more like lima beans and ice cream. Climate change is vastly more complicated, with even more powerful entrenched interests to overcome.

And to reiterate this chapter's theme, uncertainty permeates all of this. For example, the temperature increases expected over the next century are frustratingly difficult to pin down, ranging between 1.5 to 4.5 Celsius (or 3 to 8 degrees Fahrenheit) if a doubling of preindustrial atmospheric carbon dioxide occurs as forecast.

The obvious question here is why? What accounts for this uncertainty?

Part of what clouds matters here, literally, is global dimming, the cooling effect that offsets greenhouse warming to a degree. For a fair part of the twentieth century, up to the 1970s, aerosols masked the true impact of climate change. Aerosols are fine particles in the air, such as dust or soot from smoke, produced mainly in the burning of fossil fuels. They scatter and absorb sunlight, which reduces the amount of light that actually reaches the ground. Unlike volcanic sulfate aerosols, though, aerosols remain confined to the lower atmosphere and fall out within days after emission stops. That means that only localized patterns of cooling develop to offset global warming, but those influence global temperature measurements nonetheless. And the bottom line is the true effects of global warming have been underestimated as a result, perhaps by as much as one degree Celsius, according to aforementioned climate modeler James Hansen.[15]

Changing precipitation patterns are another major factor. In fact, clouds are perhaps the biggest of the question marks here, according to Kerry Emanuel, professor of atmospheric science at MIT and one of "100 People Who Shape Our World" according to *Time* magazine.[16] Will they increase, bringing more water vapor and, thus, warmer temperatures? Or will clouds have a negative effect, dampening the impact of climate change as a warmer Earth could produce more low clouds that actually mimic the effect of surface ice and reflect incoming sunlight back into space?

Already we know that the impacts of precipitation will diverge widely according to geographic region. Some will receive too much water, others too little. Marked increases in tornadoes in North America will probably continue. Water normally raining down on Australia will dissipate as South Pole winds draw more and more water vapor rising from the South Pacific down to the Antarctic, which, somewhat paradoxically, at least to the layperson, may very well mean more snow on this dry continent, even as its ice shelves melt.

Some of this could easily be written off as natural variability, what we refer to as "climate noise." Unusual weather does not signal climate shifts. One event does not a pattern make, so the saying goes. But over time, a series of weather events do. As Emanuel asserts, patterns, in terms of climate, take thirty years to develop.[17] This is what we are seeing today.

Writer and reporter Elizabeth Kolbert draws an effective analogy to a rocking rowboat. When disturbed, rowboats tip somewhat, but then return to their normal position. This tipping and returning repeats for some time, but if the rocking reaches a certain point, it can no longer return to normal, and the boat flips upside down.

Positive (in a negative way) feedback loops are the rocking forces that increase the odds that this will happen. While factors such as carbon dioxide, methane, and black carbon undeniably drive climate change, feedbacks are what will determine its eventual magnitude. As Hansen succinctly states, they are the guts of the climate problem.[18]

Water vapor is the most important of these. The concentration of water vapor depends on temperature and pressure. This ratio is what we refer to as "relative humidity" and averages around 60 percent. Warmer air holds more moisture through greater evaporation, so higher temperatures mean more water in the atmosphere; thus the likelihood of more snow in Antarctica even as its ice shelf melts.

But this is not the only source. What lies beneath the permafrost is a second major feedback that complicates our climate change estimates. In the upper reaches of Canada, Alaska, and Russia, for example, trees and grasses do not fully decompose when they die; rather, they are compressed down through the snow and ice as organic matter, essentially suspended in animation for thousands of years. Grass has been found around Fairbanks, Alaska, that dates back to the last ice age. It is literally still green in the permafrost. As the permafrost melts, though, this organic matter will begin to break down and release carbon dioxide and methane into the atmosphere, lots of it.

Still another positive feedback loop (remember—in a negative way) is the ice-albedo effect. Literally meaning "whiteness," albedo is represented by ice such as the Larsen B ice shelf, which collapsed in March 2002. This can be a big deal for we are melting away ice, which reflects heat, and replacing it with much darker substances such as water or land that absorb heat. For example, a spectroradiometer measures reflected light on a scale of 1 to 0, where 1 is perfect reflection and 0 represents perfect absorption. Earth averages about 0.3 overall, meaning one-third of light is reflected back into space. In the Arctic, this average in spring, with a full coverage of ice, is between 0.8 and 0.9, but as ice melts away to leave only ocean waters in the summer, that number drops to a mere 0.07. That's not seven tenths, but seven hundredths! That means that Arctic spring ice shifts from literally the best reflector you could imagine to the worst as summer melting leaves only exposed water.

Another example of ice serving the important function of reflecting radiation and heat back into space is the Greenland ice sheet. As this ice sheet melts, less and less sunlight is reflected. At the moment, this loss of reflective capability is not that noticeable, but as Greenland ice melts faster and faster, it will become much more obvious. To lose the entire Greenland ice sheet could take another two thousand years, a recent study led by Alexander Robinson with the Potsdam Institute for Climate Impact Research in Germany contends.[19] Others, such as James Hansen, assert that this estimate is too optimistic and assumes an unlikely linear progression in the melting. He believes it is possible that Greenland could melt completely in a matter of centuries, possibly even decades. What all agree on, though, is that once begun, the process is self-reinforcing and virtually impossible to stop.

This calls to mind the driving plot of the 2004 Hollywood film *The Day After Tomorrow*, which is actually not centered on the rise in ocean levels but, rather, what happens to the Gulf Stream and the warming effect it creates on Europe and North America. Ocean water in the North Atlantic is saltier than in other parts of the globe such as the North Pacific, in part due to the abundantly salty Mediterranean water that passes through Gibraltar.

The combination of high salt content and winter cooling makes the North Atlantic surface water dense enough to sink to the ocean bottom and create a current of deep water moving south while warmer water at intermediate latitudes moves north to replace it. Introducing massive amounts of additional fresh water, as a melting Greenland would, could well shut down this conveyor belt, thus eliminating the warming Gulf stream effect and, instead, cooling the North Atlantic, although this would probably take decades if not centuries, not the mere hours depicted in the film. On top of these three feedbacks—water vapor, permafrost, and ice albedo—you could argue that a fourth and final positive feedback loop exists. Despite the significance and unpredictability of water vapor, you might even assert this fourth one is the most problematic of all. This feedback is people, specifically our energy usage. Will we continue to use more and more energy in the years ahead? From where will it come? Will alternative energy sources be further developed? Or will fossil fuels continue to dominate our needs? How humans respond to the threat of climate change will shape not only future forcings such as carbon dioxide. It will influence the other aforementioned feedback loops. If we continue with business as usual over the next decade, little hope remains.

chapter four

DARWIN, SCIENCE, AND SPIRITUALITY

WHAT EXPLAINS PEOPLE'S INTEREST in the environment? For some, it is an innate curiosity about how the life around us works. It's a pragmatic focus on science framed as a simple search for cold, hard facts. The unemotional language of chemical, physical, and biological interactions expressed in well-reasoned mathematical equations and relationships dominates this line of thinking.

For others, it's the opposite. The environment is special for the intense spirituality it fosters. Emotion defines the relationship. It's not what we know and what we are able to explain—but what we feel. Famed American naturalist John Muir highlighted this approach when he described wilderness as the recharging grounds for civilization, a space desperately needing protection if only for our own psychological health.

As different as they may at first seem, these two approaches do not inherently contradict one another. When it comes to science and spirituality, you can have your cake and eat it too. Favoring one need not come at the expense of the other.

A useful analogy in this respect is to compare this relationship to the highly touted, but often misrepresented, concept of sustainable development and its components of economic and ecological interests. With that term, at least when accurately applied, one must address both economic health and environmental protection. Indeed, lasting success in one is intrinsically dependent on achieving simultaneous success in the other. Future economic health is not possible where environmental degradation occurs, and vice versa.

When it comes to science and spirituality, similarly, many often confuse the two as diametric opposites, but one can have a strong religious faith while remaining a passionate follower and defender of science. Perhaps no one articulated this better than noted astronomer and popular science writer Carl

Sagan with his assertion, "Science is not only compatible with spirituality; it is a profound source of spirituality."[1]

Traveling through the laboratory of Charles Darwin and the origin of his theory of evolution that creationists abhor, these thoughts are on my mind, although admittedly not at this very minute. At the moment, I'm lost in my own little world, one I never dreamed existed when growing up in middle Tennessee. Here, snorkeling off Bartolomé Island, a heavily photographed but barren islet just east of Santiago in Sullivan Bay, I'm surrounded by an array of intricately colored fish I never knew existed. I even see a majestic green sea turtle out of the corner of my eye.

Diving to follow it, though, I stop dead in my tracks after only a few strokes. Directly ahead, about fifteen feet below, is a five-foot whitetip reef shark. Nothing inspires terror like a shark, even if it is a relatively small, harmless species like this one. You see whitetips top out at just over five feet in length, too small to regard people as prey. When they do bite, it's most likely a case of mistaken identity.

None of that matters to me at the moment, as I fail to process this critical information in my own muddled mind. In a matter of seconds, I experience a complete spectrum of emotions, from initial ecstasy in trailing behind such a majestic creature as the green sea turtle to literally gasping in horror and

4.1 Bartolomé Island and Pinnacle Rock.

retreating to the surface when I glimpse this shark. Despite their unaggressive nature when it comes to humans, whitetip reef sharks still possess that iconic dorsal fin and menacing, toothy grin that makes you second-guess any water outing.[2]

Surviving that encounter and returning to our ship, I get the chance to jot down a few notes in my expedition journal. As seen in Figure 4.1, Pinnacle Rock, jutting like a giant shark tooth into the sky, stands in the background as my immediate inspiration. One of the most-photographed features of the Galápagos, including an appearance in the 2002 Hollywood blockbuster *Master and Commander*, Pinnacle Rock is recognizable far and wide across the globe.

It's day four and my attention turns from the omnipresent and ominous black coal that dominates any discussion of climate change as our overall largest source of carbon dioxide emissions, to the remote former pirate haunts of James Bay off Santiago and its beautiful black sand beach. We've completed our two snorkels on tap for the day and visited two of the three different islands on the day's itinerary. Santiago was the first, and worth a detour if only for a short history lesson on the damage caused by invasive species.

A number of invasive species threaten the Galápagos, from donkeys, pigs, and cows, to cats and dogs. Aside from people themselves, however, perhaps none are more devastating than feral goats.[3] First introduced in the late 1800s, goats established a presence on thirteen islands by the 1900s. Primarily through overgrazing, they wreaked havoc on the fragile Galápagos ecosystem.

Project Isabela aimed to change this, beginning in 1998 with $6 million in funding from the World Bank's Global Environment Facility and direction from the Galápagos National Park as well as the Charles Darwin Foundation. While some 120 islands worldwide had been effectively cleared of feral goats before Project Isabela, including earlier efforts in the Galápagos on five of its smaller islands, the scale of this project was significantly larger. It addressed problems with feral goats on Santiago, a small islet off the west coast of Isabela, and on Isabela itself.[4] Isabela in particular was a daunting challenge because it is easily the largest island of the archipelago, eighty miles long from north to south and fifty miles at its widest.

In one of life's not too little ironies, to effectively protect Darwin's laboratory of natural selection, the park desperately adopted decidedly anti-Darwinian measures. Officials employed three phases in what amounted to an all-out war against this invading pest. In the case of Santiago, the ground assault came first, with teams of twelve to fifteen hunters deployed, each with two hunting dogs, for an average of two weeks. Aerial attacks followed this initial offensive, with sharpshooters and two helicopters imported from New Zealand. Park operatives killed nearly eighty thousand feral goats on Santiago, in an area more than three times the size of Washington, D.C., with these initial two tactics. Approximately 99 percent of the population was eliminated.

But that was not enough because goats are remarkably prolific. A female reaches sexual maturity when seven months old. The typical nanny gives birth to two kids at a time, on average three to four times a year for the rest of her life. Under these conditions, it does not take long for a population to get out of control. In the summer of 1982, for example, only 10 wild goats were found on Isabela. By the end of the millennium, before implementing the eradication project, more than 100,000 roamed the island. As summed up by Felipe Cruz, director of technical assistance for the Charles Darwin Foundation, the task at hand would not be easy.[5]

With this in mind, officials turned to a creative third and final phase, implemented with what became known, fittingly, as Judas goats. As innately social creatures, any surviving goats naturally sought out fellow animals. Often brightly painted and fitted with radio collars, Judas goats then led park personnel right to these remaining goats. Pointedly, Judas goats were female goats coated with hormones (induced into a long-term estrus) to give nearby male goats extra incentives to seek them out, but also sterilized to insure that any liaisons were unproductive.[6]

Aside from twenty sterile Judas goats kept for monitoring of potentially deliberate reintroductions on the island, Santiago was declared goat-free in less than a year after we left, in March 2006.[7] In an intriguing epilogue to this story, moreover, the remaining flora and the fauna that depended on it were not the sole beneficiaries of these goats' demise. Even some plant species thought extinct returned as their seeds germinated, at times literally from the decomposed stomachs of the goats that were thought to have stamped them out of existence.

As destructive as goats have been, furthermore, another species consistently does even more damage—people. Most of the over 25,000 people in the Galápagos live on Santa Cruz, and Puerto Ayora is the biggest settlement on the archipelago, with a population of roughly 6,000. It is a tourism center with beautiful surrounding beaches and considerable commerce, although it is highly dependent on the mainland.

We are not here this morning to study that, though. Located on the southern shore of Santa Cruz, just outside the heart of Puerto Ayora, is the Charles Darwin Research Station, our main target for the day. With roughly two hundred staff, scientists, and volunteers as well as some fifty research projects currently underway, the station provides a plethora of information on Galápagos marine and terrestrial species as well as restoration and social science projects. There's much to learn, but we're also here to simply see what most tourists seek out, the giant tortoises, and one in particular, Lonesome George.

While Galápagos tortoises lead a decidedly uncomplicated life, alternating their time between grazing on grass, leaves, and cactus and napping nearly sixteen hours per day, they are also one of the most devastated of all Galápagos animals. Only eleven subspecies remain, down from the fifteen that existed when Darwin first stepped ashore (there is also a giant tortoise of Seychelles and Aldabra in the Indian Ocean). As noted earlier, pirates, whalers, and merchants all exploited them as food sources. At least 100,000 were eliminated from the seventeenth to nineteenth centuries. But it's not just humans who target them. Introduced species such as rats, pigs, and dogs prey on their eggs as well as juvenile tortoises. Goats and burros damage their habitat.

Today only about 15,000 remain. Listed as endangered, they have been strictly protected by the Ecuadorian government since 1970. This, along with the captive breeding program at the Charles Darwin Research Station, is showing results. Outside of the research station, one of the best places to see them is the misty Santa Cruz highlands, which we will visit later that day. San Cristóbal, Santiago, Española, and Pinzon also boast notable populations, and the largest populations of all are found on Isabela's Alcedo volcano.

Here at the Darwin Research Station, these gentle giants display the distinctive characteristic that showcases natural selection—their shells. From the flat, dry islands come tortoises with saddleback shells adapted with high openings in front for their necks to reach up and strip away scarce vegetation. In the Santa Cruz highlands and comparable lush habitat, as seen in Figure 4.2, these iconic species have much fuller, dome-shaped shells, because food sources are more plentiful and these shells better protect them in the dense underbrush.

Lonesome George was the last of his subspecies, one of the rarest creatures in the world. He died early one Sunday morning in June 2012 at the Tortoise Breeding and Rearing Center in the Charles Darwin Research Station. A Hungarian scientist studying snails on the distant island of Pinta had

4.2 Galápagos tortoise in the Santa Cruz Highlands.

found Lonesome George in 1971, and in the spring of 1972, park wardens assigned to kill goats on Pinta captured him. Amazingly, no tortoises had been seen on the island since 1906, when explorers with the California Academy of Sciences killed three.

Lonesome George quickly became a conservation icon, literally becoming the face of conservation organizations such as Charles Darwin Foundation, the Galápagos National Park Service, and the UK-based Galápagos Conservation Trust. He lived to be well over a hundred years old, but never really overcame his first half-century-plus of isolation, preferring to keep to himself rather than socialize with others. Two female tortoises from Wolf Volcano on Isabela, who were initially considered his closest genetic match, lived with him when a new enclosure was added at the end of the tourist trail at the research station in early 1992.[8] No chemistry ever developed, though, as Lonesome George remained an ornery old man, very much set in his ways. You could say George was anything but curious.

For a brief four-month period in 1993, he did have a girlfriend, but not an Isabela lady tortoise or an Española female friend, as scientists later determined this subspecies to be a closer genetic match. Instead, it was a twenty-six-year-old Swiss zoology graduate student named Sveva Grigioni, who came closer than anyone else to stimulating George, yet even she was unable to generate results.[9] As Grigioni later explained, George never really seemed to get it. His parts worked, but his heart just wasn't into it. "He started to try copulation," Grigioni told conservation writer Henry Nicholls, "but it was like he didn't really know how."[10]

Even though he never reproduced, Lonesome George's plight gathered headlines around the world, raising much-needed funds for Galápagos conservation efforts. This is his legacy. The science conducted in his name continues to make a difference. As in the age-old tale of the tortoise and hare, slow and steady can win the race.

That's not an understatement. These tortoises are indeed slow, with typical speeds of maybe 0.2 miles per hour, and, as I pause at George's pen that morning, I am reminded that slowness is not necessarily a negative. When it comes to evolution, for example, change was long assumed to be gradual. Darwin himself thought evolution took place over hundreds if not thousands of years, that it was generally impossible to observe in a human lifetime.

That all changed when the husband-and-wife team of British evolutionary biologists Peter and Rosemary Grant arrived in the Galápagos in 1973. In their first year, they visited seven of the islands, but their focus quickly turned to Daphne Major.

Daphne Major is north of Santa Cruz and just west of the Baltra airport that the American military took over during World War II. Darwin never saw it, and neither do most tourists, as the national park service normally restricts visits to those conducting full-fledged scientific research. We are fortunate in that respect, having received special permission to make a late-afternoon landing. As nesting ground for blue-footed boobies, the crater floor remains forbidden territory, but we will be able to gaze down into it after trekking up from our landing, dodging ubiquitous coats of bird guano all the way.

By its fellow island standards, Daphne Major is relatively young, only a million years old. Even more importantly, it's emerged as an ideal laboratory for the Grants. It's small enough for the Grants and their assistants to literally know all the birds on it, but, at the same time, large enough to support a solid population study.

Encircled by two to three story-high cliffs almost all along its shoreline, moreover, the island rises above the sea like a fortress. There is no shore for boat landings, and deep waters around the island make anchoring offshore problematic. That means there is really only one way onto to the island, a spot where the cliff rim stoops down to the water level at a relatively manageable level, provided the tide is right as shown here in Figure 4.3. This wet, black

4.3 Panga landing on Daphne Major.

ledge near the waterline is our panga's target, but it's not an easy one. In this isolated laboratory along the equator, it is not only hard for subjects to leave, it's difficult for outside influences like us to invade.

The Grants' focus is the medium ground finch, *Geospiza fortis*, an ideal choice because it has few predators or competitors. The only other finch on the island, in fact, is the cactus finch, which occupies a different ecological niche with its dependence on the cactus.

In time, the Grants determined that the main factor shaping the survival of the medium ground finch was the availability of food, and that weather was what decided the bounty available to harvest. The Grants, of course, were naturally drawn to examine the beak as the bird's chief taxonomic character, and this made all the more sense as the medium ground finch eats mostly seeds with its stubby beak. They are variable in size and shape, and every year, a new generation emerges, making the medium ground finch an excellent candidate for studying evolution.

With its Latin origins, the word "evolution" refers to an unrolling, unfolding, or opening. This applies whether the driving force is natural selection or sexual selection. In either case, the great question Darwin faced was the same one addressed by the Grants, and it mirrors the one we face here in discussing the science of climate change: Why?

For Darwin, the question was, why are there so many species? For the Grants, it was, why do some finches flourish while others perish? And for us, the question is, why do people not understand climate change?

Perhaps not unexpectedly, answering each of these questions requires a paradoxical mix of simplicity and complexity. The Grants and their work provide further insight here. Writer Jonathan Weiner describes the Grants' data collection with a mix of wonder and admiration. Like Biblical scholars, they meticulously inventoried the seeds and fruit that the finches ate. They caught, weighed, and measured random samples of the finches they netted. They observed which species ate what food. Then they left. Just as they departed, though, fate intervened when Ecuadorian biologist Tjitte de Vries convinced them not to leave for a year as originally planned, but to come back again in only two months to see how different the dry season was in the Galápagos.

What a dry season that would be. Even the most thorough scientists can use a little luck. While it's certainly unfair to the species that succumbed to the drought of 1977 to characterize that event as lucky, the shock it provided to the data collection was truly fortunate. For 551 days the islands received no rain. Plants withered and died. The tiny seeds medium ground finches ate became scarce, and medium ground finches with larger beaks took advantage of the alternative food sources at their disposal with their ability to crack open larger seeds with their larger beaks. Those that could not starved to death; *Geospiza fortis* declined by 85 percent. By 1978 the average beak and body sizes had measurably increased. Shockingly, in merely a year, the birds had evolved.

This process was reinforced a few years later when the El Niño of 1982–1983 hit. Named for the time of year when it typically first appears, around Christmas, we know of El Niño for the strange weather it instigates around the globe; closer to home, winter temperatures are warmer over the northern half of the United States while the southwestern U.S. desert receives higher amounts of rainfall. The impact within the Galápagos, though, is even greater.

At irregular intervals three to seven years apart, El Niño arrives from the eastern Pacific. It's a mixed blessing. The life-giving rains initiate an explosion of growth and reproduction for a number of terrestrial species. With ten times the normal rainfall, an abundant variety of seeds, flowers, and grubs extended the medium ground finches' breeding season; instead of their normal one- to three-month period, they bred continuously for eight months during 1982–1983.

It is a different story, however, at sea. El Niño not only brings rain that floods into the normally blue ocean, creating concentric circles of dark red and brown from washed-out mud. It also ushers in warmer water temperatures and decreased nutrient levels, which spread death through the seas and those that depend on them. Marine iguana mortality, for example, increased 60 percent during the 1982–1983 event as these creatures essentially starved to death with the disappearance of their precious green algae.

To repeat an earlier refrain distinguishing weather and climate, it's difficult to conclude that climate change was the culprit in this specific event. More longitudinal data would be needed. Then again, even though climate change probably will not increase how often an El Niño hits, a 2014 study in *Nature Climate Change* suggests it may well double the frequency of super El Niño events.[11] That means death on this order is more likely in the years to come.

chapter five

IRREVERSIBLE IS NOT INEVITABLE

FILM DIRECTOR WOODY ALLEN once suggested that 80 percent of success was showing up. Think about it. Love or hate Woody Allen and his eclectic films, there is a persuasive ring of truth in that succinct, somewhat tongue-in-cheek statement.[1] You have to be present to win.

Of course, that's an incomplete motto for living. There's another 20 percent in the mix. Exactly *how* you show up makes a huge difference.

Are you prepared? Are you well rested? Are you confident?

This applies to every facet of life, from the workforce to friends and family, from academics to athletics, but the explicit analogy I want to draw here, in terms of both the 80 percent and the 20 percent, is to our understanding of climate change. Are we going to show up in terms of recognizing the climate change crisis of today? That's first and foremost. It's the most critical step of all, akin to alcoholics admitting they have a problem in the first place.

What comes after that, though, should not be understated either. How exactly are we going to show up? Are we prepared to make significant changes in our daily lives, moving away from fossil fuels as our primary energy source? Are we prepared to say no to business as usual? Or are we going to take only timid, insufficient strides in that general direction? Are we going to follow the lead of brave souls such as climatologists James Hansen and Michael Mann, challenging entrenched interests with their cutting-edge research? Or will we, as Stanford climatologist Stephen Schneider asserts, mimic the compromised April 2007 IPCC report, which left out the potentially incendiary "burning embers" diagram update (which depicts degrees of rising risk with increasing temperatures) under pressure from the governments of China, Russia, Saudi Arabia, and the United States?[2]

A similar overarching lesson permeates the history of people in the Galápagos. How are we going to show up? What will our lasting impact be? Along these lines, the threat of invasive species links with habitat loss and wider climate change to form the most significant issues shaping the Galápagos today. Indeed, as we discovered in our visit to Santiago in the previous chapter, invasive species have left an indelible imprint across the Galápagos. How you show up matters.

This point is hammered home on the oldest of the main islands of the archipelago, Española. Day six of our expedition begins on the northern coast of this isle at Bahía Gardner, with arguably my most magnificent morning snorkel to date. Although Española is a dying island one hundred miles from its hotspot origins, the Humboldt current fosters a last hurrah of sorts with its nutrient-rich, cold waters, and some five hundred species of fish traverse this plankton-rich zone. Over the next hour, a partial list of species I glimpse includes king angelfish, three-banded butterfly fish, yellow-tailed surgeonfish, Moorish idol, giant damselfish, black striped salema, blue parrotfish, streamer hogfish, panamic soldierfish, and a diamond stingray for good measure.

After returning to the *Lammer Law* for lunch and much needed rest, that afternoon we land at Punta Suarez and hike the main trail of that relatively flat island. We carefully navigate among the blue-footed boobies that nest along the path, and when we stop to admire our surroundings, a hooded mockingbird alights on one of my colleague's backpacks, underscoring the degree to which these species still lack a healthy fear of humans. Like many of us, they remain ignorant of what Rachel Carson warned about so eloquently in *Silent Spring* over half a century ago: "Only within the moment of time represented by the present century has one species—man—acquired significant power to alter the nature of the world."[3]

As we admire the nearby seventy-five-foot-plus blowhole fissure in the lava where ocean waves spurt and spray at regular intervals like Old Faithful in Yellowstone, inevitably our attention is drawn nearby to the true star attraction on the island. On the rocky southern side bluffs of this island nests the waved albatross, so named for the delicate pattern of feathers most visible when it unfurls its lengthy wings.

Española is the only place on Earth that this critically endangered species nests, aside from the few pairs on Isla de la Plata near the Ecuadorean mainland. Sadly, though, when these majestic birds feed in the waters off South America, they often risk getting caught in long-line fishing tackle. As Stanford professor Bill Durham, a frequent visitor to the Galápagos, explains, fishermen there take great care to use metallic streamers that frighten off birds above water, but the albatross dive deep under the water to capture fish already caught, thus finding themselves snagged as well.

On Española, some twelve thousand pairs mate monogamously for life, one of the few species to do so. One of thirteen species of albatross world-wide, the waved albatross has a distinctive yellowish-cream neck and head, which contrast with its mostly brownish body, and a long, bright-yellow bill that seems out of proportion to its relatively small head. At about three feet high, with a seven-foot wingspan, the waved albatross is only medium-sized for an albatross, but still ridiculously large compared to other birds and is by far the biggest bird in the Galápagos. Pairs produce one egg between April and June, which both parents incubate for the next two months.

Quite a number were visible to us that late May afternoon, not only those nesting, but those arriving and departing. Again, how one shows up matters. The waved albatross gets this. On returning from perhaps weeks or longer at sea, the dedicated albatross greets its mate with a lengthy, and noisy, courtship ritual. Known as the "sky-pointing display," it is complete with an intriguing mix of bill fencing, head swaying, and nasal honks of affection.[4]

After fledging, young albatrosses head out to sea for four to five years, never once landing on a solid surface. All this we eagerly absorb from our guide, but to me, the most interesting attribute of all, in a comic way, is the de facto runway that Bitinia points out. You see, the same characteristics that make these birds such majestic flyers doom them to decidedly awkward depar-tures and landings. In essence, as we sit watching for the next half-hour, one by one these big birds take turns wobbling clumsily to the edge of the cliff before practically throwing themselves into the gusty wind.

I quickly file away this image. Inauspicious beginnings can still lead to grand results. Perhaps our inaction to date on climate change will lead to a flurry of activity in the years to come, if only we can better understand the depth of the problem that confronts us. In any case, you have to at least show up before the other 20 percent can make a difference.

Dangerous anthropogenic interference, or DAI as it is often referenced in the literature, is quantified as a measurement of the concentration of carbon dioxide in the atmosphere. It ranges between levels as low as James Hansen's cautious 350 ppm number noted earlier to the 450 to 500 ppm figure more typically cited in press reports, at which point irreversible feedback mechanisms may well begin. As reporter Elizabeth Kolbert notes, throwing further fuel on this fire, the upper-end number is more a result of what is deemed socially feasible than what scientists actually contend,[5] and while this may take another century or two to reach, it will take a Herculean effort to stay below.[6]

Perhaps borrowing a page from the Montreal Protocol, the international treaty that dealt with ozone depletion, is useful here. That agreement is widely praised as the best example of an international environmental treaty; it actually worked. On the one hand, though, it is unfair to compare something as complicated as climate change to ozone depletion. Only one class of chemical compounds, chlorofluorocarbons, caused ozone depletion. An entire way of life, a dependence on fossil fuels for energy and transportation across the globe, causes climate change.

On the other hand, the Montreal Protocol does have several characteristics that merit replication. For one, instead of playing the "blame game" whereby one or more parties shoulder the burden of responsibility alone, both the developed and developing world agreed to address the quandary of ozone depletion together in 1987—but they did so proportionally. In other words, when it comes to climate change, the developed world cannot hold the developing world to the same standards its sets for itself, at least initially. The developing world simply cannot afford it.

At the same time, given their leading emissions status today, handing developing states a free pass dooms any efforts to limit climate change. As international relations scholars insist, negotiations can only be effective if they abandon the traditional zero-sum game mentality, the idea that a win for one is a loss for the other. Interests must merge together. In simple terms, as Abraham Lincoln assiduously argued in combating the threat of secession a century and a half ago, a house divided cannot stand. We are in this together.

Two more lessons can be drawn from the Montreal Protocol. The first was not initially an issue in the 1985 Vienna meetings leading up to the 1987 protocol, but it quickly developed thereafter. Governments require sufficient evidence of the damage already done and expected damage to follow to inspire action. Of course, the danger of irreversibility rears its ugly head at this point. If we wait for sufficient evidence, it may be too late to take meaningful action. Then again, the scientific community asserts that sufficient evidence exists. It's just a matter of convincing the political sector that this is the case.

This is where the third and final lesson from Montreal becomes relevant. Business must buy in. There must be considerable financial benefit in making adjustments. At the moment, vested fossil fuel interests have successfully argued the opposite, that money will only be lost when taking action on climate change.

We don't have to reinvent the wheel here. A simple focus on air pollution, for example, produced substantial results in California, even as their economy stands as the eighth largest in the world. Of course, this didn't come overnight, but through a steady series of policy initiatives. Beginning in 1947, for example, the state legislature passed a law "allowing counties to regulate local sources of pollution." Then, in 1959, California became the first state to establish "air quality standards" as determined by smog health impacts. Smartly turning their attention to motor vehicles' emissions, the legislature next created the California Air Resources Board in 1967. A variety of additional technical regulations followed in the years to come, but the long and short of it all was that air quality improved remarkably throughout the 1970s, even as more vehicles rolled out into the streets.[7] By the 1980s and 1990s, California cars were the cleanest in the world, and smog alerts in Los Angeles and the Bay Area fewer and farther between.[8]

It's an obvious but often ignored point that postponing policy decisions like these elsewhere in the United States is still making a decision. Waiting to see where technology will go and how bad things will become does not postpone the consequences of our inaction. In fact, one could easily argue the opposite, that we're rushing these consequences. On this point, I would add that a draw in any debate on whether to take action on climate change equates to a loss. Policy inaction, after all, is the goal of the climate deniers, as detailed toward the end of this book in my journey to Antarctica and an exploration of the political misunderstandings surrounding climate change.

So what exactly is at stake here? It may not sound like much, but the last time the Earth was two to three degrees warmer, what five hundred parts per million would bring when combined with the near one degree Celsius rise in temperature over the last century, was three million years ago. It was a different planet back then. For one, we weren't around. For another, sea levels were eighty feet higher than today. Florida, including where I live in the center of the state, was underwater. It wouldn't even take that much, though, to put central Florida underwater. Just a seventeen-foot rise above the levels of today would be enough to submerge most of our state, and most coastal cities around the world for that matter. Conversely, the Little Ice Age from 1600 to 1850, also sometimes dated as 1250 to 1850, was less than half a degree Celsius lower than the historic average.[9] Just a little bit really can make a huge difference.

This point is reinforced each time we return from an island excursion in the Galápagos. As we enter the back deck of the *Lammer Law*, we all dip our hiking boots in a saline cleaning solution designed to prevent the spread of seeds from one island to another. How you show up matters.

Entering our last full day among the islands, that message continues to resonate as we land on Point Cormorant on the island of Floreana. A picture of tranquility, dozens of the four hundred to six hundred greater flamingos found in the Galápagos quietly fill the large brackish pond before us, as seen in Figure 5.1.[10] They feed on drought-resistant brine shrimp as well as a mix of blue-green algae, mollusks, crustaceans, and seeds, which they fish out of the mud with their tongues. Equally handy is the flamingo's beak,

5.1 Greater Flamingos sifting for food on Floreana.

which is truly a feat of engineering with deep troughs and fine filters that pump out pond water while keeping key nutrients in.

Different species of flamingo range in color from pale pink to vivid vermillion. Widely considered the pinkest flamingo in the world, the Galápagos flamingo's color comes from a diet high in alpha and beta carotene.[11] Like Bugs Bunny in our first chapter, these guys cherish that key ingredient found in carrots. They're not just willing to get their feet wet for it. For seven to twelve hours a day, they literally stamp the muddy bottom of the lagoon before us, harvesting food particles.

After our requisite daily and latest once-in-a-lifetime snorkel, this one at Devil's Crown, we head for one of our last stops of the trip, Post Office Bay. Since 1793, a wooden post barrel of some sort has occupied this spot on Floreana and served as a link back to the outside world. British Captain James Colnett established the outpost as an officer in the Royal Navy, although at the time he was sailing on behalf of private whaling interests. In those days, whalers were typically out to sea for two years at a time, and the Galápagos provided a frequent stop for both inbound and outbound ships. Those heading outbound left messages in the barrel. Those sailing inbound assisted in getting messages home. Tourists now continue this tradition, and a colleague and I try our hand with a postcard back home—a journey it completes, remarkably, not too long after we ourselves return.

Much more of a lag effect exists with greenhouse gases. Recall from our earlier discussions that carbon dioxide is the biggest culprit here. As a persistent gas, it lasts hundreds of years.[12] That means future generations will continue to pay its price over not just decades, but centuries to come.

The lag effect does not stop here. Raising the Earth's temperature is not only warming our air and land. It's also melting ice and heating oceans. We've already addressed melting ice, but the heating of the oceans is a woefully underestimated development. Oceans, on average two-and-a-half miles deep, take centuries to fully warm, but as this water warms, it expands. Over the next one hundred years, sea-level rise of perhaps three feet is expected, most of which is a product purely of thermal expansion.[13]

There will be winners and losers as this unfolds. And notably, the losers won't be restricted to distant developing countries such as Bangladesh, although that impoverished state, with its vast delta plain of 230 rivers between melting Himalayan glaciers to the north and an advancing Bay of Bengal to the south, will certainly be a loser. Indeed, Germanwatch's Global Climate Risk Index ranks Bangladesh as one of the top five countries that suffered most from extreme weather events from 1993 to 2012.[14]

On the positive side of the ledger, my landlocked home north of Orlando, Florida, and roughly fifty-five miles from the Atlantic Ocean, might become beachfront property, at least for a generation or two. Then again, it might go the way of Holland Island in Chesapeake Bay. It turns out, you don't need to live half way around the world to find a recent example of the effects of climate change. You can find it on the doorstep of our nation's capital.

After years of resisting a relentless advancing tide, and with a population high of over 360 people in the early twentieth century, including two stores, a school, and a baseball team, the last of some sixty houses on three-mile-long Holland Island literally slid into the ocean during the fall of 2010. *Washington Post* reporter David Fahrenthold chronicled its destruction, part of which was due to sinking soils in the region and part of which was due to rising sea levels, on the order of over eight inches from 1880 to 2009.[15]

Again, it bears repeating that changes in the coming century will not be equally distributed. Temperatures are rising more quickly over continents than oceans. Everywhere across the globe, nighttime temperatures are increasing more rapidly than daytime temperatures. Until recently, day and night generally rose and fell in parallel, but daily carbon emissions now trap heat during the evening, preventing it from radiating back into space. A 1997 research team led by David Easterling of NOAA's National Climate Data Center found that night and winter low temperatures were rising nearly twice as fast as day and summer temperatures. Based on 5,400 observing stations around the world, Easterling called this a classic "fingerprint" of greenhouse warming and attributed the rise to higher humidity and more water vapor in the atmosphere.

As the eighth and final day dawns on our expedition, it is more and more clear to me that studies such as these by Easterling must find their way to a wider public audience. People don't understand how we our changing our environment daily. Some of this change, of course, is what you might call natural or inevitable. Like death and taxes, as American founding father and inventor extraordinaire Benjamin Franklin was fond of noting, consuming products and producing waste are inevitable. Again, though, it's that other 20 percent that makes a huge difference. How we consume and how we dispose of our waste not only impacts our surroundings, it impacts us.

In a very selfish respect, as highlighted by renowned environmental writer Rachel Carson a half century ago, we should be deeply concerned, if only because of the impact our actions have on ourselves. Interdependence must drive our thinking.

This is particularly crucial in a world where some level of climate change is inevitable. "The reality is that the climate is changing," said James W. C. White, a paleoclimatologist at the University of Colorado at Boulder, who led the nonprofit National Research Council 2013 report on abrupt impacts of climate change. "It's going to continue to happen, and it's going to be part of everyday life for centuries to come—perhaps longer than that."[16]

While the precise size and scale of this change remains very much in doubt, we already have alarm bells ringing, from the drunken forests of toppled trees around Anchorage, Alaska, as permafrost melts away beneath them, to Alaska's Kenai Peninsula, where four million acres of spruce forest were lost, the largest loss ever recorded in North America, as warmer temperatures continue to facilitate an outbreak of tree-damaging mountain pine beetles. Since the 1960s, in fact, winter temperatures have risen an astounding average of six degrees Fahrenheit in Alaska, according to the National Ocean and Atmospheric Administration. With less-frequent cold winter nights to kill off the eggs of these beetles, their populations exploded at twice their normal rate and ravaged tens of millions of acres of forests, damage so extensive it can literally be seen from space. The same type of catastrophic destruction is feared for coral reefs around the globe, as is addressed in our next set of chapters on the Great Barrier Reef and economic misunderstandings surrounding climate change.

These threats cannot be overstated. The ramifications of our actions or inactions today will be felt for generations. Paraphrasing John Muir's thoughts on ecological interdependence, our fate is deeply intertwined with our environment. Our future success depends not just on showing up, but on what we do once we show up. To borrow from the eloquent Rachel Carson: "We're challenged, as mankind has never been challenged before, to prove our maturity and our mastery, not of nature, but of ourselves."[17]

section two

SHOW ME THE MONEY!

The Great Barrier Reef and Economic Obstacles to Understanding Climate Change

The test of a first-rate intelligence is the ability to hold two opposed ideas in the mind at the same time, and still retain the ability to function. One should, for example, be able to see things as hopeless and yet be determined to make them otherwise.

—F. Scott Fitzgerald, *The Crack-Up*, 1936

chapter six

LOOKS CAN BE DECEIVING

JUST ABOUT TWO MONTHS before flying off to Australia I was rear-ended at a stoplight only minutes from my home here in central Florida. My back bumper was scratched up a bit and the trunk hatch no longer functioned. The lady who rammed into me seemed polite enough, at least initially. She apologized profusely, admitted her fault right away, and offered to pay for the damages, but, alas, as you know, first impressions can be misleading. Turns out she had enjoyed a few beverages celebrating a friend's birthday before our encounter, and, despite her assurances that she was a mother of three and a respected past PTA president of our local elementary school, this woman was little more than a smooth talker with no intention of atoning for her mistake.

My first and most significant error wasn't that I trusted her, though. That was probably my second biggest mistake, which is another lesson altogether. As you also know, people don't always tell the truth, especially when it's in their financial interest not to. That said, my biggest mistake that muggy May evening was the act of moving my car off the main road.

As we carefully exited our vehicles around ten that night, cars sped by, honking aggressively. Quickly checking to see if she was okay and asking if she had a cellphone to call in the accident, I suggested we pull off on a side street to exchange insurance information and avoid further danger and damage. She said she did not have her cellphone on her, and it simply didn't seem smart to stay on the main thoroughfare as cars continued to wiz by us.

But what made perfect sense in terms of safety was my dumbest act of all, at least legally and financially. Once I moved the car, I could no longer make a case that I was the victim. The police would not file an accident report, and my insurance agency would have to rely on cooperation from her insurance agency to process my claim. When I returned home and spoke to my agent on the phone, I realized that what had seemed like an open-and-shut case initially was going to be a lot more complicated, particularly as the insurance card she gave me referred to her husband and an altogether different vehicle.

The next morning my suspicions were confirmed. She was uninsured. I held out hope that the thousand-dollar good-faith check she wrote out to me would still be sufficient to demonstrate fault, but it turned out I was wrong on that count as well. The check itself was even worthless.

The point of describing this minor accident is not to echo President Ronald Reagan's famous adage regarding 1980s reductions in Soviet nuclear weaponry—trust but verify—although that is always a good idea. It is rather to emphasize that common sense tied to my immediate safety concerns did not match up with our legal system and my personal financial interests. Indeed, there are often inherent contradictions among these variables. In this case, my concern about getting hit by another vehicle cost me $637 after the deductible, plus additional expected increases in my own insurance premiums down the road.

The analogy here to climate-change centers on financial costs of action versus financial repercussions of inaction, as well as the legal and political structures in place that foster business-as-usual thinking, encouraging behavior counter to long-term interests. Quite simply, it costs money to avoid or, more realistically, minimize and mitigate climate change. Moving away from the greenhouse gases of coal, oil, and natural gas that power our global economy will not be cheap. The natural, self-interested reaction is to avoid seemingly unnecessary economic expenses, from the macro to the micro level.

Of course, as Australian scientist and author Tim Flannery points out, the cost of compliance is only half the equation here. The other half is the cost of doing nothing, the anticipated impact of more intense droughts, floods, fire seasons, tropical storms, hailstorms, tornadoes, heat waves, and ice storms.

We've all read about these. Some of us have experienced them firsthand. As we noted in the chapters on the Galápagos Islands, individual instances of extreme conditions are merely examples of weather, but over time, as patterns develop, they are representations of climate, a climate that is changing. One example comes from a beachside town I had the chance to spend a few weekends in summers ago, Ocean City, Maryland. The beaches there have been eroding at an astounding 16.4 feet a decade.[1] No matter whom you ask, that costs money.

And choosing to do nothing triggers additional long-term costs that will be even more difficult to act on in the future. That is, our immediate economically driven behavior handicaps larger, and longer-term, financial interests. By saving money now, we inevitably spend much more later. Exactly when this "later" is, of course, is hard to tell, as is whether we will act in time to avoid a tipping point, the moment when any action, no matter how substantial, is insufficient to make a difference.

With this in mind, it is worth drawing one more analogy to automobiles as the dominant mode of transportation in the states, particularly as cars and light trucks are responsible for nearly a fifth of our greenhouse-gas emissions, according to the Environmental Protection Agency as well as the nonprofit Union of Concerned Scientists.[2] Stated succinctly, objects in the rearview mirror are closer than they appear.

If you're of driving age in the states, you've undoubtedly heard this before, but I want to give it a little more context. You might argue that this pithy phrasing is another, perhaps earthier, interpretation of F. Scott Fitzgerald's eloquent expression opening this set of chapters. To intelligently assess your location relative to other vehicles on the highway, you need more than a quick peek in the rearview mirror. First impressions can be misleading, even deadly.

The same can be said, both figuratively and literally, when it comes to climate change. That's a big part of the problem in considering its impacts across the globe, and particularly along Australia's Great Barrier Reef noted in Figure 6.1.

The Great Barrier Reef Outlook Report 2009 says the long-term outlook for the Great Barrier Reef is "poor." Scientific study after scientific study warns of not only the increasing threats to the reef, but already substantial, quantifiable damage.[3] Still, depending on when and where you visit, and with a little luck in terms of weather and water clarity, the reef can look amazing, simply picture-perfect.

When it comes to the reef, then, two seemingly conflicting facts present themselves: the reef may look amazing but still be in serious danger.

The last time I visited the Great Barrier Reef I struggled to reconcile these two ideas. An entirely new world erupted as I plopped into the water with my eight-year-old son and eleven-year-old daughter, and together we eagerly poked our snorkel masks underwater. We were at the Moore Reef, a much-visited part of the outer reef offshore from Cairns, and it was sensory overload.

Forests of branching staghorn coral lay before our eyes, their tips glowing a majestic purple. Brilliant blue clumps of sun-loving mushroom coral nestled beside layers of randomly stacked pink plate coral as well as bulbous green brain coral that lay rooted nearby in solid blocks of limestone. Well-named honeycomb coral and broccoli coral further complemented semitranslucent sea fan coral, exotic elephant's ear coral, and brilliant fire coral, which, technically, isn't even a coral at all.

6.1 The Great Barrier Reef. Source: Wikimedia Commons.

And that's just a snapshot of the physical infrastructure that plays home to a stunning array of diversity on the reef. One of every four inhabitants of the oceans spends at least part of its life cycle on coral reefs, according to Australian scientist Tim Flannery.[4] The National Oceanic and Atmospheric Association provides additional context here, asserting that coral reefs contain literally millions of different types of plants and animals. Given its immense size, covering at least 2,200 km (1,367 miles), the Great Barrier Reef is our most notable example.

Here on the Moore Reef were sea slugs with royal insignia performing the menial yet much-needed labor of cleaning sand by eating fish poo off the sea floor. There were giant clams slowly manufacturing their precious pearls. There were bright blue starfish glistening on the ocean floor—not actually as fish at all, of course, but sea stars. And that's only a portion of the Moore Reef, a roped-off snorkel-and-diving area not much larger than a couple Olympic swimming pools.

The collective 2,900 different reefs and cays or coral islands that comprise the Great Barrier Reef are inhabited by six out of the world's seven marine turtles. There are fourteen species of breeding sea snakes, some thirty species of whales and dolphins, more than 100 species of jellyfish, 133 varieties of sharks and rays, 215 different species of birds, 500 different kinds of worms, 629 types of seaweed, 630 species of starfish and sea urchins, and 3,000 varieties of mollusks within its waters.

And then there are the fish. Thousands of them, in all shapes and colors. There are even the only males on our planet that give birth. Male seahorses, bless their little hearts, accept female eggs into their brood pouches and gestate them for several weeks before giving birth over a period of anywhere from minutes to hours. That might not sound too bad to mothers of our species, considering the standard nine-month gestation period typically capped with hours of intense labor, but, to men, it's an unfathomable sacrifice.

According to the Great Barrier Reef Marine Park Authority, there are 1,625 different types of fish on the reef, meaning just over 10 percent of the 13,000 species worldwide.[5] Some of them even a novice like me would recognize, such as the well-named clownfish that hangs out in bundles of seemingly free-flowing anemone. Actually, there are thirty-three types of anemone fish, but we know Nemo the clownfish best, thanks to the 2003 animated blockbuster by Pixar.[6]

In short, everything was beautiful on this balmy August afternoon, even where you might least expect it. With roughly 50 percent of all sand on the reef literally parrotfish poop (from the calcium carbonate on the reef they ingest), one could easily say, for example, that even fish waste on the reef is attractive. That general message was reinforced throughout our afternoon snorkel on the Moore Reef, time and time again. Each new turn around a coral colony brought a barrage of colors and a new school of fish to ID back on the *Sunlover* deck.

Even as I fought off the slight winter chill in the water, thankful for my upgrade to a "shorty" wetsuit earlier that day, a warm feeling of contentment swept over me. Better still, I could tell I wasn't alone with such thoughts, as my eight-year-old hummed continuously underwater. He was humming no song in particular, as far as I could gather. He just hummed here in Figure 6.2 because he was happy, and finning through this new amazing underwater world deserved its own soundtrack.

But there are dangers, too, out on the reef. The melody can be punctuated by the instantly recognizable *Jaws* theme. Sharks are what everyone first thinks of when it comes to the reef and danger. In certain situations, tiger sharks can definitely be a threat. The more common blacktip and whitetip reef sharks, though, are much less problematic, and everyone's favorite ocean nemesis, the great white of *Jaws* fame, doesn't even make it up to Queensland and the reef, preferring the cooler waters of the Southern Ocean.

Come to think of it, we saw many more signs warning of jellyfish during our time in Queensland than of anything else. Even the wetsuits we wore paid homage to these creatures with their nickname, "stinger suits." Among stingers, the boxed jelly is the equivalent of the great white among sharks. It's another kind of predator that deserves its own theme song. Pound for pound, packed with chemicals capable of halting the human heart in a matter of minutes, it is actually the deadliest animal in the world, but, thankfully, it, too, is not seen on the reef. A coastal-dwelling creature, the boxed jelly is only a problem along the shore, and only during the summer stinger season from November to April.

The Irukandji jellyfish, however, even though it also lives predominantly along the shoreline, is occasionally found on the reef. And in the far northern reaches of the reef, near remote coral cays and continental islands, another predator, the crocodile, lurks as an imposing threat. Fortunately, these coastal river migrants restrict themselves to areas largely off the tourist path.

Divers and snorkelers are much more likely to hurt themselves scraping coral, which can lead to infection and several months of healing time. Even worse, others face injury when they ignorantly collect the admittedly

6.2 Snorkeling at Moore Reef.

stunning textile cone snail. The predatory marine snail inside can sting and cause intense, localized pain or, in severe cases, respiratory failure and death. In fact, while other venomous creatures such as snakes and spiders produce only a few toxins, a single cone snail boasts one hundred individual poisons.[7]

Not all of these toxins are lethal, but there are enough to draw the attention of the United States Centers for Disease Control and Prevention as well as bioterrorism experts with the Department of Homeland Security.[8] Theoretically, with their needlelike harpoons poised to attack, they have enough venom to kill ten, possibly even twenty people. Fortunately, only about thirty fatalities worldwide have ever been reported. The most common injuries from textile cones are not lethal but nasty, painful abrasions on the thigh and chest, as divers surreptitiously place the pretty shells in their pockets and wetsuits. Who says nature doesn't fight back?

Getting back to the coral foundation of the reef, though, we've already noted that it assumes many shapes and colors. These colors define the reef in terms of both our vivid imagination and simple, daily life chores. Coral polyps form a critical, symbiotic relationship with the algae zooxanthellae. When this arrangement breaks down, coral lose their color and turn a ghostly white. Scientists refer to this as coral bleaching, a troubling phenomenon we will explore more in a few minutes.

Well over four hundred types of coral live in the Great Barrier Reef, including about one hundred genera of soft coral, in effect the reef's interior decorator, according to marine biologist Gareth Phillips. Even more notable, there are roughly 360 types of hard coral. This sturdier infrastructure comes in the form of pioneer species such as staghorn coral, which Phillips affectionately labels the Amy Winehouse of corals because they live fast, growing about seventy centimeters a year, but, alas, die young.

All this comes alive in the second-floor classroom of Reef Teach among a largely college crowd in downtown Cairns the night before we head out to the nearby inner reef at Frankland Islands National Park. Reef Teach is a highly recommended interpretative center that offers regular educational and entertaining programing focusing on reef outings, and Phillips is energetic and knowledgeable, using a dash of anthropomorphism here and there to relate to his audience, including my two older kids, aged eleven and eight at the time.

For eighteen dollars AU you receive an engaging two-hour combination lecture and slide show on types of coral, competition among fish, and reproduction habits along the reef, complete with what's billed as the best chocolate biscuits in town. My eight-year-old son does his best to claim his share of the latter, all while soaking up the information Phillips relays, but he faces tough competition from the college boys a few rows ahead of us.

Reef Teach also proves that how we tell stories matters. Humor and personalization better explain the complex phenomena underway. Scientific studies are integral, but the general public needs more. They need personalized context. Reef Teach does precisely this, and we are all eager to get an early start the next morning. It will be the first time back on the reef in seven years for my wife and me, and the first visit ever for each of our three children.

Nobody agrees on exactly where the Great Barrier Reef begins and ends. Running across the shallow ocean of the Coral Sea off the Queensland coast, the standard line of thinking is that the reef covers around 2,200 km and consists of over 2,900 separate reef banks and coral islands called "cays." Most pinpoint its northern top in the Torres Strait, the narrow body of water separating Australia from Papua New Guinea. From here, the reef stretches south along Australia's east coast, ending north of the world's largest sand island, Fraser Island.

In short, the reef is a big deal. It's the world's largest area of coral, and the largest structure in the world built by living organisms. Larger than the Great Wall of China, the Great Barrier Reef is the only living object visible from space. It is bigger than the United Kingdom, Holland, and Switzerland combined. It's roughly equal to Japan, or about half the size of Texas.

All that's more than a bit ironic, given how small its polyp building blocks are. Then again, it's also highly significant and illustrative of ecological interdependence, in which survival of the very large often depends on the extremely small, as when huge whales feed off tiny krill in the Antarctic or massive coral bleaching is tied to warming of ocean waters by one to two degrees.

Consistently listed as one of the seven natural wonders of the world, the Great Barrier Reef Marine Park was created in 1975, and in 1981, its 348,000 square kilometers received World Heritage designation. Unlike most other reefs, though, the Great Barrier Reef runs along a series of major population centers, including Cairns, Townsville, MacKay, Rockhampton, and Gladstone. As a result, approximately 820 permitted commercial tourism operators ply their trade in its waters, for some 1.8 to 2.1 million visitors a year.[9] Concentrated offshore from Cairns, Port Douglas, and Whitsundays, in a mere 10 percent of the

6.3 Showing off a sea cucumber at Frankland Islands National Park.

marine park, but where 85 percent of visitors travel, these operations generate around 64,000 jobs in Queensland. As such, the Great Barrier Reef Marine Park Authority recognizes that tourism and the Great Barrier Reef are inextricably linked.[10] People are part of its environment.

Late April to October is the best time to visit, when clear skies and moderate breezes predominate, so we've blocked off a good chunk of August. That places us in the water well before November, when the wet season and its accompanying stingers return for their annual visit. By January, the rains are a near-daily affair and trips to the reef much more of a gamble.

We've also planned to visit different parts of the reef, utilizing both large and small tourist operations and stretching our dollar as far as possible to compare and contrast the inner and outer reef ecotourism experiences. As a general rule, the further out your boat heads, the more pristine the diving, but that is not always the case. Sometimes weather intervenes along the outer edge of the continental shelf, affecting water quality. Conversely, the inner reef still has its own version of underwater gems.

That proves to be true when we visit the coral cay continental island of Normanby, part of Frankland Islands National Park, with about fifty other tourists one day in mid-August. The Frankland Islands were largely unaffected by mass bleaching a little over a decade ago, whereas other inshore reefs experienced 50 to 90 percent mortality in 2002. After a thirty-minute midmorning cruise down the Mulgrave River, it's a short crossing to our boomerang-tip beachhead on Normanby, and the kids are eager to take their first dip into the big, blue Coral Sea.

My wife Linda graciously lets me take the two older kids first, and we snorkel around with the marine biologist on her initial reef tour, trying to recall what we had learned the previous night at Reef Teach. Nothing beats being there in person, as Ansleigh can attest while proudly displaying the sea cucumber sample in Figure 6.3. The real treat is coming later that day, though. After an interactive, educational rock-pool tour and delightful tropical luncheon, Linda and the kids take another rotation snorkeling and quickly spot the one creature they most wanted to see, aside from perhaps a clownfish like Nemo. Paddling along the ocean floor about twenty feet down is a marvelous sea turtle. It seems to have not a care in the world, but for the kids, and Linda for that matter, it has just made their day.

Be careful, though, looks can be deceiving.

chapter seven

THE BLAME GAME

EVEN THOUGH WE PUSHED OFF that morning forty-five minutes south of it, Cairns remains the best-known gateway for tourism operations on the reef. We've reserved four-and-a-half spots (including our eighteen-month-old) for later in the week on a three-hundred passenger, eco-certified catamaran. It departs from the terminal in Cairns, where operators are lumped together rather efficiently in one building.

About an hour north of Cairns, Port Douglas is another, more upscale option, one that is a bit closer to outer bands of the reef such as Agincourt Reef. Back in 2006 my wife and I stayed in Port Douglas for several days and trekked out thirty-eight nautical miles aboard a small two-dozen-person boat called the *Calypso*. You've probably heard of the Agincourt reefs even if you don't recognize the name. Americans Eileen and Tom Lonergan were left behind on them in the late 1990s when diving off a boat roughly the size of our *Calypso*. Parts of their story were depicted in the mesmerizing indie film *Open Water* in 2003.

That film was set in shark-infested Bahamian waters, but based on the Australian tragedy. In the true story, an American couple, following a two-year Peace Corps stint in climate-change-threatened Tuvalu and another year of travels in Fiji, were just beginning a year-long journey across the globe. Australia was their first stop, and they choose Port Douglas as their debarkation point to see the reef. Taking a twenty-six-passenger boat called the *Outer Edge* in late January 1998, the two were last seen on the third and final dive of the day around 3:00 P.M.

No one noticed the Lonergans' failure to return to the boat. Even the following day, when the *Outer Edge* returned to the same site and a passenger found six dive weights resting on the bottom, no one noticed the Lonergans were missing. It was only two days after they were left behind that skipper Jack Nairn sounded the alarm when he found their bag on board with a wallet and passports.

Several months later fishermen one hundred miles north of the site found a dive slate reading: "nday Jan 26; 1998 08 am. To anyone can help us: We have been abandoned on A[gin]court Reef by MW Outer Edge 25 Jan 98 3pm. Please help us to rescue us before we die. Help!!!" [1] Despite insinuation in the film *Open Water*, sharks probably weren't the cause of the Lonergans' deaths. Inflatable dive jackets with their names etched in them later washed ashore north of Port Douglas along with tanks and one of Eileen's fins. None of the equipment showed any signs of shark attack. More likely, the couple disrobed intentionally, perhaps due to delirium, and then drowned or died of dehydration in the blazing tropical heat.

Although tragic, even more troublesome in a wider sense was how elements within the industry reacted. Not unexpectedly, damage control won the day. Rumors spread that Tom Lonergan committed a murder-suicide, and melancholy passages from a diary were unearthed as evidence. Still another line of intrigue suggested the couple faked their own deaths and sped off in a nearby boat to start a secret life. Sightings of the Lonergans subsequently streamed in across Australia.

Now obviously, fear of financial loss drove this response. It's a common reaction. Don't accept blame. Lay it elsewhere. The tragedy was due to some action by the Lonergans, some mistake or inappropriate behavior, so we're not financially liable. It wasn't just the *Outer Edge* owner who engaged in this strategy. Segments of the entire industry played along. While understandable from a short-term economic perspective, it's also incredibly shortsighted.

In the long run, what makes more financial sense is to correct what truly caused the problem. First and foremost, there was a faulty head count, but, secondly, an insufficient posttrip survey of the boat and its supplies. This is what will limit future tragedies—and ensure that tourists don't get cold feet when designing their vacation plans. This is what keeps the money rolling in. My last two trips to the reef underscored this as each boat was literally shut down during the obligatory count, with passengers forbidden to move as multiple staff double- and triple-checked their numbers.

When it comes to climate change, the lesson here is to prevent specialized economic interests from ruining bank accounts for the rest of us. Yet for the better part of the past two-and-a-half decades, particularly in the United States, the same type of misplaced economic logic has shaped our responses to climate change. Key political players fear economic loss if they act more responsibly, with a longer time horizon in mind. What they really should be thinking about, though, is economic loss if they don't act more responsibly.

Arguably, then, the most promising route to stem climate change lies in reorienting our economic thinking. Col McKenzie, executive officer of the Association of Marine Park Tourism Operators, explains, "I don't think climate change action stacks up unless you can show a businessman that there is a better bottom line." As McKenzie pointed out to me one Friday morning in a little coffee shop in the central business district of Cairns, environmentalists help no one when they harp on the moral or scientific problems that come with climate change. That only carries weight among the "greenies," those who are already worried. It's preaching to the choir. To win additional proponents of climate change action, a different tactic is needed.

Yet, too often, at least in the United States, climate-change discussions deteriorate into shouting matches fueled with religious-like zeal. One either believes in climate change or does not. Conversions are celebrated like those that take place when people are "born again" and join the faith. In truth, that's a disservice to the cold (or in this case, hot) hard facts—the Earth is getting warmer because of how we live. It's simply not an issue of belief. It's an indisputable fact.

Economic obstacles, thus, deserve a more central role in this debate, albeit one qualified by cultural, social, and political considerations that will be explored in subsequent chapters. For example, the essence of the argument from climate change deniers such as the Competitive Enterprise Institute, the Heartland Institute, and Americans for Prosperity rests upon financial interests tied to fossil fuels. ExxonMobil, for years, was a leading funder of such groups, purposely encouraging doubt about climate change by presenting alternative, non-peer-reviewed "articles" of skepticism.

The irony in Exxon's case is that they once employed top-level scientists to inform their own company executives about the true threats of climate change. As early as July 1977, for example, a senior scientist in their research and engineering division was briefing Exxon executives internally.[2] These efforts, including cutting-edge research, continued into the early 1980s, before funding was slashed in the wake of the 1982 oil price collapse. By the summer of 1988 and the famous congressional hearings in which Jim Hansen testified, Exxon was squarely in the obfuscation camp.

Interestingly, it's this earlier, previously unknown, history that may come back to haunt Exxon. To date, seventeen state attorney generals, led by New York, are deploying a legal strategy similar to that used against Big Tobacco in the 1990s and investigating whether the company misled investors on climate change.[3]

Despite the obvious financial position of Exxon outlined above, one more point deserves emphasis. To fully understand the climate denial camp, one cannot simply blame the biased economic interests supporting them. There are deeper political fears intrinsically tied to these economic interests. Enjoying a rebirth in numbers that coincided with the global financial crisis that erupted in late 2008, opposition is firmly rooted in a political economic perspective that seeks to minimize government.

For example, resistance to Waxman-Markey in 2009, the House-approved but Senate-defeated legislation that would have curbed heat-trapping gases with an emissions trading plan, was not just economic. It was ideological, too. Climate-change deniers definitely think of themselves as rebels and patriots. Even more importantly, they favor free markets with limited government and fear that godless liberals have grander designs than climate change.[4] Waxman-Markey was a Pandora's box in their mind, one that would allow much wider government intrusions in the future.

The Environmental Protection Agency (EPA) serves as exhibit A for these purposes. Armed with a landmark five-to-four decision in April 2007, the EPA later under President Barack Obama pursued climate change action through regulatory rather than legislative initiatives.[5] In delivering the opinion of the court, Justice John Paul Stevens argued that a group of states, local governments, and private organizations could sue the EPA to establish regulations that control carbon dioxide from automobiles as a greenhouse gas. The majority opinion's legal foundation was the federal Clean Air Act, which gives the EPA the power to set rules regarding air pollution.

During the summer of 2013, after a testy 136-day confirmation period, recently minted EPA Administrator Gina McCarthy alluded to this political approach favored by the Obama administration as well as its economic intentions. She argued in her first speech as the country's lead environmental official that cutting carbon emissions was a "way to spark business innovation."

McCarthy further asserted that the Clean Air Act had produced thirty dollars in benefits for every dollar spent in its name.

If one looks more closely at the numbers, one sees that she has a good point. Air pollution fell 68 percent in the United States between when the Clean Air Act was first passed in 1970 and 2011, even as GDP rose 212 percent, private-sector jobs rose by 88 percent, and population rose by 52 percent. "Can we stop talking about environmental regulations killing jobs, please? It's not a choice between the health of our children and the health of our economy," she implored.[6]

McKenzie, the executive officer of the Association of Marine Park Tourism Operators, agrees with the wider implications of this philosophy, asserting that Australian tourism operators will only react when the problem is couched within the context of its impact on their future earnings. He may well be right. The question here is whether McKenzie's colleagues will recognize their plight in time.

Quite simply, there is a shrinking window of comfort for tourism in the tropics. Once you get beyond 34 to 35 degrees Celsius, McKenzie thinks tourists won't visit. Further, climate change will probably bring stronger winds, which in turn will bring more wave action. Operators would then need to invest in bigger and stronger boats to deal with the more intense winds and waves, as well as air-conditioning on board to keep customers comfortable. Quicksilver, one of the leading reef operators, agrees and has already reengineered its main boat, with 30 percent savings in fuel costs.

Speaking of fuel costs, I have to admit again there are serious tradeoffs to touting ecotourism as a tool in combating climate change. Travel and tourism by definition require expenditure of resources and the release of greenhouse gases. Airplane travel, in particular, is one of the fastest-increasing sources of greenhouse gases. That means one had better be prepared to make the most of one's travel; otherwise, you are merely another part of the problem, rather than part of the solution.

As I fiddle with carry-on bags on the Orlando tarmac before our 2,500-mile flight to Los Angeles, these thoughts are on my mind. I better get this book published, and I've got some serious miles to log biking to work when I return home. That's amplified all the more on the nearly 7,500-mile international leg of our flight from Los Angeles to Sydney.

Australia is the smallest continent and the only country that covers an entire continent. Beyond quirky facts to ply as pleasant cocktail banter, what you really need to know about Australia is that it's isolated. It's far away, and hard to reach. Even in the twenty-first century, it typically takes two

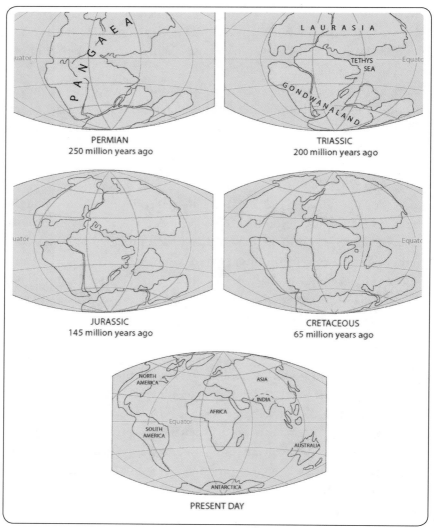

7.1 Pangea. Source: Kious, W. Jacquelyne, and Robert I. Tilling. This Dynamic Earth: The Story of Plate Tectonics. Online edition. Reston, VA: United States Geological Survey, 3 Sept. 2015 (print edition, Feb. 1996). http://pubs.usgs.gov/gip/dynamic/historical.html.

days when travelling from the States to Australia. The travel time from the East Coast is about twenty-four hours, for example, and you lose another twenty-four hours when crossing the international date line in the middle of the Pacific. Just imagine what transit was like in an earlier, preflight era.

This distance, or more precisely, isolation, dictates the uniqueness that defines Australia. Until 510 to 180 million years ago, there was just one land mass on Earth, Pangaea as depicted in Figure 7.1. This body splintered into the northern and southern supercontinents of Laurasia and Gondwana, respectively, with Gondwana including today's Southern Hemisphere with Africa, Madagascar, South America, Antarctica, and Australia, plus the Arabian peninsula and Indian subcontinent now found in the Northern Hemisphere. Then, roughly fifty million years ago, as articulated by Alfred Wegener's 1912 theory of continental drift, Australia split off from these landmasses to evolve completely on its own.[7] It bears repeating. That was fifty million years ago.

This isolation translated into uniqueness, or, in scientific terms, endemism; an endemic species is one found nowhere else. You've heard of the iconic ones in Australia—marsupials such as kangaroos (like the one in Figure 7.2), wombats, wallabies, and the cute but actually not so cuddly koalas. You may have heard of the emu or platypus. What you haven't heard

7.2 Kangaroo with joey.

about is all the other ones. About 80 percent of Australian plant species are endemic, for example. And that only counts the ones we know about. Consider the Wollemi pine. One of the oldest plants in the world, dating back to the dinosaurs, it was only discovered in the late 1990s by a bushwalker in New South Wales.

I could go on and on here. Australia has over one thousand different species of earthworms, including the world's largest, *Megascolides australis*, registering an astounding nine feet long. The important point is that Australia is not just different; it's highly unusual. That also means it is highly susceptible to invasive alien species. This helps explain why Australia routinely disinfects not just the outside of international planes but the inside as well, to reduce the likelihood of the inadvertent introduction of such species.

Perhaps the best illustration of Australian vulnerability to invasive species comes in the form of a fluffy creature not known to inspire fear—the rabbit. Indeed, the descendants of twenty-four wild rabbits imported from England in 1859 for sport hunting have wreaked havoc on the fragile Australian ecosystem ever since.

What seemed an innocuous effort to create sport by a landowner in Winchelsea, Victoria, backfired disastrously. The prolific rabbits quickly exploited their new habitat, facing no natural predators and taking full advantage of mild winters to reproduce year-around. They migrated at the rate of eighty miles a year and descended on native flora like locusts. Ballooning to an estimated ten billion in the 1920s, their voracious grazing led to soil erosion and loss of valuable topsoil across the continent.[8] Over time, they have literally cost the agricultural industry billions of dollars. Only with extensive eradication efforts, the most famous of which are probably the three rabbit-proof fences built in the early twentieth century in a woeful attempt to protect Western Australia, have numbers dropped to a still unsustainable 200 million covering 2.5 million square miles.[9]

The moral here is be careful what you bring with you in your travels, and I quickly look through our carry-on bags to verify we're in full compliance. Immigration officials take their declaration forms seriously, particularly in a place like Australia. No fruits, vegetables, or fresh meat products allowed. Not too much for me to worry about when it comes to the latter two, but especially on sleep-deprived flights such as this one, I have a bad habit of forgetting about the first and dig out any remaining fruit in my pack.

chapter eight

BUILDING BLOCKS . . . AND TEARING THEM DOWN

THE DAY AFTER LANDING, bleary-eyed, in Townsville via our Virgin Australia transfer from Sydney, the kids are itching to start. We had some unexpected hiccups with the apartment check-in the day before but finally unpacked in the late afternoon and grabbed some scrumptious fish and chips down on the Strand before collapsing in our beds early that night. Stop one of the first fully conscious day of our Australian adventure is Reef HQ Aquarium on Flinders Street, which houses the world's largest living coral reef aquarium at 2.5 million liters.

Here we learn that there are several different kinds of reefs. Fringe reefs are the youngest type and grow in shallow waters. Atolls are ringed reefs away from the shore; they often grow around the rims of sunken volcanoes. And then there are the barrier reefs, which grow in deeper water than fringe reefs and form a wall between the sea and shore. The Townsville aquarium, along the end of a bend on Ross Creek, focuses, as you might expect, on barrier reefs. It is unique not only for its size but also because it is exposed to the elements, which means its thousands of inhabitants receive natural daylight and moonlight as well as experience rain and storm events similar to those on an actual reef.

The kids love it, even the littlest one, eighteen-month-old Emerson. The minute we slide into the cool lobby, escaping the heat outside, our two eldest are busy negotiating a schedule. There's a whiteboard listing a range of activities offered that day, from the dive show and turtle talk to creature feature and animal-feeding tours, but the clear winner is the 750,000-liter predator exhibit, the shark tank.

Here an underwater viewing tunnel allows visitors to straddle the separate coral reef and predator tanks at ocean-floor level. We view iconic species such as marine turtles, blacktip reef sharks, and even a hammerhead shark, against a backdrop of a replica of the S.S. *Yongala*, north Queensland's most famous shipwreck and dive site.

As lunchtime rolls around, though, and jet lag starts to set in, our youngest is growing restless. We make it through the shark talk and dive show, in shifts at least, but realize that the turtle hospital tour, touch tank, and several other exhibits will have to come another day. Fortunately, our tickets are child friendly and allow you to come back a second time if kids start to break down, something we later discover is a welcome pattern among a number of Queensland attractions. We give one last snarl to the sharks, because, despite the claims of Bruce the shark from *Finding Nemo* (a model of him hangs above the stairwell near the shark tank), even our toddler knows that sharks are predators—and that fish are food.

Later that week, we are able to witness this firsthand during the afternoon fish feeding at the aquarium. But I have to say the real treat during that follow-up visit was touring the turtle hospital next door. The hospital is essentially a small building attached to the aquarium with an outdoor porch and a connected raised shed, both of which house a series of blue tanks dedicated to turtle rehabilitation. Since opening in August 2009, with an average stay of two to six months each, thirty-six sick and injured marine turtles have been housed and released.

Probably the most common cause of hospitalization is ingestion of plastic. Some seven billion tons of trash flow into our oceans annually, and 60 percent of this is plastic, as we will learn the following week up in Cairns at Reef Teach. There's even a plastic island in the North Pacific Gyre,[1] commonly known as the Great Pacific Garbage Patch, that is roughly the size of Texas, extends twenty feet down, and contains an astounding 3.5 million tons of trash.

This is particularly problematic for marine turtles, because plastic bags and rings look like their favorite food source, jellyfish. Once they make this mistake, turtles get much more than an unhappy surprise meal. The plastic literally blocks their digestive system, slowly killing them.

You could say, then, that oil throws a double whammy at these unfortunate sea turtles. Even before our petroleum-based economy has made the full force of its impact felt in terms of climate change, petroleum-based plastic bags are picking off these majestic sea creatures.

Over the last week, and in our preparations during the month before our trip, my family learned that many other species along the reef are temperature-dependent, not just the coral infrastructure. Microbes, seabirds, and marine turtles are, too. Having an opportunity to see marine turtles up close, though, and hearing firsthand about their trials and tribulations gives this much greater context.

Marine turtles are reptiles, coming from the same family as lizards, crocodiles, and snakes. They breathe air but spend most of their time underwater, staying below the surface for fifteen to twenty minutes at a time while feeding, then sleeping all night under water without coming up to breathe. They have strong front flippers for swimming but use their back flippers merely for steering and digging nests. The Great Barrier Reef is home to six of the seven species worldwide; only the Kemp's Ridley is not found off Queensland as it is restricted to the Gulf of Mexico.

Earlier that week, over coffee and hot chocolate in the Townsville central business district, Julie Traweek, project manager for Sea Turtle Foundation and Local Marine Advisory Council chairperson in Townsville to the Great Barrier Reef Marine Park Authority, filled me in on still more turtle details. Marine turtles migrate several hundred kilometers, sometimes over one thousand, back to the same beach where they first hatched. Exactly how they do this is poorly understood, although scientists suspect marine turtles utilize some combination of the earth's magnetic pull, reading ocean currents, and judging the angle of the sun.

Due to habitat loss tied to coastal development, light pollution, and the plastic trash noted above, not to mention rising sea levels that flood nests, marine turtles are threatened across the globe.[2] According to the IUCN Red List of threatened species, six of the seven species are vulnerable to extinction, and we have insufficient data to assess the seventh, flatbacks. Eastern Pacific leatherback populations, for example, have dropped 90 percent since the 1960s according to data kept by Las Baulas National Park in Costa Rica.

But as Traweek explains, precisely how to process these numbers presents challenges similar to those with the climate-change data discussed earlier. "We've seen a lot lower nesting numbers recently, but it's so cyclical with marine turtles that we can't really say yet," elaborates Traweek. Marine turtles live a long time and grow slowly. It takes decades to accurately assess year-to-year fluctuations. Further, marine turtles do not breed until they are thirty to forty years old, and they only breed every few years because migrating and breeding take so much energy. In short, it takes quite a while for them to reproduce. When they do, they are certainly prolific, laying between sixty and one hundred eggs in a clutch. Even with that advantage, though, predators and an assortment of challenges within the big blue ocean take their toll. Only one in one thousand baby turtle hatchlings survives to adulthood to produce hatchlings of its own.[3]

Yet another issue with marine turtle susceptibility to climate change is their gender. Marine turtle gender is determined by sand temperature during the middle third of incubation. The pivotal temperature at which an equal number of male and female hatchlings emerge hovers around 29 degrees Celsius (82 degrees Fahrenheit), but the transitional range of temperatures that produces both sexes varies according to species and geographic location.[4] In general, incubation temperatures above 33 degrees Celsius (91.4 degrees Fahrenheit) are likely to produce only females, which obviously would be a problem in terms of future generations.[5]

A few days after visiting Reef HQ and meeting with several helpful staff there, I have the opportunity to drive thirty-seven kilometers south of Townsville and tour the Australian Institute of Marine Science (AIMS) off Cape Ferguson. Started in 1972 by six scientists, AIMS has produced the longest and most comprehensive data set on the health of the Great Barrier Reef. Baseline data assessing changes in the ecosystem and the impact of human activity are available thanks to coral cores, which are analogous to tree cores and provide data stretching back to the seventeenth century.

My two-hour tour begins in the AIMS theater with a thirty-five-minute DVD introduction to marine science conducted at the facility before moving to the library, equipment workshop, and outdoor crayfish study center. Afterwards I settle down to a tasty lunch in the complex's cafeteria with science communicator Sue Lim. Between bites of mixed salad and fried barramundi she tells me about the massive $35 million ocean simulator that opened just last week. While it is not yet available to members of the public, scientists on staff are already scrambling for simulator time.

The simulator offers all sorts of new possibilities for reef scientists. Perhaps most notable is the study of synchronized spawning. Not all coral reproduce in this manner. Some don't even reproduce sexually. Asexual reproduction entails coral dividing into two, over and over again, forming exact copies of themselves. It's efficient, but the smaller gene pool reduces coral diversity.

Turning back to sexual reproduction, brooders might be called the more traditional category. After an egg is fertilized internally, an embryo develops into a free-swimming larva within the polyp, called a "planula." This accounts for approximately 15 percent of known sexual reproduction by corals. The other 85 percent are broadcast spawners that release eggs and sperm into the water column for external fertilization and development.

To complicate matters still more, though, coral can also be classified according to sexual orientation—seriously. Only about 25 percent of corals studied are gonochoric or dioecious species, meaning their colonies are either male sperm producers or female egg producers. The other 75 percent are hermaphrodites, in which a single colony produces both eggs and sperm.

AIMS new simulator will come in handy for all cases, but particularly for the broadcast spawning of stony corals, because the exact date of their release fluctuates each year depending on external stimuli. Popularly advertised by tourism operators as "sex on the reef," mass spawning was only first scientifically observed in 1981. Once a year, four to five days after a full moon in October or November, sometimes even December if storms postpone the date night, two hundred species of stony coral simultaneously spawn on the Great Barrier Reef, releasing eggs and sperm to the surface like millions of champagne bubbles. Joining together into a space capsule smaller than a pinhead, the happy couple then floats away to honeymoon on currents anywhere from a few meters to thousands of kilometers away before settling down.[6]

According to Southern Cross University coral reef expert Peter Harrison, three main stimuli determine when this happens. For starters, late each Australian spring, eggs and sperm mature within the coral only with a gradual rise in sea temperature to 27 degrees Celsius. Second, the lunar cycle and its influence on tides determine the exact day. And third, the diurnal cycle of night and day dictates final time of release, with coral, in their modesty, requiring the cover of darkness to do the deed.

Interestingly, in terms of the lunar cycle, there is a significant range between high and low tide during a full moon. Approximately five nights after a full moon, something called a "neap tide" occurs when the differences between the heights of the high and low tides are minimized. According to coral researcher Bette Willis from James Cook University, this reduces water flow and creates weaker currents, which is critical to coral spawn because calmer waters increase the chances for eggs and sperm to meet and mix before being dispersed by water currents.

The trouble is, as noted earlier, that scientists know only roughly when this will be from year to year, not the exact date. So having a simulator will allow them to replicate the spawning in a setting that is much easier to study.

This brings us back to the heart of the reef ecosystem, the coral polyp. A polyp is an animal consisting of little more than a tentacle surrounded by a mouth and a limestone carapace into which it withdraws. It is an invertebrate that ranges in size from smaller than a pinhead to up to a foot in diameter, according to the Coral Reef Alliance. Polyps become coral as they grow hard skeletons outside their bodies, building essentially a series of apartment buildings that can have incredible density on the order of 10 to 100 million plant cells (more on that in a minute) in one square millimeter. Over thousands of years, the corals build on top of their ancestors, the skeletons of earlier generations, to form a reef whose surface is covered by colonies of vibrant, colorful living coral.

Corals grow in shallow seas at a constant warm temperature. They are in the business of greenhouse gases, calcifying organisms that take dissolved material from the surrounding seawater and grow a calcium carbonate skeleton. Like trees and oceans more generally, corals are natural sinks for carbon dioxide. As Australian environmental writer James Woodford concisely states, "They turn carbon dioxide into rock."[7]

Corals are carnivorous and related to jellyfish and sea anemones.[8] Animated Reef Teach marine biologist Gareth Phillips describes them as similar to an upside-down jellyfish whose main goal in life is to attend spring break, to suntan and soak up sugars produced by its symbiotic algae partner, the protozoa zooxanthellae.

Here's where the defining relationship of reefs like the Moore Reef in Figure 8.1 comes into play. It centers on tiny protozoan algae embedded within the coral tissue of a polyp. They account for not only the signature, vibrant colors of coral but, more importantly, its very survival. Living in symbiosis, corals receive up to 90 percent of their energy from zooxanthellae, which use sunlight to turn water and carbon dioxide into carbohydrates that spur much quicker growth than if coral relied on plankton alone. In return for sharing the food they produce, zooxanthellae receive valuable shelter.

Zooxanthellae are particular about their living conditions, though. They cannot survive cold, deep water, which is why they are typically found in the tropics.[9] And they don't like hot water, either. Unusually warm waters, defined as an increase of 1.5 to 2 degrees Celsius above normal summer maximums, begin a chain reaction where photosynthesis breaks down. If the water remains warm for too long, the ability of zooxanthellae to cope with normal light levels is compromised, and they produce harmful waste products that the coral cannot withstand. The polyp then expels the zooxanthellae to avoid being damaged by these toxic chemicals.

With no zooxanthellae, the coral's tissue becomes transparent and the white external skeleton of the coral visible. Known as coral bleaching, this was little heard of prior to 1930 and only a small-scale phenomenon until the 1970s. Pollution, siltation from erosion tied to inland logging, excessive fresh water that reduces the salinity of ocean waters, and high light intensity all cause bleaching, but higher temperatures appear to be particularly pernicious when it comes to mass bleaching.[10] Some corals are still able to feed themselves by capturing plankton and particles in the water with their stinging tentacles, but most struggle to survive without their symbiotic partner.

8.1 Coral on Moore Reef.

Effects here are typically uneven. Fast-growing corals such as branching and plate coral are often the first to bleach and, thus, most likely to die. Slower-growing boulder coral takes longer to bleach and is more likely to survive.

It is also worth noting that initial bleaching does not necessarily seal the coral's fate. Death sentences can be commuted. In almost Monty Python–like fashion, some corals insist on not being dead yet. If given time and cooler waters, they can recover. It's impossible to generalize here, but coral have a chance if ocean waters fall back to normal ranges within six to eight weeks. This depends on many variables beyond temperature reductions, though, including the species of coral, strain of zooxanthellae, and geographic location.

Until 2016, the two best-known bleaching events on record were in 1998 and 2002. From 1997 to 1998 temperatures recorded on the reef were the hottest since record-keeping began in the late nineteenth century, and the resulting damage was significant. Then, in 2002, the bleaching was even worse; roughly 54 percent of reefs bleached to some extent that year, and 18 percent strongly bleached.[11]

Not to be outdone, though, the year 2016 "dwarf[ed] previous bleaching events by a long mark," according to Terry Hughes, director of the Australian Research Council Centre of Excellence for Coral Reef Studies in Townsville. In fact, only 7 percent of the reef system avoided coral bleaching entirely, with the most severe bleaching in the northernmost thousand kilometers of the reef, according to an April 2016 release by Australia's National Coral Bleaching Taskforce.[12]

The Great Barrier Reef is not alone in facing this onslaught. Across the globe, coral reefs have been hit hard, from Bahrain to the Maldives to Sri Lanka to Singapore to Tanzania. According to the United Nations Environment Program, in fact, some four hundred mass bleaching events occurred worldwide in 2002. The numbers appear to be even worse in 2016, with the National Oceanic and Atmospheric Administration declaring it the third global coral bleaching event on record.

Much will be lost. Some may recover. What does will depend on resilience, which is determined, in large part, by size. Larger reefs such as the Great Barrier Reef have an advantage here. But it also appears that some coral are better suited to adapt to environmental change.[13] The key factor is, will the rate of adaptation for these corals be able to match the rate of change in temperatures? Further, resistance and recovery depend on an array of additional variables that shape the health of the reef, including storm damage, pollutants, destructive fishing methods, and acidification.

Acidification is probably something you haven't yet heard about, yet. It's a silent killer that could be just as much a game changer as temperature increases. Oceans are naturally slightly alkaline. This helps with the calcifying process for corals and other shell creatures. Greenhouse gas emissions, though, threaten the future of these creatures as about 30 percent of the extra carbon dioxide in the atmosphere dissolves into our oceans.

On the one hand, this is good for us. It helps explain why atmospheric temperatures have not risen more. On the other hand, as our oceans absorb more and more atmospheric carbon, they are becoming more and more acidic, to the detriment of this calcifying process. In very simple terms, then, the chemistry of our oceans is changing; they are on the order of 30 percent more acidic since the beginning of the industrial era.[14]

It doesn't sound like much at first. An expected decrease of 0.4 pH units seems quite small. But when measured on a negative log scale, this translates into a 2.5-fold increase in the concentration of hydrogen ions. The growth and skeletal strength of coral is then compromised, making it all the more vulnerable to future storm damage.[15]

Indeed, acidification could very well cause the extinction of an entire class of marine organisms, the amoeba-like creatures with a shell known as "forams" or "foraminifera," according to an AIMS study published in the online journal of *Nature* called *Scientific Reports* by senior research scientist Sven Uthicke. Such extinctions do not occur in a vacuum and will very likely have impacts elsewhere along the food chain. Looking at subsurface volcanic activity and its naturally emitted carbon dioxide off the shores of Papua New Guinea, this AIMS group found localized seawater acidity changes similar to what would be expected worldwide by 2100.[16]

Beyond the twin obstacles of rising water temperatures and increasing acidification, additional human activities cannot be ignored. Sewage from resorts is a problem. Siltation from inland logging can settle like a thin brown death mask onto a reef. Irresponsible dropping of anchors does damage. Dredging of harbors is highly destructive. And as Nemo followers everywhere know, aquarium fish collecting continues.

chapter nine

HUMAN INFLUENCES—
FROM LEMONS TO LEMONADE?

THEN, THERE IS FISHING. Despite dramatic improvements over the last several years, recreational and commercial fishing are both still threats. I witnessed the recreational side of this firsthand one Sunday afternoon on the hidden gem of Magnetic Island, a mountainous triangle of an island within the Great Barrier Reef National Heritage area and five miles offshore from Townsville. I had picked Maggie, as the locals refer to it, largely because 54 percent of the island is covered by national parks, and I wanted to see a less-hyped portion of the region.

I soon found the added bonus of several activists among its 2,100 or so residents. One of these was Rick Braley, a marine biologist who specializes in giant clams and owns a quaint aquarium called Aquasearch in Nelly Bay. Rick had graciously offered to give a personal tour of his aquarium that weekend, but what he really wanted to show off were the two recently established snorkel trails on the island. His friend Colin joined us for the two-hour working snorkel that afternoon, volunteering to help with the bimonthly maintenance of scrubbing algae off the underwater site designation placards on the Nelly and Geoffrey Bay snorkel trails.

The afternoon chop at our first stop at Nelly Bay caught me off guard, and I struggled to adjust the mask my son had borrowed the previous day while keeping up with my more experienced compatriots seen in Figure 9.1. In between gulps of seawater I managed to stay within shouting distance along the trail. Everything seemed in order after the placards were wiped. We exchanged a couple fish stories, mine focusing on the distinctive black-and-white sergeant major fish I'd seen, and then moved on to the more sheltered Geoffrey Bay. Here the water quality was much better, as was my ability to efficiently follow in the wake of Rick and Colin.

9.1 Magnetic Island working snorkel.

The diversity of coral and aquatic life at Geoffrey and Nelly Bay were not what my family had seen on the outer reef, but that was expected. And despite this caveat, if you take your time, glittering treasures remain to be found practically anywhere within the marine park. Today's figurative catch was getting to visit a couple of Rick's "children," twenty-seven-year old giant clams he raised and then seeded along the trail. He pointed these out with great pride at the end of our snorkel, and, I have to admit, they were amazing. If it were not for the lateness of the hour, I would have stalled even more as we kicked back to shore, just to prolong my viewing.

Here's where the real point of relaying this segment of my story emerges. As we climbed back up the abandoned pier at Geoffrey Bay and packed up our gear into Rick's truck, Colin noticed the two couples on the boat adjacent to our trail weren't just frolicking in the cool waters. One of the males was line fishing.

The problem with that is Geoffrey Bay is not just part of the Great Barrier Reef World Heritage area. It is also in what the Great Barrier Reef Marine Park Authority classifies as a "no-take" green zone. That means anyone can enter and engage in low-impact activities such as swimming, snorkeling, or boating, but extractive activities such as collecting and fishing are prohibited. When rezoning went into effect in July 2004, the protected portions of the reef rose dramatically from 5 percent to 33.3 percent. The other side of Maggie still has a large swath of yellow, meaning single-line fishing is allowed, but here in Geoffrey Bay it is not.

Now, mind you, fishing violations such as this are less and less frequent the last several years, according to the Great Barrier Reef Marine Park Authority, and, ironically, you could very well have a cyclone to thank for that. Cyclone Hamish was a category 5 storm that hit the Great Barrier Reef in March 2009. It was not huge news for most Australians because its eye never touched the coast, but out on the edge of the outer reef, it unleashed some of the worst damage in recent memory.

Most cyclones travel east to west, restricting their impact to a smaller portion of the reef. Hamish was different. Beginning off the coast of Townsville, it traveled north to south, racing parallel to the Queensland coastline for some 310 miles and chewing up large chunks of the reef in its path. While homeowners experienced far less damage than most cat 5 storms cause, fishermen felt the brunt of this impact, particularly those specializing in coral trout grouper. In the southern half of the reef, Australian fishermen ship these light pink fish live to Hong Kong for a premium price.

But as Paul Marshall, former manager of the climate-change-response program at the Great Barrier Reef Marine Park Authority, relayed to me, for six, twelve, even eighteen months there were no fish to catch. "It was then that these fishermen realized that the biggest threat to their future was not the bloody government," as Marshall emphatically explained. "There was a massive transformation within the industry as they realized the need to take a different look at their future, that there are forces bigger than all of us."

Virtually overnight leaders within the fishing industry changed their approach to climate change. "Ever since then there has been a transformative relationship between fishing and conservation," Marshall added. "For the main part it's a constructive relationship now. Climate change is a way of talking about a future that neither one of us is responsible for. Cyclone Hamish changed the tone of conversation. It created space, allowing dialogue to occur where we had previously often struggled."

The same opportunity to make lemonade out of lemons has yet to present itself when it comes to tourism, although tourism operators are becoming more and more eco-conscious. As such, they regularly recite the mantra to "take only photos and leave only bubbles" to their clientele. Even when swimmers don't make physical contact with the reef, for example, their sweat and suntan lotion can dissolve into the water and change its chemical composition enough to cause localized damage.

When they do make contact, whether it is intentional or not, the results can be catastrophic. Coral requires an average of twenty-five years to recover from even accidental scrapes by young or inexperienced snorkelers and divers. Despite the best precautions, it happens more than you would imagine, including during our stay on the Moore Reef when one child in a group of local school children literally stood on a shallow portion of the reef to adjust his mask.

Such transgressions aside, the biggest human threat, excluding climate change and acidification, is still connected to our appetite back on land. Agricultural runoff is a serious threat to the Great Barrier Reef. Beef cattle, cotton, and bananas all do their share of damage, but the most problematic of all, with its dependence on chemical fertilizers, is sugar cane. Further farm expansion that we witness along the coast also means a loss of coastal wetlands, and thus removal of a natural filter for agricultural runoff.[1] Indeed, since European settlement, there has been a fourfold increase in nutrient and pollution-rich sediment runoff due to croplands, with plumes stretching farther and farther, as many as sixty kilometers offshore after larger storms.[2]

It is also worth noting that water runoff doesn't even have to be polluted to be a threat. In large amounts, fresh water changes ocean salinity and is problematic in its own right. The El Niño–Southern Oscillation determines how bad this can become. During La Niña, flooding onshore can result in millions of additional liters of water being dumped into the oceans. Even droughts during El Niño years are problematic for the oceans, because the loss of vegetation due to drought means increased terrestrial runoff when the rains finally do come. There simply is less vegetation to soak up excess water than there was before the drought.

Cyclones are yet another threat. The past decade in Queensland is one of the worst in recorded history, with one category 4 or 5 storm after another hitting the coast. Still, this pattern is relatively recent and impossible to link to climate change without additional data. In fact, despite what your intuition might tell you, it is scientifically unlikely that cyclones will become more frequent with climate change. That is also the case with hurricanes here in our Northern Hemisphere, even though each year in the 1990s exceeded the normal average of hurricanes. Most climatologists agree, on the other hand, that cyclones and hurricanes will become more and more intense and destructive when they do occur.[3]

Even with this in mind, there is yet another sinister villain when it comes to coral cover decline over the last seven or so years. Crown-of-thorn starfish (COTS) seen in Figure 9.2 at the aquarium in Townsville are a nearly omnipresent threat, according to the Great Barrier Reef Marine Park Authority. COTS outbreaks are not directly linked to water temperatures, although higher temperatures do make cyclones more intense. This, in turn, creates flooding and runoff problems, and COTS are directly linked to water quality that can be traced to this runoff. With that in mind, one could argue that COTS damage to the reef is an indirect product of climate change.

The overabundance of plankton that results from agricultural runoff fosters an eightfold increase in COTS egg production, raising numbers from the normal ten to twelve million to an incredible fifty to sixty million in localized outbreaks on the reef. Scientists disagree as to exactly why

9.2 Crown-of-thorns starfish on display at Reef HQ in Townsville.

outbreaks are more frequent in recent decades, but one promising theory proposed by Australian Institute of Marine Science's (AIMS) Katarina Fabricius is that outbreaks are tied to flood plumes with a time delay typically of ten years. As broadcast spawners that time their release of eggs and sperm to match ideal conditions, COTS exploit the massive nutrient pulses from agricultural runoff, allowing their production cycle to rotate much more quickly than it ever has, essentially every fifteen years now instead of the traditional sixty to eighty years.

This means coral simply don't have time to bounce back after a COTS outbreak because these voracious killer starfish literally eat the coral to death. COTS latch onto coral and dissolve polyps with their digestive juices, clearing entire tracts of the reef. Green Island was the first to see this plague in 1962. Infestations then spread southward, in 1988 reaching reefs around Bowen. An estimated 31 percent of reefs were affected by then, and scientists continue to struggle with an appropriate response, because COTS are virtually indestructible. Poisonous to other fish, they can regenerate from a single leg and small portion of their intestine.

As we pull out of Townsville driving north along the Bruce Highway to Cairns I'm trying to process all this—and draw the COTS dots together. COTS is very possibly related to agricultural runoff and water quality, which is related to flooding and storms, which is related to cyclones, which is related to climate change, which is related to us.

Hmm . . . it looks more and more like I'm a big part of this problem. Negotiating a series of roundabouts with increasing ease while taking a turn force-feeding Ozzie biscuits to our little one, I also realize there are baby steps that can be taken, behavioral changes that may lead to even larger, more meaningful societal shifts. For example, roundabouts are definitely an improvement on stoplights; the conventional car I'm driving, like most in the United States, is less efficient when idling at stoplights. Even better would be more public transportation options like the light-rail commuter line that finally started after a couple attempts in my hometown metro Orlando area in the spring of 2014.

In any case, as we pass field after field of sugar cane, I also come to the conclusion, hopefully not just rationalization, that some are more to blame than others. No matter what Australia does, for example, in terms of restricting its own greenhouse gas emissions, which on a per capita basis are embarrassingly high, it will never be enough to make a dent in the global problem. To do that, you have to look to China and the United States. We win hands down in terms of historical responsibility, roughly three times more than China, according to former director of NASA Goddard Institute for Space Studies James Hansen, but have played second fiddle to them since late 2006 in terms of annual greenhouse gas emissions.

What's really scary is this is only going to become worse. The developing world will continue to increase its emissions as both its population and economy grow, the latter particularly in China and the former particularly in India, which is on pace to pass China as the world's most populous country in 2028, according to the United Nations.[4]

While our political concerns with an international climate change treaty involve the wider developing world, China still gathers the lion's share of our attention here in the States. This is driven partly by our persistent political rivalry but also by concerns about how China is developing. They are doing as we did, not as we say they should.

In many respects, China is industrializing with the model the United States used seventy or more years ago. The kicker here is this development is on a far grander scale. With 1.354 billion people, China has four times the U.S. population. To meet the increasing energy demands of these people, expectations which are intrinsically tied to the political future of its Communist Party, China is engaging in climate-destructive practices such as building a large new coal-fired power plant every ten days.[5]

It is in this context that American policymakers often cite China as justification for our inaction on climate change. The problem will continue to worsen, we argue, even if we act, unless China is on board.

That's true. It is also true that we've been causing the problem a lot longer than China, and that there is no hope for addressing climate change unless we act, too. We'll hear much more about that toward the end of this book when we visit the Antarctic Peninsula and emphasize political misunderstandings surrounding climate change.

chapter ten

SPENDING TO SAVE

UPON REACHING CARDWELL, a small seaside town a few hours north of Townsville, we take a much needed lunchtime stop and fuel up on fish and chips, a fizzy lemon soda called "Lift," and petrol. As we stuff our newly enlarged selves back into the rental car, I continue to toss these ideas around in my head. All the while, I remind myself that Australia was a British colony until 1901, which means, despite my American-bred inclinations, I need to keep our vehicle on the left side of the highway. One trick that helps is visualizing the steering wheel near the centerline of the road, just like in the States. Over the next two weeks I avoid any dust-ups, but continually confuse the turn signals, as they too are juxtaposed, with the lever I keep mistaking as a turn signal actually controlling the windshield wipers. Let's just say we kept our windshields extra clean on this trip.

But getting back to responsibility. A postcard at the seaside diner in Cardwell caught my attention. It highlighted damage done several years ago with a twenty-three-foot storm surge at our lunch stop. A devastating category 5 storm, with wind gusts up to 290 kilometers an hour, Cyclone Yasi made landfall around Mission Beach in the early morning hours of February 2, 2011. Surrounding areas such as Tully, Silkwood, Innisfail, and Cardwell, where our café is located, were severely damaged. Hundreds of houses were made uninhabitable and thousands damaged and without power.

As with all storms, though, that was just the tip of the economic iceberg, so to speak. The majority of costs, like an iceberg itself, are hidden below, only surfacing in the weeks and months, sometimes even years, after the storm. According to the Australian Bureau of Statistics, for example, Yasi, along with extensive flooding in Queensland in late December 2010, dictated a 24.9 percent increase in fruit prices through the March 2011 quarter and an 18.7 percent increase in vegetable prices. Similarly, although its winds weakened the further inland it blew, Yasi continued to cause flooding well beyond Queensland, extending into New South Wales, Victoria, the Northern Territory, and even South Australia, bringing still further economic loss.

On a slightly different topic, that seaside diner was of note for something else as well. It offered clean and complimentary access to an item that's become a bit of a conversation piece at our home in central Florida—dual-flush toilets. Thanks to inspiration at that pit stop, we, too, now have two buttons for bodily waste, one for liquid and another for the more substantial variety. The larger button uses more water than the smaller but still less than a conventional toilet, 1.28 gallons compared to the current U.S. standard of 1.6 gallons per flush.[1] And the smaller button, reserved for liquid waste, uses even less at 0.8 gallons per flush.

Not to get too technical, but beyond these adjustments, a larger trapway, the hole at the bottom of the bowl, allows dual-flush toilets to abandon the standard toilet's water-intensive siphoning action to expel waste and rely more on gravity instead. Combining the two, the smaller flush and lack of siphoning, saves as much as 67 percent of water usage in a home, according to an independent study by the Oregon Department of Energy.

Invented by an Australian named Bruce Thompson in 1980, dual-flush toilets are widely used in Australia today as well as in Asia, Europe, and Israel. They are not too common here in the States, though. In fact, on returning from our first adventure down under several years ago, we decided to rip out our antiquated American Standard water hogs and replace them with Australian dual-flushers. Problem was we couldn't find them, at least for residential sale.

After a couple weeks of searching, Linda tracked down a company out of North Carolina that sold the Australian Caroma brand online, and, given that our toilets were antiques original to our 1964 house at five gallons to the flush, we jumped on the opportunity. First-time guests to our humble abode have taken a little extra time using the facilities ever since, often emerging with a quizzical smile affixed to their face. There was an initial cost of conversion of $306 per toilet plus installation labor, but at an estimated 11,565 gallons less per year translates to savings on the order of hundreds of dollars a year.[2]

Despite their dual-flush toilet contribution and, more seriously, the massive carbon dioxide numbers being emitted by the United States and China in comparison, Australia does not get a free pass when it comes to overall environmental footprint and its specific role in climate change. As noted earlier, Ozzies are among the worst carbon dioxide emitters in the world when it comes to individual emissions, ranking number twelve globally with 16.9 metric tons per capita according to the World Bank in 2010.[3] That places them in the happy company of the United Arab Emirates, Saudi Arabia, and, you guessed it, the United States.

Another negative in Australia's corner is the fact that it is a world-class coal enabler. Not only is coal Australia's second-largest export. Australia is also the second-largest (after Indonesia) exporter of coal in the world. It helps make greenhouse emissions possible elsewhere around the world, particularly those in China.

This exported coal, by the way, affects the reef long before its byproduct of carbon dioxide is released into the atmosphere in some distant land. To ship the coal, deep-water ports such as Queensland's Abbott Point need to be dredged, creating yet another set of water-quality issues for the reefs beyond these bays. Special interests contend that these steps are necessary because they create jobs. Again, though, espousing a one-dimensional economic side of the house is insufficient. Our economic house is multidimensional and, ideally, multigenerational.

Yes, show me the money now, but show it to me in the years to come as well. As Wendy Tubman, coordinator for North Queensland Conservation Council, explained from her airy bungalow on Magnetic Island, you have to question what jobs we are talking about, and how long they will actually last. The jobs-versus-environment argument simply doesn't work if jobs dissipate within a few years.

Saying this is one thing, of course. Convincing communities to implement a longer economic horizon is quite another. As explored in the account of the next destination, South Africa, we are culturally accustomed to taking shortcuts when it comes to economics, at least in much of the West. Cuba Gooding, Jr., and Tom Cruise scream "Show me the money!" at each other in the 1996 film *Jerry Maguire* with the here and now in mind, not the future. We want immediate results.

Convincing people to take a longer view is all the harder if wide cross-sections of a community directly benefit from existing infrastructure. Take Alaska as an example. Alaskan oil production delivers 93 percent of the state's unrestricted general fund revenues, $8.86 billion in fiscal year 2012.

That means "almost every state service, including the education system, transportation infrastructure, public health and safety services, and a host of other programs throughout Alaska" depend on the petroleum industry, according to the Resource Development Council for Alaska, Inc., an oil and gas, mining, forest products, tourism, and fisheries industry association.[4]

This economic dependence extends well beyond the public sector. Large numbers of the most reliable and highest-paying jobs are connected to extraction and related services. Then there is the Alaska Permanent Fund. Each Alaska resident, as long as they have resided in state for at least one calendar year, receives annual dividends based on a five-year rolling average of investment earnings from a $47 billion fund. The Permanent Fund was established in 1976 after the North Slope oil was discovered, and the state began distributing money from the fund to residents in 1982. In 2013 this amount was $900, but it's been as high as $2,069, in 2008, shortly before the global financial crisis hit.[5]

It's hard to ask someone to give up money like that. Any chance at success would depend on the understanding that more money will be had in the future, combined with the ability to forgo the funds now and still live with some degree of comfort.

That's a lofty goal. To achieve it, we need to better monetize climate-change mitigation. We need to show people the money. As Jeremy Goldberg, a doctoral student at James Cook University, explained to me one Friday afternoon over the phone, that's not easy. "Climate change is the perfect problem. It's invisible and abstract, with repercussions in the future, so it seems there is no immediate need to act," he stated. Chris Briggs, former director of tourism and recreation at the Great Barrier Reef Marine Park Authority, echoed this sentiment to me earlier that week in his office off Flinders Street. As Briggs noted, "Climate change can really send people into a catatonic panic. It's just too big, and they think they can't do anything about it."

These thoughts underscore the first of two characteristics that make climate change particularly daunting for our generation. For one, size matters. In Australia, a country built around its vast size, with more sheep (over 100 million) than people (23 million), this point is not easily ignored. Climate change is a really big problem. Its roots lie in the heart of our economy. They permeate all aspects of our daily lives.

As if that were not imposing enough for policymakers, secondly, as Goldberg the doctoral student pointed out, climate change is mostly a problem for the future. Yes, we already feel components of climate change today, but this pales in comparison to what is on the horizon. Taking action today, then, requires a degree of selflessness instead of selfishness.

Here's where nonprofits and nongovernmental organizations enter the picture. They fill the political space between business and governments, agitating and advocating for interests that tend to be discounted. Ecotourism Australia, for example, is a nonprofit organization in Australia that bills itself as the first environmental certification program for the tourism industry in the world. Their goal, since 1996, has been to economically incentivize more environmentally responsible tourist operations and thus reduce the environmental footprint of tourism itself.

Two levels of accreditation exist in Ecotourism Australia, standard and advanced. Operators who achieve either acquire a range of benefits, including the right to fifteen-year permits instead of only six-year permits. They literally take this benefit to the bank and refinance loans to purchase larger boats with greater income potential. With only six-year permits, according to Great Barrier Reef Marine Park Authority (GBRMPA) officials, many banks would not give these loans, so accreditation provides direct financial benefit.

While the majority of reef tourism operators have yet to earn eco-certification, according to GBRMPA, 65 percent of all reef visitors travel with eco-certified operators. That's an impact.

Moreover, as Doug Baird, environment and compliance manager at Quicksilver Group of Companies, explains to me over a late coffee one midweek afternoon on the Cairns pier, accreditation is helpful even if it only gives additional structure to the industry. A marine biologist involved in the field for over two decades, Baird believes Australian tourism has evolved over the years, and that it now goes beyond ticking off the icons. He sees operators and tourists alike as "becoming a lot more enlightened within their own world," in part because of greater publicity by groups such as Ecotourism Australia.

Speaking of enlightenment, earlier we noted that the uniqueness of Australian flora and fauna is tied to its history of continental drift. There is, of course, another, much sadder history that fundamentally shapes Australia today as well. The aboriginal experience is filled with tragedy, from the First Fleet's initial arrival at Sydney Cove in January 1788 to the systematic slaughter of aboriginals well into the twentieth century. Racism shaped British and other European immigrants' attitudes toward aboriginals, who were often treated as subhuman and beneath white civilization. Native people were marginalized to such a degree, in fact, that the federal government did not even bother to include them in the census until 1967. They simply did not count as people.

But there was another critical factor at work in this calculus as well: greed for land. Aboriginals take offense at celebrations honoring the establishment of a permanent settlement in Sydney Cove at Port Jackson as Australia Day, viewing it as an outright invasion of their continent. If you take a step back to examine settlement of Australia neutrally, that's exactly what it was. The British wanted the land, and they forcibly took it. Like proper British, they even took concerted legal steps to justify their actions, declaring Australia *terra nullius* or land belonging to nobody according to international law. Indeed, it was only in 1992 with the Mabo judgment that the Australian high court

10.1 Uluru/Ayer's Rock.

reversed this rationale, stating that British claim to sovereignty "depended on a discriminatory denigration of indigenous inhabitants."[6]

Aside from superior weaponry and the deadly diseases they transmitted, one of the key factors facilitating success for the white invaders was the sharp contrast between how aboriginals and Europeans viewed the land. Most fundamentally, aboriginal philosophy places humanity not as owners of the land, but as its caretakers. This was a concept that the Europeans recognized and successfully exploited. Aboriginals were seen as uncivilized.[7] They did not have leaders, chiefs, or councils. They did not wear clothes, build houses, sow crops, herd animals, or make pottery. And most convenient of all, they did not have any conventional sense of property, even of noted landmarks such as Uluru, previously known as Ayer's Rock, seen in Figure 10.1. Unattached to the land, at least in the European sense, they wandered from place to place as the seasons and food supplies dictated.

Almost immediately on British arrival, systematic destruction of this culture began. For example, some 250 languages were spoken among aboriginals before European settlers came. Today only about fifteen of those languages are still in use. It wasn't just languages that were dying, of course. People were too, at a horrifyingly efficient pace. When the Brits first settled, estimates on the aboriginal population range from 300,000 to over a million. By the end of the nineteenth century no more than 50,000 to 60,000 still lived on the continent.[8] European diseases such as smallpox, chicken pox, pleurisy, syphilis, and influenza claimed many, but there was also cruelty beyond imagination.

As egregious as these violent episodes were, yet another appalling atrocity that deserves our attention was not murder but theft, specifically the theft of aboriginal children. From 1909 until as late as 1970, aboriginal children were systematically stolen from their parents. Government authorities abducted these children and placed them with white families or schools and missions. The goal was to "breed the black out of them," to help them learn to become part of white society. Virtually every family across the continent was affected, which often destroyed the continuity of community relationships permanently. It should be emphasized, furthermore, that just because the practice was halted in 1970 does not mean past damages were magically undone. Dislocation drove dysfunction, and high levels of suicide as well as grief-related alcoholism can be traced to the practice. In short, the tainted legacy of the Stolen Generations will not be soon undone.

The analogy here is that we run the same risk of damaging future generations on the Great Barrier Reef if we tear away components of its ecosystem now. We cannot ignore interdependence on the reef, just as we could not in the Galápagos Islands. The ability of the reef to recover from shocks such as cyclones and COTS as well as agricultural runoff and irresponsibly implemented tourism depends greatly on our ability to reduce greenhouse gas emissions that cause coral bleaching and acidification and contribute indirectly to many of the aforementioned threats. A diverse ecosystem, like a diverse Australia, is stronger and more resilient for it.

The time to act is now. There might not be time later. This contradicts yet another historical legacy in Australia, a territory long known as the land of second chances. With the exception of the soldiers who accompanied them, initial waves of British immigrants were convicts guilty mostly of minor crimes such as theft. They were the unwanted population from Britain sent to a faraway land when prisons in their home country no longer had space for them. More than 220 crimes were once punishable by death in Britain, and as these sentences were reduced in a more liberal era, prisons became overcrowded. Australia emerged as the politically expedient housing solution, particularly after Britain lost its American colonies.

Australian historians such as Stuart Macintyre adeptly describe this transportation movement and convict experience, from penal colony origins to successive waves of increasingly diverse immigration in the nineteenth and twentieth centuries.[9] People flocked to Australia for a second lease on life. It truly was the land of second chances.

Yet second chances may not develop for Australians this time around. As the Galápagos Islands highlight, the imposing danger of irreversibility arises when it comes to climate change, at least on a human time scale.

When it comes to Australia, furthermore, one final historical label deserves particular emphasis. From the prim and proper tennis courts of Wimbledon to the silver screen of Hollywood, Ozzies are typecast as rough-and-tumble individuals whose penchant for rule-breaking is deeply embedded in their DNA. One might take this as either critique or compliment, challenging or accepting the categorization.

Regardless, the Australian persona includes a related and equally significant stereotype. As manifested in the endearing fictional film character Crocodile Dundee, Australians are stubborn yet creative. They enjoy finding solutions instead of throwing up their hands in despair. Like Americans, Australians pride themselves on rugged individualism, on breaking traditions that confine their self-interests. Take the case of John McDouall Stuart, who led the first European expedition to survive crossing mainland Australia from south to north.[10] Australians are tough. They carve out new paths from the challenging frontiers placed before them.

Australia's traditional rebellious attitude toward authority is even romanticized in the popular tune "Waltzing Matilda," which at times is mistaken as its national anthem. It is a story of a swagman (where a swag is a bundle containing bedding and cooking utensils not unlike that of the hobos in the United States during the Great Depression) who steals sheep, runs from the police, and hides out in camp at a billabong (a seasonal waterhole that occasionally floods).

Thug worship is reflected further in the legend of Ned Kelly. Known as much as a hero as a villain in Australian culture, Kelly was the son of an Irish pig thief who constituted one fourth of the infamous Kelly Gang with his brother and two others. A notorious bank robber, Kelly lived off the land and the good graces of its people until he was caught and hung in Melbourne in 1880 for killing three police officers. Yet to this day, locals invoke Ned Kelly's name as much in praise as in disgust.

Now I don't mean to encourage thug worship with this tale. What I do suggest is that the best routes for the future are probably different than what is commonly accepted today. It will take creativity and guts to be among the first to strike out on such paths. Australia has a history rooted in this ideal, and, since the late twentieth century, has become more and more comfortable embracing it as it becomes more and more multicultural, particularly in its major cities, such as Sydney.

Again, this is a lesson to apply toward the Great Barrier Reef. Diversity makes Australia stronger, more resilient. And diversity makes the reef stronger, more resilient. But climate change threatens this diversity on the reef, and the livelihood it provides for many Australians.

Homogenous ecosystems are poorly equipped to withstand future shocks to their system. When these shocks come, financial losses follow. Paul Marshall, former manager of the climate-change response program at the Great Barrier Reef Marine Park Authority, explained the relevance to me in no uncertain terms one August over coffee and meat-pie wraps at a little café near the Reef HQ. "One of the things that should never be forgotten is that the park was built on principles of multiple use, except for mining," he emphasized. When we abandon this coalition of multiple-use interests for one economic interest over another, our entire financial foundation is threatened. In short, as F. Scott Fitzgerald suggested, we have to be able to hold two conflicting ideas in our mind at the same time. We have to spend money to save money.

LIONS, RHINOS, AND HYENAS . . . OH MY

South Africa's Hluhluwe-iMfolozi and Cultural Obstacles to Understanding Climate Change

My greatest challenge has been to change the mindset of people. Mindsets play strange tricks on us. We see things the way our minds have instructed our eyes to see.

—Muhammad Yunus, 2006 Nobel Peace Prize winner

chapter eleven

INSURANCE

ARGUABLY THE BEST TIME OF THE DAY is when we are shooting down a dusty dirt road of sorts in our aging, partially white pickup truck. Dawn is breaking here at South Africa's Hluhluwe-iMfolozi provincial park, with striking specks of orange and red splashed across a quickly shifting background from black and blue, to blue and white. Amid yet another beautiful African sunrise, I'm simultaneously exchanging halting small talk with my armed Zulu guard, rechecking supplies packed in semipanic that chilly winter morning, and psyching myself up for a ten-kilometer hike through some of the most inspiring terrain in the world. Aside from the loss of sleep, what could be better?

Then it hits me: What would be better is if more days were like this. I don't mean the scenery or the conversation, although both are deeply cherished. I'm thinking bigger picture. What truly would be better is if more day-to-day decisions were made in the same vein of thought in which this project was conceived, thinking about the future as well as the present.

You see, I'm here to assist with a series of wildlife population studies at Hluhluwe-iMfolozi, the park that literally snatched the southern white rhino from the brink of extinction. It is world-renowned for its game population and park management. Every white rhino alive today traces its genetic heritage to this flagship park in KwaZulu-Natal, South Africa. Now, park officials are attempting to replicate that success with its cousin, the critically endangered black rhino.

The point I'm trying to make is that it's easy to get wrapped up in the here and now, especially when it comes to financial matters exemplified by the economic issues surrounding Australia's Great Barrier Reef. What makes just as much sense, though, provided you can place food on the table today, is to plan for the future at the same time. Culturally, Americans have some weaknesses there. We aren't the best at planning long-term.

Of course, notable exceptions exist. Take our national park system as one example. Yellowstone National Park was actually the first national park in the world, and roughly two hundred countries around the globe emulated that unique American experiment in the years that followed, including South Africa. Our national park system, America's "best idea," akin to a "declaration of independence for land," according to award-winning American documentary filmmaker Ken Burns, is a concerted public commitment to planning long-term.[1]

Admittedly, additional influences greatly shaped the creation of parks back then. With Yellowstone in 1872, for example, recreational interests linked with a powerful railroad magnate seeking an expanded customer base to make the park politically possible.[2] Of course, it didn't hurt to have land values discounted due to the geyser activity that discouraged development in this northwest corner of Wyoming. Both of these characteristics are much more than historical footnotes, by the way. They represent an important lesson in regard to combined financial interests, a lesson to which we will return in subsequent chapters focusing on the Amazon and social misunderstandings surrounding climate change.

Before going any further, though, it should be noted that South Africa's Hluhluwe-iMfolozi wasn't exactly conceived with the American ideal of egalitarian access. It also never became a national park. Despite these points, Hluhluwe-iMfolozi held one all-important characteristic in common with Yellowstone from the beginning: long-term thinking. Indeed, this futuristic perspective is perhaps the most powerful argument to make for national parks such as Yellowstone and provincial parks such as Hluhluwe-iMfolozi. It is also the easiest to understand.

Sometimes bad things happen. When they do, you need a backup plan. What's more, you are probably going to need a little help implementing that back-up plan. You need insurance.

Most Americans intuitively understand this. It's why we have life insurance. We want to be able to take care of our loved ones even when we are no longer around to do so ourselves.

But it doesn't stop there. What if a drunk driver with expired insurance rear-ends you at a stoplight? Or if your neighbor's rotten tree two doors down, in an "act of God," falls on the roof of your house? Most of us have automobile as well as home insurance with precisely these contingencies in mind. You need insurance for the big, important things in life.

That said, for the biggest, most important piece of all, our planet, we arrogantly and ignorantly continue to operate as if no insurance is needed. We keep plugging along like tomorrow will take care of itself, ignoring the increasingly obvious damage inflicted on our environment, including the atmosphere that sustains us.

As a point of fact, it bears noting that climate change won't destroy our planet. The planet will recover—albeit over long periods of time. The more immediate question is, will we?

Roaming through the Galápagos Islands helped highlight the scientific uncertainty that surrounds this query while at the same time calling attention to what we do know about the processes now under way. In essence, the trip made it clear that our climate is changing, and that much of this change is human-induced. Culturally, this is a daunting obstacle to face. Unlike in World War II or the war on terrorism we face today, we are not fighting some distant, nefarious evil-doer. We are fighting ourselves. We are the enemy.

Still, that is probably not the most constructive approach to understanding climate change, let alone taking personal steps to reduce it. Hluhluwe-iMfolozi highlights a distinctly more palatable one, shifting focus from personal character to emphasize individual or societal behavior by balancing immediate with long-term interests. In other words, from a parental perspective, it's not that we are bad children, but that we have bad behaviors. Our parents aren't disappointed with us; they are disappointed with our actions.

To drive this point home, let's take an example a little closer to home, the devastating Hurricane Katrina. In late summer 2005, Americans were blasted repeatedly with images of that tragedy here on our own soil, from the shock of its raw power, to the maddening and painful governmental missteps in both its anticipation and aftermath. While it is impossible to attribute a single event such as Katina to climate change, many Americans learned in the ensuing weeks how climate change makes severe hurricanes more likely.

For example, we learned that hurricanes draw their strength from warm ocean surface waters, and that they arise in the tropics only during the season when sea temperatures are at their highest. Further, we learned that Katrina fed off unusually warm Gulf waters late that summer, growing from its first landfall in south Florida as a category 1 storm with 80 mph winds to a frightful category 5 with 175 mph winds when it tore through the Gulf of Mexico, right before dropping to a category 3 and striking New Orleans and the Gulf Coast on August 29, 2005.

What is less known, tragically, are the desperate warnings presented years before this disaster. In October 2001, for instance, less than four years before Hurricane Katrina, a story ran in *Scientific American* describing New Orleans as a "disaster waiting to happen." It suggested, geologically speaking, that the city was sinking. It's future was not good. Yet the public response to this clarion call was predictably, and woefully, anemic.

The following year, the *Times-Picayune* published a five-part, 50,000-word series entitled "Washing Away." New Orleans wasn't simply vulnerable geologically, it asserted. People were making the city more vulnerable by pumping out its groundwater, digging for oil exploration, and eliminating surrounding wetlands. These wetlands, which serve as a critical buffer from powerful storm surges, were disappearing at the phenomenal rate of a football field every thirty-eight minutes.[3] Again, nothing was done in response.

It is here that the true lesson of Katrina lies.

Profound racial problems still constrict our country's potential. Damage from Katrina was not evenly distributed by race or class. Predominantly African American neighborhoods such as those in the Ninth Ward were devastated. To add insult to injury, if not outright racism, political ideology further bungled efforts to assist those in danger both before and after the storm.

From an environmental justice standpoint, even over a decade later, much work remains; these same disadvantaged "populations [are] more vulnerable in the rebuilding and recovery process."[4] And sadly, as noted by longstanding environmental justice advocate Robert Bullard, Katrina is symbolic of a larger problem, one where communities of color face not only chronic unemployment and poverty, but also widely disproportionate exposure to environmental risk.

Regardless of your political leanings in this context, the overarching lesson of the Katrina tragedy is that we need to go beyond living for today. We need to prepare for tomorrow.

Of course, culturally, that is easier said than done. The here and now garners our immediate attention, whether it be the less fortunate among us trying to make ends meet on a day-to-day basis, or the well to do who are understandably hesitant to waste their funds on the unknown. From either extreme, and at all the points in between, those who fail to plan ahead will be considerably less rich in both experiences and the personal and professional opportunities that flow from them.

To take a short pause here: another legitimate question is, what exactly do I mean by the term "culture"? Perhaps it is most helpfully conceptualized as "patterns of values, ideas, and other symbolic-meaningful systems" that shape our behavior.[5] But how exactly does that differ from social influences addressed in later chapters about the Amazon?

The easy answer, and a partially correct one at that, is to say the two concepts are not all that different and lump them together. Call them "sociocultural influences," if you will. But even this seemingly casual act raises a critical, not merely academic, question. By placing "socio" first are we indicating social aspects are more important, that they shape culture?[6]

To make matters a bit more complicated, it is also critical to note that culture is not constant. It is constantly evolving. As Grameen Bank founder and Nobel Prize–winning economist Mohammad Yunus asserts, "Culture is useless unless it is constantly challenged by counter culture. People create culture; culture creates people. It is a two-way street."

Turns out, this two-way street is more of an asset than a handicap in overcoming cultural obstacles to understanding climate change. Quite simply, we are not stuck with what we have now. We have the capacity to adjust culturally, to develop values and ideas that are part of the solution instead of the problem.

As referenced in the Galápagos Islands and the Great Barrier Reef, this starts first and foremost with how we produce and consume energy. A three-pronged approach to energy consumption must drive this process. Energy efficiency, alternative energy, and integration of fourth-generation nuclear energy plants must replace our current fossil fuel economy.

That is easier said than done. While no yellow brick road exists, creativity will be an undeniable asset. As esteemed American astronomer and astrophysicist Carl Sagan once asserted, "Imagination will often carry us to worlds that never were, but without it we go nowhere." In other words, we must think outside the box. We need to be creative like Carl Sagan and use our imaginations like Dorothy in *The Wizard of Oz*.

Of course, as I've argued from the beginning, to combat climate change, we first have to admit it exists, which, in turn, requires understanding why it exists. We've looked at scientific and economic explanations, with the

Galápagos Islands and Great Barrier Reef, respectively. Now it is time for a third explanation, a cultural one. I'm off to South Africa to see and taste it myself, in the land where *Homo sapiens* originated 150,000 years ago.

In terms of biodiversity, after Indonesia and Brazil, South Africa is the third richest country in the world. Ironically, though, in many ways, South Africa actually falls short as a top big-game safari destination. To many visitors, it lacks the feeling of unfettered wilderness found in Botswana or Tanzania.[7] That said, it's still a popular Big Five destination, as the number of hunters aboard my flight demonstrates. "Big Five," by the way, is a term traced to the big game hunters of the nineteenth century, and refers to the five most dangerous animals to encounter on foot in Africa: lion, black rhino, buffalo, elephant, and leopard.

What makes this destination particularly attractive is not only the thrill of sharing days and nights in the bush among the Big Five, but the chance to study the dangerous cocktail of environmental threats South Africa faces. These continue to proliferate, ranging from alien plant infestations to urban sprawl and overcrowding, to poor farming and unwise use of water for commercial crops, to the legacy of land degradation in the former homelands, not to mention the combination of international and local demand that drives poaching of its megafauna.[8]

I've volunteered for a scientific expedition in the eastern bush of South Africa at the continent's oldest declared wildlife reserve. The group that brought me here is called Earthwatch, an environmental nongovernmental organization based outside of Boston that sponsors approximately 130 scientific research projects a year in more than forty countries across the globe.

Interestingly, Earthwatch doesn't just give money to scientists conducting research. It also provides them with free labor in their data collection. More accurately, people like me pay Earthwatch for the privilege of working with their scientists. The thinking here is, as long as data gathering is kept fairly basic, the scientists receive much-needed assistance in compiling large data sets. They also gain funding from the volunteers, who essentially cover field costs. And the kicker in the equation is that Earthwatch hopes these volunteers become public advocates for the projects once they return home. In essence, Earthwatch actively encourages proselytizing in the name of biodiversity protection and climate change.

Humans began migrating from the African continent 55,000 to 60,000 years ago. I'm migrating back in just under twenty-four hours—but even that streamlined schedule is not without its own challenges. My plane leaves Orlando over an hour late, which means plans for a relaxing, two-hour layover at Dulles airport in D.C. are supplanted by a mad, sweaty dash from one terminal to the next. I arrive twenty-five minutes prior to the scheduled takeoff time—and a mere five minutes before attendants close the cabin doors. Nervously wiping beads of perspiration off my brow, I ask the more-cheery-than-normal flight attendant if my bags will make it. With supreme confidence, she replies in the affirmative, and the ensuing delay once onboard reassures me that she is not just telling me what I want to hear, that my bag really will make it.

In between a mix of action films and bouts of actual sleep, I read up a bit more on my destination, the oldest reserve on the African continent. There are three more airports to negotiate before I actually enter Hluhluwe-iMfolozi, though. The first is in Dakar, Senegal, where, as dawn breaks, we land to refuel. Technically, I've just picked up my sixth continent, although my personal qualifications are a bit more stringent. You must actually spend extended time in a place to log credit for being there, let alone truly experience what it has to offer. And since I'm a scientist—well, at least a social scientist—I've even devised a measurement for that. In a somewhat joking fashion, my criteria rest on travel's holy trinity of a good meal, a good night's rest, and a good bowel movement. Partials, in any of those categories, do not count.

From the air, the setting in Dakar seems straight out of Hollywood central casting. A foreboding grayish-brown haze hangs over the streets and haphazard collection of buildings below me, albeit interspersed with a tint of increasingly reddish dirt as the sun continues to rise higher in the early-morning sky.

With little delay on the ground in Dakar, we spend the rest of the day flying a great distance south, reaching Johannesburg, the financial capital and largest city in South Africa, roughly an hour before nightfall. Customs goes surprisingly quickly, but guess what? My checked bag never shows. After filling out the appropriate paperwork and losing the time I thought I had saved going through customs, I'm told it will be delivered to the park about this time tomorrow. That doesn't sound too bad. In fact, making lemonade out of lemons, I reason that my transfer to the hotel tonight and back to the airport for a domestic flight the next morning will be easier without the extra bag to lug around.

Then again, if the bag fails to show, it will be a long, cold night when I get into the bush. I'm in the Southern Hemisphere now, and July means winter. As if on cue, as I wait at the terminal for a shuttle to my airport lodge, an evening chill descends around me, and I witness my first African sunset, an iconic image that sends figurative shivers down my spine to match the literal, temperature-induced ones.

Turns out, I'm in for still more shivers that night as well. I'm able to charge my camera with a three-prong M-type plug and dutifully don the sweatshirt I packed in my carry-on bag, but the heater in my room doesn't seem to function. And all my additional warm clothing is in my misplaced, checked bag. Not going to get much rest tonight. In fact, it's even worse than the night on the plane. At least I was warm there. I hope this is not foreshadowing the days to come.

Arising before dawn for my two-hour domestic flight to Richard's Bay, I'm running on nothing but adrenaline by now. Fortunately, the airport at Richard's Bay is small and easily navigable, about seventy-five miles from my final destination. By late morning of August 1, along with ten of my newly acquired Earthwatch volunteer colleagues, I arrive at the eastern Nyalazi Gate of Hluhluwe-iMfolozi.

By many accounts, Hluhluwe-iMfolozi, outlined in Figure 11.1, is the earliest African reserve, proclaimed by the government of Natal in 1895 and officially instituted in April 1897, although its boundaries on the south and west remained ambiguous until 1962. Largely acacia savanna and woodland, it is situated in the eastern portion of the country and influenced to some degree by the warm waters of the Indian Ocean, so it has a largely subtropical climate.[9] At 960 square km, Hluhluwe-iMfolozi is by no means massive, yet it is still the third-largest park in South Africa. Today it is actually the marriage of two historically distinct parks, as its modern, hyphenated name implies, with the addition of a formerly unprotected linking corridor running between the two reserves in 1989.

Despite that successful union, distinct differences remain between Hluhluwe and iMfolozi. They are partners that retain their individuality. Probably the most significant of these is rainfall. The mist-enshrouded hills of Hluhluwe, for example, receive over twelve inches more rain a year than the driest parts of iMfolozi, and the lower reaches of Hluhluwe, in particular, always hold water. As such, they are thickly vegetated and ideal habitat for species such as elephants.

All this will come to mean more in the coming days. Right now I'm just struggling to learn a few polite Zulu phrases and make sure I understand the instructions for recording data on our transect walks properly. Heck, even the name of the park continues to challenge me. Turns out, as a linguistically challenged English-speaker, I'm not alone. As travel writer H. V. Morton wrote way back in 1947, for example, the name "Hluhluwe" is unpronounceable to many at first sight.[10] I only develop the art over time, with great patience from my camp manager, a devoted outdoorsmen and affable Afrikaner named Cameron, who suggests practicing with phlegm stuck in my throat.

In contrast to its northern compatriot, the iMfolozi landscape is considerably more expansive, with an openness that makes spotting game, as well as predators, much easier. Rolling savannas taper into wide banks at the Black and White iMfolozi Rivers, both of which meander throughout the

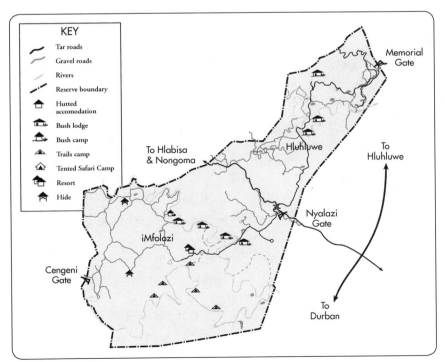

11.1 Map of Hluhluwe-iMfolozi. Source: KZN Wildlife—Design Studio.

park. Fortunately, for my sake, as I will learn shortly, they also both shrink to little more than ankle depth during the dry season from May to November.

I'm in the heart of the Zulu kingdom now, with ancient trails crisscrossing the thornveld.[11] Indeed, one major reason iMfolozi remained undeveloped in the early nineteenth century was that it served as the royal hunting grounds of King Shaka himself. Shaka would host massive hunts on these grounds, but balanced them with periods of no hunting so game populations could recover. Some even suggest he was the park's first conservator.

Although small compared to parks such as Kruger, which is literally twenty times its size, Hluhluwe-iMfolozi boasts a diversity of plant communities that support a wide range of animals, including over eighty species of mammals. What's more, its plentiful water supplies make migration less dependent on water availability than in other areas, which means animals are somewhat less inclined to attempt escape. And finally, as I shall discover shortly, Hluhluwe-iMfolozi houses all of the Big Five, the traditional most dangerous animals to hunt on the continent.

In one of life's twisted little ironies, after Shaka and the Zulu presence, the other major reason Hluhluwe-iMfolozi was spared development emerged in the twentieth century, even as iMfolozi twice lost its reserved status (although Hluhluwe never did). At times, as this story illustrates, big results come in small packages. Although each presented a considerable threat in its own right, the tsetse fly and malaria mosquito teamed together to leave a positive legacy for Hluhluwe-iMfolozi as well. They both kept human encroachment at bay, with minimal development and farming in the immediate vicinity prior to the early twentieth century.

That all changed after World War I, though, as returning veterans received land rights at Ntambanana and near Hluhluwe. Large-scale cattle introduction quickly followed, which in turn allowed the tsetse flies to flourish. Breeding in the shade of the park, these pests increasingly took sojourns outside its boundaries and began killing cattle on white ranches along the perimeter. The nagana era, named after the cattle blood disease caused by the tsetse flies, had begun.

Exasperated by their inability to quell the outbreak, the government attempted to starve out the flies within the park by eliminating their food source in the game reserves. Officials instituted a shoot-on-sight policy for all park animals but the rhino, and tens of thousands were killed. According to official park records, in fact, from December 1942 to April 1950 alone, some 70,000 creatures perished.[12] Even these drastic measures failed, however, and in 1947 officials finally resorted to spraying the entire park with DDT aerially as well as on foot. This spraying continued until 1952, when the Natal Parks Board took over administration of the park.

I guess another note to sound when trumpeting diversity in this park, then, goes well beyond boasting about how small species such as the tsetse fly and malaria mosquito steered people away in the first place. In many ways, the park and its inhabitants survived simply in spite of what people did. That's an ironically optimistic point. It is also not one we should overstate, for there is real danger in the wrong lesson being learned. Quite simply, one must avoid overconfidence in the ability of damaged areas to recover, for our own sake if not theirs.

In fact, dangerous tipping points do exist. Irreversibility, whether in terms of biodiversity loss and extinction within Hluhluwe-iMfolozi, or our overarching topic of global climate change, is an omnipresent threat. And finally, it is important to remember that Hluhluwe-iMfolozi became what it is today because many of its flagship species, the lion, elephant, and wild dogs, to name a few, were reintroduced. They were transferred from other parts of the continent. In other words, we had insurance.

Following lunch, all eleven Earthwatch volunteers dive into our orientation with one of the two principal investigators for this project, Dr. David Druce. A regional ecologist with South Zululand, Druce joined the project in April 2008, just a few months prior to my arrival. He serves as co–principal investigator with Mandisa Mgobozi, an ecologist with South East Zululand. Druce came to Hluhluwe-iMfolozi from Global Visions International, near the northern border of South Africa, and is clearly excited about his first count here.

Over twenty-three slides, Druce outlines the origin and purpose of the project, explaining how transects are cut with machetes by locals, and notes that the counts conducted along these transects provide a valuable tool in the park's biannual population census. Essentially, we are helping determine which species are declining and will require additional study, as well as which are exhibiting healthy populations and, thus, are ideal candidates for translocation. This surplus is sold annually in early spring to private parks and commercial game reserves, providing valuable funds for other park projects.[13]

All told, across South Africa, over 130,000 game animals are relocated each year, according to the Wildlife Translocation Association, a group of professional game capturers in South Africa.[14] Some of these animals come out of Hluhluwe-iMfolozi. To determine that amount, park officials conduct a census of the large herbivores every two years. Earthwatch volunteers assist with this count in four different teams, spread over the months of July, August, and September. This falls within the winter dry season of May to September, the best time to visit because vegetation cover is not as dense and animals are easier to see. In addition, the water supply is more limited, so species congregate much more. Teams of eleven individuals, then, over sixteen days, count buffalo, bushbuck, bush pig, blue duiker, gray duiker, red duiker, giraffe, impala, zebra, kudu, nyala, common reedbuck, mountain reedbuck, black rhino, white rhino, steenbok, warthog, waterbuck, and wildebeest.

Depending on the park, population count techniques vary. Aerial counts are often conducted from helicopters and fixed-wing aircraft. Ground drive counts are common as well. The standard method at Hluhluwe-iMfolozi is something different. It's called distance sampling. First developed in the 1980s, distance sampling has been successfully tested in a number of diverse environments, with a range of species, from coral reefs to whales to birds to large herbivores such as those we're focusing on.[15] The raw data we collect over the next two weeks will be entered into Druce's larger data set for these calculations.

The count itself, by the way, is only the most basic of three objectives for this study. Begun in 1996, the project is longitudinal, meaning it is conducted over a period of time, so we are also helping scientists examine wider trends in population growth and decline. And finally, our population data allows scientists to better understand interactions between herbivores, vegetation, and fire. Park officials will make a range of park management decisions based on the numbers that we and the thirty-three other volunteers this season give them.

Processing this initial information carefully, our group next tackles a short Zulu language course. Maybe it's my lack of sleep, or merely my innate linguistic deficiencies, but I struggle to grasp even the polite basics of "hello," "please," and "thank you" over the next hour or so. The only thing I'm really confident I've mastered at our closing, in fact, is the Zulu handshake, a three-step process that opens and closes with a traditional handshake but, in between, features the more informal hand clasping with thumbs around thumbs. After this class, we receive a brief tour of the renowned Centenary Game Capture Center, including a peek into the *bomas* where large species are temporarily housed during translocation, before the day closes with a traditional South African barbecue or *braai*.

The twin threats of poaching and habitat destruction due to human population growth have devastated rhinoceros populations over the last half-century. Here at Hluhluwe-iMfolozi, they have a second chance, both the white and the black species. Using the data from our daily transect walks, for example, scientists can repopulate excess numbers here into other conservation areas around the country, or the entire continent for that matter.

This practice revolves around the ingenious management of population growth. For example, black rhino reproduce at 3 percent a year when whey they populate a park at their maximum population density. When reduced to 80 percent density, though, they actually reproduce at a higher rate of 5 percent. Scientists such as Druce use this data to concentrate on maximizing growth rates, rather than relying on what the layperson would initially suspect in terms of population sizes. My role as a volunteer is to help collect the baseline data on fifteen of the larger herbivore species that makes all this possible.

As a game reserve initially, and provincial park today, Hluhluwe-iMfolozi never was a national park, let alone South Africa's first. That honor belongs to Kruger National Park, established by act of parliament in May 1926. Moreover, as alluded to earlier, from national parks to game reserves, South Africa initially followed in the elitist British tradition when setting aside land. That is, while British wildlife preservation tracts existed as early as the twelfth century, well before the United States was even a nation-state, average citizens received little to no access to them. This helps explain, at least in part, why most South African parks and reserves are no bigger than an average small farm. Many were acquired simply to protect a single endangered mammal as English sport hunters hoped to return game to numbers high enough for hunting once again.

On the other hand, the American concept of a national park, as articulated in the Yellowstone National Park Act, was fundamentally different and democratic. Its focus was to protect landscapes for the general public rather than individual species typically enjoyed by only a select few. Of course, it must be noted that such virtue was only possible due to the systematic oppression, not to mention forced relocation of Native Americans that often inhabited these very lands. This critical caveat aside, in the words of the bill President Ulysses Grant signed into law, Yellowstone was to be a "pleasure-ground for the benefit and enjoyment of the people."[16]

Hluhluwe-iMfolozi now adopts this American philosophy and is well known for a number of characteristics, from leading the establishment of wilderness areas in South Africa, to being one of the few reserves in South Africa that house the Big Five, to pioneering game-capture techniques copied the world over. This last item, in particular Operation Rhino, won the park worldwide recognition thanks to phenomenal success with the white rhino during the 1960s.

Once dipping well under one hundred individuals in the twentieth century, to perhaps as low as thirty in 1920, according to author Charlton-Perkins, the white rhino, as seen here in Figure 11.2, now boasts populations of over eleven thousand. Some 2,068 of those were based in Hluhluwe-iMfolozi as recently as early 2014.[17] What's more, with its remarkable growth over the last couple decades, the white rhino became the first species to actually be taken off the endangered list of IUCN.

This stunning success story has a number of twists and turns but starts with the leadership of Dr. Ian Player, the senior warden at iMfolozi in 1962. Player developed a revolutionary technique for drug-darting, a practice that

11.2 The southern white rhino.

allowed rangers to capture animals without injury and transport them to new environments.[18]

As noted earlier in this chapter, there are two species of rhino in Africa, white and black.[19] Each is actually the same pigment of gray, although the shade of color depends largely on local soil conditions and how much a rhino wallows around in that soil. White rhinos, which frequently curl up their tail, turn, and run if someone so much as claps their hands, are nowhere near as aggressive as black rhinos, and thus not part of the esteemed Big Five. Black rhino, on the other hand, seem to take great pleasure in confrontation. One infamous black rhino cow in Hluhluwe, in fact, gained the nickname Poking Polly for her adeptness at standing on her hind legs and trying to hook people out of the trees to which they had fled when she charged.[20]

Getting back to the name for white rhino, though, it probably comes from the Dutch word *wijd* meaning wide, an appropriate association considering their squarish mouth. English settlers, however, mistook this as "white," and before they could correct themselves, they had already named the other type of African rhino as black, even though it displayed the exact same pigmentation.

Common color aside, the two species are easily distinguished. The white rhino has wide, square lips that facilitate efficient grass grazing, whereas the black rhino has a pointed mouth, often described as a prehensile upper lip, which serves as an asset in stripping leaves from branches. As a result of these dietary preferences, even from a distance, one can hazard a fairly accurate guess as to whether the rhino is "white" or "black." White rhinos generally keep their heads low as they graze, while black rhinos keep their heads in line with their backs as they feed. The white rhino is also considerably larger than its black cousin, standing six feet at the shoulder with males weighing around 3.5 tons and registering as the second-largest land mammal (after the elephant) on the planet. The black rhino is typically less than half that.

White rhinos favor open areas, while black rhinos prefer dense, protective thickets, so much so that they often can be difficult to see. And interestingly, the white rhino calf walks in front of its mother while the black rhino calf walks behind. Finally, and perhaps most importantly, it bears repeating that the white rhino is much less aggressive than the black rhino, which is bad-tempered, extremely unpredictable, and may charge with little provocation.

It might be a bit of a stretch, but perhaps diet explains these stark mood differences a bit better. You are, after all, what you eat, right? White rhinos stick largely to grasses, but black rhinos dine on bushes, including the fleshy *Euphorbia grandicornis*, more aptly referred to by its common name, "rhino thorn," complete with five-centimeter-long thorns. That's got to hurt. It's painful enough just to watch.

Tony Pooley, a South African ranger and crocodile specialist, recounted one such jaw-dropping episode decades ago in September 1962 during the reintroduction of black rhino into Ndumu Game Reserve. White rhino had previously been reintroduced, but guards and laborers were completely unfamiliar with its black cousin. When the first black bull arrived early one spring day, it walked quietly out of its crate and began, almost immediately, to feed on the prickly rhino thorn.

One individual, the petrol attendant and workshop assistant accompanying the group for this momentous occasion, captured the sentiment of all those assembled. With a mixture of awe and fright, he exclaimed, "A creature that eats thorns like that can only be very dangerous, for when those thorns pass through its stomach and intestines, and then out of its anus, it must be painful and that animal must then be very, very bad tempered."[21]

That said, the white and black rhinos also have several characteristics in common. Each is remarkably fast and agile for its size, with the black rhino reaching speeds of thirty-five to forty miles per hour over short distances and having the added ability to maneuver surprisingly well in tight spaces. The white rhino is no klutz, either, as I will soon find out firsthand. Both also have poor eyesight, seeing nothing farther than thirty paces, although keen hearing and sense of smell compensate, to some degree, for this deficiency.

As I process all this information, one fact continues to echo in the back of my mind. The most important difference between the two species today, aside from perhaps their aggressiveness, is that white rhinos are one of the major success stories of conservation worldwide, saved from near-certain extinction. Black rhino, on the other hand, are now in desperate straits.

What happened?

To answer this question fully, let us first return to the formation of Hluhluwe and iMfolozi. These were two of the first four reserves set aside by the British colonial government in 1895, one of the few positive moves it made involving the land of South Africa according to Ian Player.[22] Two reasons Hluhluwe and iMfolozi made this list should sound remarkably familiar. For one, they were not particularly desirable given the presence of the tsetse fly and malarial mosquito. For another, environmental voices teamed with wealthy interests to form a viable political lobby after a white rhino was shot on a hunting expedition where the Black and White iMfolozi Rivers meet.

Interestingly, and ironically, it wasn't the horror of killing a member of this endangered species that generated the conservation momentum, but, rather, a sense of euphoria. White rhino, hunted by white colonialists from 1920 to 1983, first for sport and then for commercial interests, were thought to be extinct at that time. Hunters thought they were tracking what was then a common black rhino, and only discovered the opposite to be true when the creature was shot. That set in motion the declaration of the two reserves and special protection for the white rhino.

Black rhino were not similarly protected. They were much more dangerous, and there were plenty of them. In 1900, for example, there were an astounding one million black rhinos across the continent, and the species remained abundant as late as the 1970s. Over the last forty plus years, though, large-scale poaching has brought dramatic decline, on the order of 96 percent, according to the nonprofit Save the Rhino.[23] Only South Africa, Namibia, and Kenya have viable populations today.[24]

As scientists concentrated on saving the devastated white rhino population, black rhinos were unintentionally left vulnerable. You see, all rhino are prized among poachers for their horns. Etymologically speaking, it is easy to understand what makes the rhino special, the name being a form of two Greek words, with *rhino* meaning nose, and *keras* meaning horn. The rhino is a unique creature with a unique feature. Further, when you first see a rhino horn with your own eyes, with their fetching translucent color, it makes more sense why some consider them prized ornaments.

In Yemen, for example, rhino horns are used to create beautiful handles for curved daggers known as *jambiya*. Presented to boys at the age of twelve, the *jambiya* represents the transition to manhood and is symbolic of the Muslim faith more generally. While the country formally banned imports in 1982, a black market continues to prosper.

Much more of a concern than this trade, though, is the literal appetite for rhino horns, which are nothing more than the protein keratin, not unlike our fingernails and toenails, throughout parts of Asia. For centuries, rhino

11.3 Setting up camp in iMfolozi.

horn was prized for a variety of supposed healing properties, from fixing fevers to healing liver ailments. In point of fact, according to ecologist Raj Amin of the Zoological Society of London, you'd be just as well off chewing your own fingernails.[25] Yet, in Asia, from Malaysia and Vietnam to South Korea, India, and China, people pay considerable sums of money, up to $1,000,000 per kilogram, to consume crushed horn dissolved into boiling water. That makes rhino horn literally worth more than its weight in gold.[26]

What's driving such a ridiculous pricing system?

For years, it was traditional Chinese medicine. That shaped consumption for over eighteen hundred years, until the 1980s, when a series of trade bans squashed supply. By the 1990s, those actions combined with the removal of horn powder in traditional Chinese recipes to greatly restrict demand.

That all changed in 2008, though, when a rumor began circulating in Vietnam that rhino horn cured a politician's cancer.[27] Demand elevated still further when yet another faulty rumor circulated, this one suggesting rhino-horn powder cured hangovers. It quickly became a popular status symbol among a rising wealthy class, analogous to cocaine as a party drug, one that infused energy and virility. With demand rekindled in Asia, particularly countries with growing consumer classes such as Vietnam, the end result today is that a rhino is killed in South Africa every nineteen hours, a figure that translates into an average of 440 individuals a year.

This tragedy is only at the back of my mind at the moment, though, as I'm consumed with the here and now, specifically taking advantage of a rare treat that morning, precious sleep. Even with an extra hour or so, it's still pitch black when I rise at 5:30 A.M. After a quick, before-dawn breakfast, all eleven volunteers return to the Centenary Center for day two of orientation. Today is a big day. Today we get to put theory into practice.

After a short review of the Pythagorean theorem and its role in the calculations Druce will make later in the year, topped off with the requisite midmorning tea break that all former British affiliates still hold dear, we receive our data-sheets briefing and prized equipment issue. Everyone is excited to stretch their legs and begin the much-anticipated field exercises. Beginning on the grass bush-plane runway near the *boma* that we visited yesterday, I practice taking measurements with our laser range-finders and hand-held GPS devices. When rotations begin tomorrow, we'll record all study animals seen within five hundred meters of our assigned transect.

That afternoon, as our orientation ends, our party splits into two groups to depart for our respective camps for the next fortnight. Seven Earthwatch volunteers will be based in the south in iMfolozi and four in the north in Hluhluwe. In the north, they have a laptop, so their afternoons will be spent entering morning data into a series of spreadsheets. I'm starting with the larger group in the South at Thumbu (Figure 11.3), so no data entry for us just yet.

Still no word on my sleeping bag. Was it stolen in Johannesburg, simply grabbed up at the baggage carousel while I was in passport control? Security didn't seem particularly tight there, so that's entirely possible. At least our camp manager, Cameron, offered a degree of insurance in the form of these dusty wool blankets from the back of our pickup truck. In short, it pays to be a good Boy Scout, to be prepared, or in my case, to know someone who is. You never know when that insurance will come in handy.

chapter twelve

RAINBOW NATION

ARGHHH . . . I was actually sleeping for a few minutes. I think. Can't be sure on that. Maybe it was just a waking dream about sleeping. Alas, thanks to my trusty watch alarm, with its steady string of annoying beeps, those dreams have been rudely crushed. I'm crawling out of my motley, but better than nothing, rat's nest of wool blankets at the bewitching time of 4:45 A.M. Yes, 4:45 A.M.! Really, who gets up at a time like this? In my book, at least, it's downright unnatural to rise and shine before the sun signals it's okay. It's flat out disrespectful. You shouldn't ignore nature's preferred path to consciousness.

But maybe I'm a little more grumpy than usual this cold, misty morning. Without my sleeping bag, I haven't gotten much rest. It's Africa, and the temperatures can soar during the heat of the day to as high as 95 degrees F. But right now, even in our subtropical climate, it's still winter in the Southern Hemisphere, which means nights typically dip down to around 45. That's a long, cold evening without a sleeping bag.

There is one positive in my favor this morning. I'm already wearing every possible stitch of clothing from my carry-on bag, so getting dressed is a matter of simply stumbling out of my tent, after which I wander over to the camp common area to wolf down some breakfast and prepare lunch with the six other volunteers in my group.

Today is a big day. We will tackle our first transect walk. I suppose that's the common ingredient that keeps us going at such an unkind hour.

Each morning over the next two weeks, with the exception of one off day, we will pair up with an armed Zulu guide and hike six to seven miles over rolling savanna thornveld, canopy forest, and, in the southern reaches of the park, bone-dry bushland. Walks begin only when there is sufficient light to see five hundred meters (1,640 feet), the limit of our electronic range finders. Each time a target species is spotted, we stop and record its type, our GPS point, compass bearing of the transect, compass bearing to the center of the herd, distance to the herd, size of the herd, vegetation, and weather conditions. Depending on the terrain, this typically means a two- to three-kilometer-an-hour pace.

Daily essentials, beyond the obvious sufficient supply of water and food, include well-worn hiking boots and comfy socks, protective sun hat and sunscreen, rain jacket, compass, GPS, data sheet and clipboard, and, because we are tourists as well as scientific aides, a camera. Dull-colored clothing, particularly dark colors rather than light, is a daily staple as well. This allows us to blend in better with our surroundings. Of course, that benefit comes with a trade-off when late morning rolls around and temperatures heat up, for as I know all too well from hot and humid Florida, darker colors absorb rather than reflect the unwanted heat.

Overheating is the furthest thing from my mind at the moment, though. If I thought my tent was cold, the back bed of the jeep is downright freezing, at least until the sun rises at around 6:15. Arguably, this is the best part of the day, despite the considerable chill in the air. A solid thirty minutes before the sun rises you can still catch glimpses of all sorts of wildlife as the truck rushes down the gravel-and-dirt road to pick up our guards for the day. Indeed, some of our best sightings over the next two weeks will be at this time.

I'm paired with the quiet but confident Mehella and assigned to lucky number thirteen this morning, a nine-kilometer transect that starts from road R618 and cuts into the park in a north-to-south direction. It's amazing terrain and the guard's eyes sparkle with anticipation in the early morning light as we descend into our first ravine or, as its known here in Zululand, a dry riverbed known as a *donga*. *Dongas*, you see, harbor all sorts of potential danger, from snakes and spiders to wildebeest and buffalo, and, probably just as worrisome, Mehella is unsure how someone like me will respond if things get dicey.

No troubles arise on our first descent, but advancing properly with caution takes time. It also takes time to record the data we are here for in the first place, but, with each stop, I become more proficient. And day one provides plenty of practice. Twenty-three entries highlight my first day in the bush, including buffalo, which is my first encounter with one of the Big Five.

It spits light rain much of the morning, with a couple periods of steady drizzle, so the temperature stays comfortably low. We end our trek at the

Black iMfolozi River, which is quite low at this spot during the dry season. Taking off my shoes and socks, I follow my guide's expert lead across the river, but like a novice, while standing stork-like on one foot and attempting to put my socks and shoes back on, I nearly splash clumsily into the mud.

All and all it was a good first day. We didn't cross paths with any top-of-the-food-chain predators, but saw plenty and learned even more. The smell of fresh air and fresh earth is reinforced by the intermittent rain and reinvigorates what should be tired limbs. After about twenty or so minutes of small talk while waiting for our ride back to camp, I receive probably the best news a drizzle- and sweat-drenched volunteer could receive. My checked bag is finally on its way.

It rains the rest of the day after lunch, and my volunteer colleagues retreat to their tents for some much-needed rest. Naps have never been my thing, though, as I tend to feel even worse after one. With that in mind, I catch up on some reading and, admittedly, simply daydream.

My dream of visiting the African continent has been several years in the making. It's not really a coming-of-age vision, akin in some fashion to Dorothy in *The Wizard of Oz*, but I am, most certainly, searching like Judy Garland's character. I'm curious about what sorts of people volunteer for Earthwatch expeditions like this—what drives them to take such unusual working "vacations"? I'm curious about the diverse mix of people within South Africa, how their history and current struggles shape the future of this Rainbow Nation. And of course, I want to know about their environment, particularly their famous megafauna, learning firsthand with my own sights and smells as a guide. Finally, connecting all these interests is my curiosity as to how well this particular park of Hluhluwe-iMfolozi is doing when it comes to protecting species diversity, not to mention how all this connects to my overarching interest in climate change.

The rains and clouds continue throughout the afternoon, so there's no Hollywood-ending rainbow to celebrate. Over the next two weeks, though, we'll get our fair share of another dreamy display of African colors. African sunsets, featuring rich reds and oranges mixed with pink and yellows, all buttressed underneath by deep hues of purple, descend quickly but make everlasting impressions.

To me, whether you are using rainbows or sunsets as your jumping-off point, there could not be a more appropriate analogy than comparing what's happening in this provincial park within the Rainbow Nation of South Africa to our quest to better understand the cultural elements of climate change. Cultural attitudes serve as the all-important foundation in Hluhluwe-iMfolozi and South Africa more generally. Of course, economic, political, and social considerations will always be critical in understanding any nation-state, but the driving force behind South African identity is, and, arguably, always will be, cultural.

To miss this point is to misunderstand South Africa. Similarly, failing to grasp cultural attitudes that inhibit action combating climate change is to misunderstand climate change. The hope that Nelson Mandela's South Africa embodies must translate into our efforts to minimize climate change. Resistance is not futile, as the Borg of Star Trek would claim. Dreaming of "Somewhere, Over the Rainbow" is not childish, but rather, the responsible, adult course of action, for only with such inspiration can a problem as large as climate change be addressed.

Today starts much better than yesterday. I'm better adjusted to the time change now, but, even more importantly, what a difference it makes to have your own sleeping bag. Two dusty wool blankets from the back of a pickup truck only get you so far. Yes, I survived the forty-degree nights, but it wasn't pretty. Now at least I'm awaking at the ungodly hour of 4 A.M. because of my watch alarm instead of passing in and out of cold-induced consciousness. Note to self: never check your sleeping bag on an overseas flight!

This morning I am assigned to Transect A in the wilderness area with Johan, a stocky game guard who appears to be several years my senior at first glance, but once we are out in the bush he quickly disabuses me of any stereotypes about advanced age and walking pace. It's a shorter transect than the day before at only seven kilometers, but there is no actual path in these wilderness-designated areas of the park. You have only a compass, and, of course, Johan, as your guide. We are truly in the wilderness, with the seemingly omnipresent acacia thorn that I'm constantly picking out of my rain jacket. With each prick, I try to console myself with the words of Henry David Thoreau, "In wildness is the preservation of the world."[1]

In all seriousness, I deeply concur with Thoreau and those after him, such as the legendary American environmentalist John Muir, who maintained that special places such as Yosemite, or in this case Hluhluwe-iMfolozi, provide crucial spiritual sustenance. We could not claim to be civilized without them.

They recharge our spirits, peeling away what too often separates us from the natural world.

Over a half-century ago, in 1959, a fellow by the name of Ian Player, older brother of the famous golfer, Gary Player, adopted this same approach. Under his leadership, some 30 percent of the park, wedged between the White and Black iMfolozi Rivers, was reserved as primitive wilderness area, devoid of roads and any permanent structures. Only visitors on foot, horseback, or canoe are permitted still today.

Player was an admiring advocate of the wilderness concept and inspired to bring the idea to South Africa after Howard Zahniser of the American environmental organization the Wilderness Society shared documents expressing fundamental wilderness principles in the bill and 1957 Senate hearings that would create our National Wilderness Preservation Act. In fact, Player later asserted that this proposed legislation was the "most important document [he] ever received," and said it was instrumental in pushing Hluhluwe-iMfolozi to be the first to introduce ranger-led walking safaris over wilderness trails.[2]

It's another cool, misty start today. Johan and I blaze our own trail, quickly drenching ourselves, at least from the knees down, due to a combination of the morning dew and the previous day's rain. We cover a mix of terrain, from the dense thicket that black rhino seek, to the deep ravines that they visit, and finally open range reminiscent of where I grew up in middle Tennessee. The tans, browns, and beiges of late winter fill the landscape, with a constant backdrop of distinct red soil. There's even a familiar wind rustling through vegetation and an inviting briskness to the air I recall fondly from childhood.

One aspect is distinctly different, though. It's how I walk. I'm continuously watching my step once we enter the driest, almost desert-like section at the end of the morning. Shifting my gaze from upcoming grasses and bushes to my feet below, I hope to not only do my job and survive but also avoid the waste droppings virtually everywhere. Most of it is white rhino, but, at times, black rhino as well, which sets off a whole other set of nonscatological warnings in my mind, given their aggressiveness. Whether black or white, the waste decomposes much slower during these drier winter months. Then again, maybe this part of the park is temporarily running low on an unsung hero, the dung beetles that feast on it.[3]

We've finished a little earlier than expected that morning, and after waiting for pickup in Figure 12.1, on the way home, Cameron, our camp manager, takes us by Mpila Camp to sample some Namibian beer at the curio shop. Our real treat, however, is yet to come. Only half a kilometer from our campsite gate we spot four lions resting in the shade. Meandering

12.1 Waiting for pickup at the end of wilderness A transect.

12.2 Burchell's zebra heading toward water and a potential lion ambush.

toward the river behind the lions, unfortunately for their sake, and unwittingly upwind from the lions, are four Burchell's zebras, three of which are seen here in Figure 12.2.

Frequently preyed on by lions, these zebras utilize their trademark stripes, as individual as human fingerprints, for camouflage that confuses predators by distorting the outline of their figure. That benefit aside, researchers at the University of California at Davis suggest the real evolutionary drive behind a zebra's stripes is avoidance of blood-sucking flies.[4] In any case, the future is not looking bright for these particular zebras. After a short stay, snapping more grainy photos from a distance, we return to camp for our afternoon chores.

About four hours later, we reassess the situation, and the lions are still lounging lazily in the tree shade—but the zebras are nowhere to be found. Burchell's zebras possess good eyesight and, like horses, have impressive speed, so it is quite possible that they survived the potential early-afternoon ambush, particularly as lions prefer to hunt in the evening, not the heat of the day.

Later that night, I awake to an unusual sound. It's probably closer to dawn than I realize, but, in my sleep-deprived state, it's impossible to discern the difference between late night and early morning. In fact, it feels as if I just dosed off, that it's not even past midnight.

This noise is strangely familiar, yet, at the same time, unlike anything I've ever heard. With an almost hypnotic cadence, it first sounds like it's literally outside my tent flap, then on the other side of the common area to our camp, then just outside my tent again, then off behind my tent, and, presumably, behind the approximately four- to five-foot electric fence that encompasses the entire site.

Slowly it dawns on me that it's not just one creature I'm hearing, but several, and that they are probably communicating with one another. At this early hour, and with my inexperience and imagination to drive me wild, the first thought that pops into my mind is the four lions from yesterday afternoon. I envision them prowling the fence perimeter, probing to find its weak spot, and then smartly picking off the single tent on the fringe of our campsite, in other words, me.

The reality is probably not quite so fearsome. These were, indeed, large purring cats as my camp manager confirms the next morning (Thankfully, I am sane, and he heard them, too.), but these lions were probably further away than I thought and not noisily planning how to devour me. More likely, they were merely communicating with one another after a night out on the town, err bush, so to speak.

You see, lionesses easily get separated during their hunting and spend the period just before dawn calling to one another to arrange their rendezvous with the pride. Calls can range from a series of low, soft moaning coughs to a deep roar that can carry for miles. What I hear is more of the former, although it's liberally interspersed with what I can only describe as a deep, seemingly impatient purring sound, albeit from an extremely large, wild, and toothy version of the house cat. There is also, just as I put these puzzle pieces together, a deep, unmistakable roar that confirms my initial assessment. These lions are not sleeping tonight.

Turns out, lions rarely do sleep at night, despite what that catchy 1961 tune adapted by the Tokens might have us believe.[5] They also attack people quite infrequently—but that doesn't mean they never do. The infamous man-eating lions of East Africa are a case in point. A British engineer by the name of John Henry Patterson tells one of the most bone-chilling stories about lions that developed a taste for human flesh over a century ago. For nearly a year, as Col. Patterson directed a crew of mostly Indian workers in the construction of a railway bridge over the Tsavo River, these lions preyed on his railroad workers, killing well over a hundred.[6]

Much more often, though, lions target the nonhumans among us. Our principal investigator David Druce joins us for dinner later that evening with just such a lion tale to tell. It begins with a pack of wild dogs he once witnessed taking down an impala at another park before he came to Hluhluwe-iMfolozi, but we have impala as well as wild dogs here now, so the mood is appropriately set.

Impala were brought to Hluluwe during the 1930s, but quickly proliferated and today are the most common antelope found. They are gregarious creatures and tend to move in herds of females; adult males attempt to shepherd them within their territory and passionately defend those territorial boundaries from rival males. Ironically, the males announce this territorial ownership with a mixture of barks and roars, some so convincing that tourists can easily mistake them for lions.

Perhaps the impala's most distinguishing feature, though, is its swiftness of foot. Despite their weight of up to 143 pounds, with seemingly effortless ease, they can leap nearly ten feet in the air. As author Alan Duggan describes it, a startled herd dashes away with such grace and coordination that it calls to mind a well-trained ballet troupe. To catch a glimpse of this in the wild is to "witness a natural symphony of coordinated movement."[7]

Well, the one Druce saw taken down by wild dogs was not so fortunate or a fleet of foot. Quickly it was disemboweled, but, before the wild dogs could fully enjoy their meal, a lion chased them away to claim the kill. The lion then started gnawing away contently on the hindquarters of the impala, but it turned out the impala was not dead yet. Like something out of a Monty Python skit, the impala, without its back legs no less, pitifully, and fruitlessly, attempted to run away.

Getting back to our ferocious lions, they are, indeed, an impressive species. The females do the majority of the hunting, cooperating in an intelligent fashion and utilizing their powerful, fully retractable claws. Good jumpers and swimmers, they can manage without water for long periods of time. Highly social, they live in prides of up to twenty individuals and have excellent sight as well as senses of smell and hearing. One can, however, stumble on sleeping lions when heading into a stiff wind, says Clive Walker, a writer, activist, and, before that, according to noted author Lawrence Anthony, South Africa's preeminent game ranger.

Just such a wind is blowing the following morning as I set out to walk Transect 16 with my guard Mpuma, one of four female game guards recently added to the historically male force. Our first half-hour is relatively uneventful. We start at the eastern border of the park, where an electrified, cable-reinforced fence was built in the late 1970s to protect the homesteads surrounding the park as well as the game within the park. The day's planned trek is nine kilometers, but another two are added over the next four hours due to a combination of necessary and unnecessary detours.

Only forty minutes into our walk the sun is quickly rising and the morning chill dissipating, so we stop to remove excess clothing on a conveniently arranged set of boulders along a grassy, gently rising slope. The downhill wind is a pleasant relief coming off the hillside, but not enough to counter the heavy clothing I put on for the freezing, before-dawn truck ride out to our transect.

I should also mention that there's a clump of about a dozen medium-sized shrubs and trees just ahead, upwind from the four or five boulders on which we are now perched. If it were the correct continent, you'd swear it was a setting straight out of an Ansell Adams photograph. I didn't have my camera handy at that moment, but the mental image is still fresh in my mind years later. Quietly remarking to Mpuma what a beautiful morning it is, I zip up my backpack and, together, we rise in unison to continue our trek. At that very moment, prompted by either a momentary shift in the wind that allows our scent to drift uphill, or perhaps merely the sound of my backpack zipper, a deep roar arises from beyond the nearby trees. I mean, this is really close, even closer than the mixture of purring and growling from the night before. It's just around the corner, beyond the clump of trees and shrubs.

And it's not just me that is alarmed. I can see it clearly in my guard's eyes. Beads of sweat, not only from heat but also now concern, pour down her face, and we back up quickly into the grassy bush, although not so quickly as to seem to be fleeing, which might encourage the lion to charge. It's also with just enough caution to narrowly avoid falling into a small hole that could have easily done serious damage to my ankle or surgically repaired knees. After about thirty or forty feet, we slowly stride off the transect, in a counterclockwise motion, and reassess our situation.

We are in the midst of considerably higher themada grass now, which I later learn presents another set of inherent risks. Dripping wet with the odd mixture of sweet-smelling dew and our own perspiration, our focus is on the spot just beyond the boulders and clump of trees and bushes. Finally, after several anxious minutes, at about one o'clock relative to our original resting point, we see the instigator of the roar—and its companions. It's a whole pride of lions, including a female-and-male pair, the male with a truly magnificent mane, and four juveniles.

What if I hadn't stopped to remove that rain jacket? We certainly would've been a lot closer when we startled the adults, which, I might add, are particularly protective of their space when with their young. Sometimes it's simply better to be lucky than good.

When directly faced with a lion, of course, it is difficult to remain still. Primal fear and flight mechanisms naturally take over. The last thing one should do, however, is run. Males, more often than not, bluff. Lionesses, when with their cubs, are more likely to charge. Hmm, that's one strike against us.

Signals to watch for in terms of an eminent charge are a roar (that's a second strike) with flattened ears (we couldn't tell about this because we couldn't see them) or tail lashing up and down (also unknown). Your best course of action is to avoid those situations altogether—stay away from thickets and dense tall grass. Hmmm, is that the third strike? Hopefully these are true South African lions, more familiar with the batsman in cricket than the batter in baseball, so these strikes don't really matter.

Turns out lions only came back to Hluhluwe-iMfolozi over the last half-century.[8] The first one miraculously appeared of its own accord in 1958, migrating from either Kruger National Park or outside the country itself from neighboring Mozambique. Known as Nkosi, the chief, this lion negotiated approximately five hundred kilometers of terrain, in and out of homesteads, to reach his promised land.

Two adult females and two cubs were then reintroduced surreptitiously in March 1965 via an exchange with Kruger for white rhino. Without head-quarters knowing, giraffe were brought over as cover for the lionesses. Over the next decade and a half, this small population of lions faced TB and other disease problems tied to their lack of gene-pool diversity, but it grew to as many as 140 individuals in 1987, before a herbivore reintroduction cam-paign sadly dictated the shooting of nearly all lions in the northern portion of the park from 1988 to 1992. By 1999 there were only eighty lions left, none with a permanent residence in Hluhluwe.[9]

The power of the tourist dollar eventually overcame lingering official resistance, though, and, less than a decade before my visit, from August 1999 to January 2001, sixteen additional lions were brought formally into Hluhluwe-iMfolozi from Pilanesberg National Park and Madikwe Game Reserve to improve the existing population's genetic diversity.[10]

Surviving our encounter, we settle safely back into the transect walk, recording numerous sightings as we go. Little did I know, though, that our Big Five adventures had only just begun. Just as Mpuma and I are gaining back our lost confidence, we stumble on two sleeping black rhino, roughly twenty meters from our transect. Fortunately, we are now walking with the wind instead of against it, so they smell us and, with amazing dexterity for their size, scramble off to the west. Whew, that was close call number two.

In my mind, this close call also carries an important lesson, one easily generalized to virtually any other aspect of life, including our focus on climate change. Don't get too cocky. No matter what obstacles you've faced and over-come in the past, don't underestimate your next challenge.

The human exceptionalist paradigm of esteemed economist Julian Simon is an easy trap to fall into. Resist the allure. Yes, or *yebo* in Zulu, we are a damned smart species. And I'm banking on that, because this book argues an optimistic position, that our society will turn away from fossil fuels before it is too late. At the same time, I've always contended that the true sign of intelligence is to admit when you don't know something, acknowledging that you need help. In short, there is a difference between confidence and arrogance. As a society to date, at least in the States, we've been far too arrogant, if not downright ignorant, about climate change.

Less than an hour later, this message is reinforced yet again. Overconfidence is a difficult overlord to master. We are on edge now more than ever, eyes peeled for any sights or sounds out of the ordinary. Of course, in my case, as a newcomer to these parts, that means everything. Our vigilance is rewarded in short order as a herd of buffalo present themselves on the transect itself, albeit safely at a distance of several hundred meters. We pause for the obligatory count and wait another ten minutes as they meander along their way, casually enjoying tall grasses off the transect. Saddling up our supplies and heading down into a ravine, though, we promptly encounter two buffalo that had not yet left with their herd. That would definitely be close call number three. Good thing cricket's the game here instead of baseball. Otherwise we'd be out.

From a distance, late in the morning, moreover, we see a lone elephant, which brings our total to four of the Big Five that day, with only the leopard unseen. That's understandable, though, as these nocturnal creatures are seldom visible during the day, even though they often live close to civilization. An agile and powerful predator, leopards are also cunning experts in camouflage as well as master climbers.[11] I suppose, given our record today, then, it's entirely possible we passed underneath one but never saw it.

While I struggle to temper my continued Big Five adrenaline rush, one last adventure presents itself. We get lost. I know that sounds pretty stupid. How does an expert guide and her Earthwatch volunteer, who's had his own set of adventures in the woods on several other continents, get lost, with a compass to boot? It's actually a little easier than you think, and, technically, we weren't really lost. We just lost our transect.

You see, every time you go into a ravine, you not only have to worry about how you enter, but also how you exit. Since our buffalo encounter, we've been extremely cautious, so cautious, perhaps, that on this last crossing we missed the trail. In our defense, the trail is really not a trail per se. It's simply shorter grass than the tall grass around it. This grass was cut via machete roughly a month ago in preparation for the transect walks by the first Earthwatch expedition. As we are the second group this year, these grasses have had time to grow back, even in the winter season. It also seems that no other group has walked this transect since last month, and large game can always "cut" their own paths as well.

In any case, long story short, we are lost. Not completely lost because we have the compass, remember. But still, even after both Mpuma and I climb a couple trees for a higher vantage point, we are unable to locate the missing transect. This is not good. We backtrack and find two or three potential transect points heading toward the ravine. Perhaps we took the wrong one of these in our first descent? We cross over the ravine again, carefully I might add, and only after wandering around for another ten minutes or so do we find our path.

On top of that fiasco, toward the end of the morning, I temporarily lose my precious compass. In my haste to make up for lost time, I failed to stow it properly away at our last stop. We double back nearly a kilometer along the transect and, with good fortune still smiling on us, find it hanging from a branch where it was snagged by one of the omnipresent acacia thorn bushes.

The hot sun strikes down on us with full force now, and the rush of adrenaline has been replaced with a lull much like the inevitable crash that follows my youngest child's sugar highs. So I'm dragging a bit on the last half-hour of the hike. It's not just a physiological low. It's psychological, too. I'm not feeling terribly confident about my decision-making today. And to top matters off, I forgot to toss some sunscreen into my bag this morning and am feeling the results of that forgetfulness now, especially on my nose and the back of my neck.

A lot went wrong today. Similarly, a lot has gone wrong with the American approach to climate change. We just don't get it, at least not yet. That said, here in the middle of the South African bush is as appropriate a setting as any to recount Nelson Mandela's appeal, "Do not judge me by my successes, judge me by how many times I fell down and got back up again." That's a philosophy crucial to addressing climate change. Past failures do not ensure future failures, unless we refuse to learn from them.

Taking a closer look at South African history helps flesh this out. Around three times the size of California, South Africa has a moderate climate, similar in many respects to southern California. Even more notable than its natural landscape, though, is South Africa's cultural landscape, its people. The country hosts a colorful collage of ethnic, tribal, and racial differences, including the only sub-Saharan country where a significant European population took root.

The Portuguese were the first Europeans to reach the Cape of Good Hope, in 1488, but a permanent white settlement did not take hold until the Dutch arrived in 1652, thirty years after they landed on Manhattan Island here in the States. This was the golden age of the Dutch republic, and the Dutch East India Company, with its spice trade with India, drove interest in the Cape because it provided a much-needed resupply point. In due course, within its first decade, in fact, this Cape colony developed an entirely unexpected degree of autonomy.

The next blend of influence came in the 1690s, from French Huguenots seeking escape from civil war at home. The Huguenots quickly melded with the Dutch, a legacy that lives on today—the Cape's world-renowned wine-making status traces its lineage to them. Over the next century, the Dutch and French Huguenots intermingled still further with German immigrants to form what became known as the Afrikaner people. Together this population constructed a new language, one that evolved into a simplified form of Dutch that dropped certain inflections and vocabulary, modified vowel sounds, and incorporated words from other languages. Even an untrained ear like mine catches some words while remaining mystified by others in the singsong Afrikaner accent, which, incidentally, contrasts distinctly with the clicks of Zulu.

The next major influence came from the British. During the Napoleonic wars, the Dutch alliance with the French led the British to seize Cape Town, with the rationale of protecting their own sea route to India. After Waterloo in June 1815, they decided to stay. The British and Afrikaner populations subsequently engaged in a power struggle that lasted over a century, one that manifested itself periodically in deadly conflict,[12] albeit nowhere near as bloody as that of the white alliance against native African populations. These alliances were particularly brutal in targeting the Zulu of Natal in the northeastern part of the country, coincidently, where I am based at Hluhluwe-iMfolozi.

By 1836, large numbers of Afrikaner farmers sought to escape various annoyances of British rule, such as the abolition of slavery in 1834, and marched northeast into the South African wilderness. This Great Trek by Afrikaner pioneers, known popularly as *voortrekkers*, included a dramatic set of events that form the core of what South African historian Leonard Thompson labels the Afrikaner mythos. And as a critical aside, it is a surprisingly similar legend, if we can shed our own biases, to that of the American pioneers' advance west and its disastrous impact on Native Americans.[13] The December 1838 Battle of Blood River, in particular, in which three thousand Zulus were killed with literally no loss of Afrikaner life, is still commemorated on the Day of the Covenant. These farmers or Boers, a term the British used with derogatory overtones, established what became known as the Boer Republics—the Orange Free State and Transvaal, later renamed the Orange River Colony.

Before going any further in this cursory historical overview, though, it is crucial to backtrack and acknowledge the formidable Zulu military state established by Dingiswayo in the early nineteenth century. Dingiswayo introduced conscription and guided impressively disciplined battalions in formations analogous to the European model.

The legendary Shaka assumed command of these forces in 1818 and brought the Zulu reputation to new heights. Muscular and over six feet tall, with a penchant for bathing and rubbing his body with balls of raw meat, Shaka further adopted modern warfare tactics such as the half-moon pincer movement and ruled with a Machiavellian approach that firmly rooted power in fear. Men could not marry until they "washed their spear in blood," according to H. V. Morton.[14] Shaka was assassinated in 1828 and replaced by a half-brother, which might explain the disastrous results at the Battle of Blood River. Nonetheless, the Zulu remained a force to be reckoned with until they were finally conquered during the Anglo-Zulu war of 1879. This then freed up the Afrikaners and British to directly face off against one another in the first Anglo-Boer wars of 1880–1881.

That said, there is one more ethnic ingredient to add to the mix of South Africa: Indians. They began to arrive around 1860 to cultivate sugar and tea in the Natal province where I am now based, and landowners continued to import them as cheap labor until 1911. Contracted for five-year terms, individuals branched out on their own after their contract expired. After another five years, free return passage or a small land grant was possible. Still, despite those distinctions, both British and Afrikaner whites treated Indians, like blacks and indigenous Africans, as racially inferior.

This is the setting into which a relatively unknown, twenty-four-year-old, London-trained barrister by the name of Mohandas Gandhi was thrust. In 1893 he landed in Durban and boarded a train to Pretoria with a first-class ticket, as any self-respecting lawyer would, to settle a dispute between two Indian trading firms. During his journey, though, a white passenger complained about Gandhi's "inappropriate" seating, and Gandhi was ordered to move to third-class coach. When he refused, Gandhi was tossed from the train and forced to spend the night at Pietermaritzburg station.

Pointedly, Gandhi later asserted that experience was the single most important influence in determining his political career. Over the next twenty-one years he led a number of campaigns in South Africa, honing the now famous technique of passive resistance with mass protests in Natal before returning home to India in 1914, where the rest, as they say, is history. Shortly before Gandhi left, the first major step toward South African independence occurred on May 31, 1910, when all colonies of South Africa combined together to form the Union of South Africa, with the British establishing parliamentary self-government.[15]

A handful of notable dates, particularly for the route they paved to apartheid, deserve mention after this. In 1912, the Union government passed the first law of legal separation of races, not coincidentally, the same year the South African Native National Congress, which would later become the ANC, was founded.[16] Then, in 1948, the National Party won the all-white elections and established the now infamous system of apartheid. First coined by Afrikaner intellectuals in the 1930s, *apartheid* means separateness; it evolved from a racist "political slogan" to ultimately refer to a dastardly, "systematic program of social engineering."[17]

So where does this leave us with cultural misunderstandings surrounding climate change? Our situation is not unlike that of former South African leader Nelson Mandela, infamously imprisoned and nearly executed along with ANC colleagues such as Walter Sisulu in 1964. Over the next twenty-seven years he remained incarcerated, Madiba, as known to his followers, never wavered in a faith that he could make a difference.[18]

When it comes to international climate governance, you could say we've been culturally handcuffed for nearly three decades now, too, dating back to the aforementioned congressional hearings on global warming in the summer of 1988. But even in these darkest hours, as with the story of the incomparable Nelson Mandela, hope remains. Countless examples of individual heroism exist, from Jim Hansen to Mark Mann. Moreover, for all Mandela did for South Africa, he was not alone. Innumerable individuals, both in the country and outside it, made crucial contributions. The same can be said about climate change, and extending this South African model a little further provides additional insight.

From the ashes of apartheid, this former pariah state birthed a new multinational, multiparty parliamentary democracy. It's by no means perfect. No democracy is. It would be a stretch, for example, to paint South Africa as an ideal multiracial society, one where the eleven official languages are recognized as equal in practice as well as in name, or where the classic Zulu harmonies of a cappella folk groups like Ladysmith Black Mambazo are treasured by all.[19] As in the United States, racial resentment continues, and residential areas exhibit de facto segregation through unequal economic opportunities.[20] Furthermore, notable tribal and ethnic divisions remain. The powerful Zulus of Natal, for example, established the Inkatha Freedom Party in 1974 and continue to dominate politics in that province, often to the chagrin of the ANC.

Extensive population growth, like elsewhere in Africa, is a continued threat in South Africa, with over 55 million people spread over its nine provinces, according to United Nations estimates in 2016. Unequal educational opportunities, one of the great structural threats to democracy, continue to restrict vast segments of this population. Similarly, health issues are an unequal threat as 11 to 12 percent of the population is infected by HIV and one third of the population is infected with the bacterium that causes tuberculosis, according to the World Health Organization. Economic unemployment registers at 23 percent, and a two-tiered economy continues to drive stark contrasts in the population, with one rivaling the developed world and the other only able to access the most basic infrastructure.

Related to this, crime, often violent, occurs routinely. My camp manager, Cameron, maintains that many of the people he knows are leaving the country because of it. According to the U.S. State Department, South Africa has the inglorious title of the highest incidence of reported rape in the world. Assault, armed robbery, and theft are particularly high in areas surrounding hotels and public transit. Baggage pilferage is a distinct problem at Johannesburg International. Hmmm . . . scraped by on that one.

In spite of all these negatives, though, South Africa continues to stand out for its remarkable transformation in racial politics. Chaired by 1984 Nobel

Peace Prize winner Archbishop Desmond Tutu, the Truth and Reconciliation Commission led the charge here from its formation in 1996 to the completion of its reconciliation work in 2001.[21] As former thirteen-year ANC prisoner Toyko Sexwale asserts, the end of apartheid was "not only about freeing blacks from bondage, but also whites from fear."[22] It is this considerable transformation of South Africa, over the last two decades plus, that strikes a chord of hope across our globe.

This is precisely the type of cultural transformation needed in thinking about climate change. Climate change requires a long-term perspective, one guided by the interests of our grandchildren instead of our own immediate desires. South Africa proves this is possible. The key is shifting our cultural attitudes, in this case toward the most challenging threat of not only our generation, but many generations to come.

chapter thirteen

PARKS AND PEOPLE

ONE OF THE MOST important lessons to learn about Hluhluwe-iMfolozi, or any preserve across the globe for that matter, is that parks never exist without people. Indeed, it is not the flora or fauna, no matter how magnificent or unique, that determines a park's fate. It is people.

And by people, I don't mean distant governments and the regulations they pass to protect small slices of land and water. While notable, perhaps even necessary, such regulations are not sufficient for a park to be successful. Neither are the people who visit a park on occasion, or even regularly, although they, too, are a key component. What I'm most concerned about are the people immediately surrounding the park, or sometimes directly situated within it. It is this population that must commit to various restrictions on an area. It is this population that determines whether the flora and fauna truly receive special treatment.

Islands of biodiversity enveloped by a sea of poverty will never survive. If local populations see game in the park as a necessary source of meat or livelihood, or merely as a persistent nuisance they would be better off without, enforcement measures, no matter how heavy-handed, will be forever compromised. Locals require tangible economic rewards for hosting a park in their neighborhood if they are to respect the restrictions inherent to park protection. NGOs such as the World Wildlife Fund identified this need to integrate conservation with development long ago.[1]

Far too often, though, this "golden rule" is forgotten. Local populations are marginalized, with little political capital or access. Those in power come to see these populations as part of the problem instead of part of the solution.

That's what happened after World War II when a five-mile buffer zone was created around Hluhluwe-iMfolozi in an effort to control the tsetse fly.

Even those with good intentions can become easily distracted by the beauty of parks such as Hluhluwe-iMfolozi, not to mention the ethical quandaries of biodiversity protection with species such as the white rhino.

This morning, one such case presents itself as I struggle to remain in my seat while speeding, probably a bit more than we should, along a severely rutted road at the eastern edge of iMfolozi. I've been reunited with game guard Mpuma for a 10.5-kilometer hike on Transect 22. The terrain today is diverse, ranging from open fields interspersed with thickets to a dry, almost desert-like landscape with red sandy-clay soil.

We travel fast on this day, with no reprisals of the mistakes made in our first pairing, and we record an array of relatively harmless species, with the possible exception of a pair of white rhino safely off in the distance. They trot off with, once again, annoying dexterity for their size, particularly as I increasingly feel the effects of middle age each time I summon by own body from a restful state.

I have an added incentive to overcome such challenges today, though, when we return to camp. We are briefly relocating that afternoon to a different south camp at Sontuli, situated on a clearing just above the Black iMfolozi River, before heading out for the two-hour drive north to Hluhluwe and my new home at the forest bush camp of Maphumalo.

After one of my most restful nights yet, I'm paired the next morning with one of the more experienced game guides. Jericho has spent half his forty-four years as a park game guard at Hluhluwe-iMfolozi, and I am eager to learn from him along the trail. We are assigned Transect 10, which is officially listed as a little shorter than eight kilometers.

It starts as one steep climb upward but then levels out to an easy, flat, even sometimes downhill walk, for the rest of the morning. My first day in the northern ranges of the park is relatively uneventful with minimal sightings, perhaps because of the thicker vegetation. Then again, one of my Earthwatch colleagues, Lynn, nearly runs into five lions when emerging from a ravine on her transect. She later crosses paths with a number of black rhinos and is literally pulled into a tree by her guard in an effort to avoid any aggressive charges.

That afternoon, after my obligatory but tedious stint at data entry, we make a trip to the more developed and frequently visited Hilltop Camp. Following a brief dip into its frigid swimming pool, we leisurely stroll the beautifully landscaped grounds, while taking turns calling home from the lodge's main lobby. South Africa is GMT +2, which means it's seven hours later in the day here than Florida, at least when it's not daylight savings time. Thankfully, our timing and connection are both good, and I'm able to reach Linda and the kids.

Of my two children at the time, the younger seems to be okay on the phone, even impressed with my lion tale as we roar long distance to one another, but the older is audibly holding back tears as she attempts to speak. It's harder and harder to travel without them as they mature, and I vow, whenever possible, to take them with me. In part, this is for my own sake, but, as I argued in the introduction to this work, I believe it is in their interests as well. We learn so much from direct experiences. Children, in particular, soak up copious amounts of information from travel, much more than we appreciate.

I recall this as a child, myself, travelling for a few months abroad with my own parents as a youngster. Despite being a typical American with minimal language skills, my time in Turkey encouraged me to embrace words that sounded different and seek out their meaning. Similarly, I've noticed my own children are much more flexible and comfortable with change than others their age, or than I was at their age, for that matter, given that my international travels came a few years later than theirs. While other factors may be at work as well, I believe a key variable is how often these two have traveled at such young ages. They are heeding Mark Twain's advice, avoiding "vegetating in one little corner of the Earth." They are growing up as travelers.

After our phone calls, we Earthwatch volunteers return to Camp Maphumalo for a scrumptious bush dinner once again thanks to our cook, Studla, and, with full bellies, retreat to our tents in search of a full night of sleep. I'll need it. We've received our assignments for the next morning, and I've been tasked with the infamous Transect 2.

Transects typically take twelve men between five to seven days to cut. Transect 2 takes twelve men twelve days. At 8.2 km it's not any longer than many of the other transects. It's the terrain that makes it challenging and a bit of a legend among Earthwatch volunteers and game guards alike. A series of eight hills, the last of which is a veritable minefield of ankle-twisting boulders, is what lies ahead. By chance, or maybe expressly by design, I'm matched with the fleet-of-foot game guard Bheki, and together we push through the course in a supposed record time of just under three-and-a-half hours. Admittedly, also contributing to our stellar pace is a relative paucity of sightings, so our only stops are three brief rest breaks for water and photographs such as this one in Figure 13.1 at the end of our trek.

During another stop, we pause to chat about the nearby villagers I've seen working in the park today. They are helping remove triffid weed, the most abundant invasive species in the park.[2] A shrub-like plant, with the scientific name of *Chromolaena odorata*, triffid weed forms dense thickets that quickly overgrow indigenous vegetation. In fact, under the right conditions, triffid weed matures within a year and produces over one thousand seeds annually. These then spread to other regions via wind, cars, and animals. Like other invasives, in addition to its prolific reproduction, triffid weed has no natural enemies. That is, it is unpalatable to large herbivores.

The likely source of this infestation is one of the usual suspects, the British. During the Boer War, the British found that their horses were often too weak to survive conditions in the bush of Natal. Being enterprising imperialists, and overseeing an empire on which the sun literally never set, they drew on reserves of horses from across the Atlantic in Argentina. Illustrating

13.1 Game guard Bheki with the infamous (at least among Earthwatchers) Transect 2, visible in background.

how interdependence may arise in unexpected and unwanted ways, triffid weed was probably mixed in the feed that came with those horses, arriving first in Durban at the turn of the twentieth century.

Triffid weed is not just a threat because it crowds out indigenous species, however. It also uses significant amounts of water. That is the real impetus behind the Chromolaena Clearing Project that Bheki and I witness, in part, this morning. Begun in 2003, it is the single biggest project in South Africa clearing invasive species. Some 20 million rand (over 1.5 million dollars) have been funneled through the Department of Agriculture and Environment Affairs, which is then managed by Ezemvelo KZN Wildlife to fund public works programs. Removal is back-breaking work with a machete and the liberal application of a reddish-pink chemical that is painted or sprayed on each hacked trunk to prevent regeneration.

Typically over five hundred people from communities around the park are employed at a time, and we witness a number of younger employees busily sharpening their machetes at the North Gate while on route to my transect early that morning. Only one person per household is employed, in an effort to spread income among a community, and preference is given to single-headed households and those infected with HIV/AIDS.[3]

That night, all eleven Earthwatch volunteers briefly reunite with both camp managers at the famous Hilltop Restaurant, complete with real plates and cloth napkins. I'm grateful for the meal and luxurious setting, but the irony of my surroundings is inescapable. While I dine comfortably among abundant big game in this world-renowned park, an impoverished population labors to make ends meet outside it. The meal is delicious, yet this most surely is not a recipe for success.

The Natal Parks Board (KZN) wholeheartedly agrees with this assessment, and the Chromolaena Clearing Project is one example of their attempt to weave poverty reduction into daily environmental protection efforts. Another example is how KZN allows local communities to periodically harvest thatching and weaving material as well as fish and game animals from the parks.

With the white rhino snatched from the brink of extinction as their official logo, KZN remains a leader in developing techniques for relocating wild animals. Just as importantly, though, it is also a leader in reaching out to local communities around the parks and enhancing their economic opportunities.

Healthy people make healthy parks. This interdependence, this complex web of connections, permeates the history of Hluhluwe-iMfolozi.

The rinderpest virus is another case in point. A disease of cattle that occurred naturally in Asia, rinderpest was introduced in Ethiopia by cattle brought from India by Italian invaders in 1887. Soak that in for a minute. It was an Asian disease brought to Ethiopia by Italians with Indian cattle—in the nineteenth century no less. Imagine the challenges of globalization today.

The disease spread first west, then south through eastern Africa in the 1890s, reaching the Cape by 1896. A pandemic ensued, killing 95 percent of all cattle on the entire continent.[4] Two to three years after the cattle pandemic, human famine hit, and future epidemics arose every ten to twenty years from 1900 to 1963, before cattle vaccination finally eliminated the disease. All this illustrates that cattle health, and by extension game species susceptible to cattle diseases, shaped the health of the human population. People and parks were, again, intrinsically related.

It is this idea that drives the community levy that I and all other tourists that visit Natal parks must pay. Our visit helps make the lives of local populations at least incrementally better with this direct economic investment. Of course, this benefit is no silver bullet. Assuming it actually makes its way through the potential pitfalls of graft and mismanagement, there is even a risk that park funding will become too dependent on foreign assistance. Whether from "big fish" such as the World Bank and nongovernmental organizations such as the World Wildlife Fund, or small fry like myself, this remains a common concern.

While it is always hard to turn down funding, famed Kenyan archaeologist Richard Leakey points out the very real danger of becoming an overly dependent welfare recipient when relying too heavily on these sources of income.[5] You need to make your own money, a point reinforced by the World Bank with its research project to evaluate the links between nature tourism and conservation in northeastern KZN from 2000 to 2002.[6]

We've now reached the halfway point in our expedition, which means we've earned a much-deserved day off from our volunteer duties. By chance, our recreation day falls on August 9, National Women's Day in South Africa. That means most stores are closed today, but we still have the opportunity to visit St. Lucia iSimangaliso Wetland Park thirty-one miles east.

South Africa's first World Heritage site, listed in December 1999, St. Lucia iSimangaliso encompasses eight interlinking ecosystems with at least a seven-hundred-year-old fishing tradition, according to the promotional literature I receive. My group of ten volunteers signs up for a two-hour boat ride with the provider Advantage Cruiser, complete with an educational talk on the wetlands and the enticing promise of crocodile and hippopotamus sightings. Our guide more than delivers as we enjoy a relaxing series of minilectures on Egyptian geese, African fish eagles, and, of course, the hippo and croc. Each is a treasured sight, but the hippopotamus is what we really all came to see.

Adult hippos consume as much as 180 kg (just over 396 pounds) of food a day, mostly in the form of grasses and young reed shoots. They feed mainly at night and spend most of the day underwater because they are not able to withstand high temperatures. In winter, however, you may find them sunbathing on sandbanks. Living forty to fifty years, a hippo bull may attain a weight of as much as 1,500 kg (over 3,300 pounds). Hippo calves suckle on land or underwater, but must surface at regular intervals of less than a minute to breathe. Interestingly, they run underwater on the bottom of riverbeds as fast as people walk, but, most importantly for our sake, they account for more human deaths in this part of Africa than any other creature aside from the malaria mosquito.

That brings me to another topic altogether: malaria. This frightening disease is transmitted by the seemingly harmless bite of a mosquito infected with the malaria parasite. Symptoms include fever, chills, sweats, headache, body aches, nausea, vomiting, and fatigue. Hmmm. That's how I've been feeling the last three nights, excluding nausea and vomiting.

Symptoms kick in at least seven to nine days after being bitten by an infected mosquito. If not treated promptly, the disease gets even more serious, leading to kidney failure, coma, or even death. Hluhluwe-iMfolozi has very low risk for malaria, but St. Lucia is more questionable. That is what prompted me to begin taking antimalarial meds, despite my usual pharmaceutical conservatism, the other day. In fact, my entry pamphlet to Hluhluwe-iMfolozi advises visitors to consult a physician about preventing malaria.

Unlike for my Galápagos adventure, this time around, I've actually done that. I consulted a physician before leaving the country. I wasn't going to take any malaria-prevention medicine, but my doctor at the time vociferously

encouraged a prescription. I was a good patient and deferred to his expertise. So why am I experiencing these symptoms now? Did I not start taking
the meds in time? You are supposed to take them before entering an infected
area. I think I did that. Maybe I just have the flu. I was without a sleeping
bag for two nights, after all.

The irony to all this is that, if you read the warning label on my medicine
bottle carefully, possible side effects include a litany of complications, from
upset stomach and nausea, to vomiting and loss of appetite, to stomach pain
and fever, to hair loss and ringing in the ears, to dizziness, drowsiness, and
lightheadedness, to headaches and diarrhea. Sound familiar? Many of those
correspond to the symptoms of malaria itself.

To add insult to injury, or, more accurately, yet another injury to a pre-
existing injury, taking the medicine over time, which you are instructed to do
for at least four weeks after a visit as well as several days before and weekly
throughout a visit, may affect your liver and eyes. That's interesting, unfortunately in a decidedly negative way. The very reason I'm taking these meds
is to prevent malaria from attacking my liver, and oh yeah, killing me.

I actually left out two final possible side effects from my malaria medicine: insomnia and strange, violent dreams. That last one is the kicker, for
it facilitates self-diagnosis and, now, hopefully, speedy recovery. Night sweats
over three evenings in the north were puzzling. But I'm not ill during the day,
so this can't be the flu or malaria. I never would have even finished the infamous Transect 2 with either of those. That said, this lack of sleep is sapping
my strength. It's just a matter of time before I come down with something
if I keep shivering awake drenched in soggy clothing each night.

Turns out my doc gave me a generic version of maladrone called mefloquine. The 250-mg tablet I took a few days ago in anticipation of the trip
to the wetlands park is the source of my "illness." I suspected it all along,
but the twisted vision I had two nights before of a woman beating another
woman's head on a rock seals it for me. I jettison all remaining pills, and
swear allegiance to long clothing and high-DEET insect repellent as my sole
preventative measures from here on out.

Good intentions don't always pan out. Taking mefloquine certainly
didn't for me; it became a downright handicap. A similar argument can
be made when it comes to climate change. Good intentions do not always

yield the best results. Quite unintentionally, they can forestall the deeper commitments needed when it comes to mitigating climate change.

That's the standard case against recycling, which, helpful as it is in reducing garbage disposal needs, does nothing to address the root of the problem and its link to climate change, unsustainable consumption. In fact, one could contend that recycling actually makes our problem worse by curtailing efforts to shift consumption patterns under the mistaken theory that merely recycling is enough. It's not. Recycling only addresses the symptoms of our disease, the nausea and vomiting.

To tackle the actual disease, the malaria, you have to deal with either the mosquito or the parasite itself. You have to deal with people and our insatiable and decidedly unsustainable consumption. Academics such as Ernie Yanarella and Dick Levine have been writing about this for years, pointing out that improved efficiency standards can postpone or even prevent us from addressing larger systemic problems such as fossil fuel addiction.[7]

More lessons on climate change resonate in the bush the next day. Game guard Njbula is my partner for Transect 8, a beautiful 9.5-kilometer walk with a dozen different sightings, including Burchell's zebra, giraffes, white rhinos, nyalas, blue wildebeests, warthogs, buffalo, and red duikers.

There's also the return of one species that is not recorded, it being a carnivore—remember our study here in Hluhluwe-iMfolozi focuses on large herbivores.

Roughly seven hundred meters from the end of our walk, Njbula catches first sight of them, to our right at about one o'clock, only fifteen meters off the transect. He saw the movement in the tall grasses, a couple fierce heads slowly and cautiously lowering down. I missed them, but, as Njbula loads his rifle in an effort, not to shoot, but scare them away with its distinctly dangerous sound, I catch a glimpse of one impressive lioness.

There are five lions, one male and four females. They growl and pace a bit, then, after about forty-five seconds to a minute, they run off, allowing us to pass along the transect as originally planned. My earlier point of being a good Boy Scout here deserves repeating. In the bush it pays to be prepared—or at least have a trusty game guard at your side who is.

This is a lesson the warthog knows well. Warthogs are grazers that dig for roots and tubers with their tusks, but also live on berries and wild fruits.

They have snouts much like a pig and, like pigs, they are fond of wallowing. Warthogs are also undeniably ugly. They have poor sight, but acute hearing and a good sense of smell. Found mostly in family parties, they are diurnal and retreat at night to sleep in abandoned aardvark holes. Here's where the climate-change lesson lies. These guys prepare for the future by always entering their hole backward—in case a rapid escape is necessary.

What's our escape plan when it comes to climate change? Is the warthog smarter?

Another lesson on the trail that is reinforced today is to never lose sight of posterity, no matter what distractions arise during daily living. Nine giraffes gracefully make this point halfway through our walk. As renowned author and economist Hazel Henderson, among others, once eloquently stated, we do not inherit the Earth from our ancestors, we borrow it from our children. The giraffes seem to get this. As Njbula patiently explains, six of the nine giraffe before us are adults. Together, they form a distinct perimeter of protection for their three young, which are then free to frolic among the adults. Concern for their young drives the adults' actions.

Just as we stop to admire these daycare duties, the adults smell, see, or hear us. Perhaps it is all of the above, for giraffes have remarkably keen capabilities when it comes to scent, sight, and hearing. They stop browsing and stand alert, at full attention, for several minutes before finally determining we are not a threat and returning to browsing.

Even at a distance of several hundred meters, the height of these creatures is impressive. Fully grown, in fact, the bull giraffe is the tallest creature on Earth, at nearly twenty feet. Indeed, the Zulu word for giraffe, *indwamithi*, translates as "he who is taller than the trees." This gentle giant with a patchwork hide blends into its surroundings and fears only one natural enemy, the lion. A giraffe's large hooves are a formidable weapon, though, and offer a degree of protection from even lions. Nevertheless, the more common defense is to run away, and adults reach speeds of fifty kilometers (roughly 31 miles) an hour.

A giraffe's long neck is another impressive feature, and prime illustration of natural selection at work. The longer one's neck, the larger the food supply. Giraffe feed mostly on acacia leaves, making expert use of their amazing eighteen-inch tongue. As they feed, to solve the problem of a rush of blood to the brain every time it lowers its head, they have developed some ingenious plumbing. Their aortic blood pressure is twice that found in man, and they have a series of one-way valves that prevent blood from flowing back to the brain.[8]

My brain is still processing this amazing anatomy the next day as I'm paired once again with the slender Bheki, this time on Transect 11. Our three-hour morning hike is filled with good sightings, including lots of giraffes, one sleeping black rhino, and six white rhinos trotting together. The best sighting of all, though, is before we even reach the transect—a spotted hyena, below in Figure 13.2, making his last rounds before the sun rises.

One of the premier undertakers of the African savanna, spotted hyenas are efficient scavengers, but equally good hunters, capable of bringing down prey as large as zebra. Blessed with excellent sight, hearing, and sense of smell, they also possess powerful jaws that crunch their prey's bones with ease. By many accounts, they grow extremely bold when hungry. That's not a very comforting fact, considering that this fellow in our taillights is neither frozen with fear nor itching to run off into the last shadows of the night. He seems overly curious, perhaps pausing in the eerie light before dawn to question whether we taste as bad as we surely smell.

Hyenas are also quite noisy. In fact, they are probably best known for their hair-raising, lunatic laughter, which is actually a cry of triumph after

13.2 A spotted hyena returning from its nightly hunt and scavenging session.

a successful hunt. They utter many other inflections, though, from moans to shrieks. A total of seventeen distinctive sounds have been recorded, ranging from high-pitched howls linked to congregating before a hunt, to angry screams over competition for a carcass.[9] After lingering a moment or two longer, this one offers no such sound sample and disappears quietly into the bush.

My last day in the north has been a good one, but I'm also excited for the trip back down south to Camp Santuli that afternoon. Returning to the theme of parks and people, it may help to think of future conservation efforts as a combination of both protected areas and community-based conservation, instead of an either/or proposition. This is the route ecologist and author Anthony Sinclair recommends for the massive Serengeti ecosystem. It seems only appropriate here as well, for while Hluhluwe-iMfolozi is only one-twentieth the size of Kruger National Park, it is the biggest of over seventy-five reserves in the province of Natal.

chapter fourteen

ALL POLITICS IS LOCAL, BUT . . .

FORMER U.S. SPEAKER OF THE HOUSE Tip O'Neill once famously quipped, "All politics is local." No matter what one achieved at the national or international level, if constituents back home found fault with your position, trouble would follow. Re-election, first and foremost, depended on a happy base. Those who forgot this fundamental precept of politics found themselves unceremoniously tossed out of office.

Now, there's a rationale to this system, but I'll get to that in a minute. Let's examine the negative impact first. In essence, elected officials become so beholden to public opinion that they fail to engage with unpopular policies, even when they are in the long-term interests of their constituents. And further, this obsession with public opinion commits offices with shorter election cycles, such as the U.S. House of Representatives, to a de facto continuous election cycle. Even though they serve for two-year terms, our representatives don't run every two years. They run every year, throughout the year. All that time running for re-election, of course, means less time for the actual business of running the country.

To a certain degree, that is the point. By constitutional design, House members are encouraged to be in touch with their constituents on a regular basis, to be more available than their counterparts in the Senate, and to be more beholden to public opinion. That public opinion, though, is parochial and restricted to the interests of a limited region, which at times directly conflict with larger national interests. This helps explain why members of Congress, at least those who play this game well, can have such high popularity ratings individually, while Congress overall often receives a dismal ranking.

In many ways, this is the same quandary that faces conservation. Parochial interests concerned with protected areas too often conflict with national and international interests. Failing to address this ignores the fact that conservation is a form of politics.

As such, all effective conservation initiatives must have local roots. Park needs cannot be sufficiently addressed if community needs are not met as well. If the community is not happy with a park and its protected status, it's never going to work, not even the first time, let alone having a chance at "re-election." This is the precise line of reasoning applied by 2004 Nobel Peace Prize winner Wangari Maathai with her Greenbelt Movement in Kenya.[1] Mobilizing poor women since 1977 to plant over 51 million trees, she thinks globally, but acts locally.[2] The Greenbelt Movement is a classic example of melding women's rights with sustainable development—and grassroots programs making a difference as a result.

You might say that I, too, am preoccupied with the local at the moment. It's a little before 6 A.M., and I'm paired with game guard Jacob for a 7.7-km hike along Transect 14 this morning. As we jostle along in the back of our pickup truck, though, my thoughts return home.

Dorothy from *The Wizard of Oz* summed it up best. There truly is no place like home. I've been busy enough to keep my mind off it for most of the trip to date, but today is my son's birthday. I'm going to be home in five days to celebrate with him, but that is not enough. It hurts to miss today, and I'm on a mission to find a phone once my morning and afternoon obligations are completed. I couldn't track down a phone card yesterday at the wetlands, with the holiday closing down the main stores, so it will be a credit-card call from one of the pay phones up at the Mpila Camp supply shop instead.

It is exhilarating to see and learn about new places. As argued from the beginning, travel also helps us better understand where we come from. Experiences abroad reinforce an appreciation for what is special about the United States, from its economic opportunities and legal framework to its grand cultural and biological diversity. Then again, travel also points to shortcomings at home, areas where the United States could learn from others, from how to better develop public transportation to enhancing multilingual education opportunities.

Traveler extraordinaire Rick Steves, who has spent a third of his adult life living out of a suitcase, offered a similar line of argument in a TEDx Talk a few years back, suggesting that *travel abroad makes us better Americans*.[3] You might even contend that travel makes us better people. The incomparable

Mark Twain, for example, famously asserted, "Travel is fatal to prejudice, bigotry, and narrow-mindedness."[4]

In my present travels, it's another good day in the bush. My game guard Jacob has a gruff attitude initially, curtly dishing out instructions and outlining an array of command signs he plans to use throughout our morning trek. By the end of the morning, though, as the temperature continues to rise, he has warmed up considerably, both literally and figuratively, shedding his olive-green sweater and standoffish demeanor with it.

Jacob seems to appreciate my curiosity and willingness to follow his lead. Deferring to him along the trail, I learn much as he shows me a number of different types of spoor, including a perfect lion print in the sand by the Black iMfolozi River. We frighten off a black rhino in the last three hundred meters, but the real scare for us is just after that, when Jacob pauses near the end of the transect. Concerned about a movement he catches out of the corner of his eye, he thinks it might be a predator, or perhaps even a poacher, but it is nothing more than innocuous shrubbery blowing in the wind.

14.1 My best view of an elephant, entirely unexpected as we returned from a morning transect hike.

After clambering aboard the back of the Earthwatch pickup truck and gathering up our last volunteer and game guard duo, the sun is at it's midday highpoint, so we aren't expecting much in terms of game sightings on the ride back to camp. About halfway back, though, we are pleasantly surprised by a large elephant casually grazing just off the side of the road to our right. As we wisely pause to cede him the right of way, he crosses directly ahead of us with a confident gait, as seen in Figure 14.1.

Elephants were reintroduced into Hluhluwe-iMfolozi in 1982, brought from Kruger National Park after an absence of almost a century in Zululand. It was a big step. Elephants can be unpopular in surrounding communities because they cause great damage to crops, sometimes even killing people in their fright. Then again, as Charlton-Perkins asserts, "The presence of elephant automatically confers great prestige on a game park,"[5] and elephants were the last piece in giving Hluhluwe-iMfolozi the honor of hosting all of the Big Five within its borders.

Elephants were common in the area until around 1850, but were completely wiped out when the last creature was shot on the banks of the Black iMfolozi in around 1890. Today the park boasts around 380. That's no small feat, because elephants require a wide range of territory.

Translocating these elephants wasn't easy. Initially, game wardens had little to no success. Adults were difficult to catch, and, when caught, they often escaped their new surroundings to return home. You might say they shared Dorothy's opinion that there is no place like home.

Adapting to this complication, parks such as Hluhluwe-iMfolozi moved away from targeting adults and brought in adolescents instead. The thinking was that younger elephants would be less inclined to attempt arduous returns home, but younger elephants presented their own difficulties. Most notably, the eight young bulls brought from Kruger to Hluhluwe-iMfolozi behaved like teenagers, complete with throbbing hormones. When they went into musth, they became destructive. Only later did Hluhluwe-iMfolozi successfully retain a more mature bull, one that performed his fatherly duties well and calmed down the younger males.

You see, a male bull in heat is a big deal. It looks—and acts—like a mess. An oily secretion exudes from its temporal glands and streams down the side of its face. Frequent and uncontrolled urination blackens its back legs. Even more importantly, its testosterone levels go through the roof, and a teenage bull becomes inordinately aggressive. In short, it is best avoided.

Elephant once crisscrossed the continent from the Cape of Africa to the edge of the Sahara desert. They have decidedly less room to roam now, of course, hemmed in by the twin threats of habitat destruction and an explosion in human population. An estimated 600,000 remain in Africa, but these are isolated in relatively small parcels of land, at least in elephant terms. In earlier times, herds were so large that there was always at least one female in estrus to solve the hormonal issue of musth. Not so today. Estrus lasts two to six days, but only occurs every three to five years, while a mature bull stays in musth for four to five months.[6] Even when feeding and territorial needs are met, then, many reserves simply aren't large enough for hormonal needs to balance out appropriately. There just are not enough elephants to do the trick.

That can make for some downright dangerous situations. Even when not in musth and not adolescent males, elephants can be unpredictable and unsafe. You simply don't want to spook an animal with that much weight to throw around. Females tip the scales at four tons and males at six, although most weigh around five tons, or ten thousand pounds.

With this massive girth come equally large ears, the biggest in the animal kingdom, but elephants still have surprisingly poor hearing. Their eyesight is not much better, which is yet another reason to avoid light-colored clothing in the bush. You want an elephant to know you are there in advance, not be startled by your sudden appearance.

Bulls, when not in musth, tend to be more tolerant than cows, which are seemingly nervous by nature, especially when with their young. Even in these situations, though, one can often drive elephant away by clapping your hands loudly or tossing clods of dirt in front of them.

Elephants live up to seventy years, depending on the health of their teeth. When worn, teeth are pushed out from behind and replaced. With six sets compared to our two, elephants repeat this process several times. When resting, they don't lie down to sleep, but lean against trees. Cows have an unenviable gestation period of twenty-two months, with calves weighing around 120 kg (about 264 pounds) at birth.

As adults, elephants spend between sixteen and eighteen hours a day eating, with adult bulls consuming 181–270 kg (399 to 595 pounds) of fodder a day, or roughly 5 percent of their body weight.[7] As author and southern Africa safari leader Allen Bechky points out, this raises yet another issue when it comes to elephant population management: within increasingly constricted quarters, how do you prevent them from eating themselves out of house and home?[8]

It's not an easy task, complicated all the more by how intelligent the species is. Elephants have the biggest brain of any land animal, and it shows. Without anthropomorphizing, it is clear that elephants have self-awareness, periodically displaying kindness and regret, as with the handling of bones of their dead. They even display outright retribution.[9] When elephants were first introduced into Hluhluwe-iMfolozi, for example, some rhinos bullied the adolescent elephants, even killing a few. When those that survived grew older and larger, they remembered which rhinos these were and took their revenge.

Elephants are gregarious and have a highly developed social structure. Life revolves around a family group headed by a matriarch with female relatives and offspring. They are typically found in groups of ten to twenty, but at times, even fifty or more. Bulls leave the family unit at puberty, between the ages of ten and thirteen years.

Elephants don't have sweat glands, so they either flap their ears to keep cool or submerge themselves in water. In fact, even though they can go days without it, elephants are highly dependent on water, covering great distances in search of it. When they find it, they are able to down two hundred liters (over 52 gallons) in a single slurp and are quite fond of wallowing in water as well as mud, which is seen as a spa treatment of sorts that protects against both sunburn and insects. The holes made by elephants for such water activities provide sustenance to a variety of antelopes, warthogs, baboons, and birds, not to mention an array of invertebrates.

This brings us to probably the most intriguing part of an elephant, other than perhaps its tusks. The trunk is an unusual fusion of an elephant's top lip and nose. Utilized for a range of practical tasks, including drinking, smelling, food gathering, and even as a weapon, this highly sensitive organ is comprised of an estimated 150,000 muscles.[10] That helps explain why young elephants do not master full control of their trunks very quickly.

Bulls have rounded foreheads, whereas cows' are angular. Both sexes in the African species carry tusks,[11] which are actually their incisors. Interestingly, one side of these incisors always shows more wear than the other—elephants are left- or right-tusked much like we are left- or right-handed.

Even more interestingly, famed South African ranger and author Clive Walker swears only half-jokingly that elephants are telepathic. In reality, elephants are able to hear infrasound, sound at frequencies too low for humans to hear.[12] It enables them to communicate as far as six miles apart, even through heavy vegetation.

All this brings us to the current vulnerable status of the African elephant. South Africa's position differs greatly from that of countries in eastern Africa such as Kenya, which lost 80 percent of its elephant population during the 1980s, and Uganda and Sudan, which both lost 90 percent.[13] While its Department of Environment Affairs and Tourism sees culling as a last resort, South Africa still employs the tactic from time to time. The ivory from a Kruger elephant cull, for example, is prized as a key source of income for the entire national park system.

Moreover, the other options on the table when it comes to elephant overpopulation issues in South Africa do not make any money. In fact, they cost money, significant amounts of it. For one, contraception is expensive to South Africans at roughly 1,000 rand ($US75) a year for a female. Translocating is even more expensive, between 10,000 and 20,000 rand ($US750 to 1,500), plus another 25 rand per km in transportation costs. It's also nowhere near as easy as culling. Translocating a species of that size takes a small army.

The only other solution is an imposing challenge as well. With more conservation corridors and transfrontier parks, as former Wilderness Foundation founder and renowned South African conservationist Ian Player once asserted, elephants could move as they once did from southern to central Africa. At the moment, though, much like in the United States with wolves, there seems to be neither sufficient space nor the political will for territorial expansion.

When it comes to political will, the Convention on the International Trade in Endangered Species (CITES) is a prime test case. Established in 1973, it groups species into three different categories, known as appendices, according to their threatened status. Appendix I is the highest designation, with Appendix III the weakest. CITES protects roughly 5,600 species of animals and 30,000 species of plants; states voluntarily restrict trade in goods derived from these species, whether the goods are the animals themselves, alive or dead, or products made from them, such as leather goods, musical instruments, tourist trinkets, and real as well as supposed medicines.

The key word here is "voluntarily." For years, even that protection was limited, because the African elephant was classified as an Appendix II species, one "not necessarily now threatened with extinction but [one] that may become so unless trade is closely controlled." Then, in October 1989, that designation changed at CITES's seventh Conference of the Parties meeting when, after heated debates, the African elephant was given Appendix I status, and three months later, in January 1990, international trade in ivory was banned. Overcoming the pro-trade position of neighboring states Botswana, Namibia, Zambia, Zimbabwe, and South Africa, East African states gathered widespread international support. The driving force was a dramatic drop in the continent's elephant numbers during the 1980s, from an estimated 1.3 million to 600,000.

In the years that followed, the CITES Conference of the Parties meetings held every three years[14] have been a battleground. For example, in September 2007, less than two decades after its upgrade, and proving once again that all environmental policy victories are temporary, southern Africa states overturned part of this designation. Exceptions to Appendix I are now made for the elephant populations of Botswana, Namibia, South Africa, and Zimbabwe, bumping the listing down to Appendix II status for those states.[15]

"Although there are many sources of ivory, such as walruses, rhinoceros [technically not ivory but keratin], and narwhals," as Rebecca Rosen, senior editor at *The Atlantic*, writes, "elephant ivory has always been the most highly sought because of its particular texture, softness, and its lack of a tough outer coating of enamel."[16] That said, any type of horn fetches a considerable sum on the black market. Ounce for ounce, from the streets of Vietnam to China, even the rhinoceros horn is more valuable than gold. For most of us in the West, that's hard to believe, considering its keratin material is the same fibrous protein in our own fingernails. The late environmental author and ranger Anthony Lawrence, for example, tongue firmly planted in cheek, suggests that we save our finger and toenail clippings to send to the East for them to chew on.[17]

More serious solutions to combat poaching have been proposed, of course, including dehorning, poisoning only the horn, and even legalizing the sale of horns in an effort to flood the market and crash the price. Each of these suggestions comes with problems, though. Dehorning animals probably would not save them, because poachers would still kill them, so as to not waste time in the future by returning and tracking the same worthless rhino. Poachers would also be tempted to extract any remaining horn underneath the doctored rhino's skin, which would also entail killing them. Secondly, when poisoning a horn, it would be tricky to avoid damaging the rest of the creature, even though the horn itself has no link to the rhino's bloodstream. Legalizing trade in rhino horn probably wouldn't work either because there simply aren't enough rhino to safely cull and lower price sufficiently to deter poaching of the remaining individuals.

In this context, the lesson of Hluhluwe-iMfolozi is a simple one: Don't inaccurately discount the future. When it comes to climate change, we need to think ahead.

This afternoon we are practicing a bit of that. We are thinking ahead, ironically by utilizing a blind. We are off to the Mphafa Hide, what we in the states would call a blind, to view wildlife undetected at a safe distance. The hide itself is a fantastic setup featuring two comfortable wooden benches enclosed in a shelter of reed walls and a thatched roof, all perched high above a popular watering hole. During the dry season, the water becomes some-what salty but still potable. All sorts of animals frequent it, from predators to prey. We don't catch any leopards or lions this afternoon, but we do get our best view yet of another of the Big Five, the buffalo.

Even this small triumph holds a lesson worth fleshing out. These buffalo didn't just waltz up to the waterhole to quench their thirst and pose for our photo shoot. Our predecessors, the park staff specifically, prepared a setting with this hide where this might be possible, provided we were patient. Good things come to those who wait.

This message on the merits of preparation is reinforced again later that night around our campfire. Our camp manager, Cameron, recounts a story showcasing the time-tested formula for humor: tragedy, or near-tragedy in this case, plus time.

Cameron's tale is about two spotted eagle-owl chicks without their mother a few years back. A friend raised the chicks with the intent to return them to the wild, so he fed them live mice each evening. When they were old enough, he released them. One he never saw again, but the other would come nightly to his garden and take a mouse out of his hand as he dangled it by the tail. Then, all of a sudden, the second one stopped visiting, too.

Several months went by, and the friend thought nothing more of it. Then, one dark night, he was having some friends over for a *braai* much like ours that evening. Someone else was in the loo, so this fellow decided to take his leak in the garden. Just as he was finishing he heard the telltale whoosh of the eagle-owl in flight. In a rush, he zipped up his pants just in time, only getting nicked on the hand, as the young owl swooped past.

I suppose the moral of this lesson is actually twofold. Good things do come to those that wait—the return of the young spotted eagle-owl—but it also pays to be quick about how you respond when they do!

Of course, being prepared requires not only due diligence, but sacrifice as well. While it would be erroneous to argue that species protection is a zero-sum game, where one's gain only comes at another's loss, there are often trade-offs involved. There are no free lunches so to speak.

That evening, as if on cue, we encounter over a dozen wild dogs heading out for the night in search of the pack's next meal, but also conveniently illustrating this point. Wild dogs struggle with competition from lions and are also vulnerable to diseases such as distemper carried by domestic dogs. Hluhluwe-iMfolozi has fifty-three wild dogs; there are only two thousand to four thousand still living worldwide.[18] Fearless hunters with impressive stamina, wild dogs can continue a chase for several kilometers, overwhelming considerably larger prey such as antelope with sure weight of numbers. They communicate with soft clicking sounds as well as deep, hoarse barks, and maintain a well-ordered social structure with packs typically numbering thirty to forty individuals. With long legs and unusually large ears, wild dogs are easily distinguishable from their domestic kin. Each has a white-tipped tail and splotches of black with a white-and-tan body, although no two animals have the exact same markings.

These wild dogs before us are curious but wary of our vehicle, dispersing after a few minutes. The fleeting glimpse reminds me that my time in Hluhluwe-iMfolozi will soon be over, with only three days remaining now.

I'm back in the wilderness area the following morning, this time hiking Transect 20. Again, there is no path, with only four GPS waypoints, a compass, and of course my trusty game guard Jacob, as a guide. We drive to the far end of the park, literally at the electrified fence border where a handful of homesteads are within view on the opposite hillside, and begin our nine-kilometer (roughly 5.5 miles) trek. The walk proceeds along a hill next to the river, then meanders horizontally through high grass along a rocky slope, before climbing an extensive hillside for an incredible view of the landscape and the White iMfolozi River below. Our last 1.5 kilometers are through a dense thicket, with good sightings to fill up my data sheet all along the way.

The next day, my second-to-last in the park, I return to the regular section of iMfolozi. Transect 17 is a short 140-minute walk over 6.4 kilometers (just under four miles) with game guard Biella, a no-nonsense fellow who carries his rifle at attention nearly the entire time. We see a number of white rhino along the way, but the real highlight was that morning's sunrise as we waited in solitude to begin the transect walk.

This is a special time of the day, if only because it provides a few moments alone for reflection. My thoughts return to the previous afternoon and our trip to a local school on the outskirts of the park. Our assistant camp manager, Abednig Mkhwanazi, sponsors a community-development project at the school and wanted to show us a little of what lay beyond the park's borders, even if just for a few hours that afternoon. Many of the children attending this school were orphans whose parents had succumbed to HIV, and it was heartwarming to see their faces light up when we arrived. They were so excited to have visitors and interact with us, hesitantly testing their English skills and giggling with delight as we stumbled awkwardly with a handful of partially accurate Zulu phrases.

The more formal part of the program, though, unfortunately degenerated into essentially a public-relations event as we visited a physical sciences classroom for older teenage children. Our visit became more of a show than a cultural exchange, with adults in the room taking center stage rather than the kids themselves. The saddest part of all this is that we were more to blame than the South Africans. It was certainly understandable that the school principal wished to show us a sample lesson and proudly proceeded to lecture the kids for twenty minutes or so. Less acceptable, to my mind, was that one of my colleagues, a confident schoolteacher from California in her late twenties, insisted on reciprocating with a lesson of her own, even though it had no context to our visit. It wasn't even clear the children understood enough English to grasp what was said.

To me, the entire experience underscored the degree to which arrogance and hubris can destroy the best of intentions. We in the West must continually remind ourselves that we don't always have all the answers.

It doesn't really help to lecture a local population on how to do something. As bright and as wealthy as we may be, we are rarely blessed with sufficient local experience to efficiently apply that knowledge or funds in a local context. To ignore the significance of local expertise just isn't smart. Even as we give assistance, we need assistance in giving it. Only a true partnership between North and South, between developed and developing countries, can make a difference with problems such as poverty, education, health, and conservation. Simply stopping for a superficial visit or throwing a lot of money around as Western institutions such as the World Bank are wont to do, won't make a difference.[19]

My final walk with African wildlife is listed as 9.3 kilometers along Transect 21. Game guard Mandela and I sprint out at a five-kilometer-an-hour pace for the first half, thanks largely to flat terrain, but an astounding 242 sightings, along with two or three substantial hills, slow us down in the second half of the morning. There is also a brief period where Mandela becomes visibly concerned, motioning me to crouch down as he, too, squirms behind a log and scours the horizon. After a few moments, he is confident that the suspected poacher's dog is actually outside the park fence. He feared that we were in the proximity of the single greatest threat in the park, my fellow man, but this time it turned out to be a false alarm.

Poachers claim all sorts of wildlife in parks and game reserves across the African continent. To young African men, poaching can be a form of initiation, a way of proving their manhood. During the apartheid era, poaching was also a way of getting back at the racist government. And regardless of context, to this day, the bush provides valuable protein sources, with the added bonus that the meat simply tastes good, as Ian Player recalls from his days with the Natal Parks Board.[20] Yet by far, the most problematic poachers of all over the last two decades are those linked to a burgeoning international trade in animal parts. They are particularly fond of rhino and elephant, although local contacts receive a small fraction of the eventual take, often less than one-tenth of the exorbitant selling price in Asian markets.

That market imbalance doesn't curtail the illegal activity, though. Executive officer of the U.N. Wildlife Enforcement Monitoring System, Thomas Snitch, maintains that poachers picked off some 1,004 rhinos in South Africa alone in 2013.[21] According to the Center for Conservation Biology at the University of Washington, extrapolating data from the 46.5 tons of African elephant ivory seized in 2011, up to 50,000 African elephants a year are lost across the entire continent.[22] If those rates continue, both species could be extinct within two decades.

It's not just wildlife that meet the poacher's bullet. At least a thousand park rangers perished in the past ten years while defending these animals.[23] According to the nonprofit Thin Green Line, the numbers are even higher, with some thousand park rangers across Africa shot dead annually by poachers.[24] Regardless of the true number, this conflict is increasingly an unfair fight. A number of poaching operations resemble small armies, and they are much better supplied than their park-official counterparts. They work with helicopters, military-grade weapons, and night-vision goggles.[25] In this context, Mandela's consternation is completely understandable.

He and I chat a bit about these dangers and a number of other issues that morning, including his famous name. The game guards have been much more talkative during our rest stops this past week, as they have become more comfortable testing out their English and teaching us a bit more Zulu along the way. Mandela once worked as a game guard in St. Lucia before coming to Hluhluwe-iMfolozi. During that tenure, he was struck with malaria and hospitalized for fourteen days. He took a full month to recover. Mandela learned an important lesson from that brush with death, one we would all be wise to follow. Life doesn't always present second chances, but when it does, take full advantage.

I've tried to do that during this trip. Over the last two weeks, I've confronted not only four of the Big Five but also an assortment of rocks, roots, and boulders. My boots, which were probably not broken in as much as they should have been, have held up well, the lone worry being a blister that formed on my heel about halfway into this adventure. Specialty socks and a handy camel pack for water have been a huge asset on the trail, keeping my body in decent shape for nearly everything the bush threw at me. And the lions never ate me, despite at least two encounters on foot. All and all a good showing, if you ask me.

But this type of physical assessment only scratches the surface of my travels, the outer journey of a two-part trip if you will. You see, coming to Africa is an inner expedition as well, a mental trek that helps you take stock of where you are in life and where you want to go. Really, any sort of ecotourism can fit this bill, and working for Earthwatch certainly does its part, too. I'm learning more about myself, where I come from, and, like Dorothy in *The Wizard of Oz*, learning to appreciate it all the more.

Furthermore, to take full advantage of this opportunity with Earthwatch I need to assess not only the particulars of this eco-adventure, but also what lessons can be generalized from it. In terms of the cultural dimension, I've had my appetite whetted over the last seventeen days but not fully quenched. That will require much more reading and follow-up once I return home. That's always the case with experiential learning, though. You learn firsthand, which sparks additional research that builds on that initial foundation.

To me, what is most interesting about South Africa is how they progressed from Nelson Mandela's prison release in February 1990 to my visit in July and August 2008 and now nearly a decade later. What happened culturally over the last quarter-century or so to transform the country? And what lessons from that remarkable transformation might apply to climate change?

One point that jumps out at me is that new nations, like new problems, require unifying symbols to move forward. There needs to be intrinsic motivation. Madiba, Nelson Mandela's endearing nickname, understood this well and embraced the sport of rugby during the first part of his presidency as a medium to mend South Africa's frayed fabric, to stitch together a true Rainbow Nation as the country prepared to host the Rugby World Cup in 1995. It was the first major sporting affair South Africa would host since the end of apartheid, not to mention the first one in which they were allowed to participate in many years. When they triumphed in the finals, in an astounding upset over the formidable and heavily favored New Zealand squad, Mandela declared it the happiest day in his life. Yes, after all that he had been through, victory in a sport, one largely identified prior to that date with the oppressive white apartheid regime, was the happiest day in his life.

How could this be? Is it possible that, like me, Mandela was utilizing a physical or outer journey to capitalize on the mental or inner journey his nation so desperately needed to make? Sport often brings out the best and worst in people. Really, competition of any sort does; it's just more obvious on the playing fields of sport. Mandela rightly recognized that sport offers unique avenues for diplomacy. U.S. President Richard Nixon famously took advantage of this potential with a travelling table-tennis squad and what is often termed "ping-pong diplomacy" with China in the early 1970s. Mandela was now doing this in his own country with rugby.

Of course, sport is not the only medium to unify a country. Interestingly, national parks are another. As author Jane Carruthers explains, "The national park is not merely a physical entity, a geographical area, or a suite of ecosystems and species, but a mirror of society and a vigorous symbol."[26] Many rural Zulus had little regard for rugby or for parks under the apartheid regime. They associated them, and the concept of conservation more generally, with their white oppressors. Yet that too changed over the last twenty-plus years, with park expansion increasing after Mandela assumed office in 1994. Parks and reserves have become a rallying symbol for all of South Africa, a unifying point for constructing its national identity.

A similar rallying symbol is needed when it comes to identifying climate change. Recognizing this, environmental groups such as the Sierra Club have employed the polar bear, with its precarious position as precious sea ice melts in the Arctic, as the poster child for climate change, one that presents a clarion call to action. That tends to stir the hearts of the deep believers, those already committed to combating climate change, but what about nonbelievers or even the agnostics? Is there any common ground within the American political spectrum that can spur action when it comes to climate change?

Maybe it won't be a sporting event for us. Then again, with increasingly obvious threats to the winter sports industry, maybe it will be. Or maybe it is more about that unique American gift to the rest of the world, the very idea of national parks. More specifically, how about the ominous threats presented to Glacier National Park, as discussed in our introduction? It's very likely that there will be no more glaciers in Glacier National Park by 2020! If South Africa can dismantle apartheid, albeit with important obstacles still remaining for many of its impoverished citizens, perhaps asking Americans to face climate change is not as impossible as some would have us believe.

I know one route that won't facilitate any progress. It is said that Zulus hate being the bearer of bad news, perhaps a holdover from when Shaka's messengers could be killed for reporting something he did not want to hear. We are flirting with that same twisted logic in the West today when it comes to our head-in-the-sand attitude toward climate change. Worse, as we shall see in my visit to Antarctica later in this book, the politics of climate change are such that powerful elements within our society indeed mimic Shaka with attempts to "kill" the messenger.

That is not a behavior we can afford to imitate. As many before have argued, we have a Faustian bargain with fossil fuels. Our addiction cannot last. There simply isn't enough oil to power us through the twenty-first century. On the other hand, unfortunately, coal is a different story. There's lots of it, particularly here in United States, and it's cheap to boot.

Of course, fossil fuels such as coal are inordinately cheap because we do not account for their true cost to society. Coal is particularly dirty; its byproducts of mercury, arsenic, and sulfates are a major source of air and water pollution. Dependence on coal has also led to increased birth defects, impaired intelligence, asthma, and a variety of other respiratory and cardiovascular diseases. Does that sound good to anyone? Should we continue down this route?

Lengthy coal trains, roughly a hundred carloads each, enough to power a large power plant for a day, passed only blocks from my office here in Winter Park, Florida, until just a few years ago. Now they move along a different line several miles away, supposedly improving traffic flow and reducing noisy, early-morning disruptions. Out of sight and sound, should not mean out of mind, though. These coal trains are still running, just on a different rail line—and continuing to feed our addiction to fossil fuels like hundreds of thousands of coal trains across the rest of our land.

Maybe we should be more creative, as Carl Sagan suggested, and give more than mere lip service to alternative energy here in the United States, where only 3 percent of our electrical needs come from renewable energy sources such as wind, solar, and geothermal.

Maybe we should reconsider nuclear power. That's not something I suggest lightly. I've shared, with many other environmentalists, an aversion to nuclear power for a number of years, at least since Three Mile Island in 1979. That's the type of sentiment that prevented any new nuclear power plant construction here in the States for over thirty-five years. But the nuclear power plants now possible are not the same as the existing second-generation light-water plants we depend upon for 20 percent of our electrical needs today. The ones that represent the future are the fast-reactor, fourth-generation nuclear power plants that James Hansen, former director of NASA's Goddard Institute for Space Studies, recommends as part of our energy equation.[27]

This transition will not be easy. As Muhammad Yunus, the 2006 Nobel Peace Prize winner from Bangladesh, suggests, "My greatest challenge has been to change the mindset of people. Mindsets play strange tricks on us.

We see things the way our minds have instructed our eyes to see." The first step, then, is to recognize the inherent difficulties before us. Namely, if we can better understand the cultural context in which short-term interests often obfuscate long-term interests, our eyes may see anew.

I HAVE A DREAM

Tambopata Research Center and Social Obstacles to Understanding Climate Change

One of the great liabilities of history is that all too many people fail to remain awake through great periods of social change. Every society has its protectors of [the] status quo and its fraternities of the indifferent who are notorious for sleeping through revolutions. Today, our very survival depends on our ability to stay awake, to adjust to new ideas, to remain vigilant and to face the challenge of change.

—Martin Luther King, Jr.

chapter fifteen

TRAVELING ALONE

I'VE BEEN ITCHING TO VISIT the Amazon since I was a young child, although admittedly, like many children with far-flung ambitions, I never fully considered the consequences if my dreams were actually translated into reality. Back then my vision was, like most daydreams, one that conveniently edited out the hardships of heat and humidity, not to mention the unwelcome advances of legions of bloodthirsty insects. Instead, my dream was akin to a comfortable recreation room romp, set in vivid Technicolor and prominently featuring a magically diverse array of species from the mysterious Amazon jungle.

Although I found tales of Spanish conquistadors and other European explorers equally fascinating and frightening, in my mind, people were not the main attraction. The legendary city of El Dorado and its mythical leader, who was reputed to be sprinkled in gold dust each morning before bathing in ceremonial waters, always took a back seat to the primary draw of the Amazon, its true wealth, its biodiversity.[1]

Now I have that rare opportunity to live out a childhood dream, to experience the Amazon for myself, or at least the southwestern Amazon basin. Encompassing more than 2.6 million square miles across eight different states, the Amazon basin, as seen in Figure 15.1, is truly massive, approaching the size of the continental United States. Nearly 70 percent of it is in Brazil, but portions also occur in Bolivia, Colombia, Ecuador, Guyana, Suriname, and Venezuela as well as my destination, southeastern Peru. Together, its waters drain eastward through a fanlike network of streams and rivers, ultimately disgorging an astounding 170 billion gallons of water into the Atlantic Ocean every hour.[2]

But I'm getting a little ahead of myself here. Let me make one more point about dreaming before diving into this next travel tale. It's important

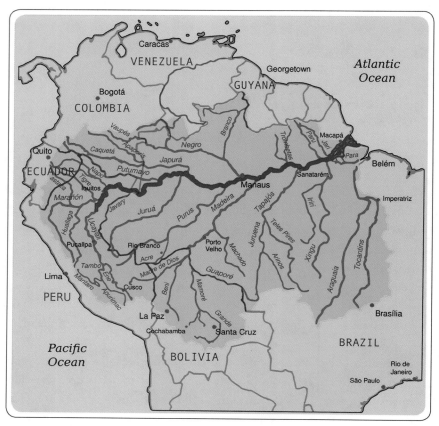

15.1 The Amazon River Basin.
Source: This file was derived from amazonrivermap.png by Karl Musser.

not to lose that precious attribute as we age, the ability to dream. Those who dare to dream, whether of personal or professional goals, create their own opportunities. Dreams are the engines that drive creativity, no matter what stage of life we are poised to enter.

And as we've seen already, that significance translates from the individual to the societal level when it comes to addressing climate change. We're in dire need of a healthy shot of creativity on this subject. Without it, we'll remain stuck in a social malaise that condemns us to the decidedly unsustainable model of business as usual.

Something has to give. Either we change, or the climate changes. It's that simple. As Martin Luther King, Jr., warned, even as he inspired us to dream,

"Our very survival depends on our ability to stay awake, to adjust to new ideas, to remain vigilant and face the challenge of change." Indeed, King and the civil rights movement, like Mandela and his fight against apartheid, provide not only inspiration in our darkest hours, but also a potential path for future climate-change policies to emulate. Combining eloquent idealism that emphasizes the equality of race with the pragmatic self-interest of employment needs, King set his sights on building a better society for all, whether black or white in skin tone.

To minimize anthropogenic climate change, we need a similar perspective today, one rooted in robust, equitable social relationships. All segments of society must buy in for this to be effective. Climate change is not merely a green issue, just as, decades ago, the civil rights movement was much more than a black issue. Similarly, just as segregation inevitably collapses on its own rotten foundation, ignorance of the interdependence of humanity, isolating climate change as a problem for others to address is destined to fail. Climate change is a problem for us all, regardless of station or geographic location.

As highlighted later during my Antarctica adventures, it should also be noted that climate change is not what some might label a "watermelon issue," green on the outside but red on the inside. Climate-change policies are not a power grab by government, what some critique as socialism in disguise. While the issue of climate change is complicated by what ecologist Garret Hardin describes as the tragedy of the commons, where public resources are exploited to their eventual ruin in the name of private interests, the rationale for addressing climate change rests firmly in the concept of protecting private interests. Quite simply, as esteemed early-twentieth-century legal scholar Judge Learned Hand once asserted, your freedom to swing your fist ends at the bridge of my nose. In other words, my freedom from injury depends on restricting your freedom to harm.

As you well know, there's been much figurative swinging of the fist in the Amazon rainforest the last several decades, not to mention disturbingly literal and fatal swings as well, such as the infamous murder of Brazilian rubber tapper and trade union leader Chico Mendes in 1988. With that in mind, I'm back with the nongovernmental organization Earthwatch to learn more about the rainforest in a slice of the Amazon basin in southeastern Peru.

Specifically, I've enlisted to help a scientist on a project entitled Macaws of the Peruvian Amazon. For approximately a decade, four times a year, typically during the rainy, non-peak-tourist months of November, December, January, and February, Earthwatch sends teams of twelve to sixteen individuals near the border of Bolivia. Most tourists come to this part of Peru between May and October, which roughly corresponds to a weak dry season from April to September, but we Earthwatchers aren't most tourists. We are coming, not when it's most pleasant, but when research is most effectively conducted. It also helps that the ecotourism operation hosting us has more vacancies during this time, when 80 percent of the annual average rainfall of 3,300 mm comes, so it makes more financial sense for them as well.[3]

Our destination is the Tambopata Research Center, nestled within the nearly 700,000-acre Tambopata National Reserve in southeastern Peru. This reserve serves as a critical buffer zone for Bahuaja-Sonene National Park, and together their 3.7 million acres comprise an area roughly the size of Connecticut, or 1.5 times the size of Costa Rica. The reserve portion was a notable addition in 1990 by the national government, although one should note that the Peruvian protected areas system treats reserves more like we treat parks here in the States, with the commercial use of natural resources legally permissible, provided appropriate national approval and oversight exist.[4]

The key here is not necessarily the lesser protective classification, but more broadly, to ensure that the relatively newly established Ministry for the Environment in Peru, which assumed control of protected areas from the Agriculture Ministry on its creation in 2008, be given a free hand to control its affairs and effectively resist inevitable economic development pressures. For when it cannot, all too often, conventional wisdom usually takes a George Bailey-esque attitude toward the value of tropical nature, that it's worth more dead than alive. Sadly, to flesh out this metaphor further, unlike that character from the holiday classic *It's a Wonderful Life*, there is no angel-chaperoned do-over when it comes to burning the rainforests. As we shall see over the next couple of chapters, there are no second chances in this soil. If you use it, you loose it.

International and local grassroots conservation-oriented operations, including Rainforest Expeditions, with which Earthwatch partners, were instrumental in establishing these 1.5 million hectares, 700,000 of which are completely uninhabited. The reserve protects the entire watersheds of the Tavara and Candamo Rivers and most of the watershed of the Tambopata. Habitat ranges from the Andean highlands around the rivers' headwaters, through some of the last remaining intact cloud forests, to the lowland rain-forests of the Amazon basin. It's difficult terrain and not easily accessed, which historically has been an asset to conservation interests attempting to stave off development. My final destination of Tambopata Research Center, noted here in Figure 15.2, is truly isolated, roughly eight hours upriver from the nearest city of Puerto Maldonado.

Despite such remoteness, in an earlier century, this area was one of many in the Amazon that played host to the infamous rubber boom. Rubber, one of the most sought-after raw materials of the Industrial Revolution, and one that literally drives our current predicament, originated from these very Amazonian rainforests. In fact, the unlikely transformation of a tree's natural insect repel-lent into the white gold of rubber is one of the great ironies in history.

For centuries *seringueiros* and their forefathers before them honed the craft of bleeding the milky white sap of the rubber tree by softly scratching its

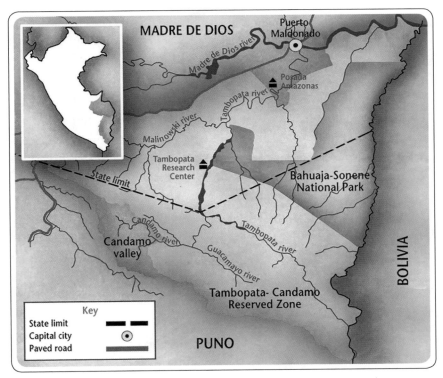

15.2 Location of Tambopata Research Center. Source: Jeff Cremer, Rainforest Expeditions. at http://www.perunature.com/map-of-peru.html.

bark. This latex, which evolved as protection against termites and other boring insects, flows through small channels half an inch or so beneath the bark. When released, its gummy quality efficiently plugs the mouth of the offending insect.

As the story goes, the Western discovery of this remarkable product dates back to 1736 and a pair of scientists sent by the French Royal Academy to help resolve a debate about the shape of the Earth. According to Newton's law of gravity, the planet was not a perfect sphere, but rather fat at the equator and flattened at the poles. Two teams, one to the Arctic and one to the equator, were sent out to make precise celestial measurements and compare them to one another. Charles Marie de La Condamine, a thirty-five-year-old geographer and naturalist, and Pierre Bouguer, a thirty-eight-year-old astronomer and mathematician, drew the equatorial assignment.

As chance would have it, though, an arguably even more influential discovery was in the making, demonstrating the often-serendipitous nature to our most meaningful learning experiences. As the two Frenchmen waited for their guides in a village along the Peruvian coast, the unique, two-foot-long torches lighting their rooms made a considerable impression on them. Unlike traditional candles, these torches produced a bright, steady light that was only half burned after a constant twelve hours of use.

Western curiosity being ignited, there followed a series of attempts to cash in on this intriguing material. Yet it was not until over a century later that such efforts bore fruit, when an American with the familiar name of Charles Goodyear developed vulcanization, the chemical process of heating rubber with sulfur to increase its elasticity, strength, and durability. The stage was set, and a viable rubber industry soon emerged.

Of course, there was further exploitation and intrigue, and a final historical footnote to the nineteenth-century portion of this tale is how control of rubber was wrested from its Latin American origins. Recognizing its financial potential, British traveler and continually aspiring entrepreneur Henry Wickham surreptitiously shipped seventy thousand Para rubber tree seeds out of Brazil to Queen Victoria's London in 1876. Only three thousand actually germinated, but a year later a handful of these seedlings arrived in Singapore to become the foundation of British rubber plantations throughout Southeast Asia. A modern monopoly was born.[5]

Nicknamed the biodiversity capital of the world by Peruvians, Tambopata is home to more species of plants and animals per square kilometer than recorded anywhere else on Earth.[6] These high levels of biodiversity are attributable to dramatic variations in climate, altitude, and forest type, not to mention the expected microhabitats endemic to tropical rainforests across the globe.

The area includes ninety species of frogs; some two hundred mammal species, including the world's largest rodent, the capybara;[7] twelve hundred species of butterfly, including the electric blue morpho once described by naturalist Frank Chapman as the "bluest things in the world;" and over ten thousand different species of plants. Indeed, these tropical forests contain between twenty to eighty-six different species of trees per acre, an astounding ratio considering temperate forests average only about four per acre.[8]

And that's just setting the table, so to speak. We haven't even gotten to the main denizens of the rainforest, the bugs. The Smithsonian Institution's Terry Erwin estimates, for example, that each species of rainforest tree supports 405 unique insect species, meaning 20 million or more insect species exist throughout tropical rainforests alone.

Unlike Erwin, though, I'm not here for insects. I'm here for the birds. There are thirteen hundred different species of birds in Tambopata, including thirty-two different parrot species, 10 percent of the world's total. Now, as you may recall from my earlier Galápagos travels, I'm not a passionate birder, but if I were, this would be paradise. There are more bird species here than on any other comparable tract of land in the world.[9]

More specifically, my targets are macaws, the largest of the parrot family of nearly 350 species, and the most readily distinguished from others in that family by their long tails and powerful bills.[10] Renowned American ornithologist Charles Munn began the first detailed studies of macaws in the wild in 1984 with the New York Zoological Society, now known as the Wildlife Conservation Society, and the scientist I am working for followed his lead.

Macaws and parrots generally, for that matter, are some of the most endangered species in the world, with nine of the world's seventeen macaw species in danger of extinction. Sadly, a major driving force in this precipitous decline is their popularity as pets, which is all the more problematic as macaws behave remarkably like people. Like people, they make good companions, not good pets. As journalist Tim Sullivan asserts, they simply are too demanding.[11]

Found in tropical forests from central Mexico to northern Argentina, they have dramatically colorful plumage with hues of blue, green, red, and gold.

They can fly great distances and as fast as thirty-five miles per hour, regularly offering impressive acrobatic aerial displays. Brains complement this beauty; macaws display innate curiosity and the ability to use tools, not to mention the remarkable ability to mimic human speech.

Noisy and social in the wild, macaws usually mate for life. Mated pairs preen each other and their offspring for hours, removing ticks and lice. In captivity, with a lifespan of fifty to seventy years, they often outlive their owners,[12] while a combination of disease, parasites, eagle attacks, and old age often claim their lives in the wild after thirty to forty-five years.

Alas, many fail to reach even this age, dying before fledging, and the original objective of the Tambopata Research Center focused on reproductive problems among three of the largest eight macaws that occur in the region. I'm here to continue that tradition, targeting specifically the rainbow-colored scarlet, the turquoise-winged blue-and-yellow, and the big-headed red-and-green. For the next two weeks, I'll assist a biologist from Texas A&M,[13] Dr. Donald Brightsmith, who began directing the center in 1999, to study their mating and migration as well as feeding and population trends.

What makes this place so unusual and a prime macaw research site, aside from the aforementioned biodiversity, is the presence of the world's largest known mineral clay lick a mere 1,640 feet from the Tambopata Research Center lodge. Formed by erosion of the Tambopata River, this lick is about 1,500 feet long and sixty-five feet high. Hundreds of parrots and macaws, up to fifteen different species daily, regularly queue up to sample clumps of clay.

Yes, that's right; they come to eat the clay. Aside from addressing the obvious question as to why, we're helping document differences over the years in clay lick usage as well as seasonal changes and the effects of climatic anomalies such as El Niño.

But before my Earthwatch adventure begins I've set aside a few days to see the heart of the Incan empire in nearby Cuzco as well as Machu Picchu, "the face of Peru" according to many, including Rainforest Expeditions guide Katherine Torres. Indeed, half a million tourists visit Machu Picchu each year. By coincidence, I stumbled on an enlightening article on South America's best-known archaeological site in *USA Today* as I changed flights in Houston, illustrating once again that serendipity can be a major player in our learning process.[14]

That's worth repeating. Learning does not always proceed as planned. Indeed, some of the greatest leaps in knowledge occur due to the unexpected twists and turns life presents. Sometimes learning simply happens. The trick here is to mold that learning, to shape it in the context of other information. And in some cases, as with climate change, that task comes with added urgency, to mold that learning before it is too late to make a difference.

Back to my airplane article. Yale historian Hiram Bingham, backed by the National Geographic Society, rediscovered the mountaintop city of Machu Picchu in 1911 and returned in 1912 and 1915, carting out thousands of artifacts. While then–Peruvian President Augusto Leguía supposedly granted permission for their removal, by the beginning of the next century, calls for their return were growing louder. In 2008 Peru formally sued in U.S. federal court, seeking return of the artifacts, and by late 2010 secured an agreement for their return in several stages over the next two years.[15] Persistence is powerful.

Departing Houston, I land around midnight at Jorge Chávez International airport in Lima, then transfer for a few hours of sleep at the nondescript Hotel Manhattan before a quick one-hour flight early the next morning to Cuzco. With assistance from Rainforest Expeditions, I'll spend three nights in the quaint Casa Andina Catedral, using it as base for my day trip to Machu Picchu.

Cuzco, which in Quechua is known as Tawantinsuyo, meaning the four quarters of the Earth, is literally surrounded by Andean peaks and itself is eleven thousand feet above sea level. Since I'm coming from a state where the highest point is a mere 345 feet,[16] I need to be extra cautious about altitude adjustment for the next several days. That afternoon, as I tour the city, I'm careful not to exert myself and risk altitude sickness, which would endanger the real purpose of the entire trip, assisting the scientist in Tambopata.

Unlike last year with my Galápagos adventure, and knowing the stakes involved, I've come much better prepared pharmaceutically this time around. To ease acclimatization, the process by which our body adjusts to the lower amounts of oxygen available at higher altitudes, I'm taking a 125-mg dose of Diamox twice daily with food as well as drinking plenty of water, at least four quarts per day. Each of these preventative measures increases my need to track down restrooms, never an easy proposition in the poorer sectors of Latin America, but the additional side effects of tingling in hands or feet, dizziness, lightheadedness, loss of appetite, drowsiness, confusion, malaise, and depression are, thankfully, all absent.

The architecture in Cuzco, on first impression, reflects Spanish colonialism, with red-tiled roofs rampant around Plaza de Armas and the colonial arcades that surround it. But there are also buildings from an earlier era in the form of massive foundations of Incan stone throughout the city.

The Church of Santo Domingo, known locally as Coricancha or Temple of the Sun, is a great example. The church itself was built over what once was arguably the most magnificent temple in all the Americas. Courtyards filled with life-sized gold and silver statues represented the flora and fauna of the Incan empire. Alas, Pizarro's men unceremoniously looted these riches at the end of the Incan reign, part of the royal ransom for the last Incan ruler Atahualpa.

Nearly as impressive, at least by virtue of its longevity, are the Incan walls still standing, walls on which the Spanish plastered their own structures. When an earthquake hit the city in 1950, much of the church was destroyed, with the exception of the master Incan stonework. Additional sturdy foundations are found throughout the city, a testament to their craftsmanship.

After a few hours in the city, my tour group takes a bus ride to the hills surrounding Cuzco, topping out around twelve thousand feet to visit the ruined fortress of Sacsayhuaman two kilometers from the city. Here again, huge walls are constructed of stones, the largest of which stands over twenty-seven feet high and weighs 361 tons; the stones are distributed in a zigzag pattern that creates three platforms. Pachacuti, the Incan ruler who built this fortress, employed twenty thousand men over fifty years to complete it. More on him in a minute.

As I climb the steps of my hotel to my room that night, I realize it has been a long day, and I have sufficient reason to be tired. Maybe it's just my mind playing tricks on me, but I'm suddenly struck by the possibility that this could be something more. Maybe it's the altitude?

In any case, despite having a decided distaste for tea since early childhood, I decide to play it safe and try the local recommendation for acclimatization, *mate de coca*, essentially a tea infused with coca leaves. Yes, that's the same coca that goes into cocaine. In this case, though, the leaves themselves are not addictive and have no narcotic effect. It's even legal in Peru, although illegal in most neighboring countries, and it would certainly set off alarm bells if I were taking a drug test.

Of course, the best way to avoid acute mountain sickness is to move up in altitude slowly, day by day. Going from Orlando to Lima and now Lima to Cuzco in less than twenty-four hours, I haven't exactly followed that prescription, rising over ten thousand feet or essentially two miles in elevation. I did have yesterday to adjust, so now it's been forty-eight hours since sea level, and, fortunately, the next day of my trip requires relatively little exertion with a bus ride through the Urubamba River Valley. It's a lovely drive, stopping first at the picturesque Andean village of Pisaq, famous for its twice-a-week indigenous market, and then on to finish at Ollantaytambo, a strategic town at the northern end of the gentle valley where the river begins to plunge into the Amazon. Here the valley narrows to a well-defined gorge, which allowed the Inca to defend Cuzco from attacks by jungle tribes to the north.

After a good rest that evening back in Cuzco and an early breakfast, I catch a 6:00 A.M. train heading for the eastern edge of the Andes. My destination is the famed Machu Picchu, which in Quechua refers to Old Mountain, the inspiring 9,060-foot peak looming over the site. Although less than seventy miles away from the old Incan capital, it takes nearly four hours through field after field of traditional Andean crops such as maize and potatoes (yet another Incan legacy) to reach the village nearest to Machu Picchu, Aguas Calientes. And even though we feel closer to the gods in this ancient cloud city, we're only at 7,700 feet, about 3,000 less than Cuzco. I'm going to be more active today, though, so altitude concerns are still on my mind.

At Aguas Calientes we transfer to a bus for the final leg of the trip, a winding unpaved road of endless switchbacks up the mountain to the Lost City of the Incas. Conquering Spaniards never found it, even after bloodily dispatching the Incan civilization in the late 1500s, so when Yale Latin American historian Hiram Bingham rediscovered it in 1911 it was quite a find. Experts estimate the population of the well-preserved, cloud-enshrouded ruins once ranged between 500 and 750 individuals, with more in the winter months when an imperial entourage descended to its lower altitude, and thus warmer climate, to escape the chill of Cuzco.

Believe it or not, I initially hesitated to add this side trip to my itinerary. Even though I'm traveling on the cheap, I'm going into debt for this detour, because it's not covered by my generous grant for the Earthwatch study. Still, being this close to such an historical landmark, it would be a shame to miss it. Sometimes you have to spend money to make it. Or at least in this case, while not making any money, I am gaining figurative currency. And the kicker, of course, is that the experience itself is priceless.

The reasons why Machu Picchu was built remain under debate.[17] In his day, Bingham dramatically suggested that the city, perched precariously one thousand feet above the Urubamba River below, housed a cult of vestal virgins seeking refuge from lustful conquistadors. More recently, some argue Machu Picchu was built and populated by the aforementioned Incan ruler Pachacuti, probably between 1450 and 1470.[18] This school of thought compares Machu Picchu to a Camp David, where royals relaxed and entertained foreign dignitaries.

Still others propose that the principal purpose of the city was to maintain a reliable supply of the aforementioned coca leaves for priests and royals in Cuzco. And a final school contends that, because it is located at the confluence of a number of trails, the city served a mixture of strategic and administrative purposes. One suggestion is that Machu Picchu was a district center charged with administering to recently conquered tribes of the Amazon. Another argues that it served as a center for teaching and brainwashing the children of those recently conquered by the Inca.

Intermingling with fellow tourists and the occasional llama, I wander through a maze of hundreds of stone terraces that litter the landscape. Amid the tombs, sundials, and baths, I pause at the Temple of Three Windows, which indicated the exact location of sunrise, and Intihuatana, or Hitching Post of the Sun, that the Inca used to determine the two equinoxes.

Machu Picchu was never a full-fledged city, at least in the modern sense of the word. It held no factories, no shops, not even any markets. It is unlikely there was ever any commerce at all. Still, people clearly lived here, and a section of grassy plazas separates the city into two distinct sectors, one urban and the other agricultural. This makes perfect sense if you know Inca culture. As Alfredo Valencia Zegarra, a distinguished Peruvian archaeologist, notes, "The Inca envisioned all things in duality: male and female, life and death, right and left, the upper world and the lower world."[19]

There is a similar line of thought when it comes to climate change. There are those who think it's a problem and those who do not. Of course, it's a bit more complicated than that, and to position the debate as that simple is a great disservice. We'll return to that topic again during my trip to Antarctica.

After judiciously making the rounds and snapping the obligatory tourist photos, I find a quiet space to sit and ponder the mystery of these stones, and whether there are any lessons in them. Life is short, I conclude, so maximize your opportunities. Okay, not exactly profound. It's been said many times before, but somehow here in the majestic clouds of Machu Picchu it seems to carry a bit more cachet.

I do think there is another lesson within Machu Picchu, though, that is particularly relevant when it comes to climate change and the social obstacles to addressing it. It's this simple: things change. Here before me was a once-thriving community. It was lost to the jungle for centuries, then rediscovered just over a hundred years ago. We are still trying to piece together answers to a series of questions about this chain of events.

As we've noted already, climate changes naturally, but change for the last two hundred–plus years, particularly the last four or five decades, is different. Just as notably, for our own selfish interests, we are socially ill-equipped to handle this change.

One key to minimizing the inevitable disruptions from climate change is to create a more equitable social environment, from the local to the international level. The United States, with our multiethnic society, could be a leader in this effort. Diversity is one of our greatest strengths, as it is in the rainforest I'm finally due to visit tomorrow. Of course, the Inca empire was multiethnic as well, and Machu Picchu itself, according to Lucy Salazar, archaeologist and co-curator of the Yale's 2003 travelling Machu Picchu exhibition, was a microcosm of that empire. Clearly then, even if such a quality is a necessary component for resilience, it is not sufficient. Diversity for the Incas and Machu Picchu wasn't enough. Something more is needed.

With that thought still in my mind, I hustle to catch one of the last buses back down to Aguas Calientes. A local boy reinforces this idea that greater social equity is needed as he races our vehicle, avoiding the switchbacks and dashing barefoot through the forests in a straight line down the mountain, only pausing each time he catches us back on the road with an exaggerated, demonstrative wave. When we finally reach the bottom, the young teenager is waiting confidently for us, with a huge grin and hardly a sweat. As if on cue, the bus driver opens the door, allowing him aboard to collect some well-deserved earnings from the impressed audience. Much more is needed, indeed.

Day five of my journey starts with a short fifty-minute midday flight from the cobbled streets of Cuzco to the steamy frontier town of Puerto Maldonado. The ride is a bit bumpy, and, at times, downright frightening. Still, I've been on worse, and the touchdown into a small, nondescript airport is, thankfully, uneventful. The heat and humidity, in contrast to Cuzco, although not unlike my summers at home in Florida, splash across my face as I descend onto the open tarmac and proceed to the processing gate. Here I show my required yellow-fever inoculation certificate to airport officials, a hint that the journey to come will be less simple, and link up with a cheery Rainforest Expeditions staffer.

Puerto Maldonado stands at the confluence of the Tambopata and Madre de Dios Rivers; the latter flows into the Madiera River, one of eleven hundred tributaries that feed the Amazon. Starting at eighteen thousand feet above sea level, in the Andean snows of southern Peru beyond the continental divide, the Amazon meanders a total 4,007 miles, making it the second-longest river in the world (the Nile ranking first).

But that's not the half of it. When it comes to its array of impressive statistics, the Amazon has no match. In terms of volume, it's the largest river in the world, accounting for approximately one-fifth of all river flow on Earth. Some of its tributaries are longer than the Mississippi. The distance between banks on the Amazon is often five miles or more, and as much as thirty miles in places during the wet season. At its mouth lies Marajo, a grassy island the size of Switzerland. And finally, for more than one hundred miles from its Brazilian coast, the Amazon's waters remain fresh, with unmixed Amazon water lying above the denser salt water of the ocean.

I'm at what you might say is a tributary to a tributary here in Puerto Maldonado, a booming and bustling tropical frontier town. Historically, the principal activities were the usual extractive enterprises of gold mining, logging, and agriculture, along with some Brazil-nut collecting; ecotourism was added recently to this mix.

After a brief stop at the Rainforest Expeditions office here in town, we clamber aboard a company truck for nearly an hour drive along a deeply rutted dirt road to the Infierno Community port. There we transfer to a motorized dugout canoe, the eighteen-wheelers of the Amazon, for another hour trip up the winding, muddy brown Tambopata River. My destination for the next two nights is the award-winning Posada Amazonas jungle lodge.

Set in a remote location and used as a dropping off point for those heading farther up the river, Posada Amazonas was named one of the top ten jungle lodges in the world by *Audubon* magazine several years back.[20] It's easy to see why so many speak highly of it, including *Condé Nast Traveler* magazine's best ecotourism operator award and Conservation International's ecotourism excellence award. Constructed from locally harvested wood, palm fronds, and wild cane, it is spacious and awe-inspiring, with large open "windows" in common areas and bedrooms alike. Heck, even a delightful bunch of bananas hang in a corner of the lobby, the sweetest and freshest I ever tasted, and a worthy conversation piece.

That night, as an assortment of odd noises emanate from my own open walled room, I reflect on the pluses and minuses to traveling alone. One obvious drawback, of course, is loneliness. There is nothing quite like visiting someplace for the first time without friend or family, or even mere acquaintance. It can try the soul.

But trials also make us stronger, enhancing our efforts on the roads ahead. Assuming your loneliness is not constant, everyone should try traveling alone at least once. Indeed, on occasion, I highly recommend it, finding it particularly instructive as a contrasting bookend to traveling with young children, as described earlier along the Great Barrier Reef. At least in small doses, as the saying goes, absence makes the heart grow fonder. You better appreciate what you have left behind after venturing out on your own.

Another benefit is that traveling alone allows you to develop a keener sense of other travelers, not to mention the locals themselves. Traveling alone makes you more socially aware. You are not as preoccupied with your own traveling party, and thus are more likely to reach out to strangers in conversation. After all, we are all fundamentally social creatures. We crave social interaction.

That has certainly been my experience on the road over the years, and I have toyed with this theory the last couple days, first from Lima to Cuzco, then onward to Machu Picchu and finally Puerto Maldonado. By the time I reach Posada Amazonas, I'm unabashedly eager for the camaraderie of my fellow Earthwatch volunteers, hopeful to establish a relationship that will last longer than a half-hour or two. As luck would have it, I'm paired up with three like-minded Earthwatchers at Posada Amazonas, including my future bunkmate at Tambopata Research Center, an engaging Welsh banker with the international firm Hong Kong Shanghai Bank Corporation (HSBC).

chapter sixteen

AMID THE DEAFENING SILENCE

SILENCE IS NOT ALWAYS GOLDEN. Sometimes circumstances dictate the need to speak up, whether you are a social activist or not. In fact, choosing to remain quiet as others suffer, whether intended or not, implies tacit agreement. Still another powerful quotation from Martin Luther King, Jr., captures this sentiment. As he eloquently asserted during the civil rights movement in the United States, "History will have to record that the greatest tragedy of this period of social transition was not the strident clamor of the bad people, but the appalling silence of the good people."

The examples don't stop there. During the Holocaust, for instance, a sad silence permeated not just Germany, but many parts of Europe, as six million Jews were led to nauseatingly systemic slaughter. While Hitler and his minions executed their Final Solution with maniacal precision, the Nazis received unspoken assists almost daily in the form of inaction among the wider, "innocent" civilian populace. It's not that the entire German public, or the European public for that matter, was innately evil. Many feared for their own lives. Total war encompassed the entire continent and a sense of helplessness discouraged resistance.

Helplessness is a familiar refrain, from continent to continent and time period to time period, when deconstructing the causes of inaction in the face of seminal societal struggles. For example, in the United States, fear and intimidation prevented countless individuals from standing up to racial violence, particularly in the South, as thousands of African-Americans were killed by the Ku Klux Klan during the Reconstruction era after the Civil War and again in episodes of the KKK's rebirth, not to mention various spinoff hate groups during the twentieth century. Martin Luther King, Jr., himself perished at the hands of a white supremacist during the civil rights movement in the 1960s, as we well know.

In the midst of this tragedy, though, voices multiplied and a turning point in American society began, a move away from our racist past. We have considerably more work ahead of us, as headlines each month unfortunately bear out, but the social context today, more often than not, is an asset instead of a handicap, supporting those who speak out rather than suppressing them. The biggest threat to continued progress, one might argue, is becoming satisfied with partial progress to date. Our society must avoid the temptation to rest on our laurels. We need to stay hungry.

When it comes to the issue of climate change, though, we're not even at that social stage. We haven't reached a tipping point. And hopefully, when we do, that's not dependent on violence. If it is, we probably will be too late. Indeed, while the violence from climate change is less direct and the fatalities not as obvious, at least to those of us in the developed world, the final tally of casualties from climate change will probably dwarf those from all previous conflicts. Indeed, as global environmental politics scholars such as American University's Paul Wapner increasingly point out, considerable climate-related suffering has already begun.[1] With this in mind, the time to speak out is now. It is socially irresponsible not to.

It's my first full day in the jungle. A symphony of sounds serenaded me the previous night, actually starting before nightfall with the so-called six o'clock cicadas providing the initial steady cadence, building to a crescendo as the sun went down. In the darkness, amid an assortment of sounds, a chorus of frogs showed off their range and vocal stamina through the wee hours of the night, only tapering off just before daybreak, when the expected bird as well as unexpected monkey sections jumped in.

With all the squawks and whistles as well as hoots and hollers, my 4:00 A.M. wake-up knock the next morning seemed a bit superfluous. Nevertheless, as I gather with a half-dozen other tourists for a quick jungle breakfast of breads and fruit, I'm pinching myself. In part, it is to stay awake, and in part, to make sure I'm not actually dreaming, but rather am living out that childhood daydream mentioned before. I'm truly in the heart of a rainforest now. (Tropical rainforests, by the way, occur in three major regions around the globe: Asia, Africa, and the Neotropics of South and Central America as well as the Caribbean.)

Early explorer naturalists often recounted their visits in religious terms, like paying respects in a natural cathedral with a great green canopy as its vaulted ceiling. Now I'm better at appreciating these descriptions.

The Amazon is the Mecca of all rainforests. One in every four plants on Earth grows here. Our destination today is Tres Chimbadas, an oxbow lake less than an hour from our lodge. Oxbow lakes are old remnants of a river that are cut off by the effects of erosion and the constant shifting of river channels, and this one houses an array of interesting characters.

The hike through the jungle is magnificent, with our guide pointing out highlights along the way, such as cocoa trees with their pale green fruit somewhat incongruously growing directly out of the tree trunk, like this one in Figure 16.1, rather than at the end of branches. These cocoa fruits are about the size of an avocado but shaped like a football with their ribs protruding on the outside along parallel lines. It's the first time I've seen real cocoa, and I stop briefly to gawk at the origin of what made so many childhood Easter mornings, not

16.1 Cocoa tree.

to mention later Halloween nights, chocolate nirvana.

After a fifteen-minute boat ride and another thirty-minute walk, we arrive at a serene lake setting. There we board a weathered but still functional catamaran, powered by muscle with a unique rotary oar system. The lake is beautiful in the early morning dawn just before six—and it is filled with piranha.

Four species of these ragged-toothed fish live in the Tambopata region, the largest of which, the black piranha, grows to nearly a foot long. These guys are omnivores, eating everything from small fish to fruit to insects to seeds and aquatic plants. At least according to the Tambopata Research Center, their reputation as a threat to people is overrated. These particular fish are largely kept in check by the primary predator of these waters, giant otters literally the length of a human. Still, when hungry or stressed, the piranha can be aggressive. They are typically found near lake shores, so I've been advised to avoid swimming close to shore, especially if I'm bleeding. Trust me. Never crossed my mind.

Attacks on humans are largely anecdotal, but one worth noting was on Christmas Day 2013 in the Parana River in Rosario, Argentina. Amid hundred-degree heat, bathers seeking cool relief endured an unprecedented attack by similar piranhas, with several sacrificing their fingers.[2]

Later, we actually catch, then release, several of them at Tres Chimbadas. After all, wouldn't want to hurt those little toothy guys, would we? The fish are fairly bony and not often eaten by locals. I get several strong bites on my makeshift stick rod, but don't fully understand the technique and fail to jerk the string quickly enough to hook them when they bite. Our well-practiced guide, of course, has much better luck, as shown in Figure 16.2.

We also glimpse a spectacled caiman at the lake around eight that morning. Relatives of our better-known alligator, four species of caiman live around Tambopata. Both the dwarf and smooth-fronted caiman do not

16.2 Piranha ready to chomp.

exceed 1.5 meters (just under five feet) and are very rare. The spectacled or white caiman may reach four meters long, but their average length tends to top out at two. This is also the caiman most commonly seen along rivers, although they tend to shy away from humans. Turns out, this is with good reason, as evidenced by the sale of caiman ceviche from where I just departed downriver in Puerto Maldonado.

The black caiman, on the other hand, is the real reason to be wary of swimming in lakes around here, as if the presence of piranha weren't enough. Here they reach as large as six meters, almost twenty feet. Most locals have a healthy respect for a creature that size. A rusty old pair of binoculars back on the bar at Posada Amazonas tells a different story. Allegedly, it was rescued from the gut of a giant black caiman from nearby Coco Cocha—all that remained from a guide who took an ill-conceived solo swim.

German ecologist E. J. Fittkau has a more appreciative perspective on these beasts, suggesting that they play a valuable role as "nutrient concentrators" in lakes and swamps off the main body of a river. To put it simply, their rather substantial excrement provides a significant food source for plankton, which, in turn, offers sustenance to young fish that hatch from these backwater egg-laying sites. In other words, fewer caimans translates into fewer fish.

Still, the highlight of the morning, for me, at least, is the family of giant river otters that frequent Tres Chimbadas. Previously hunted for their pelts or killed by local fishermen to reduce competition with their own fishing, these impressive creatures are highly endangered, declining from an original estimate of 20,000 to little more than 250 still alive in Peru today. Reaching lengths over eight feet, they are taller than most humans in the region. Six or seven are visible from our boat, and we sit silently in awe of this rare creature.

Later that afternoon, after returning to Posada Amazonas, I have the opportunity to climb into the canopy for the first time. Doing so, though, means missing a trip to the ethnobotanical center, where the local community has been registering uses for medicinal plants from its elders since 1996. Didn't want to miss that, but you can't have everything, as many a parent has said. That's something we seem to have forgotten when it comes to the adjustments necessary to curb climate change.

My sacrifice, this time at least, is quickly forgotten. It's another world unfolding before my eyes as we climb the huge thirty-five-meter tower at the end of our forest walk. Seeing the rainforest canopy for the first time is a bit like my first dive into the shallows of a coral reef. Certainly the analogy holds up in terms of the biodiversity each holds, even as deeper in the shadows below, less and less grows where little light penetrates.

There are spectacular views of the river and surrounding forest, with a continuum of trees ranging in height from 50 to 160 feet. It's a completely different perspective from the forest floor, showcasing what the great Amazonian explorer-naturalist Alexander von Humboldt called the forest above a forest.

Indeed, five strata of vegetation exist in rainforests. At the top, there are a handful of large emergent trees like those now before me. Below this is the main canopy, with trees between 100 and 130 feet high. A subcanopy falls between 50 and 80 feet above the floor, and then a sparse understory of shrubs and nonwoody plants as well as seedlings constitutes the second-to-last layer, before the forest floor itself.

At dinner that night at Posada Amazonas, we learn there will be no night walk. The details are a bit hazy, but apparently armed men are roaming about a mile from the lodge, and the staff doesn't want to take \any chances. They are probably only poachers, for although it was prevalent during the 1980s, terrorism has been all but eliminated in Peru. In fact, the infamous *Sendero Luminoso* or Shining Path, a Maoist guerilla insurgent organization, has been in steady decline since its founder was captured over two decades ago in 1992, and then nearly eliminated in 2012 when the Peruvian army announced that its mission against them was complete, but episodes of violence still flare up from time to time. Less than three weeks before our visit, for example, a group of rebels ambushed a police patrol, killing eight, albeit nearly five hundred miles away in the Huánuco region.[3]

The trouble could also be coming from neighboring Bolivia. After winning a landslide election less than four weeks earlier, president-elect Evo Morales announced plans to nationalize Bolivia's gas reserves, redistribute land to poor farmers, and adjust rules for the United States war on drugs in his country. It's that last one, in particular, that raises caution flags across the border, because it sounds like these new rules will be more to the bad guys' liking.

But I digress. Aside from the Amazon itself, the real reason I chose to focus on this particular operation in southeastern Peru is its unique social relationship. You see, Posada Amazonas is jointly owned by the Lima-based ecotourism company Rainforest Expeditions and the Ese'eja native community within the community of Infierno. The Ese'eja were traditionally dispersed throughout the Amazonian lowlands of Peru and Bolivia, but the Peruvian government gave them title to this community nestled next to Tambopata in 1976.[4]

Some five hundred people in approximately 150 families live adjacent to the northwest corner of the Tambopata Candamo Reserve Zone, which itself is adjacent to the 10,914-square-km Bahuaja-Sonene National Park. Tambopata, in fact, is a buffer zone of sorts to the park, and that status is a large part of why Rainforest Expeditions selected this location. In addition to serving as a lodge in its own right, Posada Amazonas was seen as a necessary overnight resting place for those journeying on to the Tambopata Research Center.

What complicates matters a bit, though, is the fact that it's not only Ese'eja that live here now. They account for approximately 20 percent of the population, but another 21 percent are Andean immigrants, 23 percent are local immigrants, and 34 percent are mestizos. Many of these immigrants, often descendants from the rubber-boom era, have been living in the area for decades. Some became official members of the Native Community of Infierno (CNI) and, as such, were granted the right to extract and produce from the communal lands of the community, which at times stirred ethnic tensions.

As alluded to in the previous adventure in South Africa, local people are often initially resentful of conservation efforts, viewing them as evidence that wealthy Westerners, and even their own governments, value the lives of everything from birds to rhinos more than they value the local people's lives. When designed correctly, however, as Tambopata proves, conservation empowers a local community. Profits from Posada Amazonas, for example, are fairly split, with 60 percent going to the community and 40 percent to the company. Further, at least in theory, management is divided fifty-fifty. A critical tenet here was that community members be actively involved not only as day-to-day operating staff—housekeeping, dining services, guiding, and boat driving—but also as higher-level management, from administrators to planners to outright owners. Alas, this has proven to be easier to propose than to achieve.

Lack of experience combines with social conditioning about class and race hierarchies to discourage the community from challenging the more-educated elite from Lima. Reaching the ideal is still a work in progress as the community struggles to interact with its Rainforest Expeditions partners as equals.[5] For example, while the committee that runs the operation is balanced with five Rainforest Expeditions representatives and five members of the community elected by its communal assembly, in practice, many day-to-day decisions are made outside these monthly meetings. By 2002, an exasperated community nearly kicked Rainforest Expeditions out due to this lack of consultation.

These growing pains aside, each party has benefited from the relationship since the lodge opened in 1998, and, from most accounts, both appear to embrace the continually evolving relationship. For example, in 2016, after twenty years of operation, according to the original Keieway Association in Participation contract, the native community of Infierno was set to own the entire operation, but both parties subsequently agreed to postpone a complete transfer until a later date.[6]

This is the type of partnership worth examining further, perhaps even emulating across the globe. Much as the late environmental author and economist E. F. Schumacher noted in his seminal work *Small Is Beautiful,* too often there is a danger of disconnect between a company's interests and the community's. To be sustainable, to truly benefit a community over the long haul, corporations must have long-term interests in these communities. Reward systems must not be based solely on quarterly returns. The health of a community has to be incentivized along with the health of a stock.

Recalling and rephrasing Abraham Lincoln's assertion on the union's inability to continue half free and half slave, our planet cannot exist half sustainable and half unsustainable. We are all connected. When it comes to environmental health and climate change, it is not a zero-sum game where the gains of China are our losses in the States. When it comes to climate change, we are all in this together, current generations and future ones. Paradoxically, because an economic rationale is often cited as the reason for postponing climate-change mitigation efforts, we need to be more pragmatic about this. Borrowing yet again from Martin Luther King, Jr., we need to consider our decisions today in the context of our descendants tomorrow, our children. Decisions made today will have repercussions for generations to come.

The next day starts my formal Earthwatch commitment. For the next ten days and nights I'll be working at Tambopata Research Center. The journey to TRC, though, is still another five to six hours upriver from Posada Amazonas. While our final destination is only one hundred kilometers from Puerto Maldonado, the capital of Madre de Dios Department, in reality, we are much more isolated than that reasonable number would seem to suggest. We are literally an eight-hour boat ride from the town upriver, weather permitting.

As we shuffle down the dark path to our boat, a bamboo rat, oddly sounding like a monkey or bird, scurries along, too, just out of eyesight. I do catch a glimpse, thanks to my guide Cesar, of another creature that is considerably more dangerous. There's a small scorpion perched above our path down to the river. Maybe I'm just tired, but its diminutive size fails to engender the level of respect it deserves. More on that a bit later; life's biggest threats can come in the smallest of packages.

Along the river we break up the monotony by introducing ourselves to some of the newly arrived Earthwatchers and enjoy a scrumptious lunch. In a nod to sustainability and clever use of local resources, it is wrapped in banana leaves instead of a box. There is intermittent rain, sometimes so strong that one or both banks of the river are not visible through the sheets of water. When it clears, though, a rare treat emerges. Only 2 percent of the visitors to Tambopata have the pleasure of witnessing one, and ours is posing like a confident supermodel at the edge of the eroded riverbank.

16.3 A jaguar overlooking Tambopata riverbank.

It's a magnificent jaguar, as seen in Figure 16.3. Larger animals such as this are normally reclusive, only coming down to the river to drink or prey on others quenching their thirst. Jaguars have a reputation for being vicious, but actually have no interest in people and typically run away when encountered. Thankfully, they don't consider people as food. Like most other large predators, their "prey image" is restricted to animals they have grown up eating. Nevertheless, we are advised that if we stumble across one in the jungle, it is best, as in my previous big-cat adventure in South Africa, not to trigger their predator-prey instinct and to remain perfectly still.

A female jaguar needs at least twenty square kilometers to support herself and her cubs,[7] but to sustain a genetically viable population, some three hundred breeding females are needed over several thousand square kilometers of suitable territory, according to Duke University's John Terborgh, who heads up the Cocha Cashu Biological Station in Peru. Big cats such as these, not big birds, were what originally lured the man who started TRC into the Amazon. Eduardo Nycander decided to reorient his career after seeing a wildlife film, which illustrates not only the power of that medium but also the simple fact that life is full of unexpected starts. You never know when or where inspiration will strike.

I myself, though, have a good hunch. It's in a half-acre clearing about fifty meters from the river. We've finally arrived, and the rain is harder now as we carefully shuffle off the boat up the slippery riverbank and toward that very clearing.

Before me is a building with four interconnected roofs thatched with crisneja palm fronds. Made in accordance with traditional low-impact native architecture, the building and passageways are raised four feet off the ground on stilts of palm trunks, which comes in handy during rains like today's. The main building is thirty-three feet by one hundred and divided into thirteen bedroom lodges, each with two beds draped in mosquito netting like this one in Figure 16.4. There are three walls to each room, just like at Posada Amazonas, with the fourth open to the surrounding rainforest.

Except in the kitchen and research room, we have no electricity. The lodge runs mainly on propane, with kerosene lamps providing light at night; radio communication to the outside world is powered by solar energy. Once a day, a 110-volt generator is powered up to recharge batteries for cameras and flashlights, etc. We also have shared bathrooms with flush

16.4 The TRC lodge.

toilets and unheated showers. Buffet meals are served three times a day, although you always miss either breakfast or lunch while out in the field. It's late afternoon when we arrive, so our first buffet dinner at 7:30 P.M. is still three hours away, but the bar is about to open. Yes, a jungle bar. Not one to miss an opportunity, I promptly settle down there to get better acquainted with my roommate Berwyn over a true Peruvian original, the pisco sour.[8]

The next magical morning, a Friday the 13th with all the superstitions that entails, Berwyn and I awake to a different sound. It's not the chirping and screeching of the day before, but another common sound of the rainforest, rainfall gushing from the skies. It's raining in veritable sheets around the lodge, as seen in Figure 16.5, which I suppose should not come as a surprise, considering that one of the two defining characteristics of a tropical rainforest is the copious rainfall (the other is temperature). We are also in the middle of the rainy season here at Tambopata, as noted earlier, when roughly 80 percent of the rainfall for the year falls. In some tropical rainforests, there can be as much as an inch in a half-hour, forty times more than in an average shower in the northeastern United States.[9] That's a big deal. As an aside, reinforcing the significance of the omnipresent canopy in a healthy forest, there is often a ten-minute delay between when the downpour begins and when the water finally strikes the forest floor.

When it doesn't rain, that is a big deal, too. As you know, warm and wet conditions in the rainforest breed many types of life. It's a natural greenhouse,

16.5 A downpour in the rainforest.

with high rainfall and humidity that allows species to grow and reproduce all year long, particularly because no winter season disrupts this cycle. But during dry periods, a different sort of disruption occurs, and the rainforest splits into de facto islands. Over time, new species evolve within these islands. Then, when the rains return, microhabitats emerge. One tree alone may foster three to five such microhabitats. This explains the high endemism (when a species is unique to one locale) rates found in the rainforest. Diversity begets diversity.

Botanists actually distinguish thirty to forty different types of rainforests, from evergreen lowland forest and evergreen mountain forest, to tropical evergreen alluvial forest to semideciduous forest. Equatorial evergreen forests in the center of the tropical band between the Tropic of Cancer and the Tropic of Capricorn areas have an average temperature of 80 degrees and 160 to 400 inches of rainfall a year. Moving away from the equator, the climate gradually becomes more seasonal with less and less rain, eventually developing a pronounced dry season and an average of only 40 to 160 inches in tropical moist forests. Tambopata, with its lowland rainforests somewhat south of the equator, falls into this category, averaging 118 inches a year with temperatures fluctuating between 78 and 93 degrees Fahrenheit during the day, dropping to 66 to 78 degrees at night, although cold fronts during the drier season can push temperatures below 50 degrees.

We spend the better part of the first day in training, in part by design and in part because of the persistent heavy rain. As a group we work our way through a thirty-page training packet, complete with examples and written tests. The principal investigator, Donald Brightsmith, then grades these tests and reviews any mistakes by Earthwatchers in one-on-one sessions. He wants to ensure the quality of his data, of course, but more generally, to also remind Earthwatchers that their focus is volunteer-oriented rather than vacation-oriented. Nothing like a round of tests to do that. And despite the striking setting and amazing all-you-can-eat meals, 4:00 A.M. wake-up calls certainly reinforce that work objective.

Speaking of objectives, why are we studying macaws instead of some other brilliant long-tailed parrots of the Neotropics? Turns out, our answer is more than feather-deep. While these creatures are indeed a charismatic focal point for conservation, they also have decidedly big brains. As Ian Tizard, of the Schubot Exotic Bird Health Center with the College of Veterinary Medicine & Biomedical Sciences at Texas A&M, explains, "They are considered to be

among the most intelligent of all birds and also one of the most affectionate—
it is believed they are sensitive to human emotions."[10] Further, it doesn't hurt
that macaws breed from age three to thirty and live as long as sixty years
or more, providing plenty of opportunities for study. In short, they are a true
flagship species and an important ecotourism resource, as hinted by the
Rainforest Expeditions logo depicting their silhouettes since its inception
in 1992 by Eduardo Nycander and Kurt Holle.

Macaws exist across a range of territory in Latin America, from Panama
to eastern Brazil and Bolivia, but, like many parrots worldwide, they are
declining or locally extinct in much of that range. Indeed, according
to the International Union for Conservation of Nature, the parrot family,
Psittacidae, has the highest number of threatened species of any bird family.[11]
Approximately 30 percent of all parrot species are threatened globally, and
that figure rises to 37 percent of Neotropical parrots. Currently, five species
of macaws are extinct, and of the remaining seventeen species, three are critically endangered, four endangered, two vulnerable, and one near threatened.[12]

Such dismal numbers drive the research here at Tambopata. They have
from its very humble beginnings, when Eduardo Nycander, a former architecture student in Lima, partnered with Kurt Holle to open the Tambopata
Research Center in 1989. The two, using earlier work by legendary specialist
Charles Munn with the Wildlife Conservation Society (WCS), an organization
for which each of them had served as research assistants in Manu National
Park in the late 1980s, found that part of the bird's low rate of reproduction
was attributable to insufficient nesting holes in the virgin rainforest. After
landing funding for a pilot project from WCS, Nycander changed gears from
designing houses for people to creating humble abodes for birds. The first
attempts in 1990 featured 650-pound palm trunks hollowed out by machete,
but soon evolved to be much more manageable.[13]

Donald Brightsmith, fresh off his PhD in zoology at Duke University,
took over the operations in 1999 and established four areas of research: nest
monitoring, success of natural nests compared to artificial ones of PVC
or wood, avian use of the clay lick, and observation of tourist activity. During
my stint with Brightsmith, Tambopata hosted thirty-four nests for macaws.
Twenty-one of these were active, with eighteen in use by scarlet macaws, two
by red-and-green macaws, and one by a chestnut-fronted macaw. Half of these
were natural, with another fourteen made of PVC and three more of wood.

My task was to observe daily behavior and reactions to tourists at one of these active nesting sites or the clay lick itself. Each volunteer was paired daily with a partner and assigned either a six-hour morning or six-hour afternoon shift, which together covered all daylight hours under the canopy. Our directions were clear. Speak only in whispers to avoid being a distraction, and avoid eye contact with your partner as you alternate eyes on the nest every five minutes. To miss an entry or exit from the nest would compromise Brightsmith's data set.

In terms of specific data, we record the arrivals and departures of the nesting adults as well as number in the nest, weather (sun, rain, fog, cloudy), and the presence of potential competitors or predators. The data we gather helps determine incubation, brooding, and feeding time schedules for other parts of this Tambopata project. It also shapes additional studies on the effectiveness of nest boxes and annual reports on the impacts of tourism. Five-minute shifts don't sound like a tall task, but it's easy to get distracted amid the 150-foot trees, not to mention the plethora of enchanting epiphytes and lianas. Even though the name "liana" might be unfamiliar, the uninitiated would still recognize them as an iconic jungle image. These long-stemmed woody vines are rooted in soil at ground level and exploit nearby trees for support, reaching toward sunlight at the top of the canopy.

One strategy that helps Earthwatchers retain our focus is to continually remind ourselves that this is an urgent project. Macaw numbers have been decreasing since the 1960s due to three major threats. One is local hunting, either for food or merely decorative feathers. A second threat is basic habitat loss. Macaws require slow-growing, century-old trees for nesting. These are the trees with deep, dry nest cavities large enough for big birds, and one square mile of virgin rainforest typically holds as few as one to two such nest sites.[14] Clearing for crops, ranching, and logging makes matters all the worse. More than an acre and a half of tropical rainforest is lost every second, in fact, according to Rainforest Action Network.

The third threat is the most devastating of all, the pet trade demands from North America and Europe. This is despite a 1973 Peruvian law forbidding the export of rainforest birds. There is also the United States ban on the import of wild macaws thanks to the Wild Bird Conservation Act in 1992. Further, the Convention on International Trade in Endangered Species (CITES) shifted the scarlet macaw to Appendix I in August 1985,[15] which allows trade only of birds bred in captivity. Still, while legal trade numbers decreased notably, at least in the United States, over the past two decades, a thriving black market continues to foster parrot smuggling in many quarters.[16]

To corral their valuable targets, which may be worth as much as $30,000 each, poachers often resort to cutting down nesting trees to reach the chicks, reducing the already narrow reproduction options for the remaining macaws that escape the poacher's clutches.

Total worldwide black market trade in wild and exotic animals generates billions each year, according to the nonprofit group TRAFFIC.[17] After guns and drug trafficking, Interpol lists illicit wildlife third among lucrative illegal enterprises, averaging $10 billion annually.[18] But it's worse. Of the several million individual birds calculated in these numbers, only those that actually reach the pet market alive are reflected in the tally. For each that survives, another ten die during capture and transit. These birds are literally being loved to death.

And as if that were not enough, all this is complicated by low reproduction rates. Esteemed ornithologist Charles Munn found that, of one hundred macaw pairs, only ten to twenty even attempt to reproduce annually. From this pairing, as few as six chicks fledge, meaning they fly away from the nest. Now Brightsmith, with ample acknowledgment of his predecessors, is finding that 60 percent of the nests in Tambopata are fledging. Still, without intervention, for every two chicks that fledge, one dies of malnutrition. In his studies of one-chick versus two-or-more-chick broods, Brightsmith found that chicks that starve weigh only a third as much as their oldest nest mates. Armed with this knowledge and the understanding that the first seven days after hatching are most crucial, he implemented a supplemental feeding protocol to save younger siblings.[19]

This is on my mind as I ponder the days ahead. I'm also thinking about the blueprint Tambopata provides for other operations. The TRC model demonstrates that tourism and research can be mutually beneficial. Researchers receive much-needed funding for logistical support, from food and lodging to work space, transportation, and even permit assistance, not to mention free labor. At the same time, tourist operations win uniquely valuable windows into conservation research, ones they readily exploit in marketing materials. Still, as Brightsmith asserts, "Ecotourism is not the silver bullet. It's not going to solve all your problems, but you can turn that money around to make a difference."[20]

Conservation biology emerged as a discipline in the 1980s, and ecotourism followed shortly thereafter. Billed as conservation holidays or tourism with a conscience, ecotourism essentially meets three key characteristics highlighted back in our introduction: it focuses on the outdoors, minimizes its ecological footprint, and directly enhances the economic fortunes of those who live in these locales, not just a corporate headquarters in a distant land.[21]

But ecotourism is not always uncontroversial. Neither is the work Earthwatch does immune from critique. For years, Earthwatch, although itself not an ecotourism operation, drew criticism about the reliability of the data gathered by its volunteers. Even as that criticism diminishes, the scientists Earthwatch funds struggle to find the right balance between typical volunteers and those that can stay longer than two to three weeks, offering a richer payback for each investment made in training time. Over nearly ten years, from December 2000 to July 2012, Brightsmith estimates his 407 volunteers were worth the investment, and Earthwatch offered a consistently reliable source of funding.[22]

By Saturday morning the rain clears and everyone is excited for the first day of observations—alas, everyone but me and one other unlucky soul. Instead of the field, I'm assigned, along with Ellen, a herpetologist with her own Earthwatch grant in Brazil's Pantanal, to enter observation data from three years earlier. Everyone will get a shot at that unwelcome task, we just happened to draw the unfortunate straws today. Although tedious, it's necessary for the study, and it turns out to be a beneficial window into the daily activities of Brightsmith, because Ellen and I are holed up for a good portion of the morning in the research room with him.

Brightsmith, who reminds me of a confident graduate professor of mine several years back in both his accent and mannerisms, is much more of a fix-it man than I would have expected. Breaking any stereotype of a stodgy scientist one might have, he eagerly jumps from task to task, including scaling a young sapling outside our window to improve radio reception for the lodge, for example.

The morning assignment also allows me to learn about my compatriot in data entry and her own project in the Pantanal, one of the world's largest wetlands at 150,000 square kilometers. Similar to the Amazon, two-thirds of the Pantanal is in Brazil, but this time the remaining third is split between only two countries, Bolivia and Paraguay. The main threats to its environment stem not from within the Pantanal but the highlands outside it as residue from farming pesticides and fertilizer inevitably flow into these waters. Earthwatch brought my fellow volunteer here to Tambopata to observe another of its funded sites, and later that week she gives us an engaging evening presentation about it.

During and between meals that day, I also learn about my other fellow volunteers, four of whom are from the international financial services corporation, Hong Kong Shanghai Bank Corporation (HSBC). It turns out that HSBC is now Earthwatch's largest corporate sponsor. Its first partnership, a five-year program from 2002 to 2006, sent some 2,000 of its 270,000 employees on expedition trips around the globe. As Simon Martin, head of Group Corporate Sustainability at HSBC, explains, "Through our partnership, many thousands of HSBC employees have been involved first-hand in tackling climate change and environmental issues. They have contributed to making HSBC a more sustainable business and have gathered invaluable data to improve scientists' understanding of the global environment. This activity makes a real difference and is at the heart of HSBC values."[23]

More approaches like this are needed. It might not seem like much at first, just a proverbial drop in the bucket for a corporate giant like HSBC. The rationale might not even be the reasons Mr. Martin asserts, the purpose instead being mere corporate "greenwash," an astute public relations move that exploits growing popularity of all things green. The truth is it doesn't really matter, at least in this case. What matters is what HSBC employees do after their experiences and whether HSBC continues such programs down the road. Returning to Martin Luther King, Jr.'s, pearls of wisdom, "History will have to record that the greatest tragedy of the this period of social transition was not the strident clamor of the bad people, but the appalling silence of the good." We need more folks like these well-placed HSBC Earthwatchers to speak out if we are ever going to reach the requisite tipping point to take more meaningful action against climate change. Continued silence won't cut it.

chapter seventeen

NURTURING NATURE—AT THE NEST

WHAT STRIKES MOST PEOPLE initially about a healthy tropical rainforest probably isn't the heat. In fact, with generous cover from the canopy above, it's usually not as hot as people expect, with temperatures typically hovering in the mid-eighties. That unexpected relief shapes first impressions of the rainforest, but it's the darkness, even in the middle of the day, that really catches people off guard.

Trees need light, of course, and in the rainforest there is great competition for it. Trees grow high and wide, which helps prevent competitors from shading them out. The end result, for those of us restricted to the forest floor, is that hardly any sunlight filters through the dense canopy, as little as 1 to 2 percent of it hitting the ground below.[1] Strong sunlight only penetrates where there has been a disturbance, where older, long-established trees have fallen.

This is where another misconception arises, especially when we use the popular synonym for rainforests: "the jungle." One of the first images the term conjures up is the stuff of Tarzan legend, a web of dense, interlocking vines impeding your every move. In fact, the term *jungle* comes from the Sanskrit word *jangala*, meaning "impenetrable." The reality is much different, though. With so little light penetrating the canopy, the so-called jungle floor is essentially free of undergrowth, and, thus, relatively easy to navigate. It's only where trees have been removed that secondary growth takes hold, creating a labyrinth of impassable vegetation.

But something even more bothersome develops when trees are removed in large numbers. The health of the entire ecosystem suffers. To understand why, let's take a quick look at the other end of the trees, the soils in which they are rooted. One of the great ironies of the rainforest is that its soils, those that support the most diverse ecosystem on Earth, are surprisingly thin and poor.

This never dawned on early explorers. With such an abundance of diversity, they assumed they were among the richest soils in the world. Like many more to follow, and even some today, they were deceived. The reason is that the rainforest is a closed ecosystem; the soils depend entirely on the trees themselves for their replenishment. As Russ Mittermeier, the head of Conservation International, explains, rainforests are analogous to castles built on sand.[2]

It works like this. When leaves fall, they decompose rapidly in the humidity of a rainforest. Here in southeastern Peru, a little more than a dozen degrees south of the equator, for example, it takes just a few weeks for them to decompose, compared to the months it takes in the temperate forests of New England. And of course, when this happens here in the tropics, the nutrients are quickly sucked back into the surrounding vegetation. So what you smell is not just the pungent aroma of death and decay, but the sweet scent of life. You smell both death and rebirth together.

Of course, if there is nothing left to die, there can be no more rebirthing. If you clear a large tract of rainforest, it will never really regenerate. Its sources of nutrition have been stolen, just like the aboriginal children in much of twentieth-century Australia. Only in the younger soils of volcanic regions such as Central America, which have not yet lost mineral nutrients through thousands of years of leaching, is regeneration within cleared tracts of rainforest even possible.[3]

The remaining nutrients that are released into the soil, particularly when tracts have been burned, are then washed away during intense tropical rains; they no longer have tree root systems to hold them in place. This means that initially productive farming on these extensively cleared soils is often compromised still further—it almost never continues beyond a season or two. That's usually when the cattle ranchers come in, but the typical rule of thumb there is, after three to five years, these newly created pastures no longer support enough cattle to turn a profit either.

What does turn a profit, increasingly, is something very different. Rainforests are a veritable first-aid kit of medicinal plants waiting to be discovered. The key here is their richness in secondary metabolites, particularly alkaloids, a category of chemical compounds most commonly found in tropical plants. Tropical plants produce alkaloids to protect themselves from insect attacks and disease. As famed ethnobotanist Mark Plotkin asserts, "Whenever you're in the rainforest, you are in the middle of chemical warfare that has been ongoing for hundreds of thousands, if not millions of years."[4]

That translates into a library of tremendous medicinal potential. The United States Cancer Institute, in fact, identifies three thousand plants with anticancer potential; 70 percent of those hail from rainforests across the globe. Just two of note within the Amazon are the root of a rambling ground vine called "suma," or as it's known in the States, Brazilian ginseng (*Pfaffia paniculata*), and the inner bark of a huge canopy tree, Pau d'arco (*Tabebuia avellandae*), which is often called "purple lapacho" for its stunning purple flowers.

Applications aren't restricted to cancer. Additional medicinal benefits include compounds used to treat arthritis, bronchitis, diabetes, dysentery, glaucoma, heart disease, hypertension, malaria, muscle tension, and tuberculosis; there are also anesthetics, cough suppressants, enzymes, hormones, laxatives, and antiseptics. Fully a fourth of all prescription drugs today contain ingredients derived from tropical plants, according to Pace University Fellow and former *New York Times* environmental reporter Andrew Revkin.[5] Yet, despite such numbers, less than 1 percent of more than a quarter-million known plant species have been thoroughly tested for medicinal potential.

One that has is quinine, an alkaloid from the bark of the cinchona tree. Used to treat malaria, the miracle compound was discovered by two French doctors in 1820, albeit fully two hundred years after Jesuits first learned of its powers and centuries more after indigenous medicine men identified its curative properties. In deference to their predecessors, Joseph Pelletier and Joseph Caventou named the alkaloid "quinine," after the Indian name *quinaquina*, meaning "bark of barks."[6]

Of course, none of that is on my mind at the moment. I'm too busy trying to manage a barrage of safety warnings from my well-meaning Earthwatch briefing.

For starters, there's heat and humidity to deal with in the Amazon. While it's not as hot as you might expect, it's still pretty darn warm. And you need sunscreen when emerging from beneath the canopy, at the river's edge or on the embankment across from the clay lick.

Even more important, with the constant humidity, you need water, and lots of it. As one quickly finds out, you sweat even when sitting, and even under the shaded canopy. Dehydration is a constant threat, and one must continually gulp down liquids to avoid headaches, disorientation, or worse. Thankfully, living in central Florida prepares me well, and only my camera suffers any ill effects, its extension lens becoming less and less responsive to my manual adjustments each day.

Next on my list of precautionary measures is an array of stinging and biting creatures. I've already mentioned scorpions as a potential nemesis. Beyond them, there are ants, bees, and caterpillars to contend with, not to mention snakes and spiders. Heck, there are even stinging trees down here, with black, toothpick-sized spines in the *Astrocaryum* palms, for example, that are sharper than sewing needles. It's apparently an adaptation to discourage climbing mammals from eating its fruit. Certainly works for me.

The tree trunks aren't your only worry, though. One of the more common injuries in the rainforest stems from their impressive root system. With such poor soil, roots here don't dig deep. They stretch wide, extending like giant's veins across the forest floor. A fifteen-foot radius of tangled roots sticking out above ground is not uncommon, serving a vital function of sucking up as much nutrients as possible in the top couple of centimeters of soil, plus the added benefit of buttressing the top-heavy tree during violent storms.

It's easy to take your eyes off these low-lying hurdles, to get distracted by something at eye level or above. Inevitably, people trip. They turn an ankle or cut themselves falling.

That's what makes it all the more ludicrous for me to accept our guide Reuben's offer a few days later to go for an afternoon run along the Tambopata trails. He runs the trails regularly, though, and I trust he'll do his best to minimize my chances of self-destruction. I don't regret the decision. The five-kilometer or so jaunt is truly exhilarating, a welcome counterbalance to my high-caloric buffet dinners the last couple days, and I emerge unscathed, thanks to diligent concentration on the path before me, and probably a little luck.

Then again, as Louis Pasteur stated in late 1854, chance favors the prepared mind. Whether racing through the trails of Tambopata or preparing my next class lesson back home in the States, the odds of something going badly decrease as you become better prepared. It's not rocket science. It's so simple, in fact, that my youngest has understood it since age two. Why is it, then, that we as a society so stubbornly resist calls to better prepare for the risks presented by climate change?

Again, it's not like it is rocket science. Maybe the pain isn't intense enough yet? Or maybe we need a more visceral image of what the pain could be?

I'll tell you one risk that usually startles folks to attention, at least newly minted visitors to the Amazon like myself. Talk about visceral images of pain. It's something called the canero, a fish that is apparently attracted to urine and has the disturbing ability to swim up the urethra, where it unfurls a nasty set of spines and attaches itself to the urinary tract. A parasite, it feeds on blood and body tissue, expanding to perhaps twice its original size. Thin and shaped like a four- to sixteen-inch eel, the canero is also virtually translucent and difficult to see. Nevertheless, you can avoid it by not urinating in the water, by swimming with swim trunks, or by avoiding swimming altogether. Chance favors the prepared mind. I'm opting for the last option.

Of course, in listing safety issues within the Amazon, we still haven't mentioned half of them. When legendary British biologist J. B. S. Haldane was asked toward the end of his distinguished career if he had learned anything about the Creator, he famously retorted, "Yes, he seems to have an inordinate fondness for beetles." Beetles and other insects, as you may know, represent more than half of all known living organisms, and perhaps as much as 90 percent of animal life on Earth.[7] Most of them live here in the tropics.

That means insects are first and foremost on my mind when it comes to safety on this journey, especially the further I get through my briefing. Turns out, insects fly straight up after striking you, so it's always best to tuck in your long-sleeved, light-colored (mosquitoes prefer dark colors!) shirts and pants. Tucking in your shirt certainly makes you look presentable, but it looks more than a little funny to tuck my pants into my white athletic socks and sandals. Then again, I'm not out here to win style points.

For the next two weeks, my newfound fashion statement is complemented, without compromise, by a healthy dose of mosquito repellant, one with at least 35 percent DEET in it. Of course, the adjective healthy is up to a bit of interpretation here. If this precautionary chemical can corrode my plastic ironman watchband in a matter of weeks and kill pesky mosquitoes in a matter of minutes if not quicker, what else is it doing to me?

I guess life is full of trade-offs, a continual carousel of decisions as to which action is less risky or more rewarding. The problem when it comes to climate change is that many of us don't fully understand the risks and rewards being presented. In fact, in many cases, these risks and rewards are misrepresented—or we aren't even given the option of making a decision ourselves. Instead, it's a select few financial interests that directly conflict with our own interests who make the decision for us: the fossil fuel industry.

Well, at least nobody ever came down with malaria in Posada Amazonas or Tambopata Research Center, that is, not to Brightsmith's knowledge. Then again, it takes six to eight weeks to show symptoms of malaria, and Earthwatch volunteers don't stay that long. It's more than possible that someone came down with it well after leaving, without him knowing.

Actually, more than malaria, my biggest threat here at Tambopata is a small biting fly, or more accurately, the protozoan transmitted by this fly. Affectionately known as Lucy by my roommate Berwyn, the protozoan causes the disease leishmaniasis. Fortunately, it is only carried by a small percentage of these flies, which cannot penetrate clothing and are only active when the sun goes down, from roughly 5:30 P.M. to 7:00 A.M. That said, there is no vaccination against it, and the cure entails a full twenty-one days of painful injections of glucantime. Needless to say, evenings at the lodge, which the fly is known to frequent, are spent encased in a protective cocoon of long pants and long-sleeved shirts, all not-so-stylishly tucked in. And bathroom trips are kept to a bare minimum.

Speaking of vaccinations, I wracked up $425 worth in shots in the months before making the trip down here and am slated for another round, albeit not quite as expensive, on returning to the Northern Hemisphere. This covers me for tetanus, diphtheria, typhoid, yellow fever, and hepatitis A and B as well as measles, mumps, and rubella.

Yellow fever, in particular, is apparently a big deal down here, as proof of vaccination is required when you land in Puerto Maldonado. I'm told they won't turn you away if you can't provide a validated yellow international certificate, but, instead, vaccinate you right there at the airport.[8] Of course, while it lasts ten years, the vaccination does not fully kick in until ten days after you receive the shot, so I'm not sure that's an ideal option. Again, chance favors the prepared mind. My advice for any type of international travel is to consult the CDC travel information website at least a half-year before you depart.

Yellow fever is a serious disease caused by a virus spread by infected mosquitoes. Found in certain parts of Africa and South America, it can cause fever, flu-like symptoms, vomiting of blood, and jaundice, a yellowing of the skin and eyes. Even scarier, yellow fever can cause liver, kidney, and respiratory or other organ-system failure, leading to death, according to my pamphlet from Orlando Regional Health.

Still another disease of concern is tuberculosis, which, ironically, I'm being tested for as I write these pages, years after my Amazon visit. TB comes from bacteria that typically affect the lungs, spreading from person to person through the air. When someone with TB coughs, sneezes, or spits, they propel TB germs. Inhaling just a handful creates a new infection. After HIV/AIDS, it's the second-greatest killer due to a single infectious agent.[9] Thankfully, unlike AIDS, unless it's the drug-resistant variety, TB is not only preventable but curable.

None of that is on my mind at the moment, though. I'm too excited to get out in the field and explore the TRC trails outlined in Figure 17.1. For today's assignment I've drawn an afternoon shift, which means the rare treat of sleeping till after sunrise and enjoying a hearty breakfast buffet, complete with an array of fresh juices. This morning it's a choice between pineapple and papaya. Being an American, I go with both. After gorging myself as usual, I don some rubber boots and enjoy a beautiful morning stroll with our guide Reuben and my roommate Berwyn.

Reuben has a wealth of experience, and I'm eager to learn as much as possible from him. He was a park ranger years ago in the early 1990s, becoming a guide in 1999 and moving over to the macaw project in 2003. Striking out on the series of interconnecting trails that spin like a cobweb from the lodge, it helps to be quiet when seeking out wildlife. Even better, it helps to have a companion who knows the forest, and Reuben definitely fits that bill. Over a couple-hour stroll, we see an owl butterfly, squirrel monkey, and a ruddy quail dove, among other species.

With white goggle-like eyes contrasting with its head and mouth area, the squirrel monkey, shown in Figure 17.2, is a small, dexterous creature, able to easily leap through trees over distances of more than eight feet. Its yellow arms and legs are balanced by a black tail, although unlike its larger cousin the spider monkey, it is not a prehensile tail, meaning it's not able to hold objects. In much of the Amazon, monkeys such as these have been heavily hunted and quickly learned to keep their distance from people. Thankfully, the absence of hunting for decades now in Tambopata means they have no reason to fear us, and I am able to get a couple stellar shots. This group of maybe two dozen moves quickly through the lower canopy, periodically mixing foraging with play and announcing their presence with remnants of their meal crashing to the forest floor around us.

17.1 TRC trail map. Source: Jeff Cremer, Rainforest Expeditions at http://www.perunature.com/map-of-peru.html.

In yet another example of interdependence, when squirrel monkeys disappear, it's bad news for people, too. Mosquitoes frequent the zones well above the forest floor where monkeys reside and provide them with a consistent blood supply. Without monkeys, mosquitoes must search out new sources toward the forest floor, sources such as people. That means that where monkeys disappear, malaria invariably spikes.

Another impressive find that morning comes from the plant kingdom. It's the parasitic strangler fig. Interestingly, strangler figs begin life as an epiphyte that is not parasitic—they merely use trunks, trees, and leaves for support and to collect water and nutrients without actually directly harming their hosts. Strangler figs start as seeds excreted by birds or monkeys high in the canopy. They then unfurl long, thin roots that reach the forest floor and thicken over the years into a fused mass that, eventually, completely encases its host tree. In the end, this gracious host dies and decays inside the strangler's death grip, providing still more nutrients with its passing.

When we return to the lodge, I quickly jot down some notes from the morning hike and scramble to pack a sack lunch with my supplies for the afternoon nest-observation assignment. I have some borrowed binoculars, a clipboard, data sheets, pencils, and a comfortable deck chair, all for my six-and-a-half-hour sit. While the work is relatively low-tech, it's decidedly labor intensive, not in terms of physical exertion but because of the concentration required over long stretches watching the nests.

Just as we are heading out on the trail, an amazing sound resonates through the thick tropical air. It sounds like a gale-force wind. I

17.2 Squirrel monkey.

immediately look up, expecting a dark foreboding sky, but there's no sign of an approaching storm. There's not even a breeze. Then, out of the corner of my eye, I catch a splotch of fur in the green lower canopy on the edge of the clearing. It's a red howler monkey.

Red howler monkeys such as the one in Figure 17.3, covered in reddish-brown fur except for the gray encircling their mouths, eyes, and ears, are a must-hear in any visit to the Amazon. Actually, they are kind of difficult to miss, being the second-loudest creature on Earth and all.[10] With calls as loud as ninety decibels, nearly as loud as a train, they can be heard up to five kilometers away.[11] Their long howl builds into a crescendo that sounds remarkably like wind rushing through a tunnel.[12] Famed ethnobotanist Mark Plotkin describes the call as "an unearthly din that one explorer imaginatively likened to the sound of a jaguar making love to a dragon."[13] In reality, it is merely one howler calling to another to mark its nesting tree.

Wow, I never would have expected a noise like that from such an un-assuming creature. I snap a couple quick photos with my film SLR and hustle to catch Reuben. My roommate Berwyn and I are assigned nest 16, named the "Macario nest" on Trail C, near a small kapok tree just beyond a pedestrian bridge. It has one scarlet macaw egg in it.

17.3 Red howler monkey.

Scarlet macaws traditionally nest in the hollows of emergent trees, but this one is a vertical PVC construction. Brightsmith continued the practice of his predecessor of using fake nests of wood or plastic. The macaws seem to be fine with them, and it is much easier for researchers.

We are keeping track of how much time the adults spend in the nest by recording every time a bird goes in or out from the nest.[14] This means we work in pairs. Someone is always watching while their partner records the observations. Every five minutes, Berwyn and I switch roles from observer to scribe. To date, Brightsmith has found that 95 percent of the time at least one bird is in the nest before the eggs hatch. Once a chick hatches, the parents spend more time away. Quite simply, as chicks grow, they require more and more feeding effort by their parents.

We notice when the macaws do emerge they appear a bit roughed up, but Brightsmith warned us that battered tail feathers are a physical sign of nesting. Interestingly, males and females look alike, so macaws can only be distinguished during breeding and nesting when the female incubates for four weeks while the male brings home food that he regurgitates into her mouth. Since pairs typically mate in December, our team is well positioned in mid-January to see a range of chicks and eggs. Siblings tend to hatch one to five days apart, but the eldest always enjoys a competitive advantage and is fed first at every meal, not incidentally another reason why we are here in the first place. With birds this endangered, we want to give all the chicks the best opportunity to survive, including the younger ones.

The next morning is a full-dark jungle experience. Actually, it was the night before, too, during an after-dinner walk with Cesar, and this morning feels like an extension of that evening. We awake at 4:00 A.M. that morning, leaving the lodge at 4:30 and arriving at nest 22, known as "Odio," in time to start observations right after 5 A.M. After all, the early bird gets the worm.

All along the walk to the nest, I'm taking care to avoid the ubiquitous tree roots and juggling a collection of clipboards and data sheets, cameras and camp chairs, and food and water, not to mention the requisite flashlight. We negotiate Trail C to Trail B, one of the longer hikes to a nest at approximately 1.5 miles. I know that doesn't sound like much, but, trust me, in pitch-black darkness, and with hours of lost sleep, it seems like forever.

Odio is another vertical PVC nest, this one with one thirty-day-old scarlet macaw chick. I'm partnered with Berwyn again, and, as we chat away the early morning hours, we notice a long line of tiny green leaf pieces marching in single file right through our observation site. We aren't quite sure what to make of it at first, but then it dawns on us. These are leaf-cutter ants, one of many ant species of the rainforest; in fact, esteemed entomologist E. O. Wilson once identified forty-three species of ant on a single Peruvian rainforest tree.

More commonly seen at night, leaf-cutter ants are no direct threat, but we remain cautious, as they have been known to experiment with more than leaves. It's not unusual for them to sample, for instance, tents, clothes, and bags, so we quickly move our belongings several feet away from this impromptu conga line.

These little fellows clutch snippets of leaves, often an astounding fifty times their own weight, high above their heads en route back to underground nests, where they then chew their samples into pulp. In total, a single colony may house a million ants, displacing as much as twenty cubic meters of soil.

Here's where it gets even more interesting. Leaf-cutter ants cannot digest the leaves themselves, so they cultivate a fungus on this pulp, and this fungus becomes their dietary staple. Their larvae feed exclusively on it, and adults require the enzyme the fungus produces to digest their main food source, the sap from the collected leaves.

To make all this possible, leaf-cutter ants don't just plant fungal gardens, though. They actively manage them, fertilizing their crops with fecal matter and producing hormones to accelerate fungal growth as well as

17.4 Peruvian climber checks the nest.

17.5 Aldo, at the time a veterinarian from Lima, quickly measures the young chick.

antibiotics to keep out undesirable bacteria. As Mark Plotkin succinctly summarizes, "Ants cannot live without the fungi, nor fungi live without ants."[15]

It is precisely this web of interactions among species that makes our world so fascinating. It is also yet another factor in what makes the long-term implications of climate change so difficult to anticipate. Some species will do well in a warmer world. Others will not. Yet, even with this knowledge, we do not fully appreciate the overall impact of interdependence on the extinction ledger. Just how bad will it become? How much worse than the current spasm we created, one thousand to ten thousand times the natural background rate, can it get?

Some seeds, for example, don't even germinate until they pass through the digestive systems of certain animals. These seeds are physically damaged, or scarified, so they can absorb water and become metabolically active. The calvaria tree's perhaps partial dependence on the dodo bird is an unfortunate case in point; once that flightless bird from the island of Mauritius became extinct in 1861, calvaria seeds seemingly struggled to germinate.[16] The more we learn, the more we realize how much we have still to learn. That lesson, though, is not fully understood when it comes to climate change.

Amid all this, it is important to remember, of course, that change is natural. It is the one constant in life. Indeed, dynamism literally defines nature for conservation biologist John Terborgh, from predation to pollination, parasitism to seed dispersal.[17] It's the rate of change today that is so concerning. That is what is unnatural.

So sometimes nature needs a helping hand, a little nurturing of its own. Toward the end of our shift, we get to witness a small piece of that in action. Working in pairs just like Berwyn and I, longer-term volunteers are also assisting Brightsmith. Known with awe by Earthwatchers simply as "the climbers," young Peruvians, such as Jericho in Figure 17.4, check nests here at Tambopata twice a day for the first fourteen days after hatching, then every two to three days after that until the chick fledges. With each visit they weigh the chicks, as you see in Figures 17.5 and 17.6 and feed those that are malnourished.

It's eye-opening to glimpse the wider implications of our monotonous morning of nest observations, and I return to camp that afternoon with renewed appreciation of what it means to be an Amazon researcher. To top that off, Berwyn and I end the perfect day hiking with Reuben once again, this time on a four-mile round trip to the swamp palm forest and its forty-five-foot tower leading into the canopy, but more on that a bit later. For now, suffice it to say, it's clear that even here in remote southeastern Peru, the hand of man is having an impact. What's neat about today is that it was mostly a helping hand, nurturing nature.

17.6 Weighing in: Odio I submits to the scale.

chapter eighteen

AT THE COLPA COLORADO

DESPITE THE EARLY HOUR, I shoot straight out of bed at the sound of the gentle knock outside our room. I'm finally off to the lick this morning, or as it is more commonly referred to in the local Quechua language, the *colpa*.[1] With chunks of shoreline sliding away here each year due to natural erosion, newly exposed riverbanks such as this are found throughout the Amazon basin. At five hundred meters long and twenty to thirty meters high, though, Colpa Colorado is not just any lick. It is the largest known lick in the world, complete with a convenient natural blind roughly 150 meters across from it, an island rising out of the light chocolate-brown Tambopata River.

I'm paired with Brenda, at the time curator of birds from the San Francisco Zoo, but now curator for the Steinhart Aquarium at the California Academy of Sciences. We're assigned to record first arrivals and conduct telemetry that morning. Late each nesting season, Brightsmith traps a handful of macaws in artificial nests and fits them with lightweight radio collars, each with an estimated battery life of twenty-four to forty-two months. Our task, every fifteen minutes throughout the day, is to locate each of these collared birds. Macaws do not migrate in the traditional sense, but track food sources nomad-ically, eating different plants at different times of the year. That essentially means that they migrate short distances each year, and Brightsmith is trying to determine whether this is seasonal by compiling data on how often indi-vidual birds use this lick at different times of the year.

We arrive a little after 4:30 A.M. and set up with two others assigned to the morning shift of observations on the lick, but we are by no means alone. In fact, over the next ten minutes or so, another two dozen tourists from down the river set up an elaborate array of photographic equipment right beside us along the island's edge.

Within moments, rays of sunlight begin to light the lick, steadily brightening more and more of its red surface. As if on cue, a dozen or so chestnut-fronted macaws and red-bellied macaws start screeching. They gather in small groups, perched among aguaje palm and iron trees. Then, with this foreshadowing just a few minutes old, the appropriately named "dance" begins. Smaller parrots are usually the first to fly around the lick, and a group of the aforementioned red-bellied macaws and chestnut-fronted macaws are the initiators today.

Within a couple minutes, a pair of the red-bellied macaws lands first, and a free-for-all ensues shortly thereafter. There's a veritable explosion of color on a canvas of red dirt, as seen in Figure 18.1. For the next thirty to forty minutes, parrot after parrot shoves thumb-sized clumps of clay into their beaks. Yes, they are really eating the dirt!

Our task is to record when the dance begins and what species are responsible for it, as well as what species landed first and at what time. Every five minutes after that, we record the types and numbers of each species currently feeding. New entries must also note the weather and details about the visiting tourists, including their arrival and departure times, the number in the group, the name of the company, and the estimated distance from the lick

18.1 Midmorning clay snack at the Colpa Colorado. Source: Photo by Jeff Wilson, Earthwatch volunteer.

(some remain in their boats rather than joining us on the island). To date, Brightsmith hasn't found any significant negative impact from these visits.

On occasion, a falling leaf or long shadow will startle the entire coterie of birds into the air, quite a colorful sight. And regardless, every half minute or so, there's a rotation, so numbers are constantly changing in the early morning hours. By 8 A.M., the action is tapering off, and we leave the regular shift to test the telemetry. In a few hours, a number of large macaws will return for their late-morning snack, but for all intents and purposes, the feeding frenzy is over.

As with nest-observation crews, Earthwatch volunteers, in two shifts, stay at the lick throughout daylight to document the pattern of lick use by the large macaws. The two on the morning observation shift stay until 11:30 A.M., although from 5:00 to 7:30 A.M. a more experienced staffer typically assists them. Training for the clay lick is more difficult than nest observations, but, again, after 7:30 it's much easier, because usually only large macaws, cobalt-winged parakeets, and a few others stop to sample the sodium.

Brightsmith finds that birds use the lick year round, but most heavily during the breeding season when they feed soil to their chicks, too. On some days, over thirteen hundred parrots touch down.

Lick use falls into two seasons: high season from August to January and low season from February to July. The reason why birds leave is not fully understood, because this doesn't match up precisely with wet and dry seasons. Data from nearby Manu National Park, however, suggest that low lick use and parrot migration away from the lick correspond with low fruit availability periods.[2]

Brightsmith also finds that the size and sociability of parrot species influences the ways birds use the lick.[3] Many of these behaviors, further, seem to reduce the risk of predation. Smaller species favor the sheltered southern end of the lick, for example, while larger parrots and macaws prefer the larger, more open portion toward the northern end. Parakeets, which normally travel in larger social groups, are flexible regarding the time they use the lick, as are large macaws, which use it nearly throughout the day.

Thinking back to three nights ago and the clay lick lecture after dinner by Brightsmith, this is still all unusual behavior. Most parrots around the globe are not migratory. Neither do they eat soil. Called *geophagy*, the intentional consumption of soil by vertebrates is known among several species of mammals worldwide, including deer and rodents as well as primates such as humans. Among birds, though, geophagy is less understood. Of those that are known to eat soil, parrots and pigeons are the most common.

Two main theories exist as to why. One centers on the need for basic mineral supplementation. Since sodium concentration is low in most plants, herbivorous animals may have trouble getting enough in their diet. Yet, as we know, sodium is vital for an array of animal functions, from maintenance of osmotic balance to nerve transmission.

A second theory focuses on the absorption of dietary toxins. Macaws eat fruit, flowers, and leaves, but their ultimate targets are seeds. With mammal-like dexterity, each of their feet has four clawed toes, two facing forward and two backward, which allows them to break through fruit pulp to access the seeds within.[4]

Yet, as we have already seen, many plants in the Amazon have toxic defense chemicals that prevent animals from eating them. These include compounds in the seeds and unripe fruits that comprise the main diet of parrots such as these macaws. In fact, research by U.C. Davis's James Gilardi indicates that the dirt digested by parrots in southeastern Peru neutralizes the toxicity of alkaloids by attaching to them and facilitating their expulsion from the body.[5]

Legendary ornithologist Charles Munn suspects a third rationale may be at work, too, with licks serving a social as well as a physical function. As I witness the lick for the first time and think back to my earlier solo travels, his theory sounds pretty convincing to me. Then again, I'm just a social scientist. Nevertheless, I'm of the same mind as photographer Frans Lanting, who astutely states, "To assume that macaws go to the lick only to eat clay would be like saying that people go to the pub just because they're thirsty."[6]

Looking to the macaw's diet, we find more precise answers. Of approximately nine hundred species of trees in the Madre de Dios region, over one hundred offer food for macaws and parrots, and, from these, macaws ingest an array of valuable minerals. In a 2004 study of bird crop samples, for example, Brightsmith determined natural levels in the diet of phosphorus, potassium, sulfur, sodium, calcium, magnesium, copper, zinc, manganese, iron, and boron. Further, chick crop samples showed much higher levels than are found in clay lick soils for all of these minerals, with the sole exception of sodium. On the other hand, sodium levels at the clay lick show the inverse relationship, reaching 4.5 times higher than the chick crop samples and indicating to Brightsmith that sodium at the lick was the main attraction for these birds.

Recall that the three large macaw species peak here in Tambopata in January, because of increased food supplies, in anticipation of breeding, or both. From this, Brightsmith drew two hypotheses. First, clay lick use may increase during breeding because females require more calcium to make their eggs. Second, adults may need to feed clay to their chicks to compensate for mineral deficiency or toxicity exposure. Mining his data carefully, Brightsmith found that lick use spikes in December just as chicks hatch, then drops in February around a month before the majority of them fledge, indicating it was precisely during the first few weeks of life that chicks consumed soil the most. Brightsmith thought this might be due to low resistance to the toxicity of their diet at such an early age, or to overall nutrient needs. Given that macaw chicks grow so quickly when young, with their weight matching that of adults at around nine hundred grams roughly fifty days after hatching, the latter appears to be key.

Later, I enjoy yet another afternoon hike with our guide Cesar, returning in time to interact with one of the local resident celebrities. Macaws usually lay two to four eggs asynchronously, and they have an incubation period of twenty-six to twenty-eight days. Hatching, too, is asynchronous, which leads to only one or two hatchlings developing to maturity, with fledging occurring roughly eighty-six days after hatching.

Early in the research center's history, scientists tried to save the third and fourth eggs, raising the chicks by hand. The first of these was called Chico, meaning "kid" in Spanish, and all subsequent hand-raised chicks were named similarly in his honor. In total, of the eggs saved in those early years, thirty-two chicks were hand-raised.[7] It was no easy task, akin to raising babies according to Nycander, because the researchers would wake up every hour and a half to birds screaming for formula.[8] Thirteen survived, and seven branched out to live in the wild with mates.

Now, these surviving birds fly freely through the jungle, albeit with their fear of humans gone. This means that many return to the lodge on occasion, gliding through the open-air dining room in search of a prized piece of shiny jewelry or a tasty snack, as seen in Figure 18.2.

The next two days I'm back on nest observations, one an afternoon shift at nest 3, a vertical wooden box named "Hugo" that houses two scarlet macaw chicks, and the other a morning shift at nest 6, a vertical PVC nest named "Invisible." The former is with an interesting older Earthwatch volunteer named Carol, who reminds me in both her diminutive stature and vivacious personality of my grandmother. She is a kind soul with impressive drive, having overcome a serious car accident earlier in her life. Typical of retired Earthwatch volunteers, she is innately curiously and driven to make a difference in the world around her.

18.2 Chico visiting the lodge.

My partner the next day, for what turns out to be my last nest-observation shift, is equally impressive. He works for the same banking conglomerate as my roommate, but that is not what catches my attention. Instead, at least initially, it's his quirkiness and Canadian accent, but quickly thereafter I note his consistently positive demeanor. As I think back on that day and others spent with Jim, I can recall nothing but a smile on his face. My final image will always be of him grinning ear to ear as he distributed handfuls of virtually brand-new gear to the local guides the day we departed. In fact, if I remember correctly, Jim was distributing more than gear I'd seen him use. My guess is he brought many of those supplies purely for donation.

I relay this story because Jim is no longer with us. Approximately a year after returning to his home in Canada, Jim was diagnosed with bone marrow disease, and, despite a valiant fight, his bone marrow transplant failed within a half year. Chemotherapy bought him a few more months, but Jim suffered a heart attack, caught pneumonia, and suffered a serious leg infection, before passing in the summer of 2008.

Jim's story reminds me that life is short, and the material possessions many like me covet are not as valuable as we often think. Jim modeled an adventurous spirit and positive nature we would all be wise to copy.

The story of climate change fits right into this moral. For one, we can get by with less—much, much less. Indeed, we can more than get by. We can be all the happier for it, just as Jim was. Small truly is beautiful, as British economist E. F. Schumacher once asserted. Second, it is crucial that we do not sit around, waiting for things to happen as life passes us by. Instead, take the bull by the horns. Mimic the adventurous spirit of Jim and see the world, establish new relationships and deepen old ones. Third, and perhaps most importantly, remember that perspective shapes not only our day-to-day activities, but also our long-term options. Jim intuitively knew this, whether tackling his Earthwatch duties or fighting for his life against long odds. Like Jim's final battle, confronting climate change is no easy task, but to approach it without optimism is self-defeating—and condemns future generations outright.

Later that afternoon it's back to the palm swamp to view the preferred habitat of the blue-and-yellow macaws. PVC nest boxes have not worked with this species. Blue-and-yellow macaws are quite particular, seeking nest holes narrow enough to discourage predators, but deep enough to be rainproof and protect their eggs and chicks from chilling rain. They show particular affinity for the aguaje palm, what nineteenth-century German naturalist Alexander von Humboldt labeled the "tree of life." Aguaje palms have an array of applications. Their durable fibers are woven into hammocks, and their nutritious fruit is as rich in vitamin C as citrus and richer in vitamin A than carrots or spinach.

More specifically, blue-and-yellows prefer tall, *dead* aguaje palms within healthy swamps such as this one. Brightsmith manages a small section of this swamp, believed to be a remnant of a long-since-receded oxbow lake, and encourages nesting by periodically clearing out understory vegetation and cutting off the tops of a handful of aguaje palms. These dead palms remain standing another four to seven years, providing ideal nesting habitat. Indeed, he finds that 24 percent are occupied by nesting macaws.[9]

From an aging, forty-five-foot scaffolding tower, we gain a 360-degree view of this part of the swamp, including a nearby dead aguaje palm with an ideal hollowed-out hole in its trunk about sixty feet up. It has met the approval of a blue-and-yellow macaw pair colonizing it, and I catch a fleeting glimpse of one.

Sadly, outside of this protected natural wetlands, many other aguaje palms, namely the females, have been chopped down by locals in search of what is widely considered one of the most nutritious fruits of the jungle, one that is also tasty as jam, juice, and in ice cream. It is even fermented into wine. Yet the popularity of the fruits is probably not their most significant threat. Despite being a staple food source in wide swaths of the Amazon basin, the aguaje palm's habitat is disappearing, increasingly seen as more desirable for conversion into rice paddies.

The next morning I'm back at the Colpa Colorado for a full morning shift of monitoring with Carol. It's a reprise of my visit a few days before, but this time we stay till lunch and better grasp what an entire half-day at the lick feels like.

The day concludes with an afternoon hike through the jungle with Cesar and Berwyn, including a glimpse of a tapir, or least what once was a tapir, as this fellow had died at least a half day earlier. Tapirs are South America's largest terrestrial mammal, with adults growing to over five hundred pounds. Shy and usually nocturnal, they are odd-looking beasts, with the body of a pig and the hooves of a horse, along with the snout of a rhinoceros and the ears of a hippopotamus, which is actually its nearest relative. As esteemed ethnobotanist and author Mark Plotkin describes, the tapir "looks like it was pieced together from spare parts found in a taxidermist's attic."[10]

Our time is coming to an end by now, and it's only natural to grow retrospective about the entire experience. There's still a final day of activities and nearly two days of travel to reach home, including a dreadful redeye back to the States, complete with the requisite sleepwalking through customs.

All along the way, though, I think about what core lessons Tambopata offers to the subject of climate change. One is fairly easy. The literature is littered with critiques of development, each of which starts first and foremost with a condemnation of road construction within the Amazon.

More destructive than logging, in fact, are the events road-building sets in motion. Some 80 percent of deforested land lies within thirty miles of a road.[11] It's what I call the Kevin Costner's *Field of Dreams* effect. Build it, and they will come. When it comes to the rainforest, there are no yellow brick roads of salvation. Indeed, as John Terborgh contends, more often, "Roads are the death knell of the rainforest."[12] "The roads bring destruction, under a mask called progress," concurs Jaime da Silva Araujo, a rubber-tapper leader from Amazonas.[13]

Interestingly, Tambopata doesn't have a road. It has a river, which highlights an important caveat to the green critique of roads, even in remote regions of the world such as this. Some degree of access is necessary. Environmentalists cannot fall into the trap former California Governor Arnold Schwarzenegger so eloquently labeled as that of the prohibitionist at a fraternity party. You can't always say no. We must recognize that ideals mean nothing without practical opportunity.

Unfortunately, the reverse is also a constant threat, with practical opportunity too often trumping ideals. For example, in most Latin American countries, practical opportunity dictates removing the rainforest. It's the simplest way to establish title to unoccupied territory, because deforestation legally improves the land. That's a mistake, too, of course. We have to change that faulty calculus. Rainforest lands should be valued not for what is done to them, like farming, but for what is not done to them. Yet, sadly, slash-and-burn agriculture continues, decade after decade.

In the 1970s, Brazil's military dictatorship epitomized this practice, promoting an occupy-it-or-lose-it philosophy with the Amazon. Tens of thousands were encouraged to escape poverty in Brazil's overpopulated south and northeast. If they failed to develop their land productively within five years, they forfeited rights to permanent ownership and control reverted to the federal government. As governmental lawyer Felicio Pontes suggests, this demonstrated a "predatory, unsustainable model of development," one based on timber extraction and cattle.

To make matters worse, Brazil encouraged deforestation further with its well-utilized 50 percent rule. Here, while only half one's land can be cleared legally, a massive loophole allows owners to sell their uncleared half to someone else, who then clears half and sells half, with iterations continuing on and on. At that rate, it's easy to see how jaw-dropping deforestation figures develop. The annual global rate of tropical deforestation, for example, according to the global research organization World Resources Institute (WRI), is thirteen million hectares per year, an area approximately the size of Greece.[14] At that rate, the last tree is predicted to fall by around 2045.[15]

This is a problem for many reasons we have already discussed. It's also important for one more, perhaps the most significant of all. Deforestation intensifies climate change. You see, the Amazon produces half its own rainfall by releasing moisture into the atmosphere. If you take away the trees, you take away rain. The remaining trees, in turn, dry out. Those that are burned represent still another climate-change problem, for less carbon dioxide is soaked up by the remaining forests, not to mention that which is released into the atmosphere through burning. In short, as Stephan Schwartzman of Environmental Defense contends, "Tropical deforestation is a classic example of market failure."[16]

For more on solutions to this predicament we turn to our next set of chapters, but one point is obvious from my Amazon journey. We need to adjust our current social relationships. This is true at every level, from the local to the international, whether here in the Peruvian Amazon as modeled with the Infierno community or back home in the industrial world.

We must embrace change, even drive it, not remain content to merely watch as it passes us by. Returning once more to Martin Luther King, Jr.'s, warning, "One of the great liabilities of history is that all too many people fail to remain awake through great periods of social change. Every society has its protectors of status quo and its fraternities of the indifferent who are notorious for sleeping through revolutions. Today, our very survival depends on our ability to stay awake, to adjust to new ideas, to remain vigilant and to face the challenge of change."

Exactly who shapes this change, of course, is key. We as consumers play a leading role, but so, too, do business and government.

Look back at the oil interests that shaped the mass production and mass consumerism of the twentieth century. The social environment then privatized freedom in the form of a house, car, family, and yard with a "steady expansion of suburban geographies."[17]

More specifically, take the example of the great streetcar scandal in the early twentieth century.[18] Amid the recessionary early 1920s, with the fear that the consumer market for private automobiles was becoming saturated, General Motors's chief executive Alfred Sloan created the front company

National City Lines in 1922.[19] He wanted to facilitate the transformation of public transportation from electric streetcars to diesel-fired internal combustion buses, and, by the mid-1930s, National City Lines had evolved into a holding company that included Standard Oil of California, Phillips Petroleum, and Firestone Tires (with the ironic rubber connection to tires).

Over the next decade or so, between the mid-1930 and late 1940s, this de facto auto-petroleum industrial complex bought out the supply contracts for dozens of municipal public transit systems, including those of Los Angeles, St. Louis, Detroit, and Phoenix. They promptly destroyed the infrastructure for their new possessions, removing rail lines and throwing away their streetcars. In Los Angeles, some were even dumped into the Santa Monica Bay. National City Lines then replaced these streetcars with GM-manufactured buses, all of which were supported, of course, by products from the other companies.[20] Private industry dictated what public choices existed.

Admittedly, there is a key caveat to this General Motors conspiracy. Public transit ridership peaked in the United States in 1923, considerably before the dismantling of the public transit system began. In reality, then, this shift was much more a social one, albeit aided and abetted by nonneutral corporate interests. From the beginning of the auto age, for example, a steady campaign sought to contrast private automobiles as vastly superior to congested and unreliable mass public transit.

This rightly places our focus on a larger social picture. Alfred Sloan and National City Lines didn't help matters, but neither were they the primary causal agent. As geography professor Matthew T. Huber contends, "mass consumption of oil . . . emerged out of a wider social context, through which massive amounts of workers [could] actually afford single-family homes, automobiles, and the multitude of other petroleum-derived products that saturate[d] everyday life."[21]

The more general lesson, then, is that we must be more discerning consumers when it comes to climate change, especially with the stakes so high. We cannot be passive bystanders. We must convert dreams into action, all while heeding the advice of Martin Luther King, Jr. With that in mind, we now turn to an exploration of the Antarctic Peninsula and our final, perhaps most imposing hurdle to better understanding climate change, the politics that swirl around it.

THE ROAD NOT TAKEN

The Antarctic Peninsula and Political Obstacles to Understanding Climate Change

Two roads diverged in a wood,
and I—I took the one less traveled by,
And that has made all the difference.

—Robert Frost, *Mountain Interval*, 1920

chapter nineteen

KICKING THE CARBON HABIT

IT'S EARLY DECEMBER with a bit of a chill in the Florida air as temperatures dropped into the upper forties. I know. That sounds ridiculous. But to those unaccustomed to northern winters, this is a bona fide cold spell down here in the Sunshine State, especially once you've acclimated to our balmy climate as I have. Hmm . . . maybe I should rethink this Antarctic expedition?

Yes, I'll have modern comforts that renowned explorers Shackleton, Scott, and Amundsen a century before me lacked, but even with waterproof, breathable Gore-Tex it is still "The Ice," as researchers affectionately label the frozen continent. It's still Antarctica. It might be the peak of summer down there, but it's still is going to be cold.

Our fall semester is winding down, and I'm set to fly out of Orlando this afternoon, transferring first in Atlanta and then Buenos Aires, before landing in the southernmost city of the world, Ushuaia, Argentina. Ushuaia is one of six gateways to Antarctica. Over the years, thanks to significant government investment and strategic proximity to the seventh continent, it's become the most popular point of disembarkation.

Sandwiched between the Beagle Channel and the Martial range of Tierra del Fuego, Ushuaia benefited from a substantial injection of government funds in the 1980s. Development accelerated after 1991 when the city became administrative capital of a newly defined province in Argentina. A $10 million extension of the mooring quay in the late 1990s didn't hurt, either. Despite the influx of funds and corresponding population increase, though, Ushuaia still has the feel of a frontier town. And indeed it should, for along with space and the deep seabed, the continent of Antarctica, seen in Figure 19.1, is one of our last true frontiers.

Between fifty-five and fifty-six million years ago, during what is known as the Paleocene-Eocene Thermal Maximum, global mean temperature jumped five to eight degrees Celsius, or nine to fourteen degrees Fahrenheit, significantly higher than it is today. There was no ice left on Earth, and Antarctica was a subtropical forest filled with large mammals. Then, about 45 million years ago, give or take a couple million here and there, the Antarctic ice sheet, one of two major ice sheets in the world today (with the other in Greenland) began to form. A massive

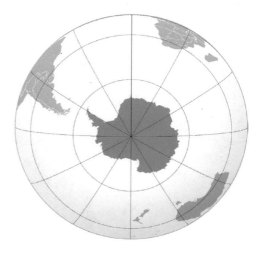

19.1 Antarctica. Source: Wikimedia Commons.[1]

frozen blanket that buries entire mountain ranges, the Antarctic ice sheet today covers 98 percent of the continent with an average thickness of seven thousand feet and a maximum in some areas of roughly fifteen thousand. That's nearly three miles.

Truth be told, Antarctica is technically two ice sheets. The larger, more stable East Antarctic ice sheet holds most of the continent's ice. If it melts, ocean levels will rise an astounding 197 feet. The West Antarctic ice sheet is smaller but much more vulnerable. It's iconic Mick Jagger–like tongues of ice lap into the ocean, submerging several hundred meters below sea level to the bedrock below. This basic difference, with the ice sheet exposed to ocean waters, makes the West Antarctic ice sheet much more dynamic, highly susceptible to break up as ocean temperatures rise. If this second ice sheet melts, sea levels would rise another 19.7 feet.

It's this peninsular portion of the vulnerable West Antarctic sheet that I'm off to see. If one visualizes the continent as a fist, the peninsula, noted in Figure 19.2, is best described as an eight-hundred-mile-long thumb sticking out of its western edge. The peninsula differs from the continent in many respects, but, most notably, its climate is less extreme, and thus it harbors more life—as well as more tourists like me. Unfortunately, jutting out into the warmer waters north of the continent, the region has also warmed an astounding 4.5 degrees Fahrenheit (2.5 degrees Celsius) since 1950.

The melt here is most definitely on.

As you recall, an array of greenhouse gases drive this process, first and foremost among them carbon dioxide; we are pumping more and more into our atmosphere each year, on average, 3 percent more per year over the last century.[2] If we are to have any hope at halting, let alone reversing, this pernicious process, our generation faces a critical choice.

Two roads diverge here. One follows further fossil-fuel addiction; 85 percent of carbon dioxide emissions (the most common greenhouse gas) originate from burning coal, oil, and natural gas.[3] The other strikes out bravely on American poet Robert Frost's less-traveled path, one that sheds our carbon dependence.

Of course, selecting this second path will not be easy. It is less traveled for a reason.

Allow me to present Exhibit A, the personal automobile. As we saw in our last chapter, the efforts of General Motors, Firestone, and Greyhound in early-twentieth-century Los Angeles helped increase initial interest in this form of transit. Still, that was not the only factor in the automobile's burgeoning popularity. Even more important, cars became a cultural symbol of modernity, representing not merely mobility but personal freedom itself, and an entire urban infrastructure was designed around them. In America, pedestrians became people who had just parked their cars.[4]

While industrial manufacturing efforts, residential and commercial electrical needs, and agricultural production all generate significant greenhouse gases, cars are arguably the biggest culprits when it comes to climate change, at least here in the States. Combining emissions from their manufacture with actual usage on a yearly basis, cars in the United States account for 60 percent of our country's emissions.[5]

19.2 The Antarctic Peninsula.
Source: NordNordWest via Wikimedia Commons.[2]

You might compare our automobile dependence, or at least our fossil-fuel-driven car dependence, to the antebellum South and slavery. Our genteel way of life is intricately interwoven within an insidious practice that will inevitably usher in our downfall. In short, as Abraham Lincoln recognized during his presidency, the time for compromises and appeasement is over.

We must face this unhealthy addiction, sooner or later. Even President George W. Bush, a well-established fossil-fuel-industry ally, acknowledged as much in his 2006 State of the Union address, albeit with a misplaced emphasis on foreign oil. Middle Eastern oil certainly remains a central player today,[6] but over the long run, geographic origin will be less and less important. The future is about negative externalities from oil use, not about from where it comes. We must break away from our fossil-fuel dependence, no matter where it originated.

Energy de-carbonization isn't as simple as moving beyond petroleum, though. While petroleum-based automobiles make an ideal Exhibit A, another fossil fuel is arguably even more problematic. For the simple reason that we have more of it, King Coal is what really keeps climate activists up at night. The U.S. Energy Information Administration estimates that 256.7 billion tons of recoverable coal reserves exist in the United States alone. Based on our coal production in 2013, at 984.8 million tons, that would last us 261 years.[7] These impressive numbers mean that coal will stay cheaper much longer than oil, which in turn translates into less intense political pressure to develop alternatives.[8] It's just not worth it.

Time is of the essence in such a scenario. The transition from wood to coal as well as that from oil to gas each required several decades. Most expect it will take at least that long to replace our extensive fossil-fuel infrastructure.[9] This is all the more likely because the United States spends $37.5 billion annually, including $21 billion in production and exploration, to subsidize fossil fuels.[10]

By the way, this number doesn't include military expenditures that ensure secure transportation of that oil from the Middle East, a figure Pulitzer Prize–winning journalist Ross Gelbspan suggests accounts for another $15 billion a year.[11] Neither does it incorporate classic economic externalities, the costs of fossil-fuel use resulting from air and water pollution, not to mention droughts, floods, and storms driven by climate change.[12] When these effects are considered, the International Monetary Fund calculates fossil-fuel companies received a global total of $5.3 trillion in subsidies in 2015. That's trillion with a T. To put that in perspective, the world spent $10 million a minute every day in 2015 to subsidize the fossil-fuel industry.[13]

Eye-popping numbers such as these underscore why former chief climate scientist for NASA James Hansen complains that the exorbitant amount of money in politics is the single biggest obstacle to solving climate change. In this context, it's fairly easy to point fingers at entrenched financial interests that oppose an energy revolution, and we should never ignore that link.

It is also important to note, though, that political opposition is not always from the usual suspects. As environmental policy experts Michael Shellenberger and Ted Nordhaus highlighted in their New Apollo Project proposal, attention should focus on jobs when debating climate-change policy. It's about employment. Almost always, that's worry number one.

Alas, too often, this fundamental financial point is manipulated without full disclosure. For example, much to the chagrin of climate deniers, coal-miner numbers in the United States have been in steady decline over the last century, well before climate activism arose. Employment opportunities have not been bright for quite some time. Climate change is only the latest threat to that livelihood. And for those with foresight, it's time to look ahead to energy alternatives such as solar and wind. They are far more attractive. Wind-energy employment surpassed that of coal years ago in 2008, according to the non-profit watchdog Center for Media and Democracy.[14] The U.S. solar industry alone employs more people than coal and gas combined.[15]

If only it were so simple. As we've already noted, climate change isn't just about money. It's also about distance. More precisely, it's about three types of distance: temporal, geographic, and causal. Each of these dampens general public concern about climate change in the United States. Prevailing sentiment foresees climate change as a problem to face down the road, someplace other than here in the United States, without fully understanding the causal links to our daily living habits.

Even drama often isn't enough to overcome these obstacles. For instance, the Larsen B, part of an ice shelf extending along the east coast of the Antarctic Peninsula on the northwest section of the Weddell Sea, lost an immense northern section some 250 meters thick and covering more than 2,500 square kilometers over a one-month period in March 2002. When it spectacularly shattered and spawned thousands of enormous icebergs, the world's attention quickly focused on it, and then just as quickly turned away. Larsen B was tangible but distant.

As if that were not enough, an arcane obsession with numbers greatly constricts public opinion as well. Limiting our increasing temperatures to two degrees Celsius higher than the pre-industrial era, for example, is more of a problem than a solution.[16] Quite simply, it's difficult for the average American to think of two degrees (with the 450 ppm threshold)[17] as significant. Two degrees just doesn't sound that bad.

And further, the truth is two might be too much. We just don't know.

Here on the white continent, in the clearer atmosphere that prevails at the bottom of the globe, and where the cold can help focus (or numb) the mind, I'm hoping to better assess these sketchy statistics.

Again, this is not an easy task. There are not only known unknowns within climate change but also unknown unknowns, nestled in relationships we have yet to uncover. Let's just focus on the known unknowns for now.

Take black-carbon aerosol, for example. These tiny particles of soot absorb sunlight, doing the opposite of liquid sulfate aerosols, which reflect it. Exactly how much this affects climate change, though, remains difficult to say. As noted in our Galápagos chapters at the outset of this book, aerosols are one of the largest sources of uncertainty in current climate-model projections.

All this brings us back to one simple point. We need alternative energy, desperately. This includes not only wind and solar but also biofuel and geothermal, perhaps even tidal.

To take this less-traveled road, we need to shift the aforementioned investments in fossil fuels to alternatives. The innovation such funding would spur, by the way, would not come overnight. U. C. San Diego political scientist David Victor anticipates that it will take two decades for relevant technology to diffuse.[18] So to repeat an earlier aphorism, time is of the essence.

Still, as seen in our second set of chapters about the Great Barrier Reef, economics and politics mix perniciously to stall action. Given that economic-growth policies win out over emissions policies every time, as Roger Pielke, Jr., a political scientist at the University of Colorado, asserts, it's nearly impossible to generate political capital to pay now for a future threat.[19] Yet, as is becoming increasingly clear, these threats, and the costs associated with them, continue to rise.

This is not to deny significant upfront costs, or the need for bridge sources of energy such as natural gas and nuclear power. Neither is it to deny the economic discount factor whereby those in the future, at least in the developed world, are often better positioned to postpone payment for action against climate change. The key to action now, rather than later, then, is a political argument that economic incentives favor climate-change action more than inaction.

It's not really a revolutionary idea. It's about spending money to make money. Money may not grow on trees, but, with the appropriate structures in place, going green is profitable.[20]

At least that's my philosophy in assuming some debt for this trip. I've come a day early to explore nearby Parque Nacional Tierra del Fuego, seen here in Figure 19.3, and to hedge my bets should there be any complications during travel, so that I could make adjustments and still arrive in time for my scheduled departure to Antarctica. After a quick, early breakfast at the comfy and conveniently situated Hotel Albatross, I meet up with Laura, my tour guide . . . to the end of world.

That's the slogan here in Ushuaia: the end of the world and start of everything. It kind of provides that extra ounce of adrenaline and anticipation.

19.3 A short hike from Lapataia is Bahía Ensenada with views of the Andes in the background.

Not that it's needed. It's a beautiful drive through a forest of beech and ever-green, terminating along a gravel road off the Beagle Channel at Lapataia Bay, which, not coincidently, is also the end of the Panamerican Highway, a network of roadways stretching over two continents and some 19,000 miles from Prudhoe Bay, Alaska to Tierra del Fuego. Asking questions and hovering near our guide throughout the day, I soak up eclectic information at every stop.

I learn, for example, that Magellan named this a land of fire for the smoke from the heating coals natives regularly burned along its shore. These natives apparently made quite an impression on Magellan. When they weren't covered in huge furs of sea lion, they invariably paraded around naked, not due to an exhibitionist nature but because that allowed them to dry off more quickly. Like my five-year-old son, though, Magellan didn't focus on the drying part. He focused on the nakedness.

That aside, one of the more unexpected tidbits I learned concerns the exotic beavers imported from Canada for hunting just after World War II. With no natural predators along this border, which Argentina shares with Chile, they are more than a nuisance. They have become a legitimate threat to the slow-growth forests in this cold climate, essentially drowning the tree roots in the ponds their dams create. One of the main reasons growth is so slow, ironically, is that death takes a long time here too, with trees taking a full century or two to decompose.

Indeed, it gets so cold here that, at least for a good part of the twentieth century, most people didn't seek out this destination on their own accord. From 1902 to 1947, for example, Argentina shipped its most dangerous crim-inals to the area. Only in 1972 did the government officially shift gears and offer special incentives to attract noncriminals, including socialized housing and tax breaks for industry. Now tourism drives the economy.

Here at the tip of Tierra del Fuego I'm searching for inspiration. What better place to ruminate on kicking the carbon habit than at the Fin del Mundo. It's the end of the world, and the start of everything. Okay, one thought tossing around in my mind must have crossed yours by this point, too. Isn't it hypocritical to expend a couple tons of carbon merely to see Antarctica? Isn't this trip in and of itself part of the problem?

Well, the short answer is yes.

As Ramon Farreny of the Autonomous University of Barcelona and seven colleagues wrote recently in *Antarctic Science*, polar tourism is extremely energy-intensive, especially because "ships represent the world's most polluting combustion sources per unit of fuel consumed." Using data from thirty-six vessels carrying 36,520 passengers from 2008 and 2009, the authors calculated the total emissions from those cruises, then added estimated emissions from commercial flights to the gateway cities of South America. They found that the average tourist trip to Antarctica spills 5.44 tons of CO_2 per passenger into our atmosphere. Approximately 70 percent of these emissions come from the actual cruise portion of a trip, with the remaining 30 percent attributable to the flight.[21] By comparison, Sustainable Travel International and the National Science Foundation find that the average individual contributes an annual carbon load of 16.82 tons.[22]

That means I've expended nearly a third of my emissions for the year on this adventure alone. Just to remain at an average emissions level for the coming year, I have some serious carbon cutbacks ahead of me. The good news is I have already begun that process, registering far below average for years thanks to my frequent habit of carpooling or commuting to work by bicycle. As I settle my predeparture jitters at Ramos Generales, a unique bakery and bar on the main drag in Ushuaia since 1906, I consider what additional commitments I must make after this trip. It's an exercise we should all employ more often.

The question remains, though: why is someone who claims to be ecologically conscious making a trip like this? I admit, there's a piece of me that is thrilled at the opportunity to set foot on my seventh continent. It's a rush. As polar explorer and entrepreneur Robert Swan asserts, adventure is the most addictive, intoxicating drug ever conceived.[23] And Antarctica is definitely one of our last frontiers, filled with life and wonderment not found anywhere else on our planet. [24] Indeed, the continent captures the popular imagination, as evidenced by a number of well-received documentaries over the last two decades.[25] Heck, *Sports Illustrated* even did a cover shoot for its swimsuit edition there.[26] Seriously.

On the other hand, it's not like I'm boldly going where no man has gone before. I'd also be hard pressed to claim I'm roughing it, given that the comfortable cruise ships of today eliminate most elements of surprise. To top all of that off, I'm just a social scientist, not conducting any cutting-edge biological science or chemistry for the greater good of society.

Then again, I am hoping to use this experience for a wider purpose, to emphasize the benefits of getting people to act on climate change. In that vein, I'd argue, like polar explorer Robert Swan before me, that tourism to Antarctica only makes sense when the mission outweighs the emissions.[27]

What's more, even in those cases, you must be extremely careful. In an ironic twist, as Swan astutely notes, this vast, unpopulated land is akin to a polar Las Vegas. What happens in Antarctica, stays in Antarctica.[28] In this land of no time zones, it's not the wildness of your transgressions that you hope remains a secret, but rather, the simple fact that time freezes to a stand-still. There are few to no decay bacteria present, so nothing organic really breaks down. The stuff we bring pretty much stays here forever, or until we melt the continent.

My top concern as a tourist, then, is to do everything possible to minimize my ecological footprint, borrowing from a term ecologist and professor emeritus at the University of British Columbia William Rees first introduced in the early 1990s.[29] Along these lines, it's also worth noting that tourists don't scar the landscape with permanent bases and trash dumps. Indeed, the most serious environmental threats within the entire Antarctic Treaty System area come from the logistical activities that support scientific research, namely transportation, the handling and use of fuels, waste disposal, etc. Heck, sometimes it's even the research itself. In 2009 a group of German and Indian scientists dumped six tons of iron into the ocean near Antarctica to evaluate its effects on absorbing carbon dioxide.

Further, unless one is reckless along the journey, much more of an ecological impact is made well before disembarking. Dr. Ian Sterling of Parks Canada, for example, in a study on the other end of the globe at the North Pole, found frighteningly high levels of industrial contaminant PCBs in the fat of polar bears. These industrial toxins, which nearly all of us must claim some responsibility for at one time or another, lodge in the fat tissues of a range of organisms. Following along the food chain, they've been migrating to both poles for decades now.[30]

Another way to think of Antarctica, then, is as our canary in the coal mine, an ironic twist of imagery considering coal's role in emissions. We keep pumping the residue of coal and other fossil fuel into the atmosphere without any sense of its impact, and Antarctica, along with the Arctic, is desperately trying to awaken us to these dangers. Let's hope it doesn't take what nineteenth-century coal miners needed, the death of the canary, to recognize the threat.

Speaking of death, it's worth noting that British Royal Navy officer Captain Robert Falcon Scott died on the Great Ice Barrier not merely because of the cold, but because his fuel supply ran out. In the intense cold of Antarctica, the gaskets beneath the caps of his fuel containers failed to seal correctly. Paraffin for his stoves then leaked out. It evaporated.

Our fuel is killing us as well. Not because we're running out, although eventually that will happen, too. Rather, it is because we are using so much of it. The U.S. tosses over six billion metric tons of carbon dioxide into the atmosphere each year, while worldwide the figure is 36.1 billion metric tons.[31]

Those numbers are unsustainable. Antarctica offers a wake-up call, a chance to focus with greater clarity, thanks to the clear atmosphere that scientists favor for their research, on the wicked problem of climate change. Indeed, Antarctica is a mirror of humanity in several respects. For one, it literally is a mirror—80 percent of the sun's heat falling on the icecap is reflected back into space. And more figuratively, Antarctica invariably spurs deeper reflection among its visitors.

With its closest neighbor of South America over six hundred miles away, Antarctica is alone at the bottom of the world, but the isolation is more than geographic. It's psychological, too, and, one hopes, not in the Jack Nicholson of *The Shining* kind of way, but more along the lines of awe and inspiration, as expressed by Ernest Shackleton's assertion, "Tongue and pen fail in attempting to describe the magic."[32] For most of us, it's as close as we will ever come to visiting another planet.

Named for what it is not, Antarctica is a place of contradictions.

The continent holds a tenth of our planet's land, yet technically, no one permanently lives here. Active volcanoes such as Mount Erebus erupt in a frozen landscape. Ice extends as far as you can see, but it almost never snows over wide stretches of the continent. An ocean surging with life surrounds a ghostly arid desert on land. While more frequent rains along the peninsula push annual continental averages up to 6.5 inches a year, in the high interior plateau of East Antarctica, precipitation averages less than 50 mm (2 inches) annually.

Antarctica is also a land of extremes.[33]

It's the coldest place on Earth, with the Russian Vostok Station registering 128.6 degrees below Fahrenheit on 21 July 1983. Even though it's classified as the largest true desert in the world, Antarctica houses nearly three-fourths of the Earth's fresh water, albeit frozen. As noted earlier, this is a big deal if only for the fact that, if all the ice in Antarctica melted, sea level would rise 210 feet.

Antarctica is also the windiest continent, with a maximum speed recorded at 200 mph at a French base in July 1972. Due to a thick layer of ice across it, it's the highest continent as well, with an average height of approximately 7,500 feet above sea level.

As I visit in the austral summer, Antarctica is 1.5 times the size of the United States, or equal in square mileage to the U.S. and Mexico combined. But during the austral winter, the formation of sea ice causes Antarctica to double in size from 5.2 to 10.4 million square miles. It's the world's biggest seasonal change, as an apron of sea ice spreads along the coastline. Interestingly, as the ocean freezes, the ice on the surface expels salty water underneath. This brine is heavier than the underlying ocean and sinks to the bottom around the margins of Antarctica, facilitating a circulation of water that contributes to life around the continent.

Amid these extremes, Antarctica's atmosphere is the most stable and transparent in the world. It's ideal for astronomical observation, but astronomers are not alone in using this as a laboratory space. Many other scientists follow for similar reasons. Indeed, Antarctica has become a Mecca for an array of collaborative sciences, from astronomy to zoology.

As you may recall, dynamic ice sheets first appeared in Antarctica roughly 45 million years ago, then began spreading inland across the continent about 34 million years ago. Around 14 million years ago, they cooled further, and the larger of the two main ice sheets, the East Antarctic Ice Sheet, became stable. Mountains known as the Transantarctic Range are responsible for this trait. They bisect the continent into a western fourth and an eastern three-fourths. To reiterate from earlier, this eastern portion, protected from invasions of warmer air currents by these same mountains, is decidedly more stable than its western portion.

The best time to travel to Antarctica is in the southern polar summer, from December to the end of February. Only the diehard scientists remain in the winter that soon follows. With a vortex of cold air circling high above it, the Antarctic winter is more like one long polar night, one with no sun for half the year. This means that summer is really the only time when weather and sunlight provide conditions appropriate for most tourist travel.

Antarctic tourists are an exclusive, albeit growing, club. Shortly before the 2008 economic downturn, some 46,000 visited in 2006–2007.[34] That number dropped more than 10,000 in the coming years, but some 36,702 visited in 2014–2015, which is still enough to raise concerns about ecological footprint.

Most of these tourists come aboard ships that feature island-hopping on Zodiacs, with the most frequent targets being the Maritime Antarctic, Peninsula, and southern islands of the Scotia arc. It's milder here than in continental Antarctica throughout the year, with longer summers that make it scenically and biologically more attractive. It's also relatively free of sea ice between early November and March, which makes travel much more pragmatic, too.

The first commercial tourist visits began in the mid to late 1950s with a tourist flight in 1956 by a Chilean operator[35] and an Argentinian vessel sailing to Antarctica in 1958. Still, it wasn't until 1966, when tour operator Lars-Eric Lindblad combined concerted education initiatives during travel with a focus on environmental preservation, that tourism really began to take hold. Favorable publicity from the International Geophysical Year of 1957–1958 and the increasing availability of modern transportation technologies helped spark this development.

In the 1970s and 1980s, ship-based tourism continued to expand, and, by 1985–1986, tourists outnumbered scientific and logistical support personnel. The 1990s brought further increases, particularly as more research vessels and even some icebreakers became available for tourism charters after the collapse of the Soviet Union.[36]

In response to this growth, seven commercial tour operators formed the International Association of Antarctica Tour Operators (IAATO) in 1991. This voluntary association, which not all Antarctic tour operators have joined, largely shapes industry behavior, as most simply see advantages in conforming to its requirements, whether they are members or not.

Those that are members, moreover, have benefited from the IAATO's participation in Antarctic Treaty Consultative Meetings, which, in turn, determine guidelines for the most heavily visited sites in Antarctica.

In 2011, for example, the Buenos Aires meeting established new guidelines prohibiting bothering wildlife as "harmful interference" and spelled out respect for penguin "highways" as well as keeping fifteen feet of distance from all birds and fifty feet from fur seals.[37]

Additional IAATO responsibilities determined over the years include the appropriate use of different transport forms, recommendations for hiring qualified staff, limits on landings to one hundred passengers ashore at a time, and an overall one-to-twenty staff-passenger ratio. The original bylaws required members not to carry more than four hundred passengers per voyage, but, in June 2001, changes allowed larger ships of five hundred to make landings, with no limit on those not landing passengers.

Landings are arguably the most invasive of all tourist activities and typically use fleets of outboard-engine-powered inflatable boats known as Zodiacs like this one in Figure 19.4. According to IAATO statistics, some 270 sites have been identified as potential landing areas within the Antarctic Treaty System (ATS), but only half are currently in use. Of these, only sixteen are visited more than once a week, with the most popular, not surprisingly, being one of our last destinations in the coming days, Whalers Bay on Deception Island in the South Shetland Islands.

19.4 Zodiac landing.

Nesting birds and basking seals are obviously vulnerable, but plant life is even more so. A footprint on a delicate moss bed may still be visible ten years later, for example, and requires perhaps a full century to regenerate.

Considering such threats, by the 1990s, increasing tourist numbers dictated a round of changes to formal policy. The 1994 site inventory identified locations that might be sensitive to over-visitation. In 2000, the IAATO implemented boot-washing and clothing-decontamination procedures. And in 2003, the IAATO published site guidelines that quantified the parameters of what locations could be visited, limits to the numbers of visitors, and time limits on their visits.

Small ships of up to 120 passengers such as the one I'm scheduled to board used to be the norm, but now more cost-effective ships of up to 250 are prevalent, not to mention more and more liners of more than 1,000 appearing each year. In total, 95 percent of tourism is by ship, with forty different ships operating in Antarctica. In actual time on land, though, tourists collectively spent only 1.07 percent of the total person-days ashore, according to a study by academics John Snyder and Bernard Stonehouse.[38] Scientists are there for far longer periods.

The caveat here is that tourists often visit the most sensitive wildlife breeding areas, where accidents are always possible. The sinking of *ARA Bahia Paraiso* off Palmer Station in January 1989 is a case in point. An Argentine naval vessel carrying eighty-one tourists, the *Paraiso* hit rocks offshore the peninsula, spilling some 250,000 gallons of diesel fuel and killing vast numbers of krill, plus penguins and other sea birds. The spill also ruined several scientific projects along the coast.

With this in mind, a number of safeguards are now in place. Drinking water is produced on ship by treating seawater. Food waste is broken down and treated before being dumped at sea. And nothing is released while in the Antarctic Treaty zone, defined as the area south of 60 degrees south latitude.

Small cruise ships such as the one I'm on use the Lars-Eric "Lindblad pattern," which evolved as the basis for IAATO guidelines and management today. On-board lectures about the environment, wildlife, and history highlight this approach, and no more than one hundred people are allowed ashore at a time, although admittedly, this limitation is dictated not so much by concern over ecological footprint, but by the need to return landing parties quickly if weather changes.[39]

In the final assessment, despite good intentions, Antarctic tourism oversight remains limited. With no provision for ecologists independent of the industry to monitor commercial transactions, the situation is not unlike that of our U.S. Nuclear Regulatory Commission. The fox is essentially guarding the henhouse. To mix metaphors, let's just hope this fox knows better than to kill the goose that lays the golden egg.

Built during the Cold War in 1976 Yugoslavia, our ship, the 328-foot *Lyubov Orlova*, seen here in Figure 19.5, is a hulky vessel strengthened against the ice and named after an early twentieth-century silent film actress from Russia. Photos of her adorn the walls of the bar where my colleagues and I will engage in contentious card games over the next week. The 4,250-ton *Orlova* was one of six built in similar style, all named for Russian actresses, and served as a cargo and passenger vessel in the North Sea for most of her career. Following refurbishment in 1999 and more extensive renovations in 2002, Quark Expeditions used her for a series of both North and South Pole tourist expeditions, each typically with a maximum of 110 passengers and a crew of 56.

There's another story about the *Orlova* I can't resist telling. Unbeknown to me at the time, the grand old girl was starting to show her age. The year before my trip, she'd had four cruises cancelled, reportedly due to an engine cooling leak and inspection failure.[40] Problems cropped up again shortly after my trip, and, in fact, my voyage in December 2009 was one of her last Antarctic expeditions.

After mechanical problems necessitated an early retirement from the Arctic season (like many tourist vessels, the *Orlova* migrated with the tourist season from pole to pole), and after five months without pay, its crew deserted her. The ship was subsequently impounded in Newfoundland in September 2010.[41] There it sat for the next eighteen months. Finally, in February 2012, apparently worth more dead than alive so to speak, it sold at auction for an estimated scrap value of $700,000.

But wait, it gets worse. The ship sat in port another eleven months before being towed out by an American tug in January 2013. Then, only a day into its journey to the Dominican Republic, the towline snapped. Thirty-five-mile-per-hour winds stymied efforts to reconnect it, but the Canadian Coast Guard continued to monitor the ship over the next week. When concern grew that it endangered offshore oil wells, they sent a larger vessel to secure it.

That ship didn't bring the *Orlova* back to port, though. It merely towed her out of Canadian waters before releasing her. The last confirmed sighting

19.5 The *Orlova*.

was in February 2013, and the British Maritime and Coastguard Agency believes she has long since sunk.

Others aren't quite so sure, arguing that because only two of the lifeboat beacons that erupt when they hit water ever sounded, the ship must still be afloat. The last beacon to send out a signal did so on March 23, 2013, about two-thirds of the way across the Atlantic, giving salvagers keen to find the *Orlova* for its scrap value continued hope.[42]

In a final comical twist to its frostbit fate, if she is afloat, thanks to over two years in dry dock, the *Orlova* is probably overrun with starving, cannibalistic rats. Drifting on the high seas with rodents reproducing like in a horror film, eating their own species, the once-proud ship has been reduced to a ghost ship, making it easy fodder for British and American headlines.[43]

Upon boarding for our 4:00 P.M. disembarkation, I quickly settle into a lower deck twin berth. Except for sleeping, though, not much time will be spent down here for the next seven days. That's not a complaint against the room. While Spartan as you might expect, given its Soviet-linked legacy, it is also admiringly efficient. It even comes with a small, scenic porthole that is sometimes above and sometimes below sea level, depending on the roughness of our waters. Still, aside from some unexpected naps due to my seasickness medication, for the next couple days, I spend most of my time in the forward lounge, site of four educational talks a day and a series of evening films for those that can stave off sleep long enough.

Of course, there is also a seemingly endless series of truly seaworthy meals, not to mention the daily afternoon teatime and requisite rounds of Uno with my colleagues. Until I discover a minigym on the third day, it is truly accurate to say, as my artist colleague wryly laments, that we are eating like hobbits, with their multiple breakfasts and lunches, and doing little to counter the effects. Perhaps this is a survival mechanism that kicks in; we've read about early explorers' need for high caloric intake on the ice as the body uses up an amazing amount of calories just to keep warm. Of course, early explorers didn't have the comfort of the *Orlova* to which to retreat, so the analogy begins to break down a bit there. Let's not get caught up in that technicality, though, even if I've never been one to turn down a good meal.

Quickly unpacking my bag, I arrange my daily essentials. There are two pairs of gloves I will wear for each outing, two pairs of socks for each outing, a balaclava for my head and face, long johns, snow pants and coat, and a series of upper and lower layers in between. None of it is cotton, though, for as they say in the polar industry, cotton kills.

It's amazing how advanced clothing has become over the last couple decades. This stuff didn't exist when I camped as a child. By the 1990s an array of fabrics like my waterproof-yet-breathable Gore-Tex hit the market, with pores larger than water molecules so the water vapor can move through them but anything as big as a raindrop cannot. It's yet another reason to pause in admiration at the amazing hardships that early polar explorers endured.

With that thought still on my mind, I stash what might be my lightest but certainly not least-needed possession on the nightstand by my bunk. This eyeshade is essential for the twenty-two hours of daylight that follow. Without it, sleep would be impossible.

Oh yes, and the meds. Ever since the Galápagos Islands, I've come prepared for this kind of thing. Scopolamine, that patch of medicine you place behind your ear, may cause blurred vision and dizziness and make your eyes more sensitive to light, but it definitely prevents seasickness. The warning label also cautions about drowsiness, something I will come to more fully comprehend over the next couple days. There are two roads to choose from on this trip: drowsiness or seasickness.

An hour later we cram into the forward lounge for an introduction to the twenty-two-member expedition staff, from scientists to Zodiac drivers to bartender. We also meet a handful of the crew, including our Russian captain, someone I'll come to fondly refer to as the World's Most Interesting Man, given his penchant for placing a fashionable sweater around his neck much like the former Dos Equis commercial character. After introductions, a mandatory lifeboat and safety briefing follows. Then, before you know it, it's time for our evening welcome dinner. With all the rush, almost nonchalantly, we enter the Drake shortly after midnight, while cruising just below our top speed at ten knots.

Oh, I don't believe I mentioned the Drake yet. Within the sheltered Beagle Channel, gliding toward Cape Horn under our two diesel engines, no signs of the notorious Drake Passage lie ahead. The Drake Passage is probably the most fearsome sea on the globe, commanding the respect of sailors since the days of its namesake Sir Francis Drake.[44] Interestingly, it's not always rough, alternating mysteriously between virtual stillness and extreme violence, or in a more colorful vernacular, between Drake Lake and Drake Shake.

Being prone to seasickness, I can't believe I've signed up for a little over four days of this water roller coaster, two going over and two coming back, but there's no turning back now.

In the midst of the second circumnavigation of the world,[45] Drake reached the Magellan Straits off South America in 1578 and was promptly blown off course from its protective environs to discover another passage farther south. That discovery enabled the English to sail around the tip of South America without acquiring Spanish or Portuguese permission to use the Straits of Magellan. This would prove handy as Queen Elizabeth I, who supported Sir Drake, sought to profit from raids on undefended settlements along the Pacific coast of South and Central America, albeit officially none against so-called Christian princes.

The gap between South America and Antarctica opened approximately 20 to 25 million years ago. Its presence means that the Southern Ocean, which begins at a latitude of about 40 degrees, is the only one to circle the globe and, thus, provides a unifying link to every other major ocean basin. That's pretty important. In fact, this continual exchange of water masses plays a major role in regulating global climate.[46] It's why scientists refer to the Southern Ocean as the "mix-master."

That's fascinating to think about, but at the moment my undivided attention is on the prominent westerly winds that regularly orbit the Earth at this latitude. Without substantial masses of land to stop them, these winds continually suck up energy from the sea, sometimes reaching hurricane levels.

It's no joke. Satellite photos consistently show impressive low-pressure zones spiraling clockwise, and these latitudes have come to be known affectionately as the roaring forties, the furious fifties and the screaming sixties. These winds also create what is known as the West Wind Drift or Antarctic Circumpolar Current, from west to east, around the continent. As it circles, it also refrigerates.

As crucial as this process is, there is one other that tops it in terms of sustenance of life in the Southern Ocean and frozen continent that abuts it, the Antarctic Convergence. The Antarctic Convergence is an area where warmer water masses from the north meet colder Antarctic waters. Within this zone, colder, denser, north-flowing water sinks beneath the warmer sub-Antarctic waters. It's an important biological phenomena because this convergence creates rich feeding grounds for a variety of marine organisms, thus influencing the distribution of plankton, fish, birds, and mammals.

Located between fifty and sixty degrees south, the convergence stretches for more than 12,400 miles around Antarctica. The exact location fluctuates, depending on a number of conditions, throughout the year, and from year to year as well as from century to century. Still, it is a sharp boundary characterized by a change in salinity, nutrient levels, and roughly two degrees cooler temperature. Even if I didn't know we were scheduled to cross the convergence at 3:30 that morning, for example, I could still literally see it with my naked eye.

Entrepreneur and intrepid explorer Robert Swan suggests that Antarctica is a harbinger of our future. I think he is right, which is both bad and good news. The bad news is that the climate change underway in Antarctica today is a warning sign of climate change across our planet. The loss of ice in western Antarctica as temperatures rise is an obvious alarm. Similarly, the growth of ice in eastern Antarctica, while seemingly counterintuitive to the uninitiated, is actually a product of increased precipitation associated with climate change.

The good news is Antarctica is also a model of what humanity can achieve. The heroic exploits of Antarctic exploration offer evidence of the power of perseverance and ingenuity in our species. Moreover, as elaborated on in successive chapters, this cold, white continent, with a relatively effective Antarctic Treaty System comprised of forty-six state signatories representing 80 percent of the world's population, also highlights the raw potential of collective action if we agree to a common purpose—and choose the road less traveled by.

chapter twenty

MARKET MECHANISMS
Cap and Trade Versus the Carbon Tax

TRUTH BE TOLD, despite my well-founded fears, there's not a whole lot of shaking going on. As they say in the business, the infamous Drake Passage, the most feared ocean in the world, was a placid Lake Drake all through the eerily lighted night. With a surprisingly high 8 degrees Celsius at breakfast (that's over 46 Fahrenheit for us Americans), this is shaping up to be more like a Caribbean pleasure cruise.

Okay, that's a bit of an exaggeration. Still, with a slight breeze registering only a two on the Beaufort wind-force scale, my morning meal goes down smoothly, and perhaps most importantly, stays down. Later that week, we'll face some decidedly rougher winds, and most of the ship, myself included, will choose not to tempt the fates and feed the fishes. What doesn't go down can't come up, right?

Ornithologist David Drummond gives the first lecture that morning, on marine birds of the Southern Ocean. I jot down a handful of intriguing notes about dimorphism, the difference in gender size within a species, as well as some tidbits about the wandering albatross. One of thirteen types of albatross worldwide, the wanderer is even bigger than its Galápagos cousin, the waved albatross we met in the first part of this book, and has the largest wingspan of any living bird at up to twelve feet, while tipping the scales at an impressive twenty pounds. It sails air currents for thousands of miles, only returning to land when sexually mature.

Next up is historian Shane Murphy's talk, "First Discoveries in the Land of Midnight Sun." I scurry into one of the last comfy seats just as he's beginning his PowerPoint presentation. The lecture is a transport back in time, both literally and figuratively, as I scramble to pay attention while faithfully recording key points. The experience reminds me of my undergraduate days decades ago, except the seats back then weren't nearly so comfortable and certainly didn't come with the soothing, sleep-aiding, side-to-side roll.

Antarctica began as an idea some 2,500 years ago. In fact, it's the only continent that was thought to exist before it was discovered. Ancient Greek mathematician Pythagoras first postulated that the Earth was round, and intellectual heirs such as Aristotle later expanded on this idea, asserting that symmetry required another southern region to prevent a top-heavy globe from tumbling over. Indeed, Antarctica's very name comes from this line of thinking, translating as "opposite Arktos," the constellation in the northern sky.

Some also suggested that Antarctica was populated, describing "antipodes" whose feet walked backward. Others proposed a frigid climate to balance out the temperate zones.[1] Only in last two hundred years, though, did anyone actually see and alight on Terra Australis Incognita.

Renowned British explorer James Cook never did. During his first circumnavigation of the globe, from 1773 to 1775, he crossed the Antarctic Circle three times, all to no avail. Cook did witness, however, an exorbitant number of seals, and his meticulous note-taking would entice many to follow in the years to come.

From 1784 to 1822, initiated by James Cook's voyage, southern ocean sealing exploded. The first wave focused on the Falkland Islands and Cape Horn region, but eventually the killing spread across the Drake to South Georgia and the surrounding islands. Over the next two decades, millions of seals were slaughtered, for their fur and skin in the case of fur seals and also for blubber in the case of elephant seals. Hunters became so proficient they could skin some sixty seals in an hour, after which, in a harbinger of globalization today, they sent them off for refinement in Canton, China, of all places.

Unlike Cook, though, due to the competitive nature of their business, sealers were a secretive lot. That means that while American captain and sealer John Davis registered the first known landing on Antarctica Feb. 7, 1821, there was probably someone before him.

After lunch and a medication-induced nap, it's time for some geology, "4.6 Billion Years in 46 Minutes," the title of the talk by resident geologist Wolfgang Bluemel. My meds are definitely starting to kick in now—either that or I'm re-enacting the less stellar, drowsy moments of my undergraduate career.

Either way, I'm struggling to keep up, and, before further embarrassment, I excuse myself to go on deck for the kind of brisk wake-up call only a polar breeze can provide. Sufficiently chilled, I return in time for marine biologist Anjali Pande's talk on the Antarctic food web. We learn about top predators such as orca and whales, but it's the leopard seals, which shuck penguins from their skin by repeatedly slapping their bodies against the water, that gain my undivided attention. Leopard seals are a keystone rather than apex predator, as at times they are preyed upon by orcas. Measuring ten feet long and weighing one thousand pounds, with an array of inch-long canine teeth, that distinction doesn't matter much to me at the moment.

We also learn the difference between secondary consumers and primary consumers. Zooplankton, miniature marine animals that drift with the current, as well as krill, fifty-mm shrimplike crustaceans like those in Figure 20.1 that eat the speck-sized algae phytoplankton (but more importantly serve as sustenance for seabirds, penguins, seals, and whales) constitute the latter.

20.1 Krill, a critical step in the Antarctic food chain.

Whales, penguins, and fish qualify as the former because they merely eat the creatures that eat the phytoplankton. That said, secondary consumers can be just as dependent on a food source as primary consumers. For example, stoking up during their Antarctic summer months for their return to the tropics for breeding, whales feast on as much as two tons of krill every twenty-four hours.

As noted in the previous chapter, the Antarctic Peninsula is warming rapidly, and thus is an ideal site to study the ecological impacts of climate change.[2] Elevated sea temperatures have greatly reduced the annual sea ice, while days have become cloudier and winds stronger. Cloudier skies mean less light filters through to support photosynthesis, while high winds turn over and mix the sea, further restricting phytoplankton by thrusting it deeper into the water and farther away from the little light that does exist. All total, the result is less phytoplankton along the northern portion of the peninsula. Given what we know now about primary and secondary consumers, less phytoplankton, of course, means fewer krill, and fewer krill means fewer seabirds, penguins, seals, and whales.

That evening, I quickly ditch a half-hearted attempt to stay up with my colleagues. I succumb to sleep, missing our 3:30 A.M. cross into the Convergence, the area where warmer water masses from the north meet colder Antarctic waters to create rich feeding grounds for a variety of marine organisms. When I awake, there's a noticeable temperature decrease on deck, roughly four degrees. Despite the invigorating air, I'm exhausted by my medication and miss both morning talks and the better part of an afternoon one as well. For all intents and purposes, my entire day has been lost to sleeping.

After all that sleep, I'm finally awake bright and early the following morning for our mandatory IAATO briefing. The International Association of Antarctic Tour Operators, as you recall, was founded in 1991 as a voluntary organization. It's also self-governed and self-policed, which means effectiveness depends entirely on rule-abiding members.

Our expedition leader, Kara Weller, runs through a range of information, taking care to emphasize that we are here to take nothing but memories and photographs. No evidence of our visit should be left ashore. That means no food or drink, other than water, is allowed off the ship. There's no smoking and no toilet usage. And of course, tourists are asked to avoid stepping on the fragile, slow-growing vegetation.

The introduction of nonnative species is also a constant concern, and boot-washing stations, similar to those in the Galápagos, are used on every return to the ship. Technically, only two species of plants exist in Antarctica, hair grass and pearlwort, but there are more than one hundred types of mosses and twenty-seven different liverworts. There are also lichens, which strictly speaking are not plants but rather a composite between fungi and algae. The peninsula has 350 different types of such lichens, but these numbers drop considerably as one moves down the coast and further inland.[3]

Remarkably, much as in the Galápagos, seals and penguins do not fear humans here in Antarctica. That does not change the protocol for interacting with these species, though, as our briefing instructions include directions to move both slowly and quietly. We are also supposed to stay low to appear less threatening. To send that message home, Kara emphasizes that fur seals are aggressive and territorial, and their bites can produce nasty infections. Tourists should avoid coming between any animal and the ocean shore, always giving them right of way and keeping at least a respectful fifteen feet distance, or fifty feet in the case of the leopard seal. When it comes to rookeries, understandably, we are restricted to the periphery.

With this briefing completed, we are now eligible for our first excursion, an exhilarating one-hour Zodiac cruise around the low-lying Melchior Islands. All 110 passengers aboard are divided into four groups for disembarkation, with ten people per Zodiac. As I stride down the inclined walkway like a grayish-black version of the puffy Michelin Man, our Zodiac driver Vladimir extends a firm sailor's grip, forearm to forearm and wrist to wrist, to pull me safely aboard.

It's a foggy day, but I quickly immerse myself in the tourist role, snapping photographs left and right with my new prized possession and absorbing all that Vladimir offers in narration.

Soon after scooting away from the *Orlova* we encounter a pod of humpback whales feasting on krill right in the center of Dallmann Bay. Part of the Palmer archipelago, these islands are covered in thick ice, with very little exposed land. Perhaps the most unexpected sight for me, though, is not the wildlife. It's not even the ice, although more on that in a minute. What is most surprising, what I failed to fully anticipate, is the beauty of the skies at the South Pole. The shades of gray are simply intoxicating. We get great gray color in Florida during the summer rainy season, but this is different.

Perhaps it's the juxtaposition of skyline and surface that really catches my attention. When it comes to the ice, the cliché response is there are no words to describe its beauty. The truth is, though, that there are lots of words from which to choose. Indeed, there are so many types of Antarctic ice, as microbiologist and New Zealand science journalist Veronika Meduna notes, the continent literally comes with its own vocabulary.[4]

Keep in mind that there are two major types of ice in Antarctica, glacial ice and sea ice. They form differently. Sea ice develops when the ambient temperature falls to the freezing point of salt water, generally about −1.9 degrees Celsius (or 28.5 degrees Fahrenheit). Of course, this varies according to the salinity of the seawater. The higher the salt concentration, the lower the freezing temperature. On the other hand, glacial ice, including the ice caps here in Antarctica, forms through the simple accumulation of snow, albeit over hundreds and thousands of years. Compressed by its own weight over time, that snow eventually becomes solid ice. It lasts decades or centuries, sometimes even millennia.

Returning to sea ice, it is important to note that it both forms and melts seasonally, although larger segments of it may last several years. The majority of sea ice occurs in a wide band around the Antarctic continent, with varying thicknesses. Commonly referred to as "pack ice," this part of the cryosphere is extremely dynamic and mobile, shifting with the prevailing currents and winds.

Further, in the summer, pack ice melt allows open water, known as "leads," to develop, although large chunks of broken ice often remain as navigation obstacles. These floes constantly change, too, which helps explain a little more of the vocabulary here. While sea ice is broadly described as "new ice," the landscape is also dotted with what are called "young ice," "first-year ice," and "old ice."[5]

An "ice shelf" is a floating ice sheet attached to the coast. Some ice shelves are so massive that they seem like countries unto themselves. The Ross Ice Shelf is perhaps the most famous of these. It's also the largest, the size of France.

Ice that floats at least five meters above sea level after breaking off a glacier is known as an "iceberg." A "tabular berg" is a flat-topped iceberg formed by breaking off from an ice shelf. On the other hand, "bergy bits" are floating ice less than five meters above sea level and not more than ten meters across.

The list goes on and on. There's "growler ice," pieces of floating ice even smaller than bergy bits. There's "brash ice," the wreckage of other ice floating as fragments under 6.5 feet across. There's the new ice floating after a heavy snowfall known as "shuga ice," or snow saturated with water. And there's always "new ice" and "old ice." Old ice has survived at least one melt season, meaning it's less saline than first-year ice, not to mention considerably stronger.

That afternoon we land at Danco Island on the southern end of the Errera Channel. It's a relatively small island stretching only a mile in length, but it is higher than one might expect at 590 feet. That means the 360-degree view from the top is spectacular, particularly as an assortment of icebergs collect in this channel after calving off heavily crevassed glaciers among the surrounding mountains.

Another draw to our attention that afternoon is the approximately 1,600 breeding pairs of gentoo penguins on Danco. Breeding high up on the slopes, these penguins' persistent waddle from their nests down to the sea below is almost hypnotic, their awkward, exaggerated gait almost comical. From such rough beginnings, though, comes a remarkable transformation. In water, these once-awkward birds metamorphosis into sleek Michael Phelps–like swimming machines.

With this thought in mind, that inauspicious beginnings can still lead to championship-level results, I find a snowy ridge off to the side to quietly contemplate the penguin highway below me. Daydreaming, my attention turns back to climate change.

Two alternative legislative actions have been proposed in the United States to date. Fee and dividend is one. Cap and trade is the other. Each has its merits and demerits.

As critical as this discussion is, though, I would argue it is of secondary importance to another often-ignored subject, at least to those of us in the developed world. Before we can talk about limiting carbon, we need to address yet another deficiency. Nearly 1.2 billion people, roughly 17 percent of the world's population, lack electricity and the indispensable basic activities such as lighting and refrigeration that accompany it, even as we are well into the twenty-first century.[6]

This deficiency can be fixed. According to the World Bank, universal access to electricity is possible by 2030. It only requires new capital investment of about $35–$40 billion a year.[7] We've made some progress over the last half-dozen or so years. In 2008, for example, over 1.5 billion were without electricity; 300 million more have access now than had it then. But it's not enough. Before the developed world can ask the developing world to take appropriate steps to combat climate change, we need to establish a level playing field. The rest of these 1.2 billion need electricity, too.

Of course, we don't have to wait until that is done before moving forward with either cap and trade or the carbon tax. We can do both at the same time, increase developing world access to electricity and decrease developed world carbon emissions.

That brings us back to our two policy options for restricting carbon emissions. Cap and trade has a number of merits. The environmental non-governmental organization Environmental Defense Fund first developed the idea of creating a market for pollution permits in the late 1980s.[8] Former vice president Al Gore championed it in the 1990s.

It works like this. Industry purchases pollution permits issued by the government, or in some scenarios, it initially accrues them cost-free. Over time, at least in theory, incremental increases in charges for these permits would continuously spur investment in alternative energy. Those that wanted to be conservative with their emissions reductions could buy additional permits on the marketplace to match their emissions. Those that wanted to be aggressive could sell their permits. Externalities finally received a tradable economic cost.

Everybody won . . . or so it seemed.

The European Union launched its ambitious version of cap and trade in 2005, but still struggles with over-allocation of permits and inappropriate pricing of carbon. In essence, cap and trade mimics one of the flaws many critics astutely point out in the Clean Development Mechanism of Kyoto. When a country (or company) finds it too inconvenient to meet its carbon emissions reduction target, it can simply purchase the right to exceed it.

Despite these complications, though, thanks to the U.S. Clean Air Act amendments of 1990, reason for hope remains. Cap and trade worked with sulfur regulation here in the States. Even though carbon trade is a considerably larger enterprise, it could work as well.

On at least a regional level, in fact, it already has. The Regional Greenhouse Gas Initiative of northeastern and mid-Atlantic states, including Connecticut, Delaware, Maine, Maryland, Massachusetts, New Hampshire, New York, Rhode Island, and Vermont, is the first mandatory market-based program in the States to reduce power-sector carbon dioxide emissions. Implementing a cap of 91 million tons in 2014, these nine states now commit to 2.5 percent declines each year from 2015 to 2020.[9]

Beyond this example, there's substantial political capital invested in cap and trade outside the northeastern and mid-Atlantic states as well, with vested economic interests who would like to see it succeed. Traders, for example, stand to make huge profits in a newly created carbon market, unfortunately, whether emissions rise or fall.

Here's where the concept of carbon offsets becomes even more problematic. Retired lead NASA climate scientist James Hansen, for one, compares offsets to the indulgences of the Middle Ages, whereby a cash donation to the church removed temporal punishment for a sin.[10] Those with means, the polluting companies of today, are happy because it allows them to continue business as usual while avoiding punishment for their sins. Meanwhile, bishops, the traders of today, love it because it directly brings in money. International relations scholar and codirector of the Laboratory on Law and Regulation at U.C. San Diego David Victor agrees with Hansen's sentiments, contending that the wealthy and most organized will channel benefits to themselves.[11]

The logical alternative in this context is the carbon tax. Akin to President Bill Clinton's failed 1993 Btu[12] tax, Nordic countries pioneered this tactic in the early 1990s, with Finland the first to implement a tax in 1990 across both industry and transport as well as private households. According to former director of the London School of Economics Anthony Giddens, though, virtually every early effort failed to reduce absolute emissions. Denmark was perhaps the lone exception, because tax revenue there was directed to subsidize energy-saving practices.[13]

This is key. Taxes assessed must be funneled directly into emissions reduction. They can't go elsewhere. Even when taxes are acknowledged as raising funds to invest in innovation, it's not an easy sell. All too often, it's the proverbial third rail in American politics.

There is precedent for public acquiescence, though, if it can be demonstrated that funds funnel directly into the public interest. The Eisenhower administration, for example, placed a tax on gasoline to build the U.S. Interstate highway system. The public supported that tax because it brought tangible benefits. Of course, politically, it is important to note, these were not benefits to be seen only generations later. They were realized right away.

Tax swaps are a variation on this idea. They are revenue-neutral, lowering other taxes to ease the pain of a carbon tax. For example, first the government levies a tax of $15 per metric ton of carbon produced. This combines with a reduction in the federal payroll tax on the first $3,660 a worker earns.[14] It's a more democratic option. All fossil fuels are taxed at their source, with fees collected uniformly in dollars per ton of carbon dioxide at the mine or port of entry for each fossil fuel. The price of goods then increases in proportion to amount of fossil fuel used for production.

This option also offers more coverage. It's less vulnerable to lobbying. Its administrative costs are lower. And the kicker is, it creates new revenue for governments to combat climate change. In short, it's the best way to control emissions, but it's also the worst way to mobilize political support. Electorates are mistrustful, unless it is crystal clear where the money goes.

Former lead NASA climate scientist James Hansen's twist on this borrows from the Alaska Permanent Fund noted in my account of the Great Barrier Reef. Hansen insists that all funds collected be redistributed equally as dividends among legal adult residents, with half shares up to two children per family. That works out to roughly $250 a month or $3,000 a year. All total, that's some $9,000 a year for a typical family of four.[15]

Of course, to work, this needs to start low, then rise continually. Phrased a little more pointedly, the only way to a high tax is to start low. Political scientist and professor of environmental studies at the University of Colorado at Boulder Roger Pielke, Jr., suggests as little as $5 per metric ton is the appropriate low number, and adds that it's best applied "upstream" when fossil fuels are first removed from the earth.[16]

But that's not going to be easy. As evidence, we need none other than the 2009 proposed carbon tax on mining in Australia. The goal was to take those funds and invest them into converting 20 percent of Australian energy into renewables by 2020. Enraged coal companies threatened to close their mines and launched an AU $22 million campaign against the tax. Even after it was watered down, it took over three years for legislation to enter force in 2012. Once it did, the tax faced constant industry attack, eventually succumbing to repeal in July 2014 under the mining-friendly Abbott government.

With this in mind, we need to better incentivize the transition from fossil fuel. Taxes may yet be an integral part of the solution, but they are not the answer in and of themselves. When it comes to encouraging investment in alternative energy, we need to mix carrots and sticks.

Research and development seed grants, for example, are a woefully underutilized option to reducing our carbon footprint. The U.S. government alone invests some $30 billion annually in medical research.[17] It spends another $80 billion on military research and development. Shouldn't we be spending more than $4.36 billion on non-defense-related energy research, as calculated in 2012 by the American Association for the Advancement of Science?[18]

To put that in a slightly different context, our entire federal appropriation for energy research amounts to less than what Americans spend annually on potato chips.[19] As Energy Secretary nominee Ernest Moniz stated during his April 2013 confirmation hearing, "We are underinvesting by a factor of three."[20] We've improved somewhat the last several years, largely in response to the debilitating 2008 financial crisis, but government investment in energy is still well below its 1970s peak. It needs to increase substantially, at least to the equivalent of the $20 to $30 billion we spent annually during the golden age of space exploration, according to former *New York Times* reporter and current Pace University Fellow Andrew Revkin.[21]

This is not to suggest that government should pick the winners when it comes to new technology. Rather, it should keep a full slate of options on the table. Government seed grants facilitate a more even playing field; they encourage full exploration of all options.

Here's where the idea of a feed-in-tariff works wonders. When effective, as in the German case first in 1991 and then again in 2000 with the German Renewable Energy Act and its subsequent amendments, this policy mechanism encourages investment in alternative energy by guaranteeing long-term, fixed price contracts for those who produce green energy such as wind or solar photovoltaic. It is the assurance of a competitive price over typically fifteen to twenty years that spurs development in alternative energies, partially inoculating investors from the vagaries of new technology and buttressing attempts to compete with existing energy sources such as coal, hydroelectric, and nuclear.

Regardless, we need a system that fundamentally shifts our energy infrastructure in the next decade, one that allows global carbon dioxide emissions to stabilize by 2025 and then begin to decline over the next quarter-century.

Along these lines, as Pielke contends, policies are infinitely more effective when they focus on causes, not consequences.[22]

The next day begins with a breathtaking breakfast cruise through the seven-mile Lemaire channel, as seen in Figure 20.2. Our destination is Pleneua Bay and Petermann Island at the southern end of the channel. Eduard Dallmann's German expedition of 1873–1874 discovered the channel, and Belgian navy officer Adrien de Gerlach first navigated it in 1898, naming it for his fellow countryman, the Belgian explorer of the Congo Charles Lemaire.

The Lemaire's narrowness makes navigation tricky. At its widest, it's merely a mile across, shrinking at one point to only a half-mile. We slow down to accommodate this difficulty, but, going northeast to southwest, the ship's deck is still soaked with spray. The sky is bright blue and filled with warming sunshine, and the temperature is rising noticeably.

Our morning Zodiac cruise explores Pleneau Bay for the next hour. We pass a series of picturesque mountain peaks with snowy slopes, and there's a brief encounter with three leopard seals. As I learned two days earlier in Anj's presentation, the leopard seal is one of four seals that breed and feed here in Antarctica.[23] They have a deserved reputation as ruthless predators, largely because they play with their food. It's not merely a poor

20.2 Lemaire Channel.

20.3 Gentoo penguins lining up to jump.

display of table manners, mind you. It's pretty gruesome stuff. You see, they often hunt close to penguin colonies such as this one in Figure 20.3, hovering by the water's edge as they wait for the first brave or foolhardy soul to dive in.

Once the first victim is caught, the "playing" begins. Hanging on with their notorious teeth, the leopard seal slaps its penguin "play toy" repeatedly on the water. In actuality, the seal is not playing. It has a far more practical intention. It is attempting to skin the penguin alive.

The three leopard seals we see, though, including this one in Figure 20.4, are merely sunning themselves on the ice. Not much action in that. Maybe the excitement was earlier, and we are stumbling upon the postmeal nap?

After giving these celebrities their red-carpet moment, my photographic attention turns to the ice. Pleneau Bay is what you might call an iceberg grave-yard, filled with hundreds of amazing "growlers," small icebergs or floes just large enough to threaten shipping.

That's not a concern for me, though. Rightly or wrongly, my faith and fate rest squarely on the shoulders of the mysterious, sweater-draped captain we catch fleeting glimpses of from time to time. I'm no early-twentieth-century heroic polar explorer; rather, I'm taking full advantage of the comforts that the *Orlova* and its captain provide us twenty-first-century tourists.

20.4 Sunning leopard seal.

And surprisingly, I feel, not like a scientific tourist, but a quasi-artistic one. These growlers come in all sorts of shapes, sizes, and even colors. My favorites are translucent light to deep-azure blue. This blue hue forms in the deepest, densest layers of icebergs. Over millions of years, the oxygen in the ice is squeezed out by the shear weight of ice above it. This extremely dense ice, if large enough, absorbs light at the red end of the light spectrum, thus glowing an otherworldly blue. From the water line to twenty feet below, these shades take on more of a turquoise to lime green hue. All are breathtaking, including this one in Figure 20.5.

That afternoon we land at Petermann Island. It's named after August Petermann, a German photographer and supporter of polar exploration. This is the southernmost point of our trip, probably the farthest south I'll ever reach in my lifetime at 65 degrees 10 minutes. On the beach near the cove where we disembark is an abandoned Argentinian refuge hut. Architecturally, it looks its age—it was built in 1955. Despite its desertion, though, it has held up well over the years thanks to the lack of moisture in this frozen, dry land. There's also a memorial cross nearby honoring three British scientists who died there in August 1982, a reminder that this climate giveth and it taketh away.

Our main purpose for this visit, though, is neither the hut nor the memorial cross. Rather, it is to pay respects to the living—the most southerly colony of gentoo penguins in Antarctica, one member of which appears below in Figure 20.6. Some 2,000 breeding pairs reside on Petermann Island, along with roughly 500 breeding pairs of Adélie penguins.

Named after the wife of nineteenth-century French explorer Jules Sebastien Dumont d'Urville, Adélies mate for life. They typically establish rock nests a mere pebble's throw from their previous season's site, and with hundreds of pairs jockeying for space, territorial squabbles inevitably erupt. Indeed, treasured pebble building blocks are frequently pilfered from nearby nests.

As we observe a number of rounds of this activity, one particularly curious penguin pauses to collect a small, plastic toy penguin a tourist in our group was photographing off to the side. We immediately realize this isn't good, but are unsure what to do. It's not like chasing after the penguin is an option. Before anyone can react, though, the toy's owner yells at the penguin, and it quickly drops the toy and continues along its way. I'd like to think she was concerned about the penguin, but, more likely, she simply feared the loss of her prized plastic possession.

This tacky tourist episode is all the more ironic considering what petroleum-based products such as this are doing to the Adélies' homes.

20.5 This breathtaking iceberg was floating just south of the Lemaire Channel in Pléneau Bay, an iceberg graveyard where pieces originating as far as the Ross Ice Shelf run aground.

20.6 Building a pebble nest.

Adélies, along with emperor penguins, are the only two true Antarctic species of penguin. These two species are the only ones that live here year around.

The problem Adélies face, if you recall from the first pages in this book, is that they rely on sea ice for survival, using ice floes as foraging platforms. A warming Antarctica is melting those essential feeding aides. Adélies arrive at their colonies in late October, in synchrony with the freezing and thawing cycle of sea ice. They are genetically programed to arrive at that time every year.[24] By early December, all their eggs are laid. The females then return to the sea to feed while the males stay back to sit on the nests. That means we are seeing only males at the moment.

Once chicks fledge, they spend five years at sea. They are visual hunters, needing daylight to forage, so during the winter months they travel with pack ice to feed in the northern Ross Sea. But warming sea and air along the north-central peninsula has reduced the distance pack ice extends offshore, cutting the annual extent of sea ice on its western edge by 40 percent since 1979. Without this ice, Adélies now swim farther offshore to reach traditional krill feeding waters, expending valuable energy previously invested in a successful breeding season.

As if that is not bad enough, Adélies are also coping with greater levels of snow accumulation on their southern-exposure nesting sites. As a result, eggs drown during summer snowmelt. Bill Fraser, president and lead investigator of the Polar Research Oceans Group, is one of the world's leading authorities on the population biology and ecology of Adélies. He finds that 12,000 to 15,000 breeding pairs have been lost, approximately 80 percent of the number that occupied this region of the peninsula only thirty-five years ago.[25]

But it's not that simple. While Adélies as well as chinstraps are struggling, gentoo penguins are climate-warming winners, expanding their southward range as temperatures rise.[26] This is a new development. An international team, led by scientists from the University of Southampton and Oxford University, has estimated both when the current genetic diversity arose in penguins and what past population sizes were.[27] In the thirty-thousand years before human activity affected our climate, they found that three species of penguin, chinstraps, Adélies, and southern populations of gentoos, all increased in numbers. Now only gentoo are benefiting while chinstrap and Adélie suffer.

To better grasp this idea of winners and losers, I hike up to the top of Petermann Island. It boasts truly stunning views. To the south lies the majestic, mountainous landscape of Graham Land. Looking north to the Lemaire Channel, icebergs dot the calm, mirror-like waters. It's hard to imagine tragedy amid such beauty. Then again, it's not such a stretch to argue that the two go hand and hand. As aforementioned environmental studies and political science professor Roger Pielke, Jr., notes, many consider climate change to be akin to an inkblot onto which people map their own hopes and values, their vision of what a better world would look like.[28]

One point is certain when it comes to climate change. Externalities must be part of our discussion. We need to price carbon. Without such pricing, the business community lacks regulatory certainty, the crucial environment that spurs private-sector investment. Only when this changes will we see concerted efforts at mitigation.[29]

That evening a group gathers on deck to disembark for camping on a small island in Leith Cove. I've been thinking long and hard about joining them for the better part of the day. Here's my chance to toss aside the toasty comforts of the *Orlova* and become a true explorer, but in the end, I calculate that it's not worth it. I'm trying to be logical about this entire experience. Even as every effort will be made to minimize the impact of these campers, including peeing in plastic bags, their presence will be felt for a long time to come. Remember, in one crucial paradoxical respect, this place is a lot like Las Vegas. What happens in Antarctica, stays in Antarctica. I'm not sure I'd gain enough from the experience to make a difference with this project. Plus, let's face it. As great a story as it may make, it's going to be really, really cold out there.

In considerably warmer environs aboard the *Orlova* that evening, I recall the astounding tales of the heroic age of Antarctic exploration. From 1895 to 1922, an array of characters carved out larger-than-life reputations. Norwegian polar explorer Roald Amundsen leads most such lists as the first man, with some one hundred sled dogs, to reach the South Pole.[30]

British Royal Navy officer Robert Falcon Scott, of course, also demands inclusion, even as a star-crossed runner-up to Amundsen. Beyond perishing with his crew on their trek back from the pole, Scott will also be remembered for the degree to which science drove his expeditions in the Antarctic. In 1911, for example, Scott sent Apsley Cherry-Garrard, Bill Wilson, and Birdie Bowers to Cape Crozier in July, the height of the winter season, to bring back eggs from an emperor penguin colony. As Cherry-Garrard writes in

The Worst Journey in the World, the three hauled their sled some sixty miles in pitch dark and temperatures of seventy below. At one point, a storm blew away their tent and the men lay in a snowdrift singing hymns while waiting to die.[31]

But they didn't. They survived, and the three eggs they lugged back to Scott's base now rest where all of us can see them in London's Natural History Museum.

And who can forget Scott's countryman, Ernest Shackleton, seen in Figure 20.7. His 497-day odyssey, from 1914 to

20.7 Legendary Antarctic explorer Ernest Shackleton during the Imperial Trans-Antarctic Expedition.
Source: Scanned from *South with Endurance* by Frank Hurley.

1916, is one of greatest survival stories ever told, one that highlights not only the in-hospitable Antarctic but Shackleton's enduring personal leadership.[32] As pack ice first gripped, then crushed his ship *Endurance*, he and his crew were marooned on the ice within the Weddell Sea, where they drifted first on ice floes and then lifeboats to desolate Elephant Island. From there, Shackleton and five others subsequently crossed eight hundred miles of open water in a makeshift boat, reaching South Georgia Island only to find they had landed on the unpopulated end and needed to march across the island interior to reach a whaling station on the other side.[33]

Drawing from this amazing journey, perhaps Sir Edmund Hillary sums it up best.[34] "For scientific discovery, give me Scott, for speed and efficiency of travel, give me Amundsen, but when disaster strikes and all hope is gone, get down on your knees and pray for Shackleton."[35] By this point, it should be pretty clear. When it comes to climate change, and drafting effective market mechanisms to combat it, relying on one savior is insufficient. We need all the above.

chapter twenty-one

FUNDAMENTALLY FLAWED?

WHEN PENGUINS NEED TO RELIEVE THEMSELVES, they let it fly. Mind you, this regular releasing of the bowels doesn't come in manageable puppy-size bits. It's more of a gooey, soupy slurry, with pinkish-brown streams squirted everywhere. Yes, everywhere. There's so much of it, in fact, you can see it from space.

I'm not kidding. Casting aside temptation for scatological embellishment, and noting that some of the excrement, depending on diet, can actually be white or even green, satellite imagery literally captures images of penguin colonies and their poo. Well, technically it's not the colonies themselves, just their poo.

"We can't see actual penguins on the satellite maps because the resolution isn't good enough. But during the breeding season the birds stay at a colony for eight months. The ice gets pretty dirty, and it's the guano stains that we can see," explains Peter T. Fretwell, a geospatial scientist with the British Antarctic Survey.[1]

These unique guano "signatures," as they are formally known, offer scientists such as those from the British Antarctic Survey valuable data sets in studying the health and size of various penguin colonies throughout Antarctica.[2] They've even facilitated the discovery of entirely new colonies.

As you might expect, from the penguin's perspective at least, there's method to this madness. Penguins defecate with purpose. They're not just dumping excess waste in and around their dutifully crafted nests.[3] They're marking territory. They are, in the most primitive sense, staking claim to Antarctica—with their bowels.

Turns out we humans aren't so different, but more on that in a minute. Let's talk a bit more about the prodigious amount of guano that drenches the spit of snow and rocks before me.

21.1 Chilean research station Gabriel González Videla.
Source: Samuel Blanc in Wikimedia Commons.

It's not just my sense of vision that is overwhelmed as I step gingerly from rock to slippery rock on Waterboat Point this morning. My sense of smell is in overdrive as well.

I'm not alone in this observation. *Sports Illustrated* columnist and writer Steve Rushin, for one, characterizes guano as the "continent's trademark smell."[4] To some degree, the scent of penguin guano is reminiscent of earthy barnyards you may recall from childhood, yet at the same time it's an entirely different stench altogether. It also lingers in your nostrils a bit more than you'd expect; even though penguins look cute and cuddly, they don't necessarily smell good, too.

Anyway, Waterboat Point is a big deal for us tourists on the boat. We've been restricted to island hopping along the peninsula, but now we can claim a true continental landing. Straddled between Paradise Harbor and Andvord Bay on the west coast of Graham Land, this is the westernmost point of the Antarctic continent.

Our stated purpose is to visit the Chilean research station Gabriel González Videla seen here in Figure 21.1. Named after the first head of state to visit Antarctica, the station was quite active over a half-century ago, but today it serves essentially as a summer base for the Chilean air force. We are told that a population census of the aforementioned poo perpetrators, gentoo penguins, continues, but the small museum with souvenirs on sale seems to indicate that tourism is the primary purpose nowadays.

This humble outcropping has historical significance under the Antarctic Treaty and served as the site where twenty-year-old geologist Thomas Bagshawe, following his record 1921–1922 overwintering with merchant naval officer M. C. Lester, wrote the first scientific study of penguin breeding. It's not a stretch to imagine that the gentoos standing before me now are the distant descendants of those noted study subjects.

Gentoos are the fastest penguin species, recording speeds up to twenty-two miles per hour under water. To put this in perspective, they're more than four-and-a-half times as fast as Olympic sensation Michael Phelps, plus they are capable of diving up to two hundred feet below water.[5] These characters are also distinctive in appearance, with a bold white stripe that looks a bit like a bonnet perched on their heads. Fully grown, they stand about three feet high, which is slightly taller than their Adélie and chinstrap cousins, both of which measure about two-and-a-half feet.

Gentoo population interests aside, though, what's really going on here, in addition to the prodigious defecation, is more of an old-fashioned "possession is nine-tenths of the law" sort of claim to the mainland—and the opportunity to let capitalism flourish at the bottom of the globe by selling small souvenirs to rapacious consumers like myself. Establishing a physical presence, setting up laboratories and lavatories alike, allows states such as Chile, not to mention Australia, New Zealand, Argentina, France, Norway, and the United Kingdom, to claim sovereignty over slices of Antarctica (Figure 21.2).[6]

As with our penguin friends, there's method to this seeming madness. While no known commercially viable mineral deposits exist in Antarctica, states recognize that the continent still holds value, and they are not ready to cede it to someone else. Unlike at its polar opposite in the Arctic,

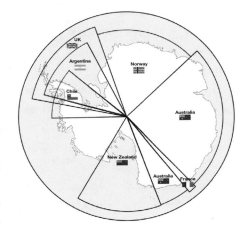

21.2 Territorial claims in Antarctica. Source: Wikimedia Commons.

though, where a veritable treasure chest of riches lies beneath the ice, here there is decidedly more room for cooperation than for competition.[7] Antarctica, much more than the Arctic, provides a potential model on how to govern a common resource.

That's the challenge with climate change, too, of course. How do we govern this common resource that's under threat? How do we govern our atmosphere?

It might help to think of this political problem as analogous to an addiction. With any addiction, the first step is to admit a problem exists. Climate-change governance, though, quickly breaks down as admission of a problem evolves into identifying who caused the problem. It's a blame game. How do we assess responsibility?

The simple fact is there are numerous ways to measure responsibility, all of which ascribe blame to different actors. If we look at per capita emissions combined with historical emissions, the key culprits are the United States and Europe, and to a lesser extent Japan, Australia, and Canada. On the other hand, developing states such as China, while relatively new to the greenhouse-gas-emissions blame game, are now the world's biggest annual polluters.

Beyond annual emissions, historical emissions, and per capita emissions, energy intensity, which calculates the amount of carbon dioxide per unit of economic output, is another measure worth noting. Before I gave a talk in Bonn, Germany, as a Fulbright Scholar years ago, the U.S. embassy asked me to highlight this statistic, which makes the United States look quite good. I obliged, but I also pointed out the atmosphere doesn't care about energy intensity the way our politicians do. It only cares about absolute amounts. If one doesn't acknowledge this, one runs the risk of engaging in statistical sleight of hand, underscoring the famous quip attributed to Mark Twain about three types of lies: lies, damn lies, and statistics.

The history of international climate-change negotiation traces back to the United Nations Conference on Environment and Development, popularly known as the Earth Summit, in Rio de Janeiro in the summer of 1992. The thirty-three-page framework convention negotiated there established common but differentiated responsibilities for greenhouse emissions.[8] All of this, however, was voluntary, and, by 1995, only the former Soviet bloc was making any progress. Of course, given that their economies were in free-fall, one could easily argue that the term progress, by definition, was inappropriate.[9]

Key rounds that followed include Berlin in March 1995, Geneva in July 1996, and, most notably, Kyoto in December 1997. Technically an addendum to the 1992 framework convention, the 1997 Kyoto Protocol to the U.N. Framework Convention on Climate Change substituted the mere goals of 1992 for mandatory commitments among thirty-seven developed states and the European Union.[10] These Annex I targets, as they are known, were for the industrialized countries, largely of the Global North, and they were to be met by reducing emissions, buying and selling emissions credits, and investing in clean development projects within countries such as India and China.

Notable numbers from Kyoto were the European Union's target of 8 percent below 1990 levels, the U.S.'s 7 percent below, and Japan's 6 percent below. In contrast, over one hundred developing countries, including China and India, were exempted during the first commitment period from 2008 to 2012. As such, Kyoto, when it finally entered force in February 2005, statistically recognized common but differentiated responsibilities.

This was not easy. As Kyoto's first commitment period expired in 2012, it's become even more challenging. Most would even assert that this hurdle of common but differentiated responsibilities was insurmountable, as numerous examples over the last decade demonstrate, including the Doha Amendment in Qatar in December 2012. You've probably never heard of this Doha Amendment, for good reason. Its attempt to establish a second Kyoto commitment period from 2012 to 2020 is not in force and probably never will be, only gathering a fraction of the necessary 144 signatories to date.[11]

Despite the model established a decade before it in Montreal under the ozone-depletion treaty, whereby developing states were recognized as less responsible and allowed a more lenient timeline to phase out offending pollutants, Kyoto and subsequent attempts to amend it remained mired in this North-South controversy for years. Attempts to replicate a delayed schedule for the developing world, one that spelled out a different timeline than their developed-state brethren, were met with opposition in the Global North, particularly the United States. Attempts to require developing states to make commitments themselves were met, until recently, with opposition from the Global South, historically with China taking the lead.

Let's take a closer look at what drove this thinking, at least from the American perspective. For starters, there is a pervasive fear that emissions, and the jobs tied to them, would leave for less-regulated realms. It's not a new argument. Over two decades ago, independent presidential candidate Ross Perot identified this phenomenon colloquially as a giant sucking sound from Mexico, one he associated with anticipated passage of the North American Free Trade Agreement (NAFTA).

When you look at the numbers, though, NAFTA did not encourage massive relocation of industry. In fact, according to the U.S. Chamber of Commerce, the agreement was a "boon to the competitiveness of U.S. manufacturers, adding more than 800,000 jobs in the four years after NAFTA entered into force."[12] Extending that analysis over twenty years and the entire economy, economists credit the arrangement with creating millions of American jobs. Of course, union and consumer advocacy groups disagree, pointing to increases in outsourcing from the U.S. and lower wages in both the U.S. and Mexico.[13]

The truth is, both are right. Gains were not equally distributed in different sectors of our economy. Losses did occur. But some of those losses would have happened regardless of whether politicians created the world's largest free-trade area. In short, it wouldn't be fair to call these charges outright lies, but scare tactics touting economic ruin are more fiction than fact.

A similar line of argument applies to Kyoto. The vast majority of our greenhouse-gas emissions come from sources that simply cannot leave the country. Are you going to go live overseas in China? Are you going to give up electricity? According to the EPA, 31.3 percent of U.S. emissions are tied to electricity generation.[14] How about your daily commute? Transportation emissions in the U.S. account for another 27.2 percent of our greenhouse-gas emissions.[15] Are you going to take that overseas too?

Turns out that only about a quarter of U.S. emissions are even candidates to leave the country.[16] Yes, some would depart for paradoxically greener pastures, and the Chinese would arguably benefit from our loss. Yet the reality is, most businesses don't even have relocation on their radar.

Another critique of Kyoto, the Clean Development Mechanism (CDM), is not so easily dismissed. While President George W. Bush's characterization of Kyoto as "fundamentally flawed" in early 2001 is not entirely fair,[17] such a label is right on target when it comes to the CDM. In theory, the CDM attempt at instituting a market mechanism helps both Northern and Southern Hemisphere states. Industrialized countries earn emission credits by investing in emission-control projects in the developing world. The developing countries receive much-needed assistance in going green.

In practice, though, the CDM is an "administrative nightmare."[18] For one, it encourages fraud with unverifiable or merely temporary adjustments such as tree plantings. As anyone who's ever planted a plant can attest, there's no assurance that once planted they will survive, let alone grow healthily. Planting is just the first of many commitments to ensure that a tree becomes a valued carbon dioxide remover. As an aside, it is also worth noting that these new investments are often indistinguishable from those that would happen anyway under normal economic development.

Most damning of all, the CDM discourages developing countries from improving energy efficiency and reducing emissions on their own. The more emissions they have, the more they have available to sell as offsets to Annex I states. Some entrepreneurs in China allegedly exploit this loophole for profit, producing CFCs solely to sell to developed countries.[19] All told, David Victor, international relations scholar and codirector of the Laboratory on Law and Regulation at U.C. San Diego, guesses that as many as one-third to two-thirds of CDM credits today fail to represent real reductions.[20]

So where do we go from here? I suggest starting over, at least with the CDM. Change the focus. Sometimes you need to take a few steps back to go forward. In this case, as argued in the previous chapter, going back involves more emissions because going forward necessitates bringing refrigeration, light, heating, and cooling to the 1.2 billion around the world still in need of electricity. As long as it's not coal, this is where initial attention must be directed.

A funding mechanism, perhaps the World Bank's Global Environment Facility, would be the first step to the requisite bargain between developed and developing states. The one caveat here is this needs to be truly an "ABC" strategy. It's an elementary requirement, one where the energy source is Anything But Coal.

By the way, in thinking about the costs to such a program, one should also consider the costs to inaction. We too often leave that part out of our calculations. According to the International Energy Agency, for example, the global costs of emission reductions increase approximately $500 billion for each year we delay investment in clean energy.[21]

This brings us back to our primary venue for climate-change governance to date. Given this need for clean energy investment, what should be done with Kyoto? It's broken. Do we attempt to fix it . . . or kick it unceremoniously to the curb?

That's a tough choice. Sometimes it is better to start over. Renovations can be more costly than entirely new construction. Then again, fundamental flaws don't necessarily condemn documents to the dustbin of history. Take our own Constitution, for example. With the infamous three-fifths rule we all learned about in secondary school, some people didn't even count as people. Sounds fundamentally flawed to me. Rip it up and start over? Few made that case then, and such an argument today would be preposterous.

I'd argue that the lesson this suggests is not that racism trumps reason. Instead, I'd assert that the Constitution, as flawed as this component made it, still had many components worth saving. An increasing number of voices, even nonconservative ones, do not share this opinion when it comes to Kyoto. Despite recent progress in Paris in December 2015, the general assessment remains that international negotiation within the U.N. framework is too unwieldy. There are just too many parties to make any real progress. It's too messy, akin to ordering a pizza with 193 friends. With those kinds of numbers, you're never going to agree on the seating arrangement, let alone the food order itself.

It is this line of thinking that drives arguments to widen, or perhaps more accurately reduce, the conventional climate governance lens. Many no longer advocate Kyoto as the central attack point in climate-change governance, turning to either smaller subsets within international organization or to limited regional activity, not to mention sub-state initiatives.

Probably the most promising parameters of all are bilateral, particularly those between China and the United States. Much of this was merely theoretical until November 2014 and an historic agreement between presidents Xi Jinping and Barack Obama. With this accord, the U.S. agreed to reduce greenhouse gas emissions 26 to 28 percent below 2005 levels by 2025, while China made its first-ever public commitment to restricting greenhouse gases, targeting 2030 as its peak year in CO_2 emissions as well as the date by which 20 percent of its energy would be from nonfossil fuel.[22] That's not enough, but it is a start, albeit one greatly compromised as President Donald Trump took office in January 2017 after openly charging the Chinese with creating climate change as a concept to damage U.S. manufacturing interests.

Despite such rhetoric, though, the November 2014 agreement still points out, just as we concluded in the previous chapter regarding market mechanisms, that climate-change governance does not have to be an either/ or proposition. We can choose all of the above. There are many shades of green. Concentrating on other options does not necessarily mean ignoring the Kyoto regime altogether. A U.N. setting can still remain relevant, a crucial player in climate-change governance, and may be worth returning to more expressly in the future. It's just not working so well for us right now.

Okay, that's a bit of an understatement. Much of the last quarter-century has been nothing short of a political nightmare when it comes to climate governance and the United Nations. I could go on and on with examples from Rio to Kyoto and Cancún to Copenhagen, even including Paris to some degree, to illustrate this point. In the interest of brevity, though, let me choose one short tale about the Madrid meeting in 1995. During this plenary session, Intergovernmental Panel on Climate Change (IPCC) scientists advocated inclusion of the word "appreciable" to describe climate change. Two entire days were wasted as the Saudi delegate blocked this single word in the "Summary for Policymakers." By one estimate, roughly thirty alternatives were debated before IPCC chair Bert Bolin finally found a term that both sides could accept, "discernible." If it takes thirty attempts over two days to decide between "appreciable" and "discernible," that's probably not the right environment to settle core differences that remain today between a new coalition of developing states that suffer from climate change and developed states that recognize the need to address it versus a few holdouts like the United States that do not.

Perhaps most frustratingly, it hasn't always been that way. Supposedly, we developed a playbook for how to address an imposing North-South divide in the 1980s. As alluded to earlier, with the Montreal Protocol on Substances that Deplete the Ozone Layer, the global community created its first truly effective international environmental law in 1987.

You've probably heard about ozone, in large part because of this success. In the lower atmosphere, ozone is a pollutant, commonly known as smog. In the upper atmosphere, though, roughly eighteen miles up from the surface of Earth, it's a welcome phenomenon in the stratosphere. It forms a protective layer that filters out harmful UV light. Unfortunately, harmful gases such as chlorofluorocarbons (CFCs), introduced commercially in the 1930s as nonflammable refrigerants like the freon formerly found in air-conditioning units, react with ozone and this sunlight.

It works like this. CFCs contain chlorine and fluorine, which are stable; that means they have a long life and don't react easily. This characteristic allows them to float into the upper atmosphere over a period of decades where they are exposed to increased solar radiation. Here the sun's rays break down these CFCs, and the chlorine atoms then break apart ozone molecules. Our protective ozone layer thins.

Without ozone, melanoma (skin cancer), cataracts, and weakened immune systems result. Incidentally, UV light also harms phytoplankton, the single-cell ocean plants that serve as a critical food source for krill. Krill, as you recall from our previous chapter, are the shrimp-like animals that serve as the major food source for penguins and whales.[23]

The Montreal Protocol targeted preservation of this protective upper atmosphere ozone, and it was resoundingly successful. Shouldn't we be able to mimic this success with climate change? Can't Montreal be a model for Kyoto? Sadly, it's a bit more complicated than that. Linking Montreal and Kyoto is not an apples-and-oranges comparison. Brussels sprouts and porterhouse steak might be more accurate. In the aftermath of Montreal, policymakers deemed certainty in science as unnecessary. They applauded incremental policy. And public opinion, never particularly intense when it came to ozone depletion, was judged to be superfluous.[24]

None of this holds true with climate change. Further, while the precautionary principle was important in Montreal, it was not the driving force. On the other hand, climate-change activism attempts to build on the precautionary principle as its foundation. As restated at Rio in 1992, "Where there are threats of serious or irreversible damage, lack of full scientific certainly should not be used as a reason for postponing cost-effective measures to prevent environmental degradation."

It turns out, then, the Montreal Model is not so easy to emulate. Ozone is a simpler example. Only a handful of large developed states contributed to that problem in the 1980s. Cost-effective alternatives were available, ironically thanks to the U.S. government forcing private industries such as DuPont

Chemical to develop them in the 1970s. Climate change, conversely, is much more complicated. Many more states are involved. Curbing it requires radical revision in our energy infrastructure. It demands a substantial shift in standard of living.

Climate meetings in Copenhagen in December 2009 made it clear that this will not happen any time soon, at least through U.N. leadership. Indeed, by nearly all accounts, Copenhagen was an unqualified disaster, its sole success being a narrow agenda item improving protection of global forests. With so much expected, why such a small result? Copenhagen fell victim to a number of flaws. Poor timing in the midst of global economic recession ensured that most delegates focused on more immediate economic needs. The United States, continuing a distressing pattern, once again failed to lead as Obama recognized that any treaty with real teeth would never receive the required U.S. Senate ratification.

And perhaps most importantly and disheartening, the U.N. process did not work. There were simply too many countries with too many issues. This created pressure to concentrate on agreement where possible, rather than carving out arrangements that actually made a difference. In short, Copenhagen made it clear that, as professor David Victor asserts, "All the canonical elements in the toolbox were wrong for global warming."[25] By the close of Copenhagen, three core points were abundantly clear. The E.U. was overly invested in a U.N. approach. The U.S. was not a credible partner to that approach. And third, and most damning of all, the U.N., at least for the foreseeable future, no longer served as the primary negotiating ground for climate-change governance.

Again, this is not an argument to toss out the U.N. altogether. It can continue to serve as an umbrella institution, fostering different experimental efforts. This does return us to an important political question, though. If not the U.N., then what? What exactly is the most appropriate level of political organization for addressing climate change?

A number of alternatives exist. For years, I've thought the bottom-up model superior to top-down ones. Maybe it's just the little guy in me always favoring the underdog. When one of my alma maters routinely cranks out basketball victories by wide margins, despite my allegiance, I frequently find myself rooting for the other team to keep it close, to keep it exciting. I suppose we all harbor a little of that sentiment, identifying with those clawing their way to the top seems more American, even if it no longer really is. More to the point, Kyoto seemed to be clear evidence that top-down models don't work when it comes to climate change. They simply don't have sufficient buy-in from the grassroots, not to mention critical support from the business community.

But I'm now convinced, after reading and speaking with countless experts, that climate-change governance needs activity at both levels, and everything in between, to be truly effective. Kyoto is not dead, but, like all of us, it will be some day. It's in the process of dying, again like all of us. That said, I ask you, isn't it a bit morbid to think of your life as the process of dying? Doesn't living life sound better? That's more than an emotional question, by the way. It's a practical one, too. We would be wise to learn from Kyoto's failures, not to euthanize it, but to allow it to survive and serve as a trusted, elder advisor.

Here's where the most recent December 2015 Conference of Parties (COP) in Paris provides promise. Most regard the twenty-first COP, in stark contrast to its predecessors, to be a resounding success. Although it is nonbinding, the deal expressly targets restrictions to "well below" 2 degrees Celsius (3.6 degrees Fahrenheit) from preindustrial levels. Widespread consensus seems to exist, with states allowed to set their own targets for emissions reductions.

Like Kyoto before it, the sixteen-page agreement signed in Paris[26] has what is known as a "dual-threshold" requirement, with formal approval by not only 55 of the original 195 signatory states and the EU but also by countries accounting for 55 percent of global emissions. The reasoning here is that small states cannot pass the agreement without large-state approval, but neither can a handful of large states force the issue without wider support across the globe. It's analogous to our Congress, where smaller states receive equal influence in the Senate while larger states hold more in the House.

Of course, with the requirement for 55 percent of global emissions, at least one of the four biggest emitters (China, United States, the European Union, and Russia) must sign on. With a combined 38 percent of emissions today, according to the environmental think tank the World Resources Institute, the most likely scenario would entail both China and the United States.

In the United States case, though, it's a bit more complicated. Yes, Secretary of State Kerry signed the U.S. up in April 2016, but, constitutionally, international treaties then require approval by two-thirds of the Senate to become law.

To avoid this political quagmire, the Obama administration, with assistance from the rest of the world, carefully crafted not a treaty but what they argued was merely an agreement between the administration and the rest of the world. As such, Obama asserted, ratification was not required. Only executive action was needed. Such diplomacy-speak serves a practical purpose on the one hand, but not one without cost. Beyond potentially dangerous precedent, this also means the agreement technically expired at the end of Obama's last term in January 2017.

Even as the Paris Agreement entered force in early November 2016, furthermore, the U.S. presidential election results less than a week later slammed the brakes on climate activists' celebratory mood. Indeed, newly elected President Donald J. Trump promises to not only extract the United States from its Paris commitment but also to dismantle Obama's clean power plan and its push to renewable energies.

With that in mind, new mechanisms beyond the United Nations format are desperately required. Most importantly, a new international financial structure is needed, with key financial levers at multiple levels. Even as these new global initiatives are pursued, moreover, bottom-up approaches require investment. Actions as mundane as individual lifestyle changes play a role here, although one must recognize that picking low-lying fruit risks postponing the crucial drive for more substantial efforts down the road.

Each of us can make a difference simply by cutting back on personal energy use. Specific adaptations run the gamut, ranging from heavier use of public transit to carpooling or even telecommuting, from converting traditional incandescent light bulbs to LED and compact fluorescent bulbs, from running dishwashers only when full to washing clothes in cool or warm rather than hot water, and from insulating hot-water heaters to keeping automobile tires properly inflated.

Of course, there's even more bang for the buck to be had at the state level, specifically the bilateral relationship between the United States and China highlighted earlier. The lessons of competition, from the Cold War to Antarctica (whose Antarctic Treaty System will be discussed shortly), underscore a mixture of promise and pitfalls here.

I see this double-edged sword of competition in my students, too. It brings out both the best and worst in them. With the appropriate structures in place, the odds that it will bring out the best are much greater. As Hampshire College political scientist and natural-resource expert Michael Klare suggests, a top-level U.S.-China energy summit modeled on the Cold War might be our best chance yet to hammer out agreement. That said, the historical stumbling block in climate-change negotiations, consensus on common but differentiated responsibility for greenhouse gas emissions between the developed and developing world, is further complicated as China increasingly carves out its own interests independent of much of the developing world.

States within the United States, not countries themselves, might also go it alone, as seen through a number of non-Kyoto initiatives over the years. Our system of federalism, with power sharing between national and state governments, allows states such as California to carve out meaningful climate-change policy. Former California Governor Schwarzenegger, for example, earned a reputation as the Carbon Terminator with passage of that state's Global Warming Solutions Act in 2006. This law requires the California Air Resources Board to oversee reductions in greenhouse gas emissions to 1990 levels by 2020, equivalent to a 25 percent reduction.

It's not just federalism that distributes power in the American system, though. Constitutional separation of powers at the federal level opens up multiple options as well.[27] While it can play the role of foe just as easily as friend, environmentalists point to the judiciary as one such example. This is tied to the simple fact that, when it comes to policymaking, courts take longer views than politicians. Courts, at least at the highest levels, don't need to worry about re-election, whereas Congress and presidents often obsesses over election cycles.

Perhaps, then, the response to our question regarding the most appropriate level for action is not an either/or answer. The strategy that makes the most sense is one that incorporates all the above. Every level is problematic. From democracy to the discount rate, the obstacles that present themselves provide nearly limitless opportunities to stall action. And despite past failures through Kyoto, we should not abandon the international arena entirely. As articulated by international relations scholars David Held et al., a dual approach advancing domestic and international negotiations is preferred.[28]

The United Nations is probably not the best place to start. Instead, starting with roughly a dozen countries, working in small sets of states rather than the global U.N. framework, makes more sense. It's what professor David Victor calls "the club approach." Over time, this group could evolve much like the General Agreement on Tariffs and Trade (the precursor to today's World Trade Organization), where progression through a series of eight rounds of deal-making proved effective.[29] Such a system allows an emphasis on carrots over sticks, fostering enabling rather than prohibitive behaviors. A race to the top would emerge.

This will be not be two-minutes-and-a-cloud-of-dust, Kentucky-Derby-type of gallop, though. It's going to take a long time. Even as immediate action is needed, it is imperative that incentives build on each other slowly, pushing individual states to make larger and larger contingent promises. As Victor further asserts, the focus here should be on policies instead of emissions, because governments can control policies more easily. The goal is to institutionalize flexibility, allowing individual governments to determine the specifics.[30]

Paris represents real progress because it does just this, provided the United States agrees to go along. If not, as Mike Hulme, founding director of the Tyndall Centre for Climate Change Research at the University of East Anglia, contends, we condemn ourselves to merely managing the problem of climate change, never solving it.[31]

And, of course, even if the U.S. does assume a leadership role, unforeseen complications may still arise. For example, this afternoon my tour group is scheduled to land along the Danco Coast at Cuverville Island, home to the largest gentoo penguin colony in the region with 4,800 breeding pairs. The island also serves as a study site for tourist impact, but alas, our landing is postponed due to gale-force winds of fifty knots (57.6 mph), strong enough to do structural damage on land. The tour company will not start Zodiac operations if winds are thirty-five knots or higher (40.3 mph), and we are required to return immediately if weather conditions worsen.

With that, weather is certainly on my mind, but the real reason I'm here, of course, involves the term too often conflated with it: climate. We've introduced only a handful of examples to date, but Antarctica is clearly a microcosm of climate change. Even the politics of climate change can be better understood with an Antarctic lens.

Take the International Geophysical Year (IGY) as an example. From 1957 to 1958, this twelve-state scientific endeavor recognized each pole as both influencing and reacting to changes around the world. For eighteen months, scientists scanned ocean and atmosphere alike. Timed to coincide with peak activity in the solar cycle, this initiative was the first scientific program to utilize earth-orbiting satellites. It also produced the first systematic measurement of greenhouse gases.

Of particular interest here, as always, was carbon dioxide, with the most famous of these studies being conducted by former oceanographer and chemist Charles David Keeling. Beginning in 1958, to escape biasing his data with local pollution, he recorded carbon dioxide concentrations atop Hawaii's 4,200-meter Mauna Loa volcano.[32] Scripps Institution of Oceanography director Roger Revelle, who organized the funding for Keeling's project, had just published a prominent paper suggesting that most carbon dioxide would stay in the atmosphere rather than be absorbed into ocean waters.[33] Keeling set out to measure whether that was accurate, and the results of his study, which continue today, are well known as the Keeling curve. As you recall from our Galápagos chapters, this graph depicts unmistakable growth in carbon dioxide within our atmosphere since 1958.

Several fortuitous developments facilitated initiatives like this under the IGY. For one, international interest in Antarctica expanded, highlighted by the rise of U.S. and Soviet influence on the continent. In essence, the two superpowers found yet another setting for their Cold War rivalry to play out. Competition brought results. Indeed, the Soviets established more scientific stations than any other IGY participant during 1957–58, and in every claimed sector of continent.[34] The following year, 1959, the Washington Conference established the Antarctic Treaty System, a decidedly complex legal regime comprised of a cluster of subregimes.

Today the ATS protects all land below 60 degrees south. It's not one treaty, but a constellation of legal agreements, evolving piece by piece over five decades.[35] Its origins date to a 1940s dispute between the U.K., Argentina, and Chile over the peninsula, one the U.S. sought to resolve by suggesting a moratorium on all sovereignty claims in the region in 1948. Some even considered placing the continent under U.N. administration.

Not to hit a global institution when it's down, but, thankfully, that never happened. On the other hand, here's where the tie to climate-change politics becomes all the more relevant. International environmental issues, across the board, are confounded by state sovereignty. The Antarctic regime is yet one more example.

Still, it's possible to make lemonade out of these lemons. As the late international legal scholar Christopher Joyner once noted, the language in the treaty serves as the legal glue by which states agree to disagree, pledging not to change the legal status quo in Antarctica.[36] It's not perfect, and many reasonably critique it as constructing a "purgatory of ambiguity." Indeed, Antarctica legally remains *res nullius*, the property of nobody. As with all nonbinding soft law, fundamental problems of monitoring and enforcement emerge in such global commons. Even as Article VII of the ATS attempts to address the monitoring issue by allowing contracting parties to inspect each other's stations and activities, for example, specific means of enforcement remain lacking.

Antarctic tourism encounters these same hurdles of state sovereignty, including dependence on domestic legislation as each tour operator applies to a specific state for permission to conduct operations. Climate-change governance is no different. It's a common pool resource issue. As such, its fundamental flaw is not the international treaty itself. It is the incentive structure that governs how states act and react. This is where attention must focus next, on changing how states, and the populations within them, think about their welfare. We need do more—with less.

chapter twenty-two

MORE WITH LESS . . .
Or, from Vicious to Virtuous Circles

THE APPROACH TO DECEPTION ISLAND is on its southeast side, through a slender opening in an ancient caldera wall known playfully as Neptune's Bellows. Nineteenth-century American seal hunter and explorer Nathaniel Palmer named it for the wind that audibly sighs as it gushes through. That bluster, along with the narrow width, can make navigation a bit tricky. But all is fine today, as our captain, the aforementioned dead ringer for the Dos Equis World's Most Interesting Man, deftly steers our craft into the sea-filled caldera of this age-old volcano.

Turns out, a few years back, the *Lyubov Orlova* was not so fortunate. It's not something you read about in the promotional literature, but the *Orlova* grounded here in Whalers Bay one late November day three years before my visit. Fortunately, a Spanish navy icebreaker came to its rescue, and, after waiting for high tide and a tortuous eight hours of towing, the *Orlova* returned to Ushuaia under its own steam, while its traumatized passengers flew back to Buenos Aires. This morning would have been decidedly more suspenseful if we had known about that beforehand. Then again, if we had known of that mishap, most of us probably wouldn't have booked the excursion in the first place.

It's 8:00 A.M., and we are a little over seventy-five miles north of the Antarctic Peninsula in the lower third of the South Shetland Islands, an ocean-sculpted archipelago of ice and black basalt. Roughly nine miles in diameter, Deception Island, seen in Figure 22.1, is a unique, ring-shaped island straddling 63 degrees south latitude. What really sets it apart, though, and helps explain its name, is an enormous sheltered harbor, which is not visible from the sea. That key characteristic, Port Foster, has shaped Deception Island since its discovery in January 1820.

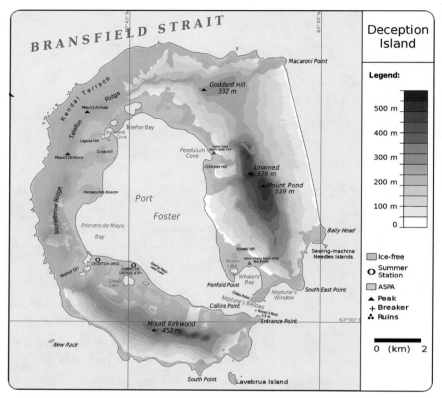

22.1 Deception Island, showing the topography and location of its stations and protected zones. Source: Wikimedia Commons author Treehill. (Modifications made by Fitzgabbro.)

Upon our landing two centuries later, most of our tourist troupe launches into individual explorations along the black beachhead of Whalers Bay, a section of Port Foster immediately starboard to its entrance. A number of us also lumber up to the notch on the eastern side of the cut known as Neptune's Window. The hike takes about a half-hour and offers glorious views atop a promontory cloaked in shrubby little fruticose lichens. As always, I watch my step with great caution, reminding myself that the stakes are all the higher given that these symbiotic alga-and-fungus organisms typically grow no more than a centimeter every hundred years.

The wind is strong here and little conversation takes place. That's fine with me as it offers an ideal opportunity for reflection. Nestled below on the muddy beach are a series of partially standing structures built a century before when this was a popular base for whaling ships. You would never know it from the serene setting before me, but a couple thousand rotting whale carcasses once littered the shoreline.[1] Indeed, in the course of only two decades in the early twentieth century, these protected waters facilitated the killing of more than 100,000 whales among the surrounding islands.[2] They say the bay was red with blood from the slaughter.

That wasn't even the first wave of wanton destruction Deception hosted. A century earlier, in the mid-1820s, Antarctic fur seals were pushed to commercial extinction by American and British fleets. The island itself didn't harbor many seals, but its shelter provided an ideal base from which to rendezvous before and after hunting raids elsewhere. Within just four years of Deception's discovery, some 500,000 fur seals had met their demise. So few remained that it was no longer commercially viable to hunt them.[3]

The primary reason we are here today, though, is not to ruminate on either of these bloodthirsty eras, even as the remains of a handful of tanks for storing whale oil lie before us. Our purpose is much more selfish. You see, this area is one of best-known active volcanoes in the Antarctic region, and the largest of three recently active volcanic centers in the South Shetlands. Its last eruption was in August 1970, but the big one was approximately 10,000 years ago, when a violently explosive eruption released some 30 cubic kilometers of molten rock.[4] With that, the volcano summit collapsed to form the caldera of Port Foster.

Most recently, in 1992, enhanced seismic activity created ground deformation as well as warmer water temperatures. Today, the floor of Port Foster, at least in geological terms, is rising rapidly and maintains long-term geothermal activity. It's classified as a restless caldera with significant volcanic risk.

Talk about significant risk, the primary reason we are here to today at exactly latitude 62 degrees 56 minutes south, complete with a defibrillator stashed to the side to stave off life-threatening cardiac dysrhythmias, is to plunge into the two-degree Celsius, slate-gray waters of this polar bay, as seen here in Figure 22.2. Admittedly, in the interest of full disclosure, the water is noticeably warmer on the edges of this black volcanic beach, precisely because of this aforementioned geothermal activity. You might say that, at least for a couple of feet along these edges, it's a veritable hot tub.

The way this works is fairly simple, if not smart. You strip down to a bathing suit under your polar gear, then dash through the frigid air and into the

22.2 Polar plunge.

initial couple feet of extra-warm water. The extreme temperature difference between air and water is not lost on me, but even as my mind is processing this contrast, the water temperature shifts quickly somewhere between ankle and waist depth (I honestly can't remember) to bone-shattering, unbearable cold.

I dive in shallowly and immediately come up gasping for air. This is a natural reflex, to hyperventilate. It's also the initial danger for those tossed overboard into chilly seas, or sanity-challenged polar dippers like me, because it can easily cause drowning. The possibility doesn't cross my mind, though. I'm consumed with nothing more than the sheer coldness of the water.

It's so cold that it stings. As author and biologist Bill Streever poignantly describes, this is the kind of cold where your whole body feels like it is being shrink-wrapped.[5] I want to say it's remarkably refreshing, but that would be a lie. I want to say at least this is the kind of cold that stimulates the senses. It's not that either.

This is the kind of cold that deadens them.

Fortunately, we don't have to test that theory. As Streever points out in his fascinating account of adventures in the world's frozen places, depending on factors such as your body fat index, it takes a full fifteen to thirty minutes before hypothermia sets in, even in icy water of this temperature.

Once your body's core drops below 95 degrees Fahrenheit, though, you are in the danger zone. Slurred speech, apathy, and pale, cold, or blue-gray skin are all early symptoms.

Even more noticeably, your brain's hypothalamus triggers uncontrollable shivering, the contracting and relaxing of one's muscles in an effort to generate heat. Shivering continues on a cycle of six to twelve times a second, burning glycogen to keep you alive. It's when you run out of glycogen (or if the body temperature drops down to 88 degrees) that the shivering stops. You don't want that. Once the shivering ends, everything else does, too.

Needless to say, I'm not pushing any limits like this. I'm in the water maybe a minute tops, plus another two or three to towel off and hastily reapply more appropriate subzero clothing. Huddled next to the abandoned ruins of the British Antarctic Survey, the same buildings Norwegian whalers inhabited before the British inherited them and were subsequently chased away when the last volcanic eruptions began in the late 1960s, I'm somewhat skeptical of that time frame. As my frozen fingers struggle with zippers and buttons, it seems a lot closer to forty minutes than four.

Skepticism can be a healthy human trait. It's an important survival mechanism. What's transpiring with climate-change politics in the United States, though, isn't skepticism. It's not contributing to our survival, either. What's happening today is outright denial and directly threatens our future.

With the exception of Russia, there's no debate in any other country as to whether climate change exists. Everywhere else that debate is over—and has been for roughly two decades. The debate that does continue today around the rest of the globe is about policy. It's about what we should do about climate change, not questioning if it really exists. Yet here in the States, we can't even start to talk about legitimate differences of policy because we can't even agree that there is a problem in the first place. You can't get to second base if you never get to bat.

How did we become so dysfunctional?

Well, the answer is both complicated and simple. The premise of this entire work, for example, is that five overlapping influences confound our understanding of climate change in the United States. From the Galápagos Islands we extrapolated core scientific characteristics that discourage agreement around climate change. The Great Barrier Reef then underscored economic hurdles to instituting effective public policy. Similarly, trips to the acacia savannah and woodlands of KwaZulu-Natal in South Africa as well as the lush Peruvian Amazon highlighted obstacles culturally and socially, respectively, to understanding climate change.

Now, here in Antarctica, we dissect perhaps the most imposing hurdle of all, the politics that envelop climate change. Central to this story are a handful of industry-funded greenhouse deniers[6] that run an extremely effective campaign of deception and disinformation, one outlined in a 2002 memorandum to the Bush White House by Republican strategist Frank Luntz. As academics Peter Jacques, Riley Dunlap, and Mark Freeman demonstrate, these anti-climate-change "experts" are not independent analysts, by any means.[7] They are hired guns.[8]

ExxonMobil, for example, has spent millions over the years to fund ideological opposition through conservative think tanks such as the Competitive Enterprise Institute. Similarly, brothers Charles and David Koch, branched out from their Koch Industries of Wichita, Kansas, the second-largest private enterprise here in the States, to spend part of their combined $44 billion fortune on an array of climate deniers. The Heartland Institute of Chicago is perhaps the most blatant and persistent of these.[9]

Increasingly, though, these exorbitant numbers don't tell even half the story. For example, Exxon, technically, has not given a publicly traceable donation to climate denial since 2008. It's harder and harder to accurately monitor the true amount of cash changing hands because so-called "dark money" flows anonymously through third-party foundations such as DonorsTrust and Donors Capital.[10] In a study covering 2003 to 2010, Drexel University environmental sociologist Robert Brulle found that 140 foundations had funneled $558 million to nearly one hundred climate-denial organizations in this fashion.[11]

By the way, climate deniers don't like that "denier" label. They prefer the term "skeptic." Too often, the media acquiesce and adopt this preference in an attempt to appear unbiased. That's not a meaningless, academic point. Semantics here are important. Calling someone a "denier" carries a decided negative connotation. Calling them a "skeptic" does not. Furthermore, in terms of strategy, skeptics enjoy the same privileges as the defense team in a criminal trial, protected by reasonable doubt. From this position, skeptics exploit the significant advantage afforded to the status quo in any policy debate. It takes energy to create momentum, to change from one policy to another. It's basic physics, Newton's First Law of Motion: A body at rest stays at rest. Climate inaction begets climate inaction.

Combine this with our U.S. political structure, one designed to prevent radical change, even create gridlock, and its easy to see how our predicament festers, how climate-change inaction continues. As Pulitzer-Prize-winning journalist Ross Gelbspan laments, drumbeats of doubt have greatly restricted

federal climate-change action over the last two decades. Often these drum-
mers were the usual suspects, those in the private sector with much invested
in the status quo, but at times, more public representatives joined the fray.
Most infamously, Senator James Inhofe (R-OK) proclaimed in the summer
of 2003, "With all of the hysteria, all of the fear, all of the phony science,
could it be that man-made global warming is the greatest hoax ever perpe-
trated on the American people? It sure sounds like it."[12]

Instead of a debate about policy, then, we've faced a war of words for the
last twenty-some years.[13] Censorship during the Bush White House brought
this to an overtly Orwellian level. Philip Cooney, chief of staff to Council
on Environmental Quality chair Jim Connaughton, was perhaps the most
notable of the protagonists here, or at least of those caught. Despite having
no formal scientific training, this former lobbyist for the American Petroleum
Institute received a free hand to alter the National Climate Assessment, a report
produced by over three hundred experts and reviewed by a panel from the
National Academy of Sciences.[14]

The Cooney story broke in March 2005, when Rick S. Piltz resigned
from his position as a senior associate in the U.S. Climate Change Science
Program, claiming Cooney edited government climate reports to emphasize
unscientific doubts. Internal White House memos leaked to the *New York
Times* later that June described repeated edits to EPA climate reports in 2002
and 2003, including de-emphasizing the link between emissions and global
warming, editing out all references to dangerous impacts from climate change
in the United States, and the addition of Cooney's own caveats that further
weakened EPA conclusions. Two days after *The Times* story broke, Cooney
resigned. Less than a week later, he was gainfully employed with ExxonMobil.
Talk about soft landings.

The EPA was not the only bureaucratic agency to draw the attention
of climate deniers. NASA endured censorship as well when its headquarters was ordered to remove global temperature analysis from the Goddard
Institute for Space Studies website.[15] In fact, lead NASA climate scientist
James Hansen was repeatedly challenged in efforts to disseminate his work
during the Bush administration. Hansen, of course, did not take this quietly,
publicly calling out conspiring political operatives.[16]

Even as Barack Obama succeeded George W. Bush in the Oval Office,
the political war surrounding climate change did not soften. In fact, in some
respects, an Obama presidency re-energized the conservative grassroots.

Within a year after Obama's election, in late 2009, an alleged conspiracy in climate science with the catchy label of "climate-gate" provided the perfect fodder to feed this fire. Indeed, "climate-gate" was a public relations disaster, "amplify[ing] distrust of the scientific process" and further inflaming belief that climate-change regulation was a Pandora's box that would lead to more and more government regulation.[17]

Before detailing this saga, though, it's important to note that there were a handful of legitimate complaints about the climate-change community. In particular, several typos in the IPCC's Fourth Assessment Report in 2007, specifically its report "Working Group II: Impacts, Adaptability, and Vulnerability," received considerable attention. For one, this document included a transcription error that predicted complete Himalayan glacier melt by 2035 instead of the correct year of 2350. The nearly three-hundred-year difference drew considerable conservative ire. Another mistake, originating from a three-thousand-page Dutch report, miscalculated sea level rise influences on the Netherlands. And perhaps most deserving of critique, when errors were identified, the Intergovernmental Panel on Climate Change (IPCC) was initially evasive toward the press, exacerbating the matter further.

In the midst of this environment, the alleged smoking gun of a climate conspiracy erupted in November 2009. Utilizing thousands of personal emails stolen from the Climate Research Unit of the University of East Anglia in Britain, unknown hackers caught scientists supposedly red-handed, cooking the books by adjusting data to meet preferred climate-change conclusions.[18]

In truth, no such conspiracy existed. Allegations were based on incorrect reading of emails with key words and phrases taken completely out of context. For example, specific references to "Mike's *Nature* trick . . . to hide the decline" actually compared standard proxy temperature reconstructions. This well-established technique had evolved to address the divergence problem within tree ring data after 1960, one where the impact of warming temperatures on trees was not as noticeable, probably because of increased pollution.

In reality, then, this was not some sinister, tight-knit coordination of reviews, editorial-board stacking, or creativity-stifling gatekeeping, but, instead, the very definition of scientific peer review. A total of five independent investigations subsequently absolved scientists of any wrongdoing whatsoever.[19] Of course, this verdict of innocence didn't carry the same weight as the initial inflammatory charges. In a familiar pattern of attacks by climate deniers, the primary purpose was merely to cast doubt. Beyond the immediate impact of these manufactured claims, the precedent fostered future abuse of the Freedom of Information Act. Signed into law by President Johnson in 1966, this legislation allows public access to government documents, which in principle applies to any federal funded science. By mid-January 2010, a group known as the National Center for Public Policy Research was even targeting renowned climate scientist Michael Mann personally, seeking revocation of his National Science Foundation grants.[20]

It does not take a crack detective to deduce that climate-gate was timed for maximum impact in the days leading up to the December 2009 U.N. climate-change negotiations in Copenhagen. Corrections and retractions, never as prominently placed as the original articles, did not appear until well after those meetings and the press that surrounded it were gone. All told, the only malfeasance within climate-gate was the actual hacking of emails. Yet, hypocritically, the far right, advocating libertarian views that stress individual freedoms and railing against governmental intrusion into individual affairs, engaged in little to no discussion of the hacking crime itself.[21]

All this illustrates how the boundaries between journalist, commentator, and paid industry advocate are easily blurred. Even official forums can fall victim, as when Senator Inhofe invited best-selling science-fiction writer Michael Crichton to testify in Congress about climate change. Yes, that's correct. Inhofe asked a science-fiction writer to serve as a lead witness on climate science. Science fiction should never be confused with science, just as skepticism should never be confused with denial.

Our final Antarctic expedition is this afternoon on Half Moon Island, a crescent-shaped, mile-and-a-half-long stretch of land between Greenwich and Livingston Islands. Moon Bay, known to sealers as early as 1821, now hosts the Argentine base Cámara in the middle of a lengthy beach. You can't miss the slowly rotting dory, remnant of a whaling expedition on the northern shore, but our focus is the more than three thousand pairs of chinstrap penguins documented years ago in a 1995 survey.

That evening we commemorate this closing chapter in the expedition, wisely timed before entering the notorious Drake, with a festive Russian dinner, a nod to the nationality of most of the crew, not to mention the ship's namesake herself. Our two-day return through the Drake Passage, ironically, occurs at exactly the same time that the IPCC meeting in Copenhagen is ending miserably in failure.

We have a new set of lectures on tap over that period, including a particularly fascinating one by historian Shane Murphy on whaling in the Southern Ocean. It's become fashionable in recent years to treasure whales as a majestic oceanic species, but that's a recent development. Herman Melville's *Moby Dick* paints a much different historical portrait, one that dates at least back to that novel's publication in 1851. Whales were never seen as underdogs. They were the villains, the nefarious creatures from depths below. In terms of pure size, this makes sense. The blue whale, for example, is the largest animal ever to have lived, larger than any of the dinosaurs.[22] That size, as long as a Boeing 737 plane and with the weight of two thousand men, enshrined their Goliath to our David status.[23]

Still, although they dwarf humans, whales have long been at considerable disadvantage in their dealings with us. Even the International Whaling Commission (IWC) was an asset more to whalers than the whales it ostensibly protected when it first began. Signed in Washington, D.C., in early December 1946 by fourteen states, the IWC took effect nearly two years later in November 1948. As its governing body states, its mission is to ensure "the proper conservation of whale stocks and thus make possible the orderly development of the whaling industry."

Can't make it much clearer than that. The end goal is to serve the whaling industry. The IWC periodically reviewed whaling and set quotas with whalers in mind, not whales. In theory, this did include some benefits for the whales. It regulated minimum catch sizes and prohibited killing certain species that were near extinction. More accurately, though, the IWC was nothing more than an exclusive big-game-shooting club, one that came together once a year before killing season started.

Here, a gentlemen's agreement would establish the sporting rules, including the ever-important date for opening the season. Killing of nursing mothers and undersized whales was prohibited, and the hunt ended immediately when the quota was reached. The only problem with all this was that no one behaved in a gentlemanly manner. No one stuck to the agreement.[24] In fact, statistically, more whales died under IWC direction than had before regulations were established. Prior to its formation, three of ten species of whales (right, bowhead, and grey whales) were "commercially extinct," meaning too few existed to be worth the expense of hunting. Now that number stands at eight out of ten.

Finally, in 1986, under U.S. leadership, the IWC instituted a moratorium on commercial whaling. This wasn't the end to whales' troubles, though. All told, three enforcement problems continued to plague the IWC. For one, member countries were free to leave the association at any time and declare themselves no longer responsible to its regulations. For another, member states could always opt out of specific regulations by lodging formal objection within ninety days of a regulation coming into force. And finally, most important of all, the IWC had no enforcement capability. Like the baleen whales it supposedly sought to protect, the treaty simply had no teeth.

From vote buying by the Japanese Fisheries Agency to flouting of aboriginal subsistence exemptions within the U.S. and Canada, many have exploited perhaps the most visible loophole in the IWC, a stipulation requiring states to fully utilize whales once scientific work is complete. Foremost among these are renegade whaling states such as Japan, Norway, and Iceland.[25] Claiming to conduct "scientific research," these states are simply stocking the luxury food in upscale Japanese restaurants, and at times even in children's school lunchrooms.

Before this luxury-meat market created demand, lighting needs as well as beauty and health products drove the early whaling industry. Ambergris, the grayish substance secreted from the sperm whale's intestines, was once a valued perfume fixative. Whale liver oil was a major source of vitamin D. For decades, spermaceti wax from the oil reservoir in the sperm whale's forehead supported candle making. By the nineteenth century, baleen, or as it was more commonly called, whalebone, brought whalers a tidy profit. Baleen, the horny substance that grows down in plates from the mouths of toothless whales, found application in buggy whips and umbrellas as well as corset stays, at least until steel stays replaced them in the late nineteenth century. Still, despite this impressive diversification, the hunt for whales invariably boiled down to one key ingredient, blubber, which once boiled into oil was used for lighting and as lubrication for machinery.[26]

From a framing perspective, early waste once seen in harbors such as that at Deception Island gave way to gruesome efficiency with the harvesting of massive amounts of whale biomass. Of course, as argued earlier concerning the difference between skeptics and deniers, framing is also an intensely political maneuver.

Failing to recognize this basic fact obscures crucial details. Take the icebergs of Antarctica as an illustration. For the uninitiated, icebergs appear to be nothing but beautifully sculpted chunks of compressed snow floating harmlessly along our ocean's currents. That's all true, with the exception of the "harmless" part. You don't see roughly seven-eighths of an iceberg's mass because it falls below the water line.[27] That can be a significant source of danger for shipping, from the *Titanic* in the North Atlantic, to the *Exxon Valdez* in Prince William Sound of Alaska, to (I hope not here today) the *Orlova* in the Southern Ocean.

Icebergs vary somewhat in density, and, due to their irregular shapes, some stretch higher above the water than others. But the fact remains that, in terms of mass, the vast majority of every iceberg remains hidden under water. It's a question of buoyancy, really, where the buoyant force on an object is equal in weight to the fluid displaced by the object.[28] We know this as Archimedes's principle, a fundamental relationship he observed 2,200 years ago while taking a bath.[29] Archimedes was so excited by his discovery that he famously shouted "Eureka" and, depending on which version you believe, either ran naked through the streets or modestly covered himself with a towel while sharing his newfound knowledge.[30]

I suppose this is a long-winded way of backtracking to my argument a few chapters earlier about the problem fossil fuels present. Be careful how you interpret what you think you see. Framing can mislead. Yes, fossil fuels are central to climate change, but like any addiction, the real enemy is not the tool employed to inflict damage. It's the person doing it. For those struggling with weight, the enemy is not food. It's your appetite for food. You are your own worst enemy. Like unsustainable development more generally, with our carbon-intensive diet, the real enemy with climate change is not fossil fuels. It is our use of them. We are the enemy.

Herein lies the root of the problem. How do you wage a war against yourself?

Let's try one more take on this. One word often employed to sum up climate change is "water." It makes perfect sense—melting sea ice, rising sea levels, increases in precipitation and evaporation, the intensification of warm-water-energized storms, and so on. There's another, equally strong contender, though, to take center stage in discussing climate change. That word is "less." I like it even better than "water" because the term "less" encapsulates how best to address climate change. "Water" tells us what is happening. "Less" tells us how to stop it.

Concentrating on "less" also directly confronts the root of our problem without demoralizing or demonizing ourselves. More specifically, the idea of "less" involves a two-tiered approach. Action requires not only investing in new technology, but even more importantly, emphasizing old-fashioned conservation. Yes, we must harness the profit motive, continually pushing the envelope with advances in our technical abilities. As Nobel Prize–winning economist and op-ed columnist Paul Krugman contends, technology can greatly temper future emissions tied to economic growth.[31] It's a huge asset, but it's not the solution in and of itself. Much like market mechanisms and taxes, technology is no more than a partial means to an end. It's a tool. As best-selling author Eric Schlosser once said, it's not something to "be celebrated for its own sake.[32]

Furthermore, advances in technology do not necessarily guarantee reductions in emissions. There is always potential for a dangerous rebound effect, the incentive to eat away at savings by simply using more. Often stated formally as Jevons's paradox, improvements in efficiency can easily create perverse incentives whereby reduced costs encourage more consumption, not less.[33] Avoiding this rebound effect will not be easy.

Let's explore this relationship a bit further. There's a measure of human impact on climate known as the "Kaya identity." Developed by a team of carbon experts and Yoichi Kaya, an engineer at Tokyo University, it has four levers: reductions in population, reductions in per-capita GDP, increases in efficiency as measured by energy use per unit of GDP, and reductions in carbon-intensive energy sources as measured in carbon emissions per unit of energy consumed.[34] Using these four levers, Kaya and his colleagues created an equation for computing future emissions scenarios used today in the IPCC's Special Report on Emissions Scenarios. Again, each component here highlights "less." Of course, this isn't how former vice president Dick Cheney would have us interpret it. Speaking to the annual meeting of the Associated Press in Toronto in late April 2001, Cheney asserted that conservation was "a sign of personal virtue, but it is not a sufficient basis for a sound, comprehensive energy policy."[35]

On the contrary, conservation, using less, is central. It is both the starting point and end goal that we seek. Idealism and social justice need not be the focus here, by the way. They are important, even useful, but climate-change mitigation goes beyond the politics of the common good to target raw self-interest as well. As we saw in our chapters on the Great Barrier Reef, climate change is about saving money—and making money. It's not merely about less, then. It's about getting more from less.

Here's where technology enters the picture once again. I don't mean carbon capture and storage and its magical solutions with carbon sequestration.[36] This attempt to bury carbon deep underground is, at best, an uncertain and expensive technology. It could easily contaminate aquifers and increase the likelihood of earthquakes. It would do untold damage to biological communities in its storage sites. And finally, according to the Union of Concerned Scientists, "Even under optimistic scenarios, it would nearly double the costs of electricity to consumers."[37]

Similarly, geo-engineering is not a particularly attractive Plan B to mitigation, at least in my mind. It amounts to planetary experimentation with partially understood variables. What if something goes horribly wrong? There are no mulligans in this game, no do-overs if we mess up.

In returning to mitigation, or for that matter adaptation technology, though, two points deserve emphasis. For one, the problem must be fixable. With an intractable problem, people shut down psychologically. It's a coping mechanism. Rather than face frustration and failure, individuals ignore the issue altogether. For another, the government cannot pick winners. This doesn't mean it can't fund projects. Indeed, creating a more level playing field actually means the opposite. As argued earlier, government spending on energy technology remains woefully low. It needs to increase.

Along these lines, roughly ten countries matter most.[38] According to political scientist David Victor, these ten account for four-fifths of world spending on research and development and 95 percent of the world's patents.[39]

Similarly, when it comes to climate-change politics, some countries matter more than others. State power in climate negotiations is a function of both current and future emissions.[40] In this regard, twelve countries, accounting for 77 percent of global emissions (treating the European Union as one), stand out, according to the Carbon Dioxide Information and Analysis Center at Oak Ridge National Laboratory in Tennessee.[41] Starting with this smaller group is much more manageable than the unwieldy U.N. process, as referenced in our last chapter addressing Kyoto.

Keep in mind that even as this process proceeds incrementally, success may still arrive unexpectedly, in the wake of what Canadian journalist and best-selling author Malcolm Gladwell famously defined as a tipping point.[42] In fact, the daunting challenges of today simultaneously present unprecedented opportunity. Much like the Chinese character for "crisis" that combines the characters for "danger" and "opportunity," the two go hand in hand.

Sometimes benefits emerge out of seemingly unconnected tragedy. One might argue, for example, that as the brutal Nazi demagogue Adolf Hitler marched across Europe, his atrocious acts actually saved whales. During World War II, for the first time in over thirty years, whaling ships withdrew from the Southern Ocean.[43] They were needed in the war effort closer to home.

If climate-change governance is to break through our political stalemate today, though, one point is certain. The key is salience, moving climate change from the back of our minds to center stage. Civil society plays a central role here, with a network of climate-change nongovernmental organizations working tirelessly to set this ambitious agenda every day. But individual travel, provided it is eco-friendly, can serve as a remarkable asset as well. Ecotourism provides context. It enhances understanding, much like experiential learning in academic settings. We learn more efficiently, and more thoroughly, through our experiences.

As we move along this path, though, as emphasized in preceding chapters, we cannot leave roughly 17 percent of the world behind. Accepting the charge to provide 1.2 billion more people with electricity as a first step, and if we incorporate the continued rate of acceleration for those already burning fossil fuels, the sad truth is that emissions are going to become worse before they become better.

That is why now is no time to wait. Continued inaction makes future action all the harder. Revisiting Frost's poem from the beginning of our Antarctic chapters, especially famed marine biologist Rachel Carson's adaptation of it in *Silent Spring*, emphasizes this point:

> We stand now where two roads diverge. But unlike the roads in Robert Frost's familiar poem, they are not equally fair. The road we have long been traveling is deceptively easy, a smooth

superhighway on which we progress with great speed, but at its end lies disaster. The other fork of the road—the one less traveled by—offers our last, our only chance to reach a destination that assures the preservation of the earth.[44]

Here, at the bottom of the world, these words resonate with additional gravitas. Pulling into Ushuaia that morning, with three flights ahead of me, stretched across yet another twenty-seven hours of travel time, it's clear that neither I nor my country has selected the less-traveled road Carson and Frost intended. As I eagerly anticipate the holidays and an opportunity to atone for lost time with my family, a simple lesson emerges in my mind. This trip has been priceless in shaping an outline for this book, but it has come at a cost, both personal and planetary. It's important that we consider carefully the routes before us when it comes to climate change—and do more with less.

CONCLUSIONS
The Power of Travel

Travel is fatal to prejudice, bigotry, and narrow-mindedness, and many of our people need it sorely on these accounts. Broad, wholesome, charitable views of men and things cannot be acquired by vegetating in one little corner of the earth all one's lifetime.

—Mark Twain, *The Innocents Abroad*, 1869

THE STREETS OF DELHI are choked full of every manner of transit you could imagine, from well-worn construction and delivery trucks, to crowded city buses and smaller passenger vans, to luxury SUVs and an array of personal sedans covering the entire spectrum of age and condition. Motorcycles and mopeds are everywhere. Bicycles are still fairly common. And there are untold numbers of donkey carts sharing the road as well, not to mention men, sometimes even prepubescent boys, hauling heavy handcarts stocked with blocks of ice and other wares using nothing but their own sinewy muscle.

The most prolific mode of transportation, though, might be the quaint little yellow-and-green taxis known as Tuk-Tuks. Riding in one of these is nearly a full five-senses experience, delicately treading the lines between exhilaration and exasperation, not to mention sheer terror. When they aren't speeding unsafely along side streets, these glorified, albeit souped-up, riding lawnmowers sit wedged in the infamous, bumper-to-bumper Delhi traffic, belching out more than their share of greenhouse gases.

In one of the fastest-growing cities in the world, with over 25 million in its metropolitan area, the pollution inevitably increases each year. It's become so bad, in fact, that a 2014 World Health Organization study ranked New Delhi as the worst smog-choked city in the world.[1]

Yet that's not the point I want to emphasize here. I want to talk about Delhi's population and its poverty. You can read about how many people there are in Delhi and India at large, and realize that it will soon surpass China as the world's most populous country, probably in 2028. You can also view images of its ubiquitous traffic congestion in glossy magazines, daily newspapers, and online postings as the capital city continually struggles with its rapid annual growth.

But to really appreciate what millions of people crushed together means, you need to see it yourself. You need to catch the jam-packed, but blissfully chilly, Delhi metro with acclimated, nonsweaty locals during their summer morning rush-hour commute. You need to wander the heat-scorched side streets south of the ring road, Mahatma Gandhi Marg, in the middle of a weekend afternoon. You need to explore a series of shanties, known in India as *jhuggis*, on a little stretch of water stemming off the mighty Yamuna River just behind the Defense Colony Police Station.

This is what overpopulation looks like. And, in the case of many of these shanties (see Figure C.1), this is poverty. At times constructed of no more than cardboard, tin, and plastic, these shacks seem ready to collapse at any moment. Continual erosion along this particular stream bank and the presence of portions of "construction materials" amid the trash in the filthy water below suggest that this isn't an unusual phenomenon, especially once monsoon season arrives in late June.

That said, it should also be noted that many Delhi shanties last decades. More sturdily constructed with mud and corrugated iron, they integrate themselves into the surrounding neighborhood in a number of respects, even providing critical "vote banks" for local politicians. Indeed, as many as five million Delhi residents live in one form or another of unauthorized colony, ranging from slums like the one before me, to middle-class communities, and even to a handful of illegal rich enclaves.[2]

Admittedly, this brief excursion on a blistering hot day in early May is but a glimpse into the destitution that confronts significant portions of the developing world. It's an image that resonates, though, and makes it much harder for those with means to ignore. Travel like this educates us. As Mark Twain argued, it reduces prejudice and narrow-mindedness.

C.1 Shanties near Mool Chand Station.

Later that week, venturing south in the wake of four million other tourists a year to the wondrous Taj Mahal, yet another vivid example arises before me along the banks of the same Yamuna River, this time outside the city of Agra. Here, an elderly woman appears to stoop over piles of hardened mud, mud she dutifully handcrafts into pizza-sized portions before arranging them along the riverbank to dry. But this isn't mud. It's cattle dung. When you see someone her age, in hundred-degree heat, working feces with her hands, you gain a much better appreciation for what poverty really means. And hopefully, you start asking questions. You become better educated.

It turns out that some 2.8 billion people around the world still cook or heat with firewood, kerosene, or sundried patties of hand-packed cow dung. A good chunk of those come from India, where more than two-thirds of its 1.3 billion population uses carbon-emitting biomass and dung-based fuel for cooking, according to a United Nations Industrial Development Organization report released in July 2014.

After passing through an animal's gut, the residue of undigested plant matter, when it is burned, provides more than energy, though. Like any

biomass, it also emits smoke containing high concentrations of tiny particles of black carbon. This black carbon is responsible for some 4.3 million
premature deaths a year across the globe, making it more deadly than HIV,
malaria, and tuberculosis combined.

But black carbon doesn't stop there. Some suggest that it accounts
for as much as 20 percent of climate change as it darkens Arctic ice and
high-altitude glaciers, decreasing their reflective capabilities.[3] The result
is glacial melt and declining crop yields tied to climate change.

Danish economist and self-proclaimed skeptical environmentalist Bjørn
Lomborg estimates it would cost $137 billion to provide the cleanest-burning
gas-fueled stoves to those using these black-carbon-intensive sources.[4] A group
of eighty-two economists at his think tank, the Copenhagen Consensus,
then suggests that every dollar of that investment would produce two
dollars in benefits stemming from lower medical costs, cheaper fuel,
and longer lives.[5]

Lomborg and his group, of course, are not exactly proponents
of climate-change action, even though such an initiative would provide
immediate climate benefits.[6] The reason I mention their suggestion
here, though, is not to challenge their climate-change position. Rather,
it is to use this Copenhagen Consensus study as a model that demonstrates creative thinking about core handicaps within the developing
world. Lomborg and I aren't on the same page when it comes to climate
change, but we do share a wish for creative thinking about overcoming
developing-world handicaps.

He asserts that studies such as this should direct attention to an issue
ostensibly more important than climate change, something more immediate
and more realistically solved. I too contend that poverty of this magnitude
demands immediate attention, but as you recall from earlier in this work,
I argue that it deserves our attention not only in its own right but also due
to its fundamental connections to climate change. Pope Francis made the
same argument in June 2015 with his encyclical identifying climate change
as intrinsically tied to the defining feature of his papacy, the fight against
inequality and global poverty.[7]

Along these lines, I'd suggest a different take on black carbon than
Lomborg and his colleagues, asserting that replacing black-carbon energy
is deeply intertwined with the climate-change problem, not something to be

addressed instead of it. The task before us, then, to repeat a theme from Antarctica and our political discussion of climate change, is paradoxically about both more and less. We agree that this is a question of how to meet the fundamental needs of more of the disadvantaged segments of our society, but we differ in that I assert that this cannot be done without emphasizing emitting less across the globe.

As we have seen throughout this book, this is no easy task. It is further complicated by the fact that key characteristics of climate change are too often misunderstood among the general public. This is a book about why that is so—and how best to address this deficit.

More scientific information about climate change is not shifting public opinion. Becoming better informed in the traditional sense is not generating momentum for effective climate-change policy. Indeed, more knowledge only strengthens existing positions on climate change, even among those who think it doesn't exist.[8] Given this impasse, it's probably not smart to stay with the same strategy. Albert Einstein would be a bit more direct if given the chance to offer his analysis. To him, the act of doing the same thing over and over again and expecting a different result is the very definition of insanity.

Let's be more intelligent about this, then. Let's tell a better story about climate change. If more information isn't working, let's change how information is accessed. After all, it doesn't take a rocket scientist, or a theoretical physicist for that matter, to tell us that it matters how people are informed as well as who does the informing.

This is not a new idea. As you recall from the beginning of our journey, eighteenth-century French Enlightenment philosopher Jean-Jacques Rousseau and his book *Emile* emphasized the power of experiential learning, as did twentieth-century American educator John Dewey in works such as *Democracy and Education*. In a similar vein, consider the Mark Twain quote that began this chapter: "Travel is fatal to prejudice, bigotry, and narrow-mindedness." Sadly, over a century later, most Americans don't even own a passport to travel abroad. The situation is even more dire if you consider our children and their "travel" in a more parochial sense. Looking at childhood experiences as close as our own backyards, you might say we do the opposite, often requiring them to no more than, again in Twain's cutting rhetoric, "vegetate in one little corner of the earth." As *San Diego Union-Tribune* columnist and author Richard Louv writes in *Last Child in the Woods*, "In the space of a century, the

American experience of nature has gone from direct utilitarianism to romantic attachment to electronic detachment."[9]

Yes, the world is a scarier place today than when we were kids—or at least it seems that way. Traffic is more dangerous. Strangers are more prevalent. Even mosquitoes and the diseases they carry seem more threatening, a risk which, not incidentally, will only worsen thanks to climate change. But I digress.

Louv and others have noted that, thanks to these supposed increased dangers, by the 1990s, the radius in which we allow our children to roam on their own had shrunk to one-ninth of what was in 1970. The result is what Louv calls "nature deficit disorder," and the higher rates of obesity, attention deficit disorder, and depression that accompany it.

Our schools reinforce what we practice at home thanks to an increasing societal obsession with testing and the funding derived from it. With more testing comes the need for more preparation. Regular schedules must adjust accordingly. Seemingly less essential parts of the curriculum fall by the wayside. Recess time shrinks, even at times disappearing altogether.

Of course, anyone familiar with kids knows that cutting back on recess is counterproductive. Children need that unstructured break from class to build their social skills, to burn off steam, and to let their mind wonder. Heck, even my college students struggle in a "recess-free" environment. I know I still do, and I'm the professor for darned sakes.

As Louv further notes, physical, mental, and spiritual well-being are all intrinsically tied to the outdoors. Environment-based education exploits this by design. It dramatically improves standardized test scores and GPAs. It enhances problem solving and critical thinking. It stimulates creativity.

But thanks to our infinite wisdom, our children receive a double whammy of handicapping, both at home and at school, with these restrictions on access to nature.

We must reverse this trend. We've grown too complacent about the world around us. It's time to get outdoors and rekindle that sense of childhood wonder. Get your children outside—and go there with them. Play. Ponder. Relax. You don't have to make your destination Antarctica or the Galápagos Islands. A local park, even your own backyard, is an ideal starting point. The key is to venture outside and be inquisitive once you are there.

In the case of climate change, there is an added benefit to spending more time outdoors and engaging in more thoughtful travel. Experiential learning on this order might actually be the missing link in developing a critical mass to support effective climate-change policy in the States. As Canadian journalist Malcolm Gladwell eloquently argued in his best-selling work *The Tipping Point*, ideas become infectious when we break out of equilibrium by utilizing at least one of three crucial "agents of change."[10]

Of the three change agents Gladwell identifies, law of the few, stickiness factor, and power of context, I'd argue the one that stands out most when it comes to climate-change activism is the stickiness factor, the extent to which an issue resonates at an individual level. Climate change remains problematic in many minds because addressing it seems impersonal and impractical. It's not sticky. To break through our impasse today, climate change must be personalized, and the actions to counter it must be tangible and practical.

Let's take one of Gladwell's examples as a case in point. For years, the anti-smoking lobby operated under much the same assumption as climate-change activists, that misinformation drove the problem of teenage smoking (much as misinformation supposedly drives uncertainty about climate change). Tobacco companies enticed teenagers into smoking by lying to them, making it sound less harmful than it really was. As we have seen, you can easily argue that fossil-fuel companies have followed the same playbook with climate change.

In both cases, activists organized extensive campaigns to combat this misinformation from each industry. In the tobacco case, a massive public-health initiative set out to inform children of the real risk of cigarettes. Yet, as Gladwell shows, for years, more information had no positive effect. In fact, it seemed that the more adults pushed against cigarettes, the more teenagers wanted to try them. From 1988 to 2000, according to Gladwell, total teen smokers in the United States actually rose by 73 percent.[11]

This smoking increase wasn't due to lack of information. Data showed teen smokers knew the risks but smoked anyway. Instead, combating smoking was a coolness problem. As Gladwell might characterize it, smoking was sticky. The success of antismoking efforts depended on making it less so—and making antismoking efforts more sticky.

It's the same with climate change. Level of concern with climate change in the United States has been decreasing since 1989, even as the science has become more and more convincing that we should be concerned.[12] Like antismoking before 2000, the threat of climate change simply isn't sticky enough. The solution to changing public perception rests in reversing this perception, in making it stickier.

Ecotourism offers that potential.

Keep in mind that ecotourism is no magical cure-all. It is merely an asset to utilize. It's not a guaranteed game-changer. In fact, sometimes damage from climate change restricts ecotourism, preventing people from venturing out to explore the world around them. Even more importantly, as noted in earlier chapters, ecotourism also contributes, by its own emissions, to some of very problem I argue it seeks to solve. Tourism in general, for example, is responsible for 5 percent of global carbon dioxide emissions, according to the United Nations World Tourism Organization (UNWTO). The transport sector of tourism generates the largest proportion here, at 75 percent,[13] and air transport in particular is the fastest-growing source of greenhouse gases, contributing up to 10 percent of transport emissions.[14]

When ecotourism is applied carefully, however, the benefits significantly outweigh the costs. Those able to engage in ecotourism accrue decidedly more personal evidence of climate change. Their experience complements scientific and theoretical explanations by highlighting additional meaningful impacts.

Without such travel, climate-change dialogue too often succumbs to abstract numbers and graphs, to intangible numbers—350 parts per million, 80 percent reductions in carbon dioxide emissions by 2050, or, arguably most restrictive of all, the vaunted two-degree Celsius threshold. As science and environment journalist Gaia Vince asserts, this is not the path toward greater understanding. We need to get behind the headlines of climate change to humanize it. We need to hear the stories of those who are not only experiencing it right now, but also taking action to mitigate it.[15] Ecotourism provides precisely this opportunity.

Again, keep in mind that ecotourism, at least the exotic foreign-travel variety, is not for everyone. In the United States, the typical ecotourist falls between the ages of thirty-five and fifty-four, although a healthy contingent of those above fifty-four exists as well. In both subsets, this population is likely to be physically active and professionally employed with a college degree, not to mention a dedication to learning. Often, these ecotourists come from dual-income families and, thus, can afford to travel to locations that those in lower income brackets simply cannot. Finally, many hail from the subset of 30 million Americans who belong to environmental organizations or profess interest in conservation.[16]

See anything problematic with these characteristics, particularly that last one? The people predisposed to ecotourism probably already understand the implications of climate change. To date, that means that ecotourism is simply preaching to the choir. To be more effective, to reach a tipping point on climate-change awareness, ecotourism needs to tap a different demographic.

Gladwell again provides further insight. As he pointed out with his "law of the few" change agent, some people matter more than others. Not everyone needs to be an ecotourist, but a select group could make a huge difference. The trick is identifying this select group. Think of it in terms of six degrees of separation. Not everyone is connected to everyone else in six steps, as is commonly misinterpreted. It's a select subset, the Kevin Bacons of the world, who connect to everyone else in even less than six steps. Phrased differently, as Gladwell points out, your social circle is not a circle at all, but a pyramid. Some people matter more than others.

Gladwell uses the example of Paul Revere to drive this message home. No one remembers another midnight rider that evening, William Dawes. Yet we all know the name Paul Revere. Why? Because he knew which people to stop and tell in each town he passed that evening on the way to Concord, Massachusetts. William Dawes did not. Climate-change activism needs its version of Paul Revere, not, with all due respect, another William Dawes. And pointedly, this modern-day Paul Revere's primary purpose is not merely to sound an alarm but, more importantly, to stoke the fires of resistance.

Environmental nongovernmental organizations, for example, would get more bang for their buck if they offered ecotourism scholarships to a decidedly different subset of our population than those who currently engage in eco-travel. These would be the Kevin Bacon types, those who are well connected. They would also be trusted experts in their fields, those who actively seek to pass on knowledge. And they would be salesmen and saleswomen, well versed in the art of communication. This is the new demographic from which to draw future ecotourists. This is how a tipping point on climate-change awareness is more likely to come within reach.

Keep in mind, even as you consider such suggestions, that how one travels matters. All ecotourism is not created equally. Some operations claim to be eco-friendly but are not, merely green-washing and exploiting environmental sentiments for profit. To meet the true definition of ecotourism, visitors must minimize their ecological footprint, empower local populations by inserting funds directly into the local economy (not some distant international head-quarters), and develop a greater understanding of local culture, history, and environment.

It's by no means perfect, but Costa Rica's green-leaf Certification for Sustainable Tourism offers a degree of guidance along these lines. Beginning with its first edition for hotels in 1998, Costa Rica's program measures sus-tainability along three axes: environmental, social, and economic. It uses a checklist of 153 yes-or-no performance-based questions in four general categories: physical-biological environment, hotel facilities, guest services, and socioeconomic environment. The lowest score in any of these four cat-egories determines the final certification score, so companies must address all four if they seek a high mark. It's a voluntary program and free to any business seeking certification; the assessment is run and financed by the gov-ernment's tourism office.

Critics claim that it waters down real ecotourism because any tourist operation can participate. Some even suggest it sets the bar too low, because only 20 to 39 percent of yes responses are needed to earn one green leaf.[17] But regardless of your perspective, as ecotourism continues to develop, certifica-tion programs such as Costa Rica's will inevitably evolve and serve as crucial assets in aiding consumer choice.

And make no mistake. Consumer choice will be a determining factor in the struggle to define climate-change policy this century. As more than one thousand businesses now state in the climate declaration launched online in April 2013, "Tackling climate change is one of America's great economic opportunities of the twenty-first century."[18]

Not convinced? Just ask the solar industry. Their market grew by 17 percent in 2015, outpacing natural gas in terms of power capacity installation for the first time ever, according to the Solar Energy Industries Association.[19] That sounds good, but even better is the market response in terms of price. "In the last six years, solar prices have dropped by more than 80 percent, and now cost less than a new coal plant. Wind is down 60 percent, and LED lights more than 90 percent," explains Hal Harvey, CEO of the policy research group Energy Innovation.[20]

We are approaching that all-important threshold of grid parity, where renewable electricity is cheaper than fossil fuels. We would already have reached parity if not for fossil fuel subsidies being forty-two times greater than subsidies for renewables.[21] Here, then, is where we find the real promise in tipping the balance of indecision regarding climate change. The narrative must emphasize opportunity. Again, it's a framing issue—the dominant framings to date, disaster and uncertainty, have been anything but helpful.[22]

Former *New York Times* reporter and current Pace University Fellow Andrew Revkin describes past failures as often degenerating into a bird battle pitting the ostrich with its head in the sand against Chicken Little, who believes the sky is falling.[23] As Revkin contends, it is counterproductive to emphasize catastrophe if your goal is to spur action. Neither is it constructive to point out the errors of thrusting one's head in the sand. People don't like to be told they are stupid.

Trumpeting the emerging era of decoupling, cutting the link between GDP growth and carbon emissions, would be a much better place to start the discussion. A study released by the International Energy Agency in March 2016 suggests this is becoming a reality. In 2014, for the first time in the forty years both have been measured, global GDP grew while carbon emissions leveled off. That trend continued in 2015. As Nathaniel Aden, research fellow at Washington think tank World Resources Institute, explains, "It's really exciting, and it suggests that countries can sever the historic link between economic growth and greenhouse gas emissions."[24]

Again, continuing to demonize those who disagree about the threat that climate change presents simply doesn't work. We must be hopeful instead of hopeless, as Norwegian economist and psychologist Per Espen Stoknes writes.[25] The key is to emphasize upholding rather than threatening cherished institutions. We must present policies in terms of gains from action instead of losses from inaction.

Within this context, there is plenty of room for varied approaches. Everyone need not mimic scientist turned activist Jim Hansen. Characters such as Hansen are treasured in this unfolding drama, but the climate-change tent is big enough for multiple personalities. Getting arrested is not mandatory.

Perhaps the simplest, most cost-effective way to make an individual difference is through eco-travel. In the words of incomparable travel ambassador Rick

Steves, becoming a more thoughtful traveler makes us a better citizen of this planet.[26] It educates us, and, as sixteenth- and seventeenth-century English philosopher Francis Bacon asserted, knowledge is power. Through ecotourism we become more powerful. We are better positioned to not only identify but to exploit core political relationships that inhibit climate-change action.

By the way, we in the developed Northern Hemisphere aren't merely acquiring enlightenment and power when we travel to the developing Southern Hemisphere, where significant chunks of ecotourism take place. We also bring much-needed financial support with our travels. Ecotourism brings cash and the power that comes with that cash. This money, in turn, encourages more environmentally friendly behavior by local populations seeking to protect their monetary investments, sometimes even finding its way into the creation of new environmental initiatives altogether. As codirector of the Center for Responsible Travel Martha Honey contends, at its core ecotourism, then, is about power relationships.[27]

But don't take my word for it. Go out and discover for yourself the power of travel—and learn what travel to wild places can teach us about climate change. I have only two requests as you begin your journey. For one, be thorough. Tread wisely. Don't let preconceptions restrict your investigation. For another, be cautious. Tread lightly. Don't let your search for truth become part of the problem.

NOTES

INTRODUCTION

1. Center for Economic and Policy Research. "No-Vacation Nation Revisited." May 2013, http://www.lifehealthpro.com/2013/05/24/vacation-wise-us-stands-alone-among-advanced-econo. Accessed 12 Oct. 2013.

2. Organization for Economic Co-operation and Development. "Labour Productivity Levels in the Total Economy," 10 Sept. 2013. http://stats.oecd.org/Index.aspx?DatasetCode=LEVEL. Accessed 12 Oct. 2013.

3. Rousseau, Jean-Jacques. *Emile, or On Education.* Trans. Allan Bloom. New York: Basic Books, 1979.

4. Dewey, John. *Experience and Education.* New York: Collier Books, 1938.

5. Schumacher, E. F. *Small Is Beautiful: Economics as If People Mattered.* London: Blond & Briggs, 1973.

6. Gunter, Michael M., Jr. "Be Patriotic—Purchase a Passport." *Richmond Times-Dispatch*, 1 July 2011, p. A-11.

7. National Park Service. "Glaciers—Glacier National Park," 24 Oct. 2013, http://www.nps.gov/glac/forteachers/glaciers.htm. Accessed 30 Oct. 2013.

8. The oft-cited 2030 date stems from a 2003 U.S. Geological Survey study, combined with 1992 temperature predictions by the U.N.'s Intergovernmental Panel on Climate Change. More recently, in 2009, Daniel Fagre, a USGS ecologist working at Glacier, asserts that the park's namesakes will disappear in 2020, ten years ahead of schedule. Anne Minard, "No More Glaciers in Glacier National Park by 2020?" *National Geographic News*, 2 March 2009. http://news.nationalgeographic.com/news/2009/03/090302-glaciers-melting.html. Accessed 30 Oct. 2013; Stephen P. Nash, "Twilight of the Glaciers."

New York Times, 29 July 2011, http://www.nytimes.com/2011/07/31/travel/glacier-national-park-montana-fading-glaciers.html. Accessed 30 Oct. 2013.

9. Lorenzi, Rossella. "Venice Sinking More than Previously Thought." *Discovery News* 26 (March 2012). http://news.discovery.com/earth/venice-sinking-120326.htm.

10. Isaacson, Andy. "In a Changing Antarctica, Some Penguins Thrive as Others Suffer." *New York Times*, 9 May 2001.

11. LaRue, Michelle A., David G. Ainley, Matt Swanson, Katie M. Dugger, Phil O'B. Lyver, Kerry Barton, and Grant Ballard. "Climate Change Winners: Receding Ice Fields Facilitate Colony Expansion and Altered Dynamics in an Adélie Penguin Metapopulation." *PLoS ONE* 8.4 (3 April 2013). http://dx.doi.org/10.1371/journal.pone.0060568.

12. Hoegh-Guldberg, O., P. J. Mumby, A. J. Hooten, R. S. Steneck, P. Greenfield, E. Gomez, C. D. Harvell, P. F. Sale, A. J. Edwards, K. Caldeira, N. Knowlton, C. M. Eakin, R. Iglesias-Prieto, N. Muthiga, R. H. Bradbury, A. Dubi, and M. E. Hatziolos. "Coral Reefs under Rapid Climate Change and Ocean Acidification." *Science* 318 (14 Dec. 2007), pp. 1737–42.

13. Australian Institute of Marine Science, "Coral Bleaching Events" (June 2016). http://www.aims.gov.au/docs/research/climate-change/coral-bleaching/bleaching-events.html. Accessed 15 July 2016.

14. Berkelmans, Ray, Glenn De'ath, Stuart Kininmonth, and William J. Skirving. "A Comparison of the 1998 and 2002 Coral Bleaching Events on the Great Barrier Reef: Spatial Correlation, Patterns, and Predictions." *Coral Reefs* 23.1 (April 2004), pp. 74–83.

15. Revelle, Roger, and Hans E. Suess. "Carbon Dioxide Exchange between Atmosphere and Ocean and the Question of an Increase of Atmospheric CO_2 during the Past Decades." *Tellus* 9.1 (Feb. 1957), pp. 18–27.

16. Cook, John, Dana Nuccitelli, Sarah A. Green, Mark Richardson, Bärbel Winkler, Rob Painting, Robert Way, Peter Jacobs, and Andrew Skuce. "Quantifying the Consensus on Anthropogenic Global Warming in the Scientific Literature." *Environmental Research Letters* 8.2 (15 May 2013). http://iopscience.iop.org/1748-9326/8/2/024024.

17. Saad, Lydia, and Jeffrey M. Jones. "U.S. Concern about Global Warming at Eight-Year High." *Gallup* (16 March 2016). http://www.gallup.com/poll/190010/concern-global-warming-eight-year-high.aspx. Accessed 13 April 2016.

18. Traced back to the United Nations Conference on Environment and Development in Rio de Janeiro, Brazil, in the summer of 1992, the subsequent Kyoto Protocol in Japan in late 1997 established the existing language of the treaty before it became effective in February 2005.

19. Schellenberg, Michael, and Ted Nordhaus. "The Death of Environmentalism: Global Warming Politics in a Post-Environmental World." Essay released at annual meeting of Environmental Grantmakers Association, Oct. 2004. Available online through *Grist*: http://grist.org/article/doe-reprint/

20. Cronon, William, ed. *Uncommon Ground: Toward Reinventing Nature*. New York: W. W. Norton & Co., 1995.

21. Leopold, Aldo. A *Sand County Almanac: And Sketches Here and There*. New York: Oxford University Press, 1949.

22. Carson, Rachel. *Silent Spring*. Boston: Houghton Mifflin Co., 1962.

23. Giddens, Anthony. *The Politics of Climate Change*. Cambridge, UK: Polity Press, 2009.

24. McCright, Aaron M., and Riley E. Dunlap. "The Politicization of Climate Change and Polarization in the American Public's Views of Global Warming, 2001–2010." *The Sociological Quarterly* 52.2 2 (March 2011), pp. 155–94.

25. Anderegg, William R. L., James W. Prall, Jacob Harold, and Stephen H. Schneider. "Expert Credibility in Climate Change." *Proceedings of the National Academy of Sciences* 107.27 (21 June 2010), pp. 12107–9.

26. International ecotourism consultant and Mexican architect Hector Ceballos-Lascurain is typically credited with developing the working definition of the term "ecotourism" in 1983 while heading up Pronatura, an influential conservation NGO in Mexico.

27. Gunter, Michael M., Jr. "Ecotourism." *Green Issues and Debates: An A to Z Guide*. Howard Schiffman, ed. Los Angeles: Sage Reference (May 2011 online, June 2011 print).

28. The International Ecotourism Society. "Factsheet: Global Ecotourism." Sept. 2006: http://mekongtourism.org/website/wp-content/uploads/downloads/2011/02/Fact-Sheet-Global-Ecotourism-IETS.pdf. Accessed 15 Oct. 2013.

29. The dual agenda of offering recreational space and still protecting special areas in this space is a constant threat within ecotourism and perhaps best articulated as inherently contradictory in our national parks here:

Alston Chase, *Playing God in Yellowstone: The Destruction of America's First National Park*. New York: Harcourt Brace & Company, 1986.

30. Political considerations are also fairly obvious. Less clear are social and cultural considerations, particularly as distinctions between the two are often difficult to draw.

31. Honey, Martha S. "Treading Lightly: Ecotourism's Impact on the Environment." *Environment* 41.5 (June 1999), pp. 4–9, 28–32; Honey, Martha. *Ecotourism and Sustainable Development: Who Owns Paradise?* 2nd ed. Washington, D.C.: Island Press, 2008.

CHAPTER 1

1. Sutherland, J. J. "Bugs Bunny: The Trickster, American Style." NPR, 6 Jan. 2008. http://www.npr.org/templates/story/story.php?storyId=17874931. Accessed 21 Sept. 2013.

2. Milanković was not a typical early-20-century scientist. Held prisoner in Budapest during the conflict between the Austro-Hungarian Empire and Serbia that caused World War I, he continued his work while in captivity, and, thanks to powerful friends, developed the idea known as Milankovitch cycles.

3. Plass, Gilbert N. "The Carbon Dioxide Theory of Climatic Change." *Tellus* 8.2 (1956), pp. 140–54.

4. Broecker, Wallace S. "Climatic Change: Are We on the Brink of Pronounced Global Warming?" *Science* 189.4201 (8 Aug. 1975), pp. 460–63.

5. Shabecoff, Philip. "Global Warming Has Begun, Expert Tells Senate." *New York Times*, 24 June 1988. http://www.nytimes.com/1988/06/24/us/global-warming-has-begun-expert-tells-senate.html. Accessed 3 Dec. 2013.

6. Hansen, J., I. Fung, A. Lacis, D. Rind, Lebedeff, R. Ruedy, G. Russell, and P. Stone. "Global Climate Changes as Forecast by Goddard Institute for Space Studies Three-dimensional Model." *Journal of Geophysical Research* 93.D8 (20 Aug. 1988), pp. 9341–64.

7. Parmesan, Camille, and Gary Yohe. "A Globally Coherent Fingerprint of Climate Change Impacts Across Natural Systems." *Nature* 421 (2 Jan. 2003), pp. 37–42.

8. Mann, Michael E. *The Hockey Stick and the Climate Wars: Dispatches from the Front Lines*. New York: Columbia University Press, 2012, p. 91.

9. The Fifth Assessment Report as well as past Intergovernmental Panel on Climate Change (IPCC) reports are available through their web pages at http://www.ipcc.ch/. IPCC. "Fifth Assessment Report (AR5)." http://www.ipcc.ch/report/ar5/. Accessed 24 Aug. 2016.

10. For comparison sake, mile-high Denver is a mere 5,280 feet above sea level.

11. Vonnegut, Kurt. *Galápagos*. New York: Laurel, 1985.

12. Darwin, Charles. *The Origin of Species: Complete and Fully Illustrated*. New York: Random House, 1979.

13. Species colonize islands in three ways: free floating, dispersal by wind, and transport by organisms. First proposed by Charles Lyell in 1830, the flotsam theory, an ironic twist of sorts on Noah's ark given how the islands have become a showcase for natural selection, makes the most sense for species such as the tortoise, although the gigantism must have evolved after the initial rafting trip. Further, it bears noting that 20,000 years ago, ice covered 30 percent of the Earth's surface, unlike the 10 percent today. This means that sea levels were considerably lower at that time, and many of the Galápagos islands would have been connected, allowing species to migrate more easily between what later became multiple islands. Over time, as naturalist Pierre Constant points out, they then evolved separately in these isolated conditions.

14. Galápagos Conservancy. "People Today." http://www.galapagos.org/about_galapagos/about-galapagos/people-today/. Accessed 20 Aug. 2016.

15. Constant, Pierre. *Galápagos: A Natural History Guide*. New York: Odyssey, 2000.

16. Larson, Edward J. *Evolution's Workshop: God and Science on the Galápagos Islands*. New York: Basic Books, 2001, p. 232.

17. While several species exist in the Galápagos, only *Isostichopus fuscus* is big and chewy enough for commercial exploitation.

CHAPTER 2

1. Carwardine, Mark. "The Galápagos Islands: Trip of a Lifetime." *The Telegraph*, 9 Sept. 2012. http://www.telegraph.co.uk/travel/destinations/south-america/ecuador/galapagos-islands/articles/The-Galapagos-Islands-Trip-of-a-Lifetime/. Accessed 21 Nov. 2013.

2. Nazca boobies, formerly known as masked boobies, were recognized as a new species in 2001.

3. Quasar Nautical. *The Galápagos Islands Visitor Sites*. Quito, Ecuador: Quasar Nautica, Galápagos Expeditions, 2003, p. 35.

4. Weiner, Jonathan. *The Beak of the Finch: A Story of Evolution in Our Time*. New York: Alfred A. Knopf, 1994, p. 17.

5. Fortunately, both the captain and a servant labeled their finches island by island, and Darwin used these specimens.

6. Darwin, Charles. *The Voyage of the Beagle*. New York: P. F. Collier & Son, 1909.

7. Arrhenius, Svante. "On the Influence of Carbonic Acid in the Air upon the Temperature of the Ground." *Philosophical Magazine and Journal of Science* (Series 5) 41:251 (April 1896), pp. 237–76.

8. Kolbert, Elizabeth. *Field Notes from a Catastrophe: Man, Nature, and Climate Change*. New York: Bloomsbury, 2006, p. 41.

9. The greenhouse gas effect is not all bad, of course. Without it, our Earth would freeze, with temperatures averaging zero instead of fifty-eight degrees Fahrenheit as they do now.

10. Darling, Seth B., and Douglas L. Sisterson. *How to Change Minds about Our Changing Climate: Let Science Do the Talking the Next Time Someone Tries to Tell You . . . And Other Arguments It's Time to End for Good*. New York: The Experiment, 2014.

11. Two weeks is the upper limit on predictability of weather. Emanuel, Kerry. *What We Know about Climate Change*. Cambridge, MA: The MIT Press, 2012, p. 34.

12. Similarly, ocean core sediments, specifically the shells of microscopic animals called "foraminifera," are made of calcium carbonate, which allows analysis of the proportion of oxygen isotopes.

13. Thompson, Andrea. "First Half of 2016 Blows Away Temp Records." *Climate Central* (19 July 2016). http://www.climatecentral.org/news/first-half-of-2016-record-hot-by-far-20540?utm_content=buffer571cc. Accessed 1 Aug. 2016. 14. The Southern Hemisphere has fewer temperate forests.

14. Mann, Michael E. *The Hockey Stick and the Climate Wars: Dispatches from the Front Lines*. New York: Columbia University Press, 2012.

15. Emanuel, Kerry. *What We Know about Climate Change*. Cambridge, MA: MIT Press, 2012, p. 42.

16. Mann, Michael E., Raymond S. Bradley, and Malcolm K. Hughes. "Global-Scale Temperature Patterns and Climate Forcing Over the Past Six Centuries." *Nature* 392 (23 April 1998), pp.779–87.

17. As a result, Mann and others recommend strongly against using tree-ring data as climate proxies after 1960. Before then, it remains effective. One case in point is 1816, the year without a summer that followed the eruption of Indonesia's Mount Tambora in April 1815.

18. Mooney, Chris. "The Hockey Stick: The Most Controversial Chart in Science, Explained." *The Atlantic*, 10 May 2013. http://www.theatlantic.com/technology/archive/2013/05/the-hockey-stick-the-most-controversial-chart-in-science-explained/275753/. Accessed 19 Nov. 2013.

CHAPTER 3

1. Hance, Jeremy. "Carbon Emissions in U.S. Rise 2 Percent Due to Increase in Coal." *Mongabay.com*, 16 Jan. 2014. http://news.mongabay.com/2014/0114-hance-co2-us.html. Accessed 20 Nov. 2013.

2. For those keeping a scorecard, we are still number-one in historical emissions, and among the leaders in annual per capita emissions.

3. Garside, Ben. "Global Carbon Emission Rise to New Record in 2013: Report." *Reuters.* 18 Nov. 2013. http://www.reuters.com/article/2013/11/19/us-global-carbon-emissions-idUSBRE9AI00A20131119. Accessed 2 Nov. 2013.

4. Archer, David. *The Long Thaw: How Humans Are Changing the Next 100,000 Years of Earth's Climate.* Princeton, NJ: Princeton University Press, 2008.

5. California Academy of Sciences. "American Adults Flunk Basic Science." *Science Daily.*13 March 2009. http://www.sciencedaily.com/releases/2009/03/090312115133.htm. Accessed 17 Nov. 2013.

6. National Science Foundation. "Science and Technology: Public Attitudes and Understanding," *Science and Engineering Indicators 2004.* http://www.nsf.gov/statistics/seind04/c7/c7h.htm. Accessed 17 Nov. 2013.

7. Chadwick, Jr., William W., Sigurion Jonsson, Dennis J. Geist, Michael Poland, Daniel J. Johnson, Spencer Batt, Karen S. Harpp, and Andres Ruiz. "The May 2005 Eruption of Fernandina Volcano, Galápagos: The First

Circumferential Dike Intrusion Observed by GPS and InSAR." *Bulletin of Volcanology* 73.6 (Aug. 2011), pp. 679–97.

8. At times marine iguanas also eat the feces of sea lions and even those of their own species.

9. Markowitz, Gerald, and David Rosner. *Deceit and Denial: The Deadly Politics of Industrial Pollution*. Berkeley: University of California Press, 2002.

10. The Global Warming Petition Project webpage holds additional information on the cover letter, analysis paper, and listing of signatories at: http://www.petitionproject.org/.

11. Howarth, Robert W. "A Bridge to Nowhere: Methane Emissions and the Greenhouse Gas Footprint of Natural Gas." *Energy Science & Engineering* 22 April 2014, pp. 1–14.

12. Banerjee, Neela. "Tennessee Enacts Evolution, Climate Change Law." *Los Angeles Times* (11 April 2012): http://articles.latimes.com/2012/apr/11/nation/la-na-tennessee-climate-law-20120411. Accessed 15 Dec. 2013.

13. Gelbspan, Ross. *Boiling Point: How Politicians, Big Oil and Coal, Journalists, and Activists Have Fueled the Climate Crisis—and What We Can Do to Avert Disaster*. New York: Basic Books, 2004, p. 67.

14. Ibid., p. 84.

15. BBC/Nova. *Dimming the Sun: What Does This Climate Conundrum Mean for the Future of Earth?* Kathryn Walker, narrator. DVD 56 min. 2004/2006.

16. Emanuel, p. 29.

17. Ibid., p. 36.

18. Hansen, James. *Storms of My Grandchildren: The Truth about the Coming Climate Catastrophe and Our Last Chance to Save Humanity*. New York: Bloomsbury, 2009, p. 42.

19. Spotts, Pete. "Greenland's Ice Sheet: Climate Change Outlook Gets a Little More Dire." *Christian Science Monitor* (13 March 2012). http://www.csmonitor.com/Environment/2012/0313/Greenland-s-ice-sheet-Climate-change-outlook-gets-a-little-more-dire. Accessed 1 Dec. 2013.

CHAPTER 4

1. Sagan, Carl. *The Demon-Haunted World: Science as a Candle in the Dark*. New York: Ballantine Books, 1996.

2. With plenty of natural food to select from in the rich, cool Humboldt currents, sharks in the Galápagos have no reason to attack humans. If one arches its back suddenly, though, all bets are off. This is the standard warning preceding an attack.

3. For an engaging description of the human impact on the islands see: Michael D'Orso. *Plundering Paradise: The Hand of Man on the Galápagos Islands.* New York: HarperCollins, 2002.

4. The other four inhabited islands, Santa Cruz, San Cristobal, Floreana, and Baltra, also have introduced goats.

5. Cruz, Felipe, Sylvia Harcourt, and Christian Lavoie, eds. *The Thematic Atlas of Project Isabela: An Illustrative Document Describing, Step-by-step, the Biggest Successful Goat Eradication Project on the Galápagos Islands, 1998–2006.* Charles Darwin Foundation and Galápagos National Park Service, 2007.

6. Cruz, Felipe, Victor Carrion, Karl J. Campbell, Christian Lavoie, and C. Josh Donlan. "Bio-Economics of Large-Scale Eradication of Feral Goats from Santiago Island, Galápagos." *Journal of Wildlife Management* 73.2 (Feb. 2009), pp. 191–200.

7. Pinta is another example. Aside from the lack of giant tortoises, it was essentially pristine until 1959, when fishermen released three goats. Their thinking was to create a fresh meat supply for a location so far from port. The initial population, however, exploded beyond control, reaching an estimated 40,000 by 1970. Copying the procedures of Santiago and Isabela, Pinta became goat-free in 2003.

8. It turns out, this was not the closest match genetically for George. According to a 2002 Yale University DNA study by Adalgisa Caccone and Jeffrey Powell, George's genetic sequence was, instead, almost identical to that of Española tortoises.

9. In tortoises, the penis is tucked inside the tail, convenient safe-keeping for traversing sharp lava rubble. When aroused, it emerges and becomes erect, allowing ejaculation to occur.

10. Nicholls, Henry. *Lonesome George: The Life and Loves of a Conservation Icon.* New York: Palgrave Macmillan, 2007.

11. Cai, Wenju, Simon Borlace, Matthieu Lengaigne,et al. "Increasing Frequency of Extreme El Niño Events Due to Greenhouse Warming." *Nature Climate Change* 4 (Feb. 2014), pp. 111–16.

CHAPTER 5

1. "Woody Allen Interview—Vicky Cristina Barcelona," *Collider.com* (15 Aug. 2008), http://collider.com/entertainment/interviews/article.asp/aid/8878/tcid/1/pg/2. Accessed 4 Jan. 2014.

2. Revkin, Andrew C. "Why 2007 IPCC Report Lacked 'Embers.'" *New York Times*, 26 Feb. 2009. http://dotearth.blogs.nytimes.com/2009/02/26/why-2007-ipcc-report-lacked-embers/?_r=0. Accessed 2 Jan. 2014.

3. Carson, Rachel. *Silent Spring.* Boston: Houghton Mifflin, 1962, p. 5.

4. For a fascinating clip of waved albatross courtship see the powerful three-part BBC documentary: *Galápagos: The Islands that Changed the World.* Tilda Swinton, narrator. Mike Gunton and Patrick Morris, producers. Paul D. Stewart and Richard Wollocombe, cinematography. 150 min. Sept. 2006. (DVD release 3 April 2007).

5. Kolbert, Elizabeth. *Field Notes from a Catastrophe: Man, Nature, and Climate Change.* New York: Bloomsbury, 2006, p. 128.

6. Hoffert, Martin I., Ken Caldeira, Gregory Benford, David R. Criswell, Christopher Green, Howard Herzog, Atul K. Jain, Haroon S. Kheshgi, Klaus S. Lackner, John S. Lewis, H. Douglas Lightfoot, Wallace Manheimer, John C. Mankins, Michael E. Mauel, L. John Perkins, Michael E. Schlesinger, Tyler Volk, and Tom M. L. Wigley. "Advanced Technology Paths to Global Climate Stability: Energy for a Greenhouse Planet." *Science* 298.5595 (1 Nov. 2002), pp. 981–87.

7. By 1995 some 26 million registered vehicles in California traveled 271 billion miles with nitrogen oxide and hydrocarbon auto emissions of 1.1 million tons a year. That represents a 31 percent reduction in emissions compared to 1970 levels, even with a 137 percent increase in vehicle miles, according to the California Air Resources Board. Source: California Environmental Protection Agency. "Key Events in the History of Air Quality in California" (4 Feb. 2014). http://www.arb.ca.gov/html/brochure/history.htm.

8. California Air Resources Board. "Clearing California Skies." Video. 12 min. 1998.

9. The last major Ice Age was 20,000 years ago, when an ice sheet more than a mile thick blanketed Canada and the northern United States.

10. Floreana was not always associated with tranquility. In fact, its early-twentieth-century history was far from it, revolving around an odd German dentist/vegetarian/philosopher named Friedrich Ritter who arrived on the

island with his mistress in 1929 as well as several eclectic characters that followed. For more on this 1930s murder and mystery see John Treherne, *The Galápagos Affair*. New York: Random House, 1983. For two eyewitness accounts: Dore Strauch, *Satan Comes to Eden*. New York: Harper and Brothers, 1935; Margaret Wittmer, *Florena*. Shropshire, UK: Anthony Nelson, 1989.

11. Juveniles are white.

12. By contrast, methane, which is thirty-three times more potent than carbon dioxide, only lasts about twelve years and is essentially removed from the atmosphere by chemical reaction.

13. Gillis, Justin. "The Flood Next Time." *New York Times*, 13 Jan. 2014. http://www.nytimes.com/2014/01/14/science/earth/grappling-wi th-sea-level-rise-sooner-not-later.html?_r=0.

14. Kreft, Sönke, and David Eckstein. "Global Climate Risk Index 2014: Who Suffers Most from Extreme Weather Events? Weather-Related Loss Events in 2012 and 1993 to 2012." *Germanwatch*, Nov. 2013. http://germanwatch.org/en/download/8551.pdf. Accessed 7 Dec. 2013.

15. Fahrenthold, David A. "Last House on Sinking Chesapeake Bay Island Sinks." *The Washington Post*, 26 Oct. 2010. http://www.washingtonpost.com/wp-dyn/content/article/2010/10/24/AR2010102402996.html. Accessed 8 Dec. 2013.

16. Gillis, Justin. "Panel Says Global Warming Risks Sudden, Deep Changes." *New York Times*, 4 Dec. 2013, p. A-22.

17. Carson, Rachel. "The Silent Spring of Rachel Carson." *C.B.S. Reports*, 3 April 1963.

CHAPTER 6

1. Lynas, Mark. *High Tide: The Truth about Our Climate Crisis*. New York: Picador, 2004, p. 112.

2. According to the EPA, 31 percent of carbon dioxide emissions in 2011 came from the transportation sector, and according to the Union of Concerned Scientists, 61 percent of transportation sector emissions come from light cars and trucks. Sources: EPA. "Overview of Greenhouse Gases." http://www.epa.gov/climatechange/ghgemissions/gases/co2.html. Accessed 20 Aug.

2016; Union of Concerned Scientists. "Clean Vehicles." http://www.ucsusa. org/clean_vehicles/why-clean-cars/global-warming/. Accessed 21 Sept. 2013.

3. Johnson, Johanna E., and Paul A. Marshall, eds. *Climate Change and the Great Barrier Reef: A Vulnerability Assessment*. Townsville, Australia: Great Barrier Reef Marine Park Authority and Australian Greenhouse Office, 2007.

4. Flannery, Tim. *The Weathermakers: How Man Is Changing the Climate and What It Means for Life on Earth*. New York: Atlantic Monthly Press, 2005, p. 105.

5. In comparison, the Caribbean holds about nine hundred different species of fish.

6. Much of that film faithfully portrays life on the actual reef, although biologically, Nemo's dad, Marlin, should have transformed into a Marilyn after the opening tragedy of losing Nemo's mom. Every anemone fish is born male, but the biggest and strongest become female.

7. Nelson, Laura. "News Feature: One Slip, and You're Dead." *Nature* 429 (24 June 2004), pp. 798–99.

8. Anderson, Peter D., and Gyula Bokor. "Conotoxins: Potential Weapons from the Sea." *Journal of Bioterrorism and Biodefense* 3.3 (17 Nov. 2012).

9. Tourism in Queensland has been stabilizing recently, recovering from a multiyear downturn. Beginning in 2004, a series of events conspired to discourage visitors, from SARS and high oil prices to the global financial crisis, flu epidemic, terrorist events, cyclones, and flooding. This downturn is notable for more than simply the money it brings to the overall Australian economy. Up to 20 percent of the Great Barrier Reef Marine Park Authority budget comes from the environmental management charge levied on visitors. When visitor numbers decline, the budget decreases, too.

10. Briggs, Chris, et al. "Tourism and the Great Barrier Reef: Healthy Reef, Healthy Industry." *International Cases in Sustainable Travel & Tourism*, Pierre Benckendorff and Dagmar Lund-Durlacher, eds. Oxford, UK: Goodfellow Publishers, 2013, pp. 57–70.

CHAPTER 7

1. Fickling, David. "The Cruel Sea." *The Guardian*, 22 July 2004.

2. Banerjee, Neela, Lisa Song, and David Hasemyer. "Exxon: The Road Not Taken." *InsideClimateNews*, 16 Sept. 2015. https://insideclimatenews.org/news/15092015/Exxons-own-research-confirmed-fossil-fuels-role-in-global-warming. Accessed 29 July 2016.

3. Harder, Amy, Devlin Barrett, and Bradley Olson. "Exxon Fires Back at Climate-Change Probe." *The Wall Street Journal*, 13 April 2016. http://www.wsj.com/articles/exxon-fires-back-at-climate-change-probe-1460574535. Accessed 29 July 2016.

4. *Frontline*. "Climate of Doubt." PBS. Catherine Upin, director and producer. John Hockenberry, correspondent. 23 Oct. 2012. http://www.pbs.org/wgbh/pages/frontline/climate-of-doubt/.

5. Massachusetts, et al. v. EPA et al. No. 05-1120. Supreme Court of the United States. 415 F.3d 50, 2 April 2007. Legal Information Institute, Cornell University Law School. https://www.law.cornell.edu/supct/html/05-1120.ZS.html. Accessed 24 Aug. 201.6; Eilperin, Juliet. "New EPA head McCarthy Outlines Ambitious Agenda in Harvard Speech." *The Washington Post*, 30 July 2013.

6. *Australia: Land Beyond Time*. Australian Film Finance Corporation. David Flatman, director. 42 min. 2002.

7. ABC Science. "Australia's Battle with the Bunny." 9 April 2009. http://www.abc.net.au/science/articles/2009/04/08/2538860.htm. Accessed 21 Jan. 2014.

8. Broomhall, F. H. *The Longest Fence in the World*. Carlisle, Western Australia: Hesperian Press, 1991.

CHAPTER 8

1. Gyres are large systems of rotating currents caused by the Coriolis effect. Five of them are found across the globe.

2. Spotila, James R. *Saving Sea Turtles: Extraordinary Stories from the Battle against Extinction*. Baltimore, MD: The Johns Hopkins University Press, 2011.

3. Roe, David. "Flippers and Flukes: Caring for Our Special Marine Turtles and Dugongs." Sea Turtle Foundation. Harim Series Book 1. Undated. https://www.google.com/#q=Flippers+and+Flukes:+Caring+for+Our+Special+Marine+Turtles+and+Dugongs.%E2%80%9D++.

4. Mrosovsky, N. "Sex Ratios of Sea Turtles." *Journal of Experimental Zoology* 270.1 (15 Sept. 1994), pp. 16–27.

5. Crews, D., J. M. Bergeron, J. J. Bull, D. Flores, A. Tousignant, J. K. Skipper, and T. Wibbels. "Temperature-dependent Sex Determination in Reptiles: Proximate Mechanisms, Ultimate Outcomes, and Practical Applications." *Developmental Genetics* 15.3 (1994), pp. 297–312.

6. BBC Earth. *The Great Barrier Reef.* James Brickell, writer and director. Monty Hall, narrator. 186 min. 2012.

7. Woodford, James. *The Great Barrier Reef.* Rev. ed. Sydney, Australia: Macmillan, 2011.

8. Like their kin, coral use stinging cells to defend themselves and catch a portion of their food. Their poisonous tentacles paralyze microscopic animals that ocean waters wash their way, and the coral then feed on them.

9. Coral in Scotland and Norway, for example, have no zooxanthellae, growing slowly as a result.

10. Glynn, Peter W. "Global Warming and Widespread Coral Mortality: Evidence of First Coral Reef Extinctions." *Saving a Million Species: Extinction Risk from Climate Change.* Lee Hannah, ed. Washington, D.C.: Island Press, 2012, pp.103–20.

11. Berkelmans, R., G. De'ath, S. Kininmonth, and W. J. Skirving. "A Comparison of the 1998 and 2002 Coral Bleaching Events on the Great Barrier Reef: Spatial Correlation, Patterns, and Predictions." *Coral Reefs* 23.1 (April 2004), pp. 74–83.

12. Normile, Dennis. "Survey Confirms Worst-ever Coral Bleaching at Great Barrier Reef." *Science* (19 April 2016). http://www.sciencemag.org/news/2016/04/survey-confirms-worst-ever-coral-bleaching-great-barrier-reef. Accessed 3 Aug. 2016.

13. Hoegh-Guldberg. "Coral Reefs, Climate Change, and Mass Extinction." *Saving a Million Species: Extinction Risk from Climate Change.* Lee Hannah, ed. Washington, D.C.: Island Press, 2012, pp. 261–84.

14. Emanuel, Kerry. *What We Know about Climate Change.* 2nd ed. Cambridge, MA: Boston Review/The MIT Press, 2012, p. 69.

15. De'ath, Glenn, Janice M. Jough, and Kathrina E. Fabricius. "Declining Coral Calcification on the Great Barrier Reef." *Science* 323.5910 (2 Jan. 2009), pp. 116–19.

16. Uthicke, S., P. Momigliano, and K. E. Fabricius. "Early Victims of Ocean Acidification Could Go Extinct this Century." *Scientific Reports 3*, article number 1769 (3 May 2013).

CHAPTER 9

1. Brodie, Jon, et al. "2013 Scientific Consensus Statement: Land Use Impacts on Great Barrier Reef Water Quality and Ecosystem Condition." Reef Water Quality Protection Plan Secretariat, July 2013.

2. Bellwood, D. R., et al. "Confronting the Coral Reef Crisis." *Nature* 429 (24 June 2004), pp. 827–33.

3. Interestingly, over the last decade, one could also argue that cyclones have actually stopped bleaching by stirring everything up.

4. BBC News. "UN: India to Be World's Most Populous Country by 2028." 14 June 2013. http://www.bbc.co.uk/news/world-asia-22907307. Accessed 24 Jan. 2014.

5. Murray, James. "China Power Sector Emissions 'to Peak in 2027.'" *The Guardian Environment Network*, 27 Aug. 2013. https://www.theguardian.com/environment/2013/aug/27/china-power-emissions-peak-2027. Accessed 15 June 2015.

CHAPTER 10

1. Toilets manufactured since 1994 are required to use no more than 1.6 GPF, according to federal plumbing standards passed in 1992. Those built between 1980 and 1994 use 3.5 to 4.5 GPF, those constructed from 1950 to 1980 use 5.0 GPF, and the truly ancient commodes made before 1950 gobble down 7.0 GPF.

2. Using a conversion fact sheet on indoor water efficiency from the Portland Water Bureau, I calculate we save between $600 to $800 a year, depending on the number of flushes per person per day; that is, sometimes we take extended trips away from home and thus flush less, whereas at other times we have visitors or folks are under the weather ☺ and flush more.

3. The World Bank. "CO$_2$ Emissions (Metric Tons per Capita)." Carbon Dioxide Information Analysis Center, Environmental Sciences Division, Oak Ridge National Laboratory, Tennessee, United States. 2016. http://data.worldbank.org/indicator/EN.ATM.CO2E.PC. Accessed 24 Aug. 2016.

4. Resource Development Council. "Alaska's Oil & Gas Industry: Background." 16 Oct. 2013. http://www.akrdc.org/issues/oilgas/overview.html.

5. D'Oro, Rachel. "Permanent Fund Dividend Is $900; Direct Deposits Begin Oct. 3." *Anchorage Daily News*, 17 Sept. 2013. http://www.adn.com/2013/09/17/3080873/alaskans-eager-to-hear-amount.html. Accessed 18 Jan. 2014.

6. Mabo and Others v. Queensland (No. 2). 23, High Court of Australia. 1992. 175 CLR 1; F.C. 92/014. http://www.austlii.edu.au/au/cases/cth/HCA/1992/23.html. Accessed 22 Feb. 2014.

7. Of course, considering aboriginal customs such as the walkabout and dreamtime, one could easily argue that their culture is tens of thousands of years old, and that through these traditions a distinctive culture passes down from generation to generation.

8. Bryson, Bill. *In a Sunburned Country*. New York: Broadway Books, 2000, p. 189.

9. Macintyre, Stuart. *A Concise History of Australia*. Cambridge, UK: Cambridge University Press, 2004.

10. The Stuart highway is his legacy today. Roughly following the path he traveled, it extends from Port Augusta, South Australia, north up the center of the continent through Alice Springs all the way to the top end in Darwin.

CHAPTER 11

1. Burns, Ken. "The National Parks." address at Rollins College, 7 April 2014.

2. Montana holds another 3 percent of the park, with 1 percent in Idaho.

3. Kolbert, Elizabeth. *Field Notes from a Catastrophe: Man, Nature, and Climate Change*. New York: Bloomsbury, 2006, p. 198.

4. Bullard, Robert D., and Beverly Wright, eds. *Race, Place, and Environmental Justice after Hurricane Katrina: Struggles to Reclaim, Rebuild, and Revitalize New Orleans and the Gulf Coast*. Boulder, CO: Westview Press, 2009, p. 1.

5. Kroeber, A. L., and Talcott Parsons. "The Concepts of Culture and of Social System." *The American Sociological Review* 23 (1958), pp. 582–83.

6. Well, it depends who you ask. Semantic confusion here may be traced to roots in mid-twentieth-century debates between anthropologists and sociologists. Anthropologists were holistic in their interpretations of culture, whereas sociologists saw it as a derivative of social systems. My colleague Bob Moore, an anthropologist and fellow world traveler, offers probably the best description I've heard. He describes culture as what people learn about themselves and their community. Drawing an analogy to software, Bob suggests that this cultural information is then processed through the biological hardware of the body. The result is manifest in the form of schools, families, and, more generally, how we treat one another. It is what we commonly refer to as "social relations," the way people respond to one another. Despite this powerful analogy, it is also important to recognize that cultural and social influences are heavily interwoven together, even presenting a chicken-and-egg-type relationship. Culture does not necessarily come first. Social influences can shape it, too.

7. Bechky, Allen. *Adventuring in Southern Africa: A Sierra Club Travel Guide*. San Francisco: Sierra Club Books, 1997, p. 407.

8. Brett, Michael. *Touring South Africa's National Parks*. Cape Town: Struik Travel & Heritage, 2010, p. 7.

9. The South African climate becomes drier as one moves progressively west across the Highveld plains.

10. Morton, H. V. "Pietermaritzburg, Durban, Zululand: 1947." *The Reader's Companion to South Africa*. Alan Ryan, ed. New York: Harcourt Brace & Company, 1990, pp. 120–46.

11. Veld is a local term for open land used for grazing.

12. Charlton-Perkins, William. *Great Game Parks of Africa: Hluhluwe-iMfolozi Park*. 2nd impression. Cape Town, South Africa: Struik Publishers, 1997, p. 10.

13. Once a year, Hluhluwe-iMfolozi holds an auction for its surplus game. Black rhino are the rarest species and, accordingly, receive top bids of as much as $US100,000, according to former ranger and author Lawrence Anthony, while an adult white rhino typically fetches about $US45,000. Impala are the most common and cheapest, averaging around 12,000 rand or a little less than $US1,200.

14. Wildlife Translocation Association. Heidelberg, South Africa. http://www.wtass.org/. Accessed 16 April 2014.

15. Buckland, S. T., D. R. Anderson, K. P. Burnham, and J. L. Laake. *Distance Sampling: Estimating Abundance of Biological Populations*. London: Chapman and Hall, 1993.

16. Act Creating Yellowstone National Park, March 1, 1872; Enrolled Acts and Resolutions of Congress, 1789–1996; General Records of the United States Government; Record Group 11; National Archives. Available at: http://www.ourdocuments.gov/doc.php?doc=45.

17. Earthwatch Institute. "Walking with African Wildlife." http://earthwatch.org/expeditions/walking-with-african-wildlife#daily-life. Accessed 10 March 2014.

18. Player, Ian. *The White Rhino Saga*. New York: Stein and Day, 1973.

19. There are five species of rhinoceros worldwide, including the Indian, Javan, and Sumatran rhinos as well as the white and black rhino of Africa. The Javan and Sumatran rhinos are nearly extinct.

20. Player, Ian. *Zulu Wilderness: Shadow and Soul*. Golden, CO: Fulcrum Publishing, 1998, p. 119.

21. Pooley, Tony. *Mashesha: The Making of a Game Ranger*. Johannesburg, South Africa: Southern Book Publishers, 1992, p. 211.

22. The other two are Lake St. Lucia, which I visited a week later, and Mdhletshe, which sadly no longer exists.

23. Save the Rhino. "Rhino Population Figures." 19 March 2014. http://www.savetherhino.org/rhino_info/rhino_population_figures. Accessed 13 April 2014.

24. Roughly 93 percent of black and white rhinos are in South Africa.

25. Marven, Nigel. *Nature: Rhinoceros*. 22 Aug. 2008. http://www.pbs.org/wnet/nature/episodes/rhinoceros/rhino-horn-use-fact-vs-fiction/1178/.

26. Depending on the species, horns average from one to three kilograms.

27. Guilford, Gywnn. "Why Does a Rhino Horn Cost $300,000? Because Vietnam Thinks It Cures Cancer and Hangovers." *The Atlantic*, 15 May 2013. http://www.theatlantic.com/business/archive/2013/05/why-does-a-rhino-horn-cost-300-000-because-vietnam-thinks-it-cures-cancer-and-hangovers/275881/. Accessed 13 April 2014.

CHAPTER 12

1. Thoreau, Henry David. "Walking." *The Atlantic Monthly* 9.56 (June 1862), pp. 657–74.

2. Player (1998), p. 45.

3. These creatures perform crucial sanitation engineering when they seek out poo as prized possessions, shape it into balls that dwarf them in size, and then roll it back to their nests with their spindly back legs.

4. Caro, Tim, Amanda Izzo, Robert C. Reiner, Jr., Hannah Walker, and Theodore Stankowich. "The Function of Zebra Stripes." *Nature Communications* 5.3535 (1 April 2014). http://www.nature.com/ncomms/2014/140401/ncomms4535/full/ncomms4535.html.

5. In 1939, South Africa's Solomon Linda first wrote and recorded the song, sung originally in Zulu with an improvised, wordless melody and a choir known as "The Evening Birds." It became a hit and was adapted and covered by an array of international pop and folk artists in the 1950s before *The Tokens* 1961 smash single.

6. Patterson, John Henry. *The Maneaters of Tsavo and Other East African Adventures*. London: Macmillan and Co., 1907.

7. Duggan, Alan, ed. *Reader's Digest Illustrated Guide to the Game Parks & Nature Reserves of Southern Africa*. 2nd ed. Cape Town: Reader's Digest Association of South Africa Limited, 1990, p. 21.

8. The last lion was shot by a poacher in iMfolozi in 1915.

9. Trinkle, M., N. Ferguson, A. Reid, C. Reid, M. Somers, L. Turelli, J. Graf, M. Szykman, D. Cooper, P. Haverman, G. Kastberger, C. Packer, and R. Slotow. "Translocating Lions into an Inbred Lion Population in the Hluhluwe-iMfolozi Park, South Africa." *Animal Conservation* 11 (2008), pp. 138–43.

10. As a humorous aside, although I was never able to confirm the urban legend, or perhaps more accurately the rural legend, one short story about these reintroductions deserves at least a footnote. During one of our fireside chats, when it was often difficult to distinguish truth from fictional embellishment, Cameron described one particularly dicey South African park translocation. It seems that one distinguished dignitary commemorating the event spoke too long before a drugged lion departed that day—and the lion actually woke up midflight. When the pilot landed, he desperately ran for cover, blowing the entire welcoming ceremony. In actuality, it's more likely this tale was an adaptation of a March 1965 event involving lionesses transported via land. At least one of these lionesses woke up at a petrol station en route to Hluhluwe-iMfolozi.

11. For example, they typically haul large kills into tree branch forks where their prize is out of reach of lions, wild dogs, hyenas, and even vultures.

12. The Anglo-Boer Wars of 1880–1881 and 1899–1902 are the most notable of these. English chauvinism, aggressive German diplomacy, and the discovery of gold in South Africa drove British interests, according to noted South African historian Leonard Thompson.

13. Thompson, Leonard. *A History of South Africa*. New Haven, CT: Yale University Press, 1995, pp. 87–96.

14. Morton, M. V. "Pietermaritzburg, Durban, Zululand: 1947." *The Reader's Companion to South Africa*, Alan Ryan, ed. New York: Harcourt Brace & Company, 1999, p. 130.

15. South Africa became fully sovereign in 1934 (and a republic in 1961), although it remained part of the British Commonwealth until 1968. After two-and-a-half decades of absence, South Africa rejoined in 1994.

16. Its goals were enfranchisement for blacks and elimination of restrictions based on color.

17. Thompson, p. 189.

18. Admittedly, his last years before release in February 1990 were much more comfortable than the early ones. Indeed, one might contend that a turning point began when the apartheid government began secret discussions with Mandela in 1986.

19. Formed in 1970, this group became world famous after contributing to Paul Simon's 1987 *Graceland* album.

20. Recall that, until 1991, South African law divided the population into four major racial categories: black, white, colored, and Asian. Blacks were about 80 percent of the population. Whites (the descendants of the Dutch, French, English, and German) represented 9 percent. Mixed races of early settlers and indigenous populations represented another 9 percent. Asians, descendants from Indian workers brought in the mid-nineteenth century to work the sugar estates of Natal and concentrated in KwaZula-Natal Province, provide the final 2 percent.

21. It investigated apartheid-era human rights abuses from 1960 to 1994, granting amnesty to those who committed politically motivated crimes and recommending compensation for victim abuses. The focus on confession, penance, and forgiveness, of course, contrasts greatly to the American penchant for punishment with a "high-noon, Western shootout" cultural mentality.

22. *Frontline: The Long Walk of Nelson Mandela.* Story Street Productions and Films2People. Will Lyman, narrator. 1 hr. 51 min. 1999.

CHAPTER 13

1. Boo, Elizabeth. *Ecotourism: The Potentials and Pitfalls.* Vol. 1. Washington, D.C.: World Wildlife Fund, 1990, p. 3

2. Others of note are lantana, bugweed, syringa, potato creeper, guava, and senna.

3. According to the U.S. State Department, approximately one-quarter of the South African population is infected with HIV.

4. Sinclair, Anthony R. E. *Serengeti Story: Life and Science in the World's Greatest Wildlife Region.* Oxford, UK: Oxford University Press, 2012, p. 47.

5. Leakey, Richard, and Virginia Morell. *Wildlife Wars: My Fight to Save Africa's Natural Treasures.* New York: St. Martin's Griffin, 2001.

6. Lindberg, K. "The Internal Market for Nature Tourism in South Africa: A Household Survey." *Nature Tourism, Conservation, and Development in KwaZulua Natal, South Africa.* E. Lutz and B. Aylward, eds. Washington, D.C.: World Bank, 2003.

7. Yanarella, Ernest J., and Richard S. Levine. "Don't Pick the Low Lying Fruit." *Sustainability* 1.4 (August 2008). http://pages.ramapo.edu/~vasishth/Articles/Yanarella+Aim_High_for_Sustainability.pdf.

8. Duggan, Alan, ed. *Reader's Digest Illustrated Guide to the Game Parks & Nature Reserves of Southern Africa.* 2nd ed. Cape Town: Reader's Digest Association of South Africa Limited, 1990, p. 42.

9. Ibid., p. 341.

CHAPTER 14

1. Maathai, Wangari. *The Green Belt Movement: Sharing the Approach & the Experience.* New York: Lantern Books, 2004.

2. The Greenbelt Movement. "Tree Planting and Water Harvesting." http://www.greenbeltmovement.org/what-we-do/tree-planting-for-watersheds. Accessed 24 Aug. 2016.

3. Steves, Rick. "The Value of Travel," TEDxRainer, Dec. 2011. http://tedxtalks.ted.com/video/TEDxRainier-Rick-Steves-The-Val.

4. Twain, Mark. *The Innocents Abroad*. Hartford, CT: American Publishing Company, 1869.

5. Charlton-Perkins, p. 16.

6. By comparison, young bulls in their late teens only remain in musth for a few days.

7. All this eating produces a fair amount of dung as well. Bright olive to yellow when fresh, the color changes as it dries, staying dark when up to six hours old but lightening thereafter. It has a strange, rather pleasant smell and holds a considerable amount of water.

8. Bechky, Allen. *Adventuring in Southern Africa: A Sierra Club Travel Guide*. San Francisco: Sierra Club Books, 1997, p. 125.

9. Masson, Jeffrey Moussaiff, and Susan McCarthy. *When Elephants Weep: The Emotional Lives of Animals*. New York: Dell Publishing, 1995.

10. Harvey, Keri. "Grey Matters." *Wild*, Autumn/Winter 2008, p. 21.

11. With Asian elephants, only males have tusks.

12. Anthony, Lawrence (with Graham Spence). *The Last Rhinos: My Battle to Save One of the World's Greatest Creatures*. New York: Thomas Dunne Books, 2012, p.169.

13. Payne, Katy, Iain Douglas-Hamilton, Vivek Menon, Cynthia Moss, Joyce Poole, and Andrea Turkalo. "Lifting the Ivory Ban Called Premature." NPR, 31 Oct. 2002. http://www.npr.org/templates/story/story.php?storyId=3879214.

14. Most recently, CoP-17 was in Johannesburg, South Africa, in September and October 2016.

15. For CITES listing details see: http://www.speciesplus.net/#/taxon_concepts/4521/legal?taxonomy=cites_eu.

16. Rosen, Rebecca J. "What Is It about an Elephant's Tusks that Make Them So Valuable?" *The Atlantic*, 6 Sept. 2012.

17. http://www.theatlantic.com/business/archive/2012/09/what-is-it-about-an-elephants-tusks-that-make-them-so-valuable/262021/.

18. Anthony, p. 256.

19. Wild dogs are best represented in Botswana.

20. To its credit, the World Bank, responding to its critics and past environmental failures, now employs some microcredit operations in addition

to its favored large-loan operations. These, by definition, better integrate local expertise.

21. Player (1998), p. 62.

22. Snitch, Thomas. "Poachers Kill Three Elephants an Hour. Here's How to Stop Them." *The Telegraph*, 13 Feb. 2014. http://www.telegraph.co.uk/earth/environment/conservation/10634747/Poachers-kill-three-elephants-an-hour.-Heres-how-to-stop-them.html.

23. "Tracking Poached Ivory: Research Overview," Center for Conservation Biology, University of Washington. 15 April 2014. http://conservationbiology.uw.edu/research-programs/tracking-poached-ivory/. Accessed 28 April 2014; Bergenas, Johan, and Monica Medina. "Opinion: Break the Link between Terrorism Funding and Poaching." *The Washington Post*, 31 Jan. 2014.

24. Kasterine, Alexander. "Africa's Anti-Poaching Problem." *Foreign Affairs*, 5 Feb. 2014. http://www.foreignaffairs.com/articles/140718/alexander-kasterine/africas-anti-poaching-problem. Accessed 22 Feb. 2014.

25. Wyler, Liana Sun, and Pervaze A. Sheikh. "International Illegal Trade in Wildlife: Threats and U.S. Policy." *Congressional Research Service*, 23 July 2013. http://www.fas.org/sgp/crs/misc/RL34395.pdf.

26. Carruthers, Jane. *The Kruger National Park—A Social and Political History*. Pietermaritzburg, South Africa: University of Natal Press, 1995.

27. Hansen, p. 200.

CHAPTER 15

1. For a classic reading of conquistador exploitation see Hemming, John. *The Search for El Dorado*. London: Michael Joseph Ltd., 1978.

2. Revkin, Andrew. *The Burning Season: The Murder of Chico Mendes and the Fight for the Amazon Rain Forest*. Boston: Houghton Mifflin, 1990, p. 7.

3. Brightsmith, Donald J. "Effects of Weather on Parrot Geophagy in Tambopata, Peru." *Wilson Bulletin* 116 (2004), pp. 134–45.

4. Solano, Pedro. "Legal Framework for Protected Areas: Peru." IUCN-EPLP No.81, May 2009. http://cmsdata.iucn.org/downloads/peru_en.pdf.

5. Jackson, Joe. *The Thief at the End of the World: Rubber, Power, and the Seeds of Empire*. New York: Viking, 2008.

6. Stronza, Amanda. "Learning Both Ways: Lessons from a Corporate and Community Ecotourism Collaboration." *Cultural Survival Quarterly* 23.2 (Summer 1999).

7. With a heavy, barrel-shaped body, but disproportionately small head, the capybara is definitely distinctive.

8. Caufield, Catherine. *In the Rainforest: Report from a Strange, Beautiful, Imperiled World*. Chicago: University of Chicago Press, 1991, p. 59.

9. Tveten, John L. "Tropical Forests of Peru's Tambopata Reserve Hold Treasure—Trove of Life." *Houston Chronicle*, 7 Feb. 1987.

10. Half the species of parrots are kestrel-size or smaller and weigh a pound or less. Larger parrots such as the macaws can be more than three feet long, with their impressive tails as long as their bodies.

11. Sullivan, Tim. "In Awe of the Macaw." *The Oregonian*, 19 April 2004.

12. Nature. "The Real Macaw." PBS. Caroline Brett, director and producer. Howard McGillen, narrator. 26 Feb. 2004. http://www.pbs.org/wnet/nature/episodes/the-real-macaw/introduction/2729/.

13. At the time of my visit, Brightsmith retained an attachment to Duke University, only making the move to A&M after my volunteer stint at Tambopata.

14. Harman, Danna. "Peru wants Machu Picchu Artifacts Returned." *USA Today*, 6 Jan. 2006, p. 10-A.

15. Orson, Diane. "Yale Returns Machu Picchu Artifacts to Peru." *All Things Considered*, NPR, 15 Dec. 2010. http://www.npr.org/2010/12/15/132083890/yale-returns-machu-picchu-artifacts-to-peru. Accessed 13 April 2014.

16. Britton Hill is in the panhandle of Florida.

17. NOVA and National Geographic Television. "The Ghosts of Machu Picchu." Craig Sechler, narrator. 2009. http://www.pbs.org/wgbh/nova/ancient/ghosts-machu-picchu.html.

18. Regarded as the greatest Inca ruler, Pachacuti reigned from 1438 to 1471 and is credited with creating the administrative system that maintained the empire. He was held in such high regard that an attendant reportedly burned his clothes after he wore them, "so nothing touching his body was contaminated by contact with lesser mortals." Rergus M. Bordewich, "Winter Palace." *Smithsonian*, March 2003, p. 112.

19. Bordewich, p. 110.

20. Markels, Alex. "A View with a Room." *Audubon*. Oct. 1999. http://archive.audubonmagazine.org/viewroom.html.

CHAPTER 16

1. Wapner, Paul. "Climate Suffering." *Global Environmental Politics* 14.2 (May 2014), pp. 1–6.

2. Chase, Rachel. "Argentina: 70 Injured in Christmas Day Piranha Attack." *Peru This Week*, 26 Dec. 2013. http://www.peruthisweek.com/news-argentina-70-injured-in-christmas-day-piranha-attack-101820.

3. "Rebels Kill 8 Policemen." *New York Times*, 22 Dec. 2005.

4. In 1974, the Peruvian government passed the Law of Native Communities, which outlines the process for Amazonian indigenous peoples to achieve formal land title recognition. It took them two years, but the Ese'eja were the first within the state of Madre de Dios to do so. Further, in 1987 when the community won a legal decision returning a tract of land mistakenly added to the Tambopata reserve, they agreed to the condition that three thousand hectares (equating to 30 percent of their lands) be protected as communal reserve free from hunting, logging, or any resource extraction.

5. Stronza, Amanda. "Learning Both Ways: Lessons from a Corporate and Community Ecotourism Collaboration." *Cultural Survival Quarterly* 23.2 (Summer 1999).

6. This contract also had an exclusivity clause forbidding anyone in the community from establishing a relationship with a competitor to Rainforest Expeditions, but was amended following the opening of a third lodge, Refugia Amazonas, in 2006.

7. Terborgh, John. *Requiem for Nature*. Washington, D.C.: Island Press, 1999.

8. Chile claims this cocktail as its national drink, too.

9. Caufield, p. 68.

10. "Saving the Parrots: Texas A&M Team Sequences Genome of Endangered Macaw Birds." *PR Newswire*, 8 May 2013.

11. International Union for Conservation of Nature—IUCN. *The IUCN Red List of Threatened Species*. IUCN, 2013. http://www.iucnredlist.org>. Downloaded on 7 December 2016.

12. Olah, George, Gabriela Vigo, Robert Heinsohn, and Donald J. Brightsmith. "Nest Site Selection and Efficacy of Artificial Nests for Breeding Success of Scarlet Macaws *Ara macao macao* in Lowland Peru." *Journal for Nature Conservation* 22 (2014), pp. 176–85.

13. Eckstrom, Christine K. "Homeless Macaws?" *International Wildlife* 24 (Sept./Oct. 1994), pp. 14–23.

14. Munn, Charles A. "Macaws: Winged Rainbows," *National Geographic* 185.1 (Jan. 1994), pp. 118–40.

15. CITES Secretariat. "Periodic Review of Animal Taxa in the Appendices Evaluation of Species Selected at AC15 and AC16." Convention on International Trade in Endangered Species on Wild Fauna and Flora. Seventeenth Meeting of the Animals Committee, Hanoi, Vietnam, 30 July to 3 Aug. 2001. http:// www.cites.org/eng/com/ac/17/E17-08-1.pdf.

16. Juniper, Tony. "Too Pretty." *Birder's World* 19.2 (April 2005), pp. 26–33.

17. Hartley, Richard. "Pet Trade Blues." *International Wildlife* 30.2 (March/ April 2000), pp. 40–47.

18. Gastañaga, Melvin, Ross Macleod, Bennett Hennessey, Joaquin Ugarte Nunez, Edevaly Puse, Anita Arrascue, Johana Hoyos, Willy Maldonado Chambi, Jimmy Vasquez, and Gunar Engblom. "A Study of the Parrot Trade in Peru and the Potential Importance of Internal Trade for Threatened Species." *Bird Conservation International* 21.1 (2011), pp. 76–85.

19. Vigo, Gabriela, Martha Williams, and Donald Brightsmith. "Growth of Scarlet Macaw (*Ara macao*) Chicks in Southeastern Peru." *Ornitologia Neotropical* 22 (2011), pp. 143–53.

20. Brightsmith, Donald. Personal interview. Tambopata Research Center. 22 Jan. 2006.

21. Honey, Martha. *Ecotourism and Sustainable Development: Who Owns Paradise?* Washington, D.C.: Island Press, 1999.

22. Brightsmith, Donald J., Amanda Stronza, and Kurt Holle. "Ecotourism, Conservation Biology, and Volunteer Tourism: A Mutually Beneficial Triumvirate." *Biological Conservation* 141 (2008), pp. 2832–42.

23. Earthwatch Institute. "Partner Profile: HSBC." http://earth-watch.org/corporate-partnerships/partnership-profiles/hsbc. Accessed 13 April 2014.

CHAPTER 17

1. Caufield, p. 50.

2. Plotkin, Mark J. *Tales of a Shaman's Apprentice: An Ethnobotanist Searches for New Medicines in the Amazon Rain Forest.* New York: Penguin Books, 1993, p. 38

3. Caufield, p. 66.

4. Plotkin, p. 47.

5. Revkin, Andrew. *The Burning Season: The Murder of Chico Mendes and the Fight for the Amazon Rain Forest.* Boston: Houghton Mifflin, 1990, p. 15.

6. Caufield, p. 213.

7. Erwin, Terry L. "Tropical Forests: Their Richness in Coleoptera and Other Arthropod Species." *The Coleopterists Bulletin* 36 (1982), pp. 74–75.

8. Exceptions can be made for those that have life-threatening allergic reactions to eggs, chicken, or gelatin.

9. The World Health Organization estimates that one-third of the world's population has latent TB, meaning that they are infected with the bacterium that causes the disease but not yet ill. In these latent cases, the patient is not contagious, but if the TB becomes active (which it does roughly 10 percent of the time), they become contagious. In 2012, 8.6 million people fell ill with TB, and 1.3 million died from it.

10. The animal at the top of the list, ironically, is the tiger pistol shrimp, which generates noise as a method for stunning its prey.

11. Normal human conversation registers around 60 decibels. The human threshold for pain is 120, with the eardrum rupturing at 160.

12. Hsiao, Patrick. "The 10 Loudest Animals on Earth." *Australian Geographic,* 22 Aug. 2012. http://www.australiangeographic.com.au/topics/wildlife/2012/08/the-10-loudest-animals-on-earth/.

13. Plotkin, p. 63.

14. Without rain, adults enter and leave the nest 1.69 times per hour, while during rain, the rate drops to 0.36 times per hour.

15. Plotkin, p. 39.

16. The remaining handful of trees, at least to the botanist Stanley Temple, seemed to be the last in their species line, until scientists discovered that domestic turkeys could provide the same service. Further, subsequent research challenged Temple's application of mutualism theory with the dodo bird and

suggested other species that also went extinct such as the Mauritian giant tortoise may have been the true causal agent for distribution and germination.

17. Terborgh, John. *Requiem for Nature*. Washington, D.C.: Island Press, 1999, pp.14–15.

CHAPTER 18

1. In temperate areas, a *colpa* is known as a salt lick.

2. Terborgh, John. *Five New World Primates: A Study in Comparative Ecology*. Princeton, NJ: Princeton University Press, 1983.

3. Brightsmith, Donald. "Macaws of the Peruvian Amazon," *Earthwatch Institute Expedition Briefing*. 2005–2006.

4. Macaws can also hang upside down and reach sideways with ease, their hooked beaks serving as a third foot.

5. Gilardi, James, S. S. Duffey, C. A. Munn, and L. A. Tell. "Biochemical Functions of Geophagy in Parrots: Detoxification of Dietary Toxins and Cytoprotective Effects." *Journal of Chemical Ecology* 25 (1999), pp. 897–922.

6. Munn, Charles A. "Macaws: Winged Rainbows." *National Geographic* 185.1 (Jan. 1994), pp. 118–40.

7. Researchers no longer rear chicks by hand, reasoning that partly tame parrots struggle in the wild.

8. Eckstrom, Christine K. "Homeless Macaws?" *International Wildlife* 24 (Sept./Oct. 1994), pp. 14–23.

9. Brightsmith, Donald, and Adriana Bravo. "Ecology and Management of Nesting Blue-and-Yellow Macaws (*Ara ararauna*) in *Mauritia* Palm Swamps." *Biodiversity and Conservation* 15 (2006), pp. 4271–87.

10. Plotkin, p. 34.

11. Wallace, Scott. "Last of the Amazon." *National Geographic*, Jan. 2007, p. 52.

12. Terborgh (1999), p. 206.

13. Revkin (1990), p. 121.

14. European Commission. "Combatting Tropical Deforestation: The REDD+ Initiative." 15 April 2014. http://ec.europa.eu/clima/policies/forests/deforestation/index_en.htm.

15. Wallace, pp. 40–70.

16. Ibid., p. 69.

17. Huber, Matthew T. *Lifeblood: Oil, Freedom, and the Forces of Capital.* Minneapolis: University of Minnesota Press, 2013, p. xvi.

18. Yago, Glenn. *The Decline of Transit: Urban Transformation in German and US Cities, 1900–1970.* New York: Cambridge University Press, 1984; Black, Edwin. *Internal Combustion: How Corporations and Governments Addicted the World to Oil and Derailed the Alternatives.* New York: St. Martin's Press, 2006.

19. Huber, p. 27.

20. They were convicted in federal court of violating antitrust laws in 1949.

21. Huber, p. 28.

CHAPTER 19

1. https://commons.wikimedia.org/wiki/File:Antarctic_Peninsula_adm_location_map.svg.

2. Victor, p. 40.

3. Most of the remainder comes from clearing land for agriculture such as the tropical deforestation discussed in previous chapters on the Amazon.

4. Vanderbilt, Tom. *Traffic.* London: Allen Lane, 2008.

5. Giddens, Anthony. *The Politics of Climate Change.* Cambridge, UK: Polity, 2009, p. 159.

6. Yetiv, Steve A. *Myths of the Oil Boom: American National Security in a Global Energy Market.* Oxford, UK: Oxford University Press, 2015.

7. U.S. Energy Information Association. "Coal Explained: How Much Coal Is Left." http://www.eia.gov/energyexplained/index.cfm?page=coal_reserves. Accessed 1 July 2015.

8. Of course, this is a moving number that will shift as production and reserve estimates evolve over the years with technology itself, not to mention changes in consumption patterns.

9. Hansen, p. 73.

10. Data reported as of July 2014: Oil Change International. "Fossil Fuel Subsidies: Overview." http://priceofoil.org/fossil-fuel-subsidies/. Accessed 2 July 2015.

11. Gelbspan, p. 185.

12. Stern, Nicholas. *The Economics of Climate Change: The Stern Review.* Cambridge, UK: Cambridge University Press, 2007, p. 403.

13. Carrington, Damian. "Fossil Fuels Subsidised by $10m a Minute, Says IMF." *The Guardian*, 18 May 2015. http://www.theguardian.com/environment/2015/may/18/fossil-fuel-companies-getting-10m-a-minute-in-subsidies-says-imf.

14. The Center for Media and Democracy. "Coal and Jobs in the United States." *SourceWatch*, 26 June 2015. http://www.sourcewatch.org/index.php/Coal_and_jobs_in_the_United_States#Total_coal-related_jobs. Accessed 1 July 2015.

15. UK Energy Research Center. *Low Carbon Jobs: The Evidence for New Job Creation from Policy Support for Energy Efficiency and Renewable Energy.* 10 Nov. 2014. http://www.edie.net/.

16. Mann, Michael E., and Lee R. Kump. *Dire Predictions: Understanding Global Warming.* London: Dorling Kindersley Limited, 2009.

17. It takes 7.8 Gt of carbon dioxide to increase 1 ppm.

18. Victor, p. 55.

19. Pielke, Roger, Jr., *The Climate Fix: What Scientists and Politicians Won't Tell You about Global Warming.* New York: Basic Books, 2010, p. 46.

20. UNEP. *Green Jobs.* Washington, D.C.: Worldwatch Institute, 2008.

21. Farreny, R., et al. "Carbon Dioxide Emissions of Antarctic Tourism." *Antarctic Science* 23.6 (Dec. 2011), pp. 556–66.

22. Posegate, Ann. "Measured by Carbon Footprint, Travel to Antarctica Has Tons of Impact." *The Washington Post*, 13 April 2010. http://www.washingtonpost.com/wp-dyn/content/article/2010/04/12/AR2010041203194.html. Accessed 15 July 2015.

23. Swan, Robert. *Antarctica 2041: My Quest to Save the Earth's Last Wilderness.* New York: Broadway Books, 2009.

24. Laws, Richard. *Antarctica: The Last Frontier.* London: Boxtree Limited, 1989.

25. Attenborough, David. *Life in the Freezer.* BBC. 174 min. 2006; *March of the Penguins.* Documentary film. Luc Jacquet, director. Morgan Freeman, narrator. 80 min. 2005.

26. Rushin, Steve. "Antarctica with Kate Upton." *Sports Illustrated*, 15 Feb. 2013, pp. 51–56, 200–207. http://sportsillustrated.cnn.com/vault/article/magazine/MAG1206858/index.htm.

27. Swan, p. 271.

28. Swan, p. 203.

29. Rees, William. "Ecological Footprints and Appropriated Carrying Capacity: What Urban Economics Leaves Out." *Environment and Urbanization* 4.2 (Oct. 1992), pp. 121–30.

30. Although PCB manufacture was banned within the United States in 1979, products built before then, from old electric devices, transformers, and motor oil, to plastics, cable insulation, and adhesives, continue to be available.

31. Zolfagharifard, Ellie. "Carbon Emissions Reach 40 Billion Ton High." *Daily Mail*, 21 Sept. 2014. http://www.dailymail.co.uk/sciencetech/article-2764323/China-US-India-push-world-carbon-emissions-up.html. Accessed 1 June 2015.

32. Lansing, Alfred. *Endurance: Shackleton's Incredible Voyage*. New York: Carroll & Graf, 1959.

33. Heacox, Kim. *National Geographic Destination: Antarctica—The Last Continent*. Washington, D.C.: National Geographic, 1998.

34. Malakoff, David. "Carbon Cruise." *Conservation*, 1 Sept. 2011. http://conservationmagazine.org/2011/09/carbon-cruise/. Accessed 13 June 2015.

35. While some "flight seeing" continues today, the practice is a relatively small portion of the overall picture, especially since the Nov. 28, 1979, Air New Zealand DC10 crash on Mount Erebus killed all aboard.

36. Another unfortunate trend is the retirement of older, smaller ships and their replacement with larger ones. The first of these large passenger liners hit southern waters in January 2000.

37. "Guidelines for Visitors to the Antarctic." Antarctic Treaty Consultative Meeting XXXIV, Buenos Aires. 2011. http://iaato.org/c/document_library/get_file?uuid=aed1054d-3e63-4a17-a6cd-a87beb15e287&groupId=10157.

38. Snyder, J. M., and B. Stonehouse, eds. *Prospects for Polar Tourism*. Cambridge, MA: CAB International, 2007, p. 165.

39. Snyder, J. M., and B. Stonehouse, p. 152.

40. Luck, Michael, Patrick T. Maher, and Emma J. Stewart, eds. *Cruise Tourism in Polar Regions: Promoting Environmental and Social Sustainability?* London: Earthscan, 2010, p. 62.

41. Bailey, Sue. "Debilitated Russian Cruise Ship Disappears off Newfoundland Coast." *Toronto Globe and Mail*, 23 May 2013. http://www.theglobeandmail.com/news/national/debilitated-russian-cruise-ship-disappears-off-newfoundland-coast/article12117511/.

42. Synnott, Mark. "Amid Hunt for Malaysian Plane, Ocean Swims with Missing Vessels." *National Geographic*, 19 March 2014. http://news.nationalgeographic.com/news/2014/03/140319-ghost-ship-malaysia-airliner-atlantic-ocean/.

43. Ferguson, David. "Ghost Ship Laden with Diseases, Cannibal Rats Could Crash into British Coast." *The Raw Story*, 23 Jan. 2014. http://www.rawstory.com/rs/2014/01/23/ghost-ship-laden-with-disea sed-cannibal-rats-could-crash-into-british-coast/; Hubbard, Amy. "Ghost Ship and Starving Rats Headed for Land?" *Los Angeles Times*, 23 Jan. 2014. http://www.latimes.com/nation/la-sh-ghost-ship-cannibal-rats-20140123-st ory.html.

44. Campbell, David G. *The Crystal Desert: Summers in Antarctica*. Boston: Houghton Mifflin, 1992.

45. Magellan was first, from 1519 to 1522.

46. McClintock, James. *Lost Antarctica: Adventures in a Disappearing Land*. New York: Palgrave Macmillan, 2012.

CHAPTER 20

1. Wheeler, Sara. *Terra Incognita: Travels in Antarctica*. New York: Random House, 1996.

2. Steig, Eric, et al. "Warming of the Antarctic Ice-sheet Surface since the 1957 International Geophysical Year." *Nature* 457 (2009), pp. 459–62.

3. Fothergill, Alastair. *A Natural History of the Antarctic: Life in the Freezer*. New York: Sterling Publishing Co., 1995.

4. Meduna, Veronika. *Secrets of the Ice: Antarctica's Clues to Climate, the Universe, and the Limits of Life*. New Haven, CT: Yale University Press, 2012, p. 5.

5. World Meteorological Organization. *WMO Sea-ice Nomenclature, Terminology, Codes and Illustrated Glossary*. Geneva, Switzerland: World Meteorological Organization, 1970.

6. Plumer, Brad. "Here's Why 1.2 Billion People Still Don't Have Access to Electricity." *The Washington Post*, 29 May 2013. http://www.washington-post.com/blogs/wonkblog/wp/2013/05/29/heres-why-1-2-billion-peopl e-still-dont-have-access-to-electricity/.

7. World Bank. "Energy—The Facts." Aug. 2016. http://web.world-bank.org/WBSITE/EXTERNAL/TOPICS/EXTENERGY2/0,,contentMDK:22855502~pagePK:210058~piPK:210062~theSitePK:4114200,00.html. Accessed 20 Aug. 2016.

8. Pooley, Eric. *The Climate War: True Believers, Power Brokers, and the Fight to Save the Earth*. New York: Hyperion, 2010.

9. See the RGGI website for updates on their progress: Regional Greenhouse Gas Initiative, Inc. (RGGI). http://www.rggi.org/. Accessed 12 Aug. 2016.

10. Hansen, p. 206.

11. Victor, p. 28.

12. A Btu is the amount of energy required to elevate the temperature of one pound of water by one degree Fahrenheit.

13. Giddens, Anthony. *The Politics of Climate Change. Cambridge, UK: Polity*, 2009, pp. 151–52.

14. Metcalf, Gilbert. *A Green Employment Tax Swap*. Washington, D.C.: The Brookings Institute, 2007.

15. Hansen, p. 209.

16. Pielke, Jr., p. 232.

17. Ibid., p. 227.

18. This figure does not include military spending on energy by the Pentagon, approximately $900 million in 2012. Neither does it include programs for proven technology such as tax credits for building wind turbines or loan guarantees for nuclear plants. The feds spent about $8 billion on these items in 2012.

19. Americans chomped on $5.6 billion in chips in 2013, for example: "Frito-Lay Dominates U.S. Salty Snacks, But Rising Cracker Sales Could Stall Growth." *Forbes.com*, 27 June 2014. http://www.forbes.com/sites/greatspeculations/2014/06/27/frito-lay-dominates-u-s-salty-snacks-but-rising-cracker-sales-could-stall-growth/.

20. Plumer, Brad. "Four Charts that Show the U.S. Spends too Little on Energy Research." *The Washington Post*, 9 April 2013. http://www.washingtonpost.com/blogs/wonkblog/wp/2013/04/09/three-charts-that-show-the-u-s-spends-too-little-on-energy-research/.

21. Revkin, Andrew C. "Paths to a 'Good' Anthropocene." Keynote

address at Association for Environmental Studies and Sciences, Pace University, New York, New York, 11 June 2014.

22. Pielke, Jr., p. 218.

23. The other three are the Ross, crab-eater (a misnomer considering it eats krill originally mistaken for crab), and elephant seals. Two additional seals found in Antarctica due to their feeding schedules, the Weddell Seal and the Antarctic Fur Seal, don't breed on the continent.

24. McClintock, James. "Lost Antarctica," *The Diane Rehm Show.* 18 Sept. 2012. http://thedianerehmshow.org/shows/2012-09-18/james-mcclintock-lost-antarctica.

25. McClintock, p. 172.

26. Meduna, p. 119.

27. Clucas, Gemma V., Michael J. Dunn, Gareth Dyke, Steven D. Emslie, Hila Levy, Ron Naveen, Michael J. Polito, Oliver G. Pybus, Alex D. Rogers, and Tom Hart. "A Reversal of Fortunes: Climate Change 'Winners' and 'Losers' in Antarctic Peninsula Penguins." *Scientific Reports* 4.5024 (12 June 2014).

28. Pielke, p. 62

29. Of course, there is also the issue of mitigation versus adaptation. In many sectors, for years, adaptation was seen as surrender on the mitigation front. The truth is, though, we need both.

30. Amundsen, Roald. *The South Pole: An Account of the Norwegian Antarctic Expedition in the "Fram," 1910–1912.* New York: Lee Keedick, 1913.

31. Cherry-Garrard, Apsley. *The Worst Journey in the World: Antarctic 1910–1913.* Kent, UK: Picador, 1994 (1922).

32. Nova. *Shackleton's Voyage of Endurance.* David Ogden Stiers, narrator. Sarah Holt (hour one) and Kelly Tyler (hour two), writers and producers. White Mountain Films/WGBH Educational Foundation, 26 March 2002. http://www.pbs.org/wgbh/nova/shackleton.

33. Alexander, Caroline. *The Endurance: Shackleton's Legendary Antarctic Expedition.* New York: Alfred A. Knopf, 2006.

34. Some attribute the quote, instead, to Sir Raymond Priestly, Antarctic explorer and geologist.

35. Swan, Robert. *Antarctica 2041: My Quest to Save the Earth's Last Wilderness.* New York: Broadway Books, 2009, p. 169.

CHAPTER 21

1. Fretwell, Peter T., and Philip N. Trathan. "Penguins from Space: Faecal Stains Reveal the Location of Emperor Penguin Colonies." *Global Ecology and Biogeography* 18.5 (Sept. 2009), pp. 543–52.

2. Hogenboom, Melissa. "Watching Penguins, and Their Poo, from Space." *BBC Earth*. 10 Dec. 2014. http://www.bbc.com/earth/story/2 0141210-surprising-use-of-penguin-poo.

3. Even their actual nests, incorporating as many as 1,700 small, smooth stones, set in a circle two feet in diameter in the cases of Adélie, gentoo, and chinstrap penguins, are not immune to defecation.

4. Rushin, Steve. "Antarctica with Kate Upton." *Sports Illustrated*, 15 Feb. 2013, p. 207.

5. Set at the 2008 Olympic Games in Beijing, Phelps's best record in the hundred-meter freestyle is 47.51 seconds, which equates to around 4.7 mph.

6. Another twenty-three countries, including the United States, have research stations in Antarctica but have not staked claims to territory, although the United States and Russia have expressly reserved that right at a later date.

7. Some ninety billion barrels of oil and gas equivalent, according to U.S. Geological Survey estimates, not to mention diamonds, rubies, and gold, lie under retreating land ice and sea ice in the Arctic. Conditions don't allow for it's exploitation yet, but ironically, if climate change continues, they will one day. Recognizing this, in 2007, Russia famously dropped two manned submersibles through a hole in the Arctic ice to pick up sedimentary samples three kilometers below on the ocean floor. They also planted a titanium Russian flag and declared, via Clause 76 of the Law of the Sea, the Lomonosov Ridge to be a "prolongation" of Russia's continental shelf. If accepted, this gives Russia over one-third the Arctic Ocean, including the North Pole itself.

8. Six greenhouse gases (carbon dioxide, methane, nitrous oxide, hydrofluorocarbons, perfluorocarbons, and sulfur hexafluoride) are established in the treaty, but for accounting purposes, each is converted into carbon dioxide equivalents.

9. One might argue that there were two other success stories, but these are outliers as well. Germany's "improvement" reflected its incorporation of

East Germany with its dirty, inefficient Communist-era factories. Emissions reductions in the UK were a product of more efficient North Sea gas developments replacing coal mines that closed in the 1980s. Also known as the Thatcher "dash to gas," many argue the true intent here was the conservative government's desire to crush the political power of coal unions, further underscoring the extent to which domestic political interests other than climate change initiated their emissions shift.

10. United Nations Framework Convention on Climate Change. "Kyoto Protocol." http://unfccc.int/kyoto_protocol/items/2830.php. Accessed 8 July 2015.

11. As of July 2016, only sixty-six states have ratified the amendment. The treaty requires three-fourths of its current 192 parties to agree for adoption.

12. U.S. Chamber of Commerce. *NAFTA Triumphant: Assessing Two Decades of Growth in Trade, Growth, and Jobs.* https://www.uschamber.com/sites/default/files/legacy/reports/1112_INTL_NAFTA_20Years.pdf Accessed 8 July 2015.

13. Aguilar, Julian. "Twenty Years Later, NAFTA Remains a Source of Tension." *New York Times,* 7 Dec. 2012: http://www.nytimes.com/2012/12/07/us/twenty-years-later-nafta-remains-a-source-of-tension.html?_r=0.

14. United States Environmental Protection Agency. "Greenhouse Gas Data Inventory Explorer." http://www.epa.gov/climatechange/ghgemissions/inventoryexplorer/#allsectors/allgas/econsect/current. Accessed 8 July 2015.

15. Ibid.

16. Industry accounts for 21 percent of our greenhouse emissions here in the States while commercial interests tally 6 percent, according to 2013 EPA calculations. Admittedly, a portion of the electricity and transportation emissions would be eligible to travel as well.

17. Although it never had force of law due to Senate refusal to ratify the treaty, President Bush formally withdrew the United States from the Kyoto Protocol early in the spring of 2001, saying it was not in the "U.S.'s economic best interest." By March 13, 2001, demonstrating a wider agenda, Bush was no longer seeking to cap carbon dioxide emissions from power plants.

18. Victor, David. G. *Global Warming Gridlock: Creating More Effective Strategies for Protecting the Planet.* Cambridge, UK: Cambridge University Press, 2011, p. xxix.

19. Hansen, p. 183.

20. Victor, p. 96.

21. Marsden, p. 248.

22. The White House Office of the Press Secretary. "U.S.-China Joint Announcement on Climate Change." Beijing, China. 12 Nov. 2014. https://www.whitehouse.gov/the-press-office/2014/11/11/us-china-joint-announcement-climate-change.

23. The food web is greatly compromised, then, in lands and waters most of us will never see, by actions taken years ago. As if to add insult to injury, decrease in phytoplankton activity also means a decrease in the amount of carbon dioxide converted to oxygen through photosynthesis.

24. Pielke, Jr., p. 42.

25. Victor, p. 22.

26. Text available through UNFCCC webpages at: UNFCCC. "Paris Agreement." 12 Dec. 2015. http://unfccc.int/files/meetings/paris_nov_2015/application/pdf/paris_agreement_english_.pdf. Accessed 28 May 2015.

27. Another executive angle worth noting involves security and terrorism. In the 2010 US Quadrennial Defense Review Report, for example, the Defense Department identified climate change as a threat shaping "significant geopolitical impacts around the world contributing to poverty, environmental degradation, and the further weakening of fragile governments."

28. Held, David, Angus Hervey, and Marika Theros, eds. *The Governance of Climate Change: Science, Economics, Politics, & Ethics*. Cambridge, UK: Polity, 2011.

29. Victor, pp. 245, 258.

30. Victor, p. 23.

31. Hulme, Mike. *Why We Disagree about Climate Change: Understanding Controversy, Inaction and Opportunity*. Cambridge, UK: Cambridge University Press, 2009.

32. Keeling started with measurements at the South Pole as well, but funding cuts in the 1960s necessitated an end to data collection at that location.

33. This is now known as the "Revelle factor."

34. Joyner, Christopher C. *Governing the Frozen Commons: The Antarctic Regime and Environmental Protection*. Columbia: University of South Carolina Press, 1998, p. 55.

35. These come in essentially six parts. There's the ATS itself. Beyond that, there's the recommendations adopted by ATCPs, including the 1964 Agreed Measures, the 1972 Seals Convention, the 1980 Antarctic Marine Living Resources Convention, the 1991 Antarctic Environmental Protocol (including its annexes), and, finally, the Antarctic Minerals Convention, although it is not yet entered into force.

36. See ATS's Article IV.

CHAPTER 22

1. Dibbern, J. Stephen. "Fur Seals, Whales and Tourists: A Commercial History of Deception Island, Antarctica." *The Polar Record* 46.3 (July 2010), pp. 210–21.

2. An historical plaque on Signey Island in the South Orkney group tallied 118,159 kills from 1911 to 1930 in the South Orkney and South Shetland Islands: Cool Antarctica. "Whales and Whaling–1–Whaling in Antarctica." http://www.coolantarctica.com/Antarctica%20fact%20file/wildlife/whales/whaling1.php. Accessed 10 July 2015.

3. Dibbern, pp. 210–21.

4. It was particularly active during the eighteenth and nineteenth centuries. Two short periods, first between 1906 and 1910, then between 1967 and 1970, highlight twentieth-century activity.

5. Streever, Bill. *Cold: Adventures in the World's Frozen Places.* New York: Little, Brown and Company, 2009, p. 4.

6. Dickinson, Tim. "The Climate Killers: Meet the 17 Polluters and Deniers Who Are Derailing Efforts to Curb Global Warming." *Rolling Stone,* 6 Jan. 2010.

7. Jacques, Peter J., Riley E. Dunlap, and Mark Freeman. "The Organisation of Denial: Conservative Think Tanks and Environmental Skepticism." *Environmental Politics* 17.3(June 2008), pp. 349–85.

8. MIT's Richard Lindzen, known in some circles as the dean of global-warming contrarians, is the most articulate and impressive in terms of scholarly credentials, elected early in his career to the National Academy of Sciences.

9. Standard strategy here is akin to that employed by the infamous Nazi propaganda chief Joseph Goebbels. If you repeat something often enough, people will believe it.

10. Fischer, Douglas. "'Dark Money' Funds Climate Change Denial Effort." *Scientific American*, 23 Dec. 2013. http://www.scientificamerican. com/article/dark-money-funds-climate-change-denial-effort/?print=true.

11. Brulle, Robert. "Institutionalizing Delay: Foundation Funding and the Creation of US Climate Change Counter-Movement Organizations." *Climate Change* 122.4 (Feb. 2014), pp. 681–94.

12. Inhofe, James M. "The Science of Climate Change." Floor Statement by Sen. Inhofe (R-OK). 28 July 2003.

13. Code words such as "sound science" underscore fears of a looming global bureaucracy that would greatly restrict democratic practices. The irony here is that participatory democracy would be most enhanced by decentralizing energy control, moving it away from the dominant fossil-fuel interests protecting our current infrastructure. For more see: Pooley, Eric. *The Climate War: True Believers, Power Brokers, and the Fight to Save the Earth*. New York: Hyperion, 2010.

14. The most recent of these reports is: U.S. Global Change Research Program. *The National Climate Assessment*. Washington, D.C., May 2014. http://nca2014.globalchange.gov/report. Accessed 14 July 2015.

15. Hansen, p. 124.

16. Revkin, Andrew. "Climate Expert Says NASA Tried to Silence Him." *New York Times*, 29 Jan 2006, p. A-1.

17. Maibach, E., J. Witte, and K. Wilson. "Climategate Undermined Belief in Global Warming among Many TV Meteorologists." *Bulletin of the American Meteorological Association* 92 (2011), pp. 31–37.

18. As an aside, the RealClimate website was also hacked via an anonymous server in Turkey on Nov 17, 2009.

19. Marsden, p. 215.

20. Mann, Michael E. *The Hockey Stick and the Climate Wars: Dispatches from the Front Lines*. New York: Columbia University Press, 2012, p. 228.

21. A handful of counterexamples from PBS include *The Diane Rehm Show* on Nov. 30, 2009, and *On Point with Tom Ashbrook* on Dec. 8, 2009.

22. Robertson, R. B. *Of Whales and Men*. New York: Alfred A. Knopf, 1954.

23. The blue whale's tongue alone weighs as much as an elephant. The heart, roughly the size of a VW Beetle car, weighs as much as 1,000 pounds.

24. In the 1950s, for example, Greek shipping tycoon Aristotle Onassis flouted every conceivable regulation. He even fitted the bar of his private yacht, the *Christina*, with polished whalebone and bar stools made from the penises of minke sperm whales.

25. Iceland, after rejoining the IWC in 2002, immediately began its own "scientific whaling" program, and in 2006 resumed commercial whaling.

26. It took three-and-a-half tons of blubber oil to make eighty barrels of oil. This oil was also used in the manufacture of nitroglycerin explosives for both world wars of the twentieth century.

27. U.S. Coast Guard Navigation Center. "How Much of an Iceberg Is Under Water," 17 Nov. 2015. http://www.navcen.uscg.gov/?pageName=iipHowMuchOfAnIcebergIsBelowTheWater.

28. In fresh water, precisely 91.7 percent of the ice lies below the surface. Icebergs aren't floating on fresh water, though. They're in sea water, which is denser than fresh water, so a bit more iceberg is visible.

29. Archimedes's discovery, as told by Vitruvius, a Roman architect, writer, and engineer, was outlined in a book written two centuries after Archimedes had died. Hieron II of Syracuse in Sicily became suspicious about just how precious the metals in his crown were. Hieron believed that a jeweler had charged him the price of solid gold but cheated him by utilizing gold mixed with less-expensive silver. Being both a friend and relative of the great Greek mathematician Archimedes, Hieron shared these concerns with him, but it wasn't until Archimedes's famous bath that an answer was found. Knowing that a solid, being denser than water, will lighten when immersed in fluid by the weight of the water the solid displaced was the key. After that, a simple experiment demonstrating that gold is denser than silver proved the jeweler had cheated his king.

30. NASA Quest. "Eureka! The Story of the Archimedes Principle." http://quest.nasa.gov/aero/planetary/archimedes.html. Accessed 22 June 2015.

31. Krugman, Paul. "Building a Green Economy." *New York Times*, 7 April 2010. http://www.nytimes.com/2010/04/11/magazine/11Economy-t.html?_r=0&pagewanted=print.

32. Schlosser, Eric. *Fast Food Nation: The Dark Side of the All-American Meal.* Boston: Houghton Mifflin Company, 2001, p. 261.

33. Friedrichs, Jörg. *The Future Is Not What It Used to Be: Climate Change and Energy Security.* Cambridge, MA: The MIT Press, 2013.

34. One should note that, in addition to intentional adjustment of these variables, significant historical events such as war, epidemic disease, and political transitions also shape total emissions.

35. Kahn, Joseph. "Cheney Promotes Increasing Supply as Energy Policy." *New York Times,* 1 May 2001. http://www.nytimes.com/2001/05/01/us/cheney-promotes-increasing-supply-as-energy-policy.html. Accessed 12 Aug. 2015.

36. Pielke, Jr., p. 107.

37. Gelbspan, p. 167.

38. The United States, China, and Japan account for more than half the $1.6 trillion invested around the world in R & D in 2014. Germany, South Korea, France, United Kingdom, India, Russia, and Brazil round out the top ten. Battelle Memorial Institute. "2014 Global R&D Forecast." *R&D Magazine,* Dec. 2013. http://www.battelle.org/docs/tpp/2014_global_rd_funding_forecast.pdf.

39. Victor, p. xxxii.

40. Victor, p. 9.

41. Boden, T. A., G. Marland, and R. J. Andres. "Global, Regional, and National Fossil-Fuel CO2 Emission." Carbon Dioxide Information Analysis Center, Oak Ridge National Laboratory, US Department of Energy, Oak Ridge, TN. 2010.

42. Gladwell, Malcolm. *The Tipping Point: How Little Things Can Make a Big Difference.* Boston: Little, Brown and Company, 2000.

43. Meduna, p. 211.

44. Carson, Rachel. *Silent Spring.* Boston: Houghton Mifflin, 1962, p. xx.

CONCLUSION

1. Anand, Geeta. "As Air Worsens, New Delhi Turns to Masks. The Flashier the Better." *New York Times,* 2 March 2016, p. A-4.

2. Yardley, Jim. "Illegal Districts Dot New Delhi as City Swells." *New York Times,* 27 April 2013. http://www.nytimes.com/2013/04/28/world/

asia/unauthorized-colonies-dot-new-delhi-seeking-legal-status.html?_r=0. Accessed 26 Aug. 2015.

3. Exact percentages are particularly difficult to pin down because black carbon also causes global dimming, reducing the amount of sunlight that reaches the Earth's surface.

4. Daigle, Katy. "Push for Cleaner Stoves in Poor Countries to Cut Pollution," *The World Post*, 9 April 2015. http://www.huffingtonpost.com/huff-wires/20150408/as—india-black-carbon/. Accessed 20 Aug. 2016.

5. Daigle, Katy. "Pollution Fight Targets Smoky Stoves." *Orlando Sentinel*, 12 April 2015, p. A-11.

6. Lomborg, Bjørn. *Cool It: The Skeptical Environmentalist's Guide to Global Warming*. New York: Alfred A. Knopf, 2007.

7. Pope Francis. "Encyclical Letter Laudato Si' of the Holy Father Francis on Care for Our Common Home." Vatican: The Holy See. Rome, 18 June 2015. http://w2.vatican.va/content/francesco/en/encyclicals/documents/papa-francesco_20150524_enciclica-laudato-si.pdf.

8. Kahan, D. "Fixing the Communications Failure." *Nature* 463.21 (2010), 296–97.

9. Louv, Richard. *Last Child in the Woods: Saving Our Children from Nature-Deficit Disorder*. Chapel Hill, NC: Algonquin Books, 2005, p. 16.

10. Gladwell, p. 19.

11. Ibid., p. 221.

12. Stoknes, Per Espen. *What We Think About When We Try Not to Think About Global Warming: Toward a New Psychology of Climate Action*. White River Junction, VT: Chelsea Green Publishing, 2015, p. 4.

13. Accommodations account for 20 percent, with museums, theme parks, events, and shopping covering most of the remainder.

14. Strasdas, Wolfgang. "Voluntary Offsetting of Flight Emissions: An Effective Way to Mitigate the Environmental Impacts on Long-Haul Tourism." Feb. 2007. www.ecotourismcesd.org Accessed 20 Aug. 2015.

15. Vince, Gai. *Adventures in the Anthropocene: A Journey to the Heart of the Planet We Made*. London: Chatto & Windus, 2014.

16. Honey, Martha. *Ecotourism and Sustainable Development: Who Owns Paradise?* Washington, D.C.: Island Press, 2008, p. 77.

17. Koens, Jacobus Franciscus, Carel Dieperink, and Miriam Miranda. "Ecotourism as a Development Strategy: Experiences from Costa Rica." *Environment, Development and Sustainability*, Oct. 2009, pp. 1225–37.

18. The Ceres declaration is available at: http://www.ceres.org/declaration.

19. Cronin, Melissa. "Solar Is So Hot Right Now. Check Out the Latest Numbers." *Grist*, 22 Feb 2016. http://grist.org/climate-energy/solar-is-so-hot-right-now-check-out-the-latest-numbers/?utm_medium=e-mail&utm_source=newsletter&utm_campaign=weekly-static.

20. Friedman, Thomas L. "Paris Climate Accord Is a Big, Big Deal." *New York Times*, 16 Dec. 2015. http://www.nytimes.com/2015/12/16/opinion/paris-climate-accord-is-a-big-big-deal.html?rref=collec-tion%2Fnewseventcollection%2Fun-climate-change-conferenc e&action=click&contentCollection=earth&region=stream&module=stream_unit&version=latest&contentPlacement=8&pgtype=collection.

21. Gore, Al. "The Case for Optimism on Climate Change." TED Vancouver, 16 Feb. 2016. http://www.ted.com/talks/al_gore_the_case_for_optimism_on_climate_change. Accessed 12 June 2016.

22. Stoknes, p. 110.

23. Andrew C. Revkin. "Paths to a 'Good' Anthropocene." Keynote address at Association for Environmental Studies and Sciences, Pace University, New York, New York, 11 June 2014.

24. Davenport, Coral. "Economies Can Still Rise as Carbon Emissions Fade." *New York Times*, 7 April 2016, p. A-3.

25. Stoknes, p. 220.

26. Steves, Rick. "The Value of Travel," TEDxRainer. 12 Nov. 2011. http://tedxtalks.ted.com/video/TEDxRainier-Rick-Steves-The-Val. Accessed 26 Aug. 2015.

27. Honey, Martha. *Ecotourism and Sustainable Development: Who Owns Paradise*? Washington, D.C.: Island Press, 2008, p. 447.

BIBLIOGRAPHY

Act Creating Yellowstone National Park, 1 March 1872. Enrolled Acts and Resolutions of Congress, 1789–1996. General Records of the United States Government, Record Group 11, National Archives. http://www.ourdocuments.gov/doc.php?doc=45.

Aguilar, Julian. "Twenty Years Later, NAFTA Remains a Source of Tension." *New York Times*, 7 Dec. 2012. http://www.nytimes.com/2012/12/07/us/twenty-years-later-nafta-remains-a-source-of-tension.html?_r=0.

Alexander, Caroline. *The Endurance: Shackleton's Legendary Antarctic Expedition*. New York: Alfred A. Knopf, 2006.

Amundsen, Roald. *The South Pole: An Account of the Norwegian Antarctic Expedition in the "Fram," 1910–1912*. New York: Lee Keedick, 1913.

Anand, Geeta. "As Air Worsens, New Delhi Turns to Masks. The Flashier the Better." *New York Times*, 2 March 2016, p. A-4.

Anderegg, William R. L., James W. Prall, Jacob Harold, and Stephen H. Schneider. "Expert Credibility in Climate Change." *Proceedings of the National Academy of Sciences* 107.27 (21 June 2010), pp. 12107–9.

Anderson, Peter D., and Gyula Bokor. "Conotoxins: Potential Weapons from the Sea." *Journal of Bioterrorism and Biodefense* 3.3 (17 Nov. 2012.)

"The Antarctic Treaty." Secretariat of the Antarctic Treaty. http://www.ats.aq/e/ats.htm. Accessed 23 Aug. 2016.

Anthony, Lawrence (with Graham Spence). *The Last Rhinos: My Battle to Save One of the World's Greatest Creatures*. New York: Thomas Dunne Books, 2012.

Archer, David. *The Long Thaw: How Humans Are Changing the Next 100,000 Years of Earth's Climate*. Princeton, NJ: Princeton University Press, 2008.

Arrhenius, Svante. "On the Influence of Carbonic Acid in the Air upon the Temperature of the Ground." *Philosophical Magazine and Journal of Science* (Series 5) 41:251 (April 1896), pp. 237–76.

Attenborough, David. *Life in the Freezer*. BBC, 174 min. 2006.

Australia: Land Beyond Time. Australian Film Finance Corporation. David Flatman, director. 42 min. 2002.

Australian Institute of Marine Science. "Coral Bleaching Events." June 2016. http://www.aims.gov.au/docs/research/climate-change/coral-bleaching/bleaching-events.html. Accessed 15 July 2016.

"Australia's Battle with the Bunny." *ABC Science*. 9 April 2009. http://www.abc.net.au/science/articles/2009/04/08/2538860.htm. Accessed 21 Jan. 2014.

Bailey, Sue. "Debilitated Russian Cruise Ship Disappears off Newfoundland Coast." *Toronto Globe and Mail*, 23 May 2013. http://www.theglobeandmail.com/news/national/debilitated-russian-cruise-ship-disappears-off-newfoundland-coast/article12117511/.

Banerjee, Neela. "Tennessee Enacts Evolution, Climate Change Law." *Los Angeles Times,* 11 April 2012. http://articles.latimes.com/2012/apr/11/nation/la-na-tennessee-climate-law-20120411. Accessed 15 Dec. 2013.

Banerjee, Neela, Lisa Song, and David Hasemyer. "Exxon: The Road Not Taken." *InsideClimateNews*, 16 Sept. 2015. https://insideclimatenews.org/news/15092015/Exxons-own-research-confirmed-fossil-fuels-role-in-global-warming. Accessed 29 July 2016.

Barrett, Pam. *Insight Guide: Ecuador*. Singapore: Apa Publications, 2006.

Battelle Memorial Institute. "2014 Global R&D Forecast." *R&D Magazine*, December 2013. http://www.battelle.org/docs/tpp/2014_global_rd_funding_forecast.pdf.

BBC. *Galápagos: The Islands that Changed the World*. Tilda Swinton, narrator. Mike Gunton and Patrick Morris, producers. Paul D. Stewart and Richard Wollocombe, cinematography. 150 min. Sept. 2006. (DVD release 3 April 2007).

BBC Earth. *The Great Barrier Reef*. James Brickell, writer and director. Monty Hall, narrator. 186 min. 2012.

BBC News. "UN: India to Be World's Most Populous Country by 2028," 14 June 2013. http://www.bbc.co.uk/news/world-asia-22907307. Accessed 24 Jan. 2014.

BBC/Nova. *Dimming the Sun: What Does This Climate Conundrum Mean for the Future of Earth?* Kathryn Walker, narrator. DVD. 56 min. 2004/2006.

Beah, Ishmael. *A Long Way Gone: Memoirs of a Boy Soldier.* New York: Farrar, Straus and Giroux, 2007.

Bechky, Allen. *Adventuring in Southern Africa: A Sierra Club Travel Guide.* San Francisco: Sierra Club Books, 1997.

Bellwood, D. R., et al. "Confronting the Coral Reef Crisis." *Nature* 429. (24 June 2004), pp. 827–33.

Bergenas, Johan, and Monica Medina. "Opinion: Break the Link between Terrorism Funding and Poaching." *The Washington Post,* 31 Jan. 2014. http://www.washingtonpost.com/opinions/break-the-link-between-terrorism-funding-and-poaching/2014/01/31/6c03780e-83b5-11e3-bbe5-6a2a3141e3a9_story.html.

Berkelmans, Ray, Glenn De'ath, Stuart Kininmonth, and William J. Skirving. "A Comparison of the 1998 and 2002 Coral Bleaching Events on the Great Barrier Reef: Spatial Correlation, Patterns, and Predictions." *Coral Reefs* 23.1 (April 2004), pp. 74–83.

Black, Edwin. *Internal Combustion: How Corporations and Governments Addicted the World to Oil and Derailed the Alternatives.* New York: St. Martin's Press, 2006.

Blashfield, Jean F. *Australia: Enchantment of the World.* New York: Scholastic, 2012.

Boden, T. A., G. Marland, and R. J. Andres. "Global, Regional, and National Fossil-Fuel CO_2 Emission." Carbon Dioxide Information Analysis Center, Oak Ridge National Laboratory, US Department of Energy, Oak Ridge, TN. 2010.

Boo, Elizabeth. *Ecotourism: The Potentials and Pitfalls.* Vol. 1. Washington, D.C.: World Wildlife Fund, 1990.

Bordewich, Rergus M. "Winter Palace." *Smithsonian,* March 2003, pp.107–15.

Bowles, Ian A., and Glenn T. Prickett, eds. *Footprints in the Jungle: Natural Resource Industries, Infrastructure, and Biodiversity Conservation.* New York: Oxford University Press, 2001.

Breslow, Jason M. "Investigation Finds Exxon Ignored Its Own Early Climate Change Warnings," *Frontline,* 16 Sept. 2015 . http://www.pbs.org/wgbh/frontline/article/investigation-finds-exxon-ignored-its-own-early-climate-change-warnings/. Accessed 28 July 2016.

Brett, Michael. *Touring South Africa's National Parks*. Cape Town, South Africa: Struik Travel & Heritage, 2010.

Briggs, Chris, et al. "Tourism and the Great Barrier Reef: Healthy Reef, Healthy Industry." *International Cases in Sustainable Travel & Tourism*. Pierre Benckendorff and Dagmar Lund-Durlacher, eds. Oxford, UK: Goodfellow Publishers, 2013, pp. 57–70.

Brightsmith, Donald J. "Effects of Weather on Parrot Geophagy in Tambopata, Peru." *Wilson Bulletin* 116 (2004), pp. 134–45.

———. "Macaws of the Peruvian Amazon." *Earthwatch Institute Expedition Briefing*. 2005–2006.

———. Personal interview. Tambopata Research Center. 22 Jan. 2006.

Brightsmith, Donald, and Adriana Bravo. "Ecology and Management of Nesting Blue-and-Yellow Macaws (*Ara ararauna*) in *Mauritia* Palm Swamps." *Biodiversity and Conservation* 15 (2006), pp. 4271–87.

Brightsmith, Donald J., Amanda Stronza, and Kurt Holle. "Ecotourism, Conservation Biology, and Volunteer Tourism: A Mutually Beneficial Triumvirate." *Biological Conservation* 141 (2008), pp. 2832–42.

Brodie, Jon, et al. "2013 Scientific Consensus Statement: Land Use Impacts on Great Barrier Reef Water Quality and Ecosystem Condition." Reef Water Quality Protection Plan Secretariat, July 2013.

Broecker, Wallace S. "Climatic Change: Are We on the Brink of Pronounced Global Warming?" *Science* 189.4201 (8 Aug. 1975), pp. 460–63.

Broomhall, F. H. *The Longest Fence in the World*. Carlisle, Western Australia: Hesperian Press, 1991.

Brulle, Robert. "Institutionalizing Delay: Foundation Funding and the Creation of US Climate Change Counter-Movement Organizations." *Climate Change* 122.4 (Feb. 2014), pp. 681–94.

Bryson, Bill. *In a Sunburned Country*. New York: Broadway Books, 2000.

Buckland, S. T., D. R. Anderson, K. P. Burnham, and J. L. Laake. *Distance Sampling: Estimating Abundance of Biological Populations*. London: Chapman and Hall, 1993.

Bullard, Robert D., and Beverly Wright, eds. *Race, Place, and Environmental Justice after Hurricane Katrina: Struggles to Reclaim, Rebuild, and Revitalize New Orleans and the Gulf Coast*. Boulder, CO: Westview Press, 2009.

Bulpin, T. V. *The Ivory Trail*. South Africa: Southern Book Publishers, 1988 (reprinted from 1954).

Burns, Ken. "The National Parks." address at Rollins College, 7 April 2014.

Cai, Wenju, Simon Borlace, Matthieu Lengaigne, Peter van Rensch, Mat Collins, Gabriel Vecchi, Axel Timmermann, Agus Santoso, Michael J. McPhaden, Lixin Wu, Matthew H. England, Guojian Wang, Eric Guilyardi, Fei-Fei Jin. "Increasing Frequency of Extreme El Niño Events Due to Greenhouse Warming." *Nature Climate Change* 4 (Feb. 2014), pp. 111–16.

California Academy of Sciences. "American Adults Flunk Basic Science." *Science Daily*, 13 March 2009. http://www.sciencedaily.com/releases/2009/03/090312115133.htm. Accessed 17 Nov. 2013.

California Air Resources Board. "Clearing California Skies." Video, 12 min. 1998.

California Environmental Protection Agency. "Key Events in the History of Air Quality in California." 4 Feb. 2014. http://www.arb.ca.gov/html/brochure/history.htm. Accessed 28 Feb. 2014.

Callendar, G. S. "The Artificial Production of Carbon Dioxide and Its Influence on Temperature." *Quarterly Journal of the Royal Meteorological Society* 64.275 (April 1938), pp. 223–40.

Campbell, David G. *The Crystal Desert: Summers in Antarctica*. Boston: Houghton Mifflin, 1992.

Caro, Tim, Amanda Izzo, Robert C. Reiner, Jr., Hannah Walker, and Theodore Stankowich. "The Function of Zebra Stripes." *Nature Communications* 5.3535 (1 April 2014). http://www.nature.com/ncomms/2014/140401/ncomms4535/full/ncomms4535.html.

Carrington, Damian. "Fossil Fuels Subsidised by $10m a Minute, Says IMF." *The Guardian*, 18 May 2015. http://www.theguardian.com/environment/2015/may/18/fossil-fuel-companies-getting-10m-a-minute-in-subsidies-says-imf.

Carruthers, Jane. *The Kruger National Park—A Social and Political History*. Pietermaritzburg, South Africa: University of Natal Press, 1995.

Carson, Rachel. *Silent Spring*. Boston: Houghton Mifflin, 1962.

Carson, Rachel. "The Silent Spring of Rachel Carson." *C.B.S. Reports*, 3 April 1963.

Carter, Jason. *Power Lines: Two Years on South Africa's Borders*. Washington, D.C.: National Geographic, 2002.

Carwardine, Mark. "The Galápagos Islands: Trip of a Lifetime." *The Telegraph*, 9 Sept. 2012. http://www.telegraph.co.uk/travel/destinations/

south-america/ecuador/galapagos-islands/articles/The-Galapagos-Islands-Trip-of-a-Lifetime/. Accessed 15 Oct. 2013.

Caufield, Catherine. *In the Rainforest: Report from a Strange, Beautiful, Imperiled World*. Chicago: University of Chicago Press, 1991.

Center for Economic and Policy Research. "No-Vacation Nation Revisited." May 2013, http://www.lifehealthpro.com/2013/05/24/vacation-wise-us-stands-alone-among-advanced-econo. Accessed 12 Oct. 2013.

The Center for Media and Democracy. "Coal and Jobs in the United States." *SourceWatch*, 26 June 2015. http://www.sourcewatch.org/index.php/Coal_and_jobs_in_the_United_States#Total_coal-related_jobs. Accessed 1 July 2015.

Ceres. "The Ceres Declaration." http://www.ceres.org/declaration. Accessed 24 Aug. 2016.

Chadwick, Jr., William W., Sigurion Jonsson, Dennis J. Geist, Michael Poland, Daniel J. Johnson, Spencer Batt, Karen S. Harpp, and Andres Ruiz. "The May 2005 Eruption of Fernandina Volcano, Galápagos: The First Circumferential Dike Intrusion Observed by GPS and InSAR." *Bulletin of Volcanology* 73.6 (Aug. 2011), pp. 679–97.

Charlton-Perkins, William. *Great Game Parks of Africa: Hluhluwe-iMfolozi Park*. 2nd impression. Cape Town, South Africa: Struik Publishers, 1997.

Chase, Alston. *Playing God in Yellowstone: The Destruction of America's First National Park*. New York: Harcourt Brace & Company, 1986.

Chase, Rachel. "Argentina: 70 Injured in Christmas Day Piranha Attack." *Peru This Week*, 26 Dec. 2013. http://www.peruthisweek.com/news-argentina-70-injured-in-christmas-day-piranha-attack-101820.

Cherry-Garrard, Apsley. *The Worst Journey in the World: Antarctic 1910–1913*. Kent, UK: Picador, 1994 (1922).

CITES Secretariat. "Periodic Review of Animal Taxa in the Appendices Evaluation of Species Selected at AC15 and AC16." Convention on International Trade in Endangered Species on Wild Fauna and Flora. Seventeenth Meeting of the Animals Committee, Hanoi, Vietnam, 30 July to 3 Aug. 2001. http://www.cites.org/eng/com/ac/17/E17-08-1.pdf.

Clucas, Gemma V., Michael J. Dunn, Gareth Dyke, Steven D. Emslie, Hila Levy, Ron Naveen, Michael J. Polito, Oliver G. Pybus, Alex D. Rogers, and Tom Hart. "A Reversal of Fortunes: Climate Change 'Winners' and 'Losers' in Antarctic Peninsula Penguins." *Scientific Reports* 4.5024 (12 June 2014).

Conrad, Joseph. *Heart of Darkness*. New York: Harper & Brothers, 1910.

Constant, Pierre. *Galápagos: A Natural History Guide*. New York: Odyssey, 2000.

Cook, John, Dana Nuccitelli, Sarah A. Green, Mark Richardson, Bärbel Winkler, Rob Painting, Robert Way, Peter Jacobs, and Andrew Skuce. "Quantifying the Consensus on Anthropogenic Global Warming in the Scientific Literature." *Environmental Research Letters* 8.2 (15 May 2013). http://iopscience.iop.org/1748-9326/8/2/024024. Accessed 21 Sept. 2013.

Cool Antarctica. "Whales and Whaling–1–Whaling in Antarctica." http://www.coolantarctica.com/Antarctica%20fact%20file/wildlife/whales/whaling1.php. Accessed 1 June 2015.

Crews, D., J. M. Bergeron, J. J. Bull, D. Flores, A. Tousignant, J. K. Skipper, and T. Wibbels. "Temperature-dependent Sex Determination in Reptiles: Proximate Mechanisms, Ultimate Outcomes, and Practical Applications." *Developmental Genetics* 15.3 (1994), pp. 297–312.

Cronin, Melissa. "Solar Is So Hot Right Now. Check Out the Latest Numbers." *Grist*, 22 Feb 2016. http://grist.org/climate-energy/solar-is-so-hot-right-now-check-out-the-latest-numbers/?utm_medium=email&utm_source=newsletter&utm_campaign=weekly-static. Accessed 10 Aug. 2016.

Cronon, William, ed. *Uncommon Ground: Toward Reinventing Nature*. New York: W.W. Norton & Co., 1995.

Cruz, Felipe, Sylvia Harcourt, and Christian Lavoie, eds. *The Thematic Atlas of Project Isabela: An Illustrative Document Describing, Step-by-Step, the Biggest Successful Goat Eradication Project on the Galápagos Islands, 1998–2006*. Charles Darwin Foundation and Galápagos National Park Service, 2007.

Cruz, Felipe, Victor Carrion, Karl J. Campbell, Christian Lavoie, and C. Josh Donlan. "Bio-Economics of Large-Scale Eradication of Feral Goats From Santiago Island, Galápagos." *Journal of Wildlife Management* 73.2 (Feb. 2009), pp. 191–200.

Daigle, Katy. "Pollution Fight Targets Smoky Stoves." *Orlando Sentinel*, 12 April 2015, p. A-11.

———. "Push for Cleaner Stoves in Poor Countries to Cut Pollution," *The World Post*, 9 April 2015. http://www.huffingtonpost.com/huff-wires/20150408/as—india-black-carbon/. Accessed 20 Aug. 2016.

Darling, Seth B., and Douglas L. Sisterson. *How to Change Minds about Our Changing Climate: Let Science Do the Talking the Next Time Someone Tries to Tell You . . . And Other Arguments It's Time to End for Good.* New York: The Experiment, 2014.

Darwin, Charles. *The Origin of Species: Complete and Fully Illustrated.* New York: Random House, 1979.

———. *The Voyage of the Beagle.* New York: P. F. Collier & Son, 1909.

Davenport, Coral. "Economies Can Still Rise as Carbon Emissions Fade." *New York Times,* 7 April 2016, p. A-3.

Day, David. *The Whale War.* San Francisco: Sierra Club Books, 1987.

De'ath, Glenn, Janice M. Jough, and Kathrina E. Fabricius. "Declining Coral Calcification on the Great Barrier Reef." *Science* 323.5910 (2 Jan. 2009), pp. 116–19.

Dewey, John. *Experience and Education.* New York: Collier Books, 1938.

Dibbern, J. Stephen. "Fur Seals, Whales and Tourists: A Commercial History of Deception Island, Antarctica." *The Polar Record* 46.3 (July 2010), pp. 210–21.

Dickinson, Tim. "The Climate Killers: Meet the 17 Polluters and Deniers Who Are Derailing Efforts to Curb Global Warming." *Rolling Stone,* 6 Jan. 2010.

D'Orso, Michael. *Plundering Paradise: The Hand of Man on the Galápagos Islands.* New York: HarperCollins, 2002.

D'Oro, Rachel. "Permanent Fund Dividend Is $900; Direct Deposits Begin Oct. 3." *Anchorage Daily News,* 17 Sept. 2013. http://www.adn.com/2013/09/17/3080873/alaskans-eager-to-hear-amount.html. Accessed 18 Jan. 2014.

Druce, David. "Walking with African Wildlife 2008 Earthwatch Institute Annual Field Report." 9 March 2009.

———. "Walking with African Wildlife 2012 Field Report." 11 Dec. 2012.

Druce, Dave, and Geoff Clinning. *White Rhino Report 2008: iMfolozi Sink Count Results and Recommended White Rhino Removals for IGR and HGR.* Unpublished Ezemvelo KZN Wildlife Report. 2008.

Duggan, Alan, ed. *Reader's Digest Illustrated Guide to the Game Parks & Nature Reserves of Southern Africa.* 2nd ed. Cape Town: Reader's Digest Association of South Africa Limited, 1990.

Earthwatch Institute. "Macaws of the Peruvian Amazon." *Research & Exploration Guide* 24.2 (2005).

———. "Partner Profile: HSBC." http://earthwatch.org/corporate-partnerships/partnership-profiles/hsbc. Accessed 13 April 2014.

———. "Walking with African Wildlife." http://earthwatch.org/expeditions/walking-with-african-wildlife#daily-life. Accessed 10 March 2014.

Eckstrom, Christine K. "Homeless Macaws?" *International Wildlife* 24 (Sept./Oct. 1994), pp. 14–23.

Eilperin, Juliet. "New EPA Head McCarthy Outlines Ambitious Agenda in Harvard Speech." *The Washington Post*, 30 July 2013.

Eldredge, Niles. *Life in the Balance: Humanity and the Biodiversity Crisis.* Princeton, NJ: Princeton University Press, 1998.

Emanuel, Kerry. *What We Know about Climate Change.* 2nd ed. Cambridge, MA: The MIT Press, 2012.

EPA. "Overview of Greenhouse Gases." http://www.epa.gov/climatechange/ghgemissions/gases/co2.html. Accessed 20 Aug. 2016.

Erwin, Terry L. "Tropical Forests: Their Richness in Coleoptera and Other Arthropod Species." *The Coleopterists Bulletin* 36 (1982), pp. 74–75.

Espinoza, Bitinia. *A Walk in Paradise.* CD/DVD. 2005.

European Commission. "Combatting Tropical Deforestation: The REDD+ Initiative." 15 April 2014. http://ec.europa.eu/clima/policies/forests/deforestation/index_en.htm. Accessed 1 May 2014.

Fahrenthold, David A. "Last House on Sinking Chesapeake Bay Island Sinks." *The Washington Post*, 26 Oct. 2010. http://www.washingtonpost.com/wp-dyn/content/article/2010/10/24/AR2010102402996.html. Accessed 8 Dec. 2013.

Farreny, R., et al. "Carbon Dioxide Emissions of Antarctic Tourism." *Antarctic Science* 23.6 (Dec. 2011), pp. 556–66.

Ferguson, David. "Ghost Ship Laden with Diseases, Cannibal Rats Could Crash into British Coast." *The Raw Story*, 23 Jan. 2014. http://www.rawstory.com/rs/2014/01/23/ghost-ship-laden-with-diseased-cannibal-rats-could-crash-into-british-coast/. Accessed 31 May 2015.

Fickling, David. "The Cruel Sea." *The Guardian*, 22 July 2004.

Fischer, Douglas. "'Dark Money' Funds Climate Change Denial Effort." *Scientific American* 23 (Dec. 2013). http://www.scientificamerican.com/article/dark-money-funds-climate-change-denial-effort/?print=true.

Flannery, Tim. *The Weathermakers: How Man is Changing the Climate and What It Means for Life on Earth.* New York: Atlantic Monthly Press, 2005.

Flinders, Matthew. *A Voyage to Terra Australis.* London: G. and W. Nicol, Booksellers to His Majesty, Pall-Mall,1814.

Fothergill, Alastair. *A Natural History of the Antarctic: Life in the Freezer.* New York: Sterling Publishing Co., 1995.

Fretwell, Peter T., and Philip N. Trathan. "Penguins from Space: Faecal Stains Reveal the Location of Emperor Penguin Colonies." *Global Ecology and Biogeography* 18.5 (Sept. 2009), pp. 543–52.

Friedman, Thomas L. "Paris Climate Accord is a Big, Big Deal." *New York Times,* 16 Dec. 2015. http://www.nytimes.com/2015/12/16/opinion/paris-climate-accord-is-a-big-big-deal.html?rref=collection%2Fnewsev entcollection%2Fun-climate-change-conference&action=click&contentCollection=earth&region=stream&module=stream_unit&version=latest&contentPlacement=8&pgtype=collection.

Friedrichs, Jörg. *The Future Is Not What It Used to Be: Climate Change and Energy Security.* Cambridge, MA: The MIT Press, 2013.

"Frito-Lay Dominates U.S. Salty Snacks, But Rising Cracker Sales Could Stall Growth." *Forbes.com,* 27 June 2014. http://www.forbes.com/sites/greatspeculations/2014/06/27/frito-lay-dominates-u-s-salty-snacks-but-rising-cracker-sales-could-stall-growth/. Accessed 12 Aug. 2015.

Frontline. *Climate of Doubt.* PBS. Catherine Upin, producer and director. John Hockenberry, correspondent. 23 Oct. 2012. http://www.pbs.org/wgbh/pages/frontline/climate-of-doubt/.

———. *The Long Walk of Nelson Mandela.* Story Street Productions and Films2People. Will Lyman, narrator. 1 hr. 51 min. 1999.

Frost, Robert. *Mountain Interval.* New York: Henry Holt and Company, 1920.

Galápagos Conservancy. "People Today." http://www.galapagos.org/about_galapagos/about-galapagos/people-today/. Accessed 20 Aug. 2016.

Gallmann, Kuki. *I Dreamed of Africa.* New York: Viking, 1991.

Garside, Ben. "Global Carbon Emission Rise to New Record in 2013: Report." *Reuters.* 18 Nov. 2013. http://www.reuters.com/article/2013/11/19/us-global-carbon-emissions-idUSBRE9AI00A20131119. Accessed 2 Nov. 2013.

Gastañaga, Melvin, Ross Macleod, Bennett Hennessey, Joaquin Ugarte Nunez, Edevaly Puse, Anita Arrascue, Johana Hoyos, Willy

Maldonado Chambi, Jimmy Vasquez, and Gunar Engblom. "A Study of the Parrot Trade in Peru and the Potential Importance of Internal Trade for Threatened Species." *Bird Conservation International* 21.1 (2011), pp. 76–85.

Gelbspan, Ross. *Boiling Point: How Politicians, Big Oil and Coal, Journalists, and Activists Have Fueled the Climate Crisis—and What We Can Do to Avert Disaster.* New York: Basic Books, 2004.

Giddens, Anthony. *The Politics of Climate Change.* Cambridge, UK: Polity Press, 2009.

Gilardi, James, S. S. Duffey, C. A. Munn, and L. A. Tell. "Biochemical Functions of Geophagy in Parrots: Detoxification of Dietary Toxins and Cytoprotective Effects." *Journal of Chemical Ecology* 25 (1999), pp. 897–922.

Gillis, Justin. "The Flood Next Time." *New York Times*, 13 Jan. 2014.

———. "Panel Says Global Warming Risks Sudden, Deep Changes." *New York Times*, 4 Dec. 2013, p. A-22.

———. "For Third Year, the Earth in 2016 Hit Record Heat." *New York Times*, 19 Jan. 2017, p. A-1, 8.

Gladwell, Malcolm. *The Tipping Point: How Little Things Can Make a Big Difference.* Boston: Little, Brown & Company, 2000.

Glynn, Peter W. "Global Warming and Widespread Coral Mortality: Evidence of First Coral Reef Extinctions." *Saving a Million Species: Extinction Risk from Climate Change.* Lee Hannah, ed. Washington, D.C.: Island Press, 2012, pp.103–20.

Goodall, Jane. *In the Shadow of Man.* Boston: Houghton Mifflin Co., 1971.

Gore, Al. "Unbearable Whiteness," *New Republic*, 26 Dec. 1988.

———. "The Case for Optimism on Climate Change." TED Vancouver, 16 Feb. 2016. http://www.ted.com/talks/al_gore_the_case_for_optimism_on_climate_change. Accessed 12 June 2016.

Grange, Sophie, Norman Owen-Smith, Jean-Michel Gaillard, Mandisa Mgobozi, and Dave Druce. "Population Trends and Patterns of Mortality in an African Ungulate Community after Large Predator Introductions." Unpublished manuscript.

Great Barrier Reef Marine Park Authority. "Climate Change Adaptation: Outcomes from the Great Barrier Reef Climate Change Action Plan 2007–2012." Townsville, Queensland, Australia: Great Barrier Reef Marine Park Authority, 2012.

The Greenbelt Movement. "Tree Planting and Water Harvesting." http://www.greenbeltmovement.org/what-we-do/tree-planting-for-watersheds. Accessed 24 Aug. 2016.

"Guidelines for Visitors to the Antarctic." Antarctic Treaty Consultative Meeting XXXIV, Buenos Aires. 2011. http://iaato.org/c/document_library/get_file?uuid=aed1054d-3e63-4a17-a6cd-a87b eb15e287&groupId=10157.

Guilford, Gywnn. "Why Does a Rhino Horn Cost $300,000? Because Vietnam Thinks It Cures Cancer and Hangovers." *The Atlantic*, 15 May 2013. http://www.theatlantic.com/business/archive/2013/05/why-does-a-rhino-horn-cost-300-000-because-vietnam-thinks-it-cures-cancer-and-hangovers/275881/. Accessed 13 April 2014.

Gunter, Michael M., Jr. "Be Patriotic—Purchase a Passport." *Richmond Times-Dispatch*, 1 July 2011, p. A-11.

———. "Ecotourism." *Green Issues and Debates: An A to Z Guide*. Howard Schiffman, ed. Los Angeles: Sage Reference, May 2011 online, June 2011 print.

Hall, Shannon. "Exxon Knew about Climate Change almost 40 Years Ago." *Scientific American*, 26 Oct. 2015. http://www.scientificamerican.com/article/exxon-knew-about-climate-change-almost-40-years-ago/. Accessed 2 Aug. 2015.

Halpenny, Elizabeth A. "Tourism in Marine Protected Areas." *Tourism in National Parks and Protected Areas: Planning and Management*. Paul F. J. Eagles and Stephen F. McCool, eds. Oxon, UK: CABI Publishing, 2002, pp. 211–34.

Halpern, Benjamin S., and Carrie V. Kappel. "Extinction Risk in a Changing Ocean." *Saving a Million Species: Extinction Risk from Climate Change*. Lee Hannah, ed. Washington, D.C.: Island Press, 2012, pp. 285–308.

Hance, Jeremy. "Carbon Emissions in U.S. Rise 2 Percent Due to Increase in Coal." *Mongabay.com*, 16 Jan. 2014. http://news.mongabay.com/2014/0114-hance-co2-us.html. Accessed 20 Nov. 2013.

Hannah, Lee, ed. *Saving a Million Species: Extinction Risk from Climate Change*. Washington, D.C.: Island Press, 2012.

Hansen, James. *Storms of My Grandchildren: The Truth about the Coming Climate Catastrophe and Our Last Chance to Save Humanity*. New York: Bloomsbury, 2009.

Hansen, J., I. Fung, A. Lacis, D. Rind, Lebedeff, R. Ruedy, G. Russell, and P. Stone. "Global Climate Changes as Forecast by Goddard Institute for Space Studies Three-dimensional Model." *Journal of Geophysical Research* 93.D8 (20 Aug. 1988), pp. 9341–64.

Harder, Amy, Devlin Barrett, and Bradley Olson. "Exxon Fires Back at Climate-Change Probe." *The Wall Street Journal*, 13 April 2016. http://www.wsj.com/articles/exxon-fires-back-at-climate-change-probe-1460574535. Accessed 29 July 2016.

Harman, Danna. "Peru wants Machu Picchu Artifacts Returned." *USA Today*, 6 Jan. 2006, p. 10-A.

Harris, Richard. "Sweeping Parts of Southern Seas Could Become a Nature Preserve." *Morning Edition*, NPR, 12 July 2013. http://www.npr.org/2013/07/12/201170987/sweeping-parts-of-southern-seas-could-become-a-nature-preserve?ft=1&f=1025.

Hartley, Richard. "Pet Trade Blues." *International Wildlife* 30.2 (March/April 2000), pp. 40–47.

Harvey, Keri. "Grey Matters." *Wild*, Autumn/Winter 2008, p. 21.

Heacox, Kim. *National Geographic Destination: Antarctica—The Last Continent.* Washington, D.C.: National Geographic, 1998.

Held, David, Angus Hervey, and Marika Theros, eds. *The Governance of Climate Change: Science, Economics, Politics, & Ethics.* Cambridge, UK: Polity, 2011.

Hemming, John. *The Search for El Dorado.* London: Michael Joseph Ltd., 1978.

"Hluhluwe–iMfolozi Park Integrated Management Plan." Ezemvelo KZN Wildlife. 2011.

Hoegh-Guldberg, O. "Coral Reefs, Climate Change, and Mass Extinction." *Saving a Million Species: Extinction Risk from Climate Change.* Lee Hannah, ed. Washington, D.C.: Island Press, 2012, pp. 261–84.

Hoegh-Guldberg, O., P. J. Mumby, A. J. Hooten, R. S. Steneck, P. Greenfield, E. Gomez, C. D. Harvell, P. F. Sale, A. J. Edwards, K. Caldeira, N. Knowlton, C. M. Eakin, R. Iglesias-Prieto, N. Muthiga, R. H. Bradbury, A. Dubi, M. E. Hatziolos. "Coral Reefs under Rapid Climate Change and Ocean Acidification." *Science* 318 (14 Dec. 2007), pp. 1737–42.

Hoffert, Martin I., Ken Caldeira, Gregory Benford, David R. Criswell, Christopher Green, Howard Herzog, Atul K. Jain, Haroon S. Kheshgi, Klaus S. Lackner, John S. Lewis, H. Douglas Lightfoot, Wallace

Manheimer, John C. Mankins, Michael E. Mauel, L. John Perkins, Michael E. Schlesinger, Tyler Volk, Tom M. L. Wigley. "Advanced Technology Paths to Global Climate Stability: Energy for a Greenhouse Planet." *Science* 298.5595 (1 Nov. 2002), pp. 981–87.

Hogenboom, Melissa. "Watching Penguins, and Their Poo, from Space." *BBC Earth*, 10 Dec. 2014. http://www.bbc.com/earth/story/20141210-surprising-use-of-penguin-poo. Accessed 3 June 2015.

Honey, Martha. *Ecotourism and Sustainable Development: Who Owns Paradise?* 2nd ed. Washington, D.C.: Island Press, 2008.

———. "Treading Lightly: Ecotourism's Impact on the Environment." *Environment* 41.5 (June 1999), pp. 4–9, 28–32.

Howarth, Robert W. "A Bridge to Nowhere: Methane Emissions and the Greenhouse Gas Footprint of Natural Gas." *Energy Science & Engineering*, 22 April 2014, pp. 1–14.

Hsiao, Patrick. "The 10 Loudest Animals on Earth." *Australian Geographic*, 22 Aug. 2012. http://www.australiangeographic.com.au/topics/wildlife/2012/08/the-10-loudest-animals-on-earth/. Accessed 1 Sept. 2013.

Hubbard, Amy. "Ghost Ship and Starving Rats Headed for Land?" *Los Angeles Times*, 23 Jan. 2014. http://www.latimes.com/nation/la-sh-ghost-ship-cannibal-rats-20140123-story.html. Accessed 2 June 2015.

Huber, Matthew T. *Lifeblood: Oil, Freedom, and the Forces of Capital.* Minneapolis: Minnesota University Press, 2013.

Hulme, Mike. *Why We Disagree about Climate Change: Understanding Controversy, Inaction and Opportunity.* Cambridge, UK: Cambridge University Press, 2009.

Inhofe, James M. "The Science of Climate Change." Floor Statement by Sen. Inhofe (R-OK). 28 July 2003.

Intergovernmental Panel on Climate Change. "Fifth Assessment Report (AR5)." http://www.ipcc.ch/report/ar5/. Accessed 24 Aug. 2016.

The International Ecotourism Society. "Factsheet: Global Ecotourism." Sept. 2006. http://mekongtourism.org/website/wp-content/uploads/downloads/2011/02/Fact-Sheet-Global-Ecotourism-IETS.pdf. Accessed 15 Oct. 2013.

International Union for Conservation of Nature. *The IUCN Red List of Threatened Species.* IUCN, 2013. http://www.iucnredlist.org>. Downloaded on 7 December 2016.

Isaacson, Andy. "In a Changing Antarctica, Some Penguins Thrive as Others Suffer." *New York Times*, 9 May 2001.

Jackson, Joe. *The Thief at the End of the World: Rubber, Power, and the Seeds of Empire*. New York: Viking, 2008.

Jacques, Peter J., Riley E. Dunlap, and Mark Freeman. "The Organization of Denial: Conservative Think Tanks and Environmental Skepticism." *Environmental Politics* 17.3 (June 2008), pp. 349–85.

Johnson, Johanna E., and Paul A. Marshall, eds. *Climate Change and the Great Barrier Reef*. Townsville, Australia: Great Barrier Reef Marine Park Authority and Australian Greenhouse Office, 2007.

Joyner, Christopher C. *Governing the Frozen Commons: The Antarctic Regime and Environmental Protection*. Columbia: University of South Carolina Press, 1998.

Juniper, Tony. "Too Pretty." *Birder's World* 19.2 (April 2005), pp. 26–33.

Kahan, D. "Fixing the Communications Failure." *Nature* 463.21 (2010), pp. 296–97.

Kahn, Joseph. "Cheney Promotes Increasing Supply as Energy Policy." *New York Times*, 1 May 2001. http://www.nytimes.com/2001/05/01/us/cheney-promotes-increasing-supply-as-energy-policy.html. Accessed 12 Aug. 2015.

Kasterine, Alexander. "Africa's Anti-Poaching Problem." *Foreign Affairs*, 5 Feb. 2014. http://www.foreignaffairs.com/articles/140718/alexander-kasterine/africas-anti-poaching-problem. Accessed 22 Feb. 2014.

Keller, Bill. "South Africa's Conqueror of Apartheid as Fighter, Prisoner, President and Symbol." *New York Times*, 6 Dec. 2013, pp. A1, 16–18.

Kious, W. Jacquelyne, and Robert I. Tilling. *This Dynamic Earth: The Story of Plate Tectonics*. Online edition. Martha Kiger, design. Jane Russell, illustrator. Reston, VA: United States Geological Survey, 3 Sept. 2015 (Feb. 1996 print). http://pubs.usgs.gov/gip/dynamic/historical.html. Accessed 20 Sept. 2013.

Koens, Jacobus Franciscus, Carel Dieperink, and Miriam Miranda. "Ecotourism as a Development Strategy: Experiences from Costa Rica." *Environment, Development and Sustainability*, Oct. 2009, pp. 1225–37.

Kolbert, Elizabeth. "Comment: Storms Brewing." *New Yorker*, 13 June 2011.

———. *Field Notes from a Catastrophe: Man, Nature, and Climate Change*. New York: Bloomsbury, 2006.

Kreft, Sönke, and David Eckstein. "Global Climate Risk Index 2014: Who Suffers Most from Extreme Weather Events? Weather-Related Loss Events in 2012 and 1993 to 2012." *Germanwatch*, Nov. 2013. http://germanwatch.org/en/download/8551.pdf. Accessed 7 Dec. 2013.

Kroeber, A. L., and Talcott Parsons. "The Concepts of Culture and of Social System." *The American Sociological Review* 23 (1958), pp. 582–83.

Krugman, Paul. "Building a Green Economy." *New York Times*, 7 April 2010. http://www.nytimes.com/2010/04/11/magazine/11Economy-t.html?_r=0&pagewanted=print.

Lansing, Alfred. *Endurance: Shackleton's Incredible Voyage*. New York: Carroll & Graf, 1959.

Larson, Edward J. *Evolution's Workshop: God and Science on the Galápagos Islands*. New York: Basic Books, 2001.

LaRue, Michelle A., David G. Ainley, Matt Swanson, Katie M. Dugger, Phil O'B. Lyver, Kerry Barton, and Grant Ballard. "Climate Change Winners: Receding Ice Fields Facilitate Colony Expansion and Altered Dynamics in an Adélie Penguin Metapopulation." *PLoS ONE* 8.4 (3 April 2013). http://dx.doi.org/10.1371/journal.pone.0060568. Accessed 31 May 2015.

Laws, Richard. *Antarctica: The Last Frontier*. London: Boxtree Limited, 1989.

Leakey, Richard, and Roger Lewin. *The Sixth Extinction: Patterns of Life and the Future of Humankind*. New York: Doubleday, 1995.

Leakey, Richard, and Virginia Morell. *Wildlife Wars: My Fight to Save Africa's Natural Treasures*. New York: St. Martin's Griffin, 2001.

Leopold, Aldo. *A Sand County Almanac: And Sketches Here and There*. New York: Oxford University Press, 1949.

Lindberg, K. "The Internal Market for Nature Tourism in South Africa: A Household Survey." *Nature Tourism, Conservation, and Development in KwaZulua Natal, South Africa*. E. Lutz and B. Aylward, eds. Washington, D.C.: World Bank, 2003.

Lomborg, Bjørn. *Cool It: The Skeptical Environmentalist's Guide to Global Warming*. New York: Alfred A. Knopf, 2007.

Lorenzi, Rossella. "Venice Sinking More than Previously Thought." *Discovery News* 26 (March 2012). http://news.discovery.com/earth/venice-sinking-120326.htm. Accessed 1 Oct. 2013.

Louv, Richard. *Last Child in the Woods: Saving Our Children from Nature-Deficit Disorder*. Chapel Hill, NC: Algonquin Books, 2005.

"*Loxodonta africana.*" Species+ CITES Listing. http://www.speciesplus.net/#/taxon_concepts/4521/legal?taxonomy=cites_eu. Accessed 31 Jan. 2014.

Luck, Michael, Patrick T. Maher, and Emma J. Stewart, eds. *Cruise Tourism in Polar Regions: Promoting Environmental and Social Sustainability?* London: Earthscan, 2010.

Lynas, Mark. *High Tide: The Truth about Our Climate Crisis.* New York: Picador, 2004.

Maathai, Wangari. *The Green Belt Movement: Sharing the Approach and the Experience.* New York: Lantern Books, 2004.

———. *Unbowed: A Memoir.* New York: Alfred A. Knopf, 2006.

Mabo and Others v. Queensland (No. 2). 23, High Court of Australia. 1992. 175 CLR 1; F.C. 92/014. http://www.austlii.edu.au/au/cases/cth/HCA/1992/23.html. Accessed 22 Feb. 2014.

Macintyre, Stuart. *A Concise History of Australia.* Cambridge, UK: Cambridge University Press, 2004.

Mahama, John Dramani. "Op-Ed: He Taught a Continent to Forgive." *New York Times*, 6 Dec. 2013, p. A-31.

Maibach, E., J. Witte, and K. Wilson. "Climate-gate Undermined Belief in Global Warming among Many TV Meteorologists." *Bulletin of the American Meteorological Association* 92, (2011), pp. 31–37.

Malakoff, David. "Carbon Cruise." *Conservation*, 1 Sept. 2011. http://conservationmagazine.org/2011/09/carbon-cruise/. Accessed 13 June 2015.

Mandela, Nelson. *Long Walk to Freedom: The Autobiography of Nelson Mandela.* New York: Little Brown and Company, 1995.

Mandela: Long Walk to Freedom. Justin Chadwick, director. William Nicholson, writer. Anant Singh, producer. 141 min. 25 Dec. 2013.

Mann, Michael E. *The Hockey Stick and the Climate Wars: Dispatches from the Front Lines.* New York: Columbia University Press, 2012.

Mann, Michael E., and Lee R. Kump. *Dire Predictions: Understanding Global Warming.* London: Dorling Kindersley Limited, 2009.

Mann, Michael E., Raymond S. Bradley, and Malcolm K. Hughes. "Global-Scale Temperature Patterns and Climate Forcing Over the Past Six Centuries." *Nature* 392 (23 April 1998), pp. 779–87.

March of the Penguins. Documentary film. Luc Jacquet, director. Morgan Freeman, narrator. 80 min. 2005.

Markels, Alex. "A View with a Room." *Audubon.* Oct. 1999. http://archive.audubonmagazine.org/viewroom.html.

Markowitz, Gerald, and David Rosner. *Deceit and Denial: The Deadly Politics of Industrial Pollution.* Berkeley: University of California Press, 2002.

Marsden, William. *Fools Rule: Inside the Failed Politics of Climate Change.* Toronto: Alfred A. Knopf Canada, 2011.

Marven, Nigel. *Nature: Rhinoceros.* 22 Aug. 2008. http://www.pbs.org/wnet/nature/episodes/rhinoceros/rhino-horn-use-fact-vs-fiction/1178/.

Massachusetts, et al. v. EPA et al. No. 05-1120. Supreme Court of the United States. 415 F.3d 50, 2 April 2007. Legal Information Institute, Cornell University Law School. https://www.law.cornell.edu/supct/html/05-1120.ZS.html. Accessed 24 Aug. 2016.

Masson, Jeffrey Moussaiff, and Susan McCarthy. *When Elephants Weep: The Emotional Lives of Animals.* New York: Dell Publishing, 1995.

Matthiessen, Peter. *African Silences.* New York: Random House, 1991.

McClintock, James. "Lost Antarctica," *The Diane Rehm Show.* 18 Sept. 2012. http://thedianerehmshow.org/shows/2012-09-18/james-mcclintock-lost-antarctica. Accessed 2 Dec. 2013.

———. *Lost Antarctica: Adventures in a Disappearing Land.* New York: Palgrave Macmillan, 2012.

McCright, Aaron M., and Riley E. Dunlap. "The Politicization of Climate Change and Polarization in the American Public's Views of Global Warming, 2001–2010." *The Sociological Quarterly* 52.2 (March 2011), pp. 155–94.

Mda, Zakes. "The Mandela I Knew." Op-ed in *New York Times,* 6 Dec. 2013, p. A-31.

Meduna, Veronika. *Secrets of the Ice: Antarctica's Clues to Climate, the Universe, and the Limits of Life.* New Haven, CT: Yale University Press, 2012.

Metcalf, Gilbert. *A Green Employment Tax Swap.* Washington, D.C.: The Brookings Institute, 2007.

Mgobozi, Mandisa, and Geoff Clinning. *Animal Population Control Report, Hluhluwe-iMfolozi Park, 2008/2009.* Unpublished Ezemvelo KZN Wildlife Report. 2008.

Minard, Anne. "No More Glaciers in Glacier National Park by 2020?" *National Geographic News,* 2 March 2009. http://news.nationalgeographic.com/news/2009/03/090302-glaciers-melting.html. Accessed 30 Oct. 2013.

Mooney, Chris. "The Hockey Stick: The Most Controversial Chart in Science, Explained." *The Atlantic*, 10 May 2013. http://www.theatlantic.com/technology/archive/2013/05/the-hockey-stick-the-most-contro versial-chart-in-science-explained/275753/. Accessed 19 Nov. 2013.

Morton, H. V. "Pietermaritzburg, Durban, Zululand: 1947." *The Reader's Companion to South Africa*. Alan Ryan, ed. New York: Harcourt Brace & Company, 1990, pp. 120–46.

Mrosovsky, N. "Sex Ratios of Sea Turtles." *Journal of Experimental Zoology* 270.1 (15 Sept. 1994), pp. 16–27.

Muir, John. *My First Summer in the Sierra*. Boston: Houghton Mifflin Company, 1911.

Munn, Charles A. "Macaws: Winged Rainbows." *National Geographic* 185.1 (Jan. 1994), pp. 118–40.

Murray, James. "China Power Sector Emissions 'to Peak in 2027.'" *The Guardian Environment Network*, 27 Aug. 2013. https://www.theguard-ian.com/environment/2013/aug/27/china-power-emissions-p eak-2027. Accessed 15 June 2015.

NASA Quest. "Eureka! The Story of the Archimedes Principle." http://quest.nasa.gov/aero/planetary/archimedes.html. Accessed 22 June 2015.

Nash, Stephen P. "Twilight of the Glaciers." *New York Times*, 29 July 2011, http://www.nytimes.com/2011/07/31/travel/glacier-nation-al-park-montana-fading-glaciers.html. Accessed 30 Oct. 2013.

National Park Service. "Glaciers—Glacier National Park," 24 Oct. 2013, http://www.nps.gov/glac/forteachers/glaciers.htm. Accessed 30 Oct. 2013.

National Science Foundation. "Science and Technology: Public Attitudes and Understanding," *Science and Engineering Indicators 2004*. http://www.nsf.gov/statistics/seind04/c7/c7h.htm. Accessed 17 Nov. 2013.

Nature. *The Real Macaw*. PBS documentary. Caroline Brett, director and producer. Howard McGillen, narrator. 26 Feb. 2004. http://www.pbs.org/wnet/nature/episodes/the-real-macaw/introduction/2729/.

Nelson, Laura. "News Feature: One Slip, and You're Dead." *Nature* 429 (24 June 2004), pp. 798–99.

Newlson, V. M., and B. D. Mapstone. *A Review of Environmental Impact Monitoring of Pontoon Installations in the Great Barrier Marine Park*. Technical Report No. 13. Townsville: CRC Reef Research Centre

Ltd., 1997. http://www.reef.crc.org.au/publications/techreport/TechRep13.html. Accessed 20 Sept. 2013.

Nicholls, Henry. *Lonesome George: The Life and Loves of a Conservation Icon.* New York: Palgrave Macmillan, 2007. http://www.reef.crc.org.au/publications/techreport/TechRep13.html.

Normile, Dennis. "Survey Confirms Worst-ever Coral Bleaching at Great Barrier Reef." *Science*, 19 April 2016. http://www.sciencemag.org/news/2016/04/survey-confirms-worst-ever-coral-bleaching-great-barrier-reef. Accessed 3 Aug. 2016.

North, James. *Freedom Rising.* New York: Plume, 1985/6.

Nova. *Australia: First 4 Billion Years—Awakening.* PBS, Essential Media and Entertainment. 10 April 2013. http://www.pbs.org/wgbh/nova/earth/australia-first-years.html#australia-awakening.

———. *Shackleton's Voyage of Endurance.* David Ogden Stiers, narrator. Sarah Holt (hour one) and Kelly Tyler (hour two), writers and producers. White Mountain Films/WGBH Educational Foundation, 26 March 2002. http://www.pbs.org/wgbh/nova/shackleton.

NOVA and National Geographic Television. *The Ghosts of Machu Picchu.* Craig Sechler, narrator. 2009. http://www.pbs.org/wgbh/nova/ancient/ghosts-machu-picchu.html.

Oil Change International. "Fossil Fuel Subsidies: Overview." http://priceofoil.org/fossil-fuel-subsidies/. Accessed 2 July 2015.

Olah, George, Gabriela Vigo, Robert Heinsohn, and Donald J. Brightsmith. "Nest Site Selection and Efficacy of Artificial Nests for Breeding Success of Scarlet Macaws *Ara macao macao* in Lowland Peru." *Journal for Nature Conservation* 22 (2014), pp. 176–85.

Oregon Institute of Science and Medicine. "The Global Warming Petition Project." http://www.petitionproject.org/. Accessed 24 Aug. 2016.

Organization for Economic Co-operation and Development. "Labour Productivity Levels in the Total Economy," 10 Sept. 2013. http://stats.oecd.org/Index.aspx?DatasetCode=LEVEL. Accessed 12 Oct. 2013.

Orson, Diane. "Yale Returns Machu Picchu Artifacts to Peru." *All Things Considered*, NPR, 15 Dec. 2010. http://www.npr.org/2010/12/15/132083890/yale-returns-machu-picchu-artifacts-to-peru.

Parmesan, Camille, and Gary Yohe. "A Globally Coherent Fingerprint of Climate Change Impacts Across Natural Systems." *Nature* 421 (2 Jan. 2003), pp. 37–42.

Paton, Alan. *Cry, the Beloved Country*. New York: Scribner, 1948.

Patterson, B. D. *The Lions of Tsavo: Exploring the Legacy of Africa's Notorious Man-eaters*. New York: McGraw-Hill, 2004.

Patterson, John Henry. *The Maneaters of Tsavo and Other East African Adventures*. London: Macmillan and Co., 1907.

Payne, Katy, Iain Douglas-Hamilton, Vivek Menon, Cynthia Moss, Joyce Poole, and Andrea Turkalo. "Lifting the Ivory Ban Called Premature." NPR, 31 Oct. 2002. http://www.npr.org/templates/story/story.php?storyId=3879214.

Pearson, Richard. *Driven to Extinction: The Impact of Climate Change on Biodiversity*. New York: Sterling Publishing Company, 2011.

Phillips, Kathryn. *Tracking the Vanishing Frogs: An Ecological Mystery*. New York: Penguin Books, 1995.

Pielke, Jr., Roger. *The Climate Fix: What Scientists and Politicians Won't Tell You about Global Warming*. New York: Basic Books, 2010.

Plass, Gilbert N. "The Carbon Dioxide Theory of Climatic Change." *Tellus* 8.2 (1956), pp. 140–54.

Player, Ian. *The White Rhino Saga*. New York: Stein and Day, 1973.

———. *Zulu Wilderness: Shadow and Soul*. Golden, CO: Fulcrum Publishing, 1998.

Plotkin, Mark J. *Tales of a Shaman's Apprentice: An Ethnobotanist Searches for New Medicines in the Amazon Rain Forest*. New York: Penguin Books, 1993.

Plumer, Brad. "Four Charts that Show the U.S. Spends too Little on Energy Research." *The Washington Post*, 9 April 2013. http://www.washingtonpost.com/blogs/wonkblog/wp/2013/04/09/three-charts-that-show-the-u-s-spends-too-little-on-energy-research/.

———. "Here's Why 1.2 Billion People Still Don't Have Access to Electricity." *The Washington Post*, 29 May 2013. http://www.washingtonpost.com/blogs/wonkblog/wp/2013/05/29/heres-why-1-2-billion-people-still-dont-have-access-to-electricity/.

Polgreen, Lydia. "Mandela's Death Leaves South Africa without Its Moral Center." *New York Times*, 6 Dec. 2013, p. A-14.

Poole, Joyce. *Coming of Age with Elephants: A Memoir*. New York: Hyperion, 1996.

Pooley, Eric. *The Climate War: True Believers, Power Brokers, and the Fight to Save the Earth*. New York: Hyperion, 2010.

Pooley, Tony. *Mashesha: The Making of a Game Ranger.* Johannesburg, South Africa: Southern Book Publishers, 1992.

Pope Francis. "Encyclical Letter Laudato Si' of the Holy Father Francis On Care for Our Common Home." Vatican: The Holy See. Rome, 18 June 2015. http://w2.vatican.va/content/francesco/en/encyclicals/documents/papa-francesco_20150524_enciclica-laudato-si.pdf.

Posegate, Ann. "Measured by Carbon Footprint, Travel to Antarctica has Tons of Impact." *The Washington Post,* 13 April 2010. http://www.washingtonpost.com/wp-dyn/content/article/2010/04/12/AR2010041203194.html. Accessed 15 July 2015.

Quasar Nautical. *The Galápagos Islands Visitor Sites.* Quito, Ecuador: Quasar Nautica, Galápagos Expeditions, 2003.

Rachowiecki, Rob, and Danny Palmerlee. *Lonely Planet: Ecuador & the Galapagos Islands.* Melbourne, Australia: Lonely Planet Publications, 2003.

Reader, John. *Africa: A Biography of the Continent.* New York: Alfred A. Knopf, 1998.

Reader's Digest. *Illustrated Guide to the Game Parks and Nature Reserves of Southern Africa.* Cape Town: Reader's Digest Association of South Africa (Pty) Limited, 1990.

"Rebels Kill 8 Policemen." *New York Times,* 22 Dec. 2005.

Reef Water Quality Protection Plan in 2013. State of Queensland: Reef Water Quality Protection Plan Secretariat, July 2013. http://www.reefplan.qld.gov.au/resources/assets/reef-plan-2013.pdf. Accessed 1 Sept. 2013.

Rees, William. "Ecological Footprints and Appropriated Carrying Capacity: What Urban Economics Leaves Out." *Environment and Urbanization* 4.2 (Oct. 1992), pp. 121–30.

Regional Greenhouse Gas Initiative, Inc. (RGGI). http://www.rggi.org/. Accessed 12 Aug. 2016.

Resource Development Council. "Alaska's Oil & Gas Industry: Background." 16 Oct. 2013. http://www.akrdc.org/issues/oilgas/overview.html.

Revelle, Roger and Hans E. Suess. "Carbon Dioxide Exchange between Atmosphere and Ocean and the Question of an Increase of Atmospheric CO_2 during the Past Decades." *Tellus* 9.1 (February 1957), pp. 18–27.

Revkin, Andrew. *The Burning Season: The Murder of Chico Mendes and the Fight for the Amazon Rain Forest.* Washington, DC: Island Press, 2004 (Houghton Mifflin, 1990).

———. "Bush Aide Softened Greenhouse Gas Links to Global Warming." *New York Times,* 8 June 2005.

———. "Climate Expert Says NASA Tried to Silence Him." *New York Times,* 29 Jan 29. 2006, p. A-1.

———. "Paths to a 'Good' Anthropocene." Keynote address at Association for Environmental Studies and Sciences, Pace University, New York, New York, 11 June 2014.

———. "Why 2007 IPCC Report Lacked 'Embers.'" *New York Times,* 26 Feb. 2009. http://dotearth.blogs.nytimes.com/2009/02/26/why-2007-ip-cc-report-lacked-embers/?_r=0. Accessed 2 Jan. 2014.

Robertson, R. B. *Of Whales and Men.* New York: Alfred A. Knopf, 1954.

Roe, David. "Flippers and Flukes: Caring for Our Special Marine Turtles and Dugongs." Sea Turtle Foundation. Harim Series Book 1. Undated. https://www.google.com/#q=Flippers+and+Flukes:+Caring+for+Our+Special+Marine+Turtles+and+Dugongs.%E2%80%9D++.

Rosen, Rebecca J. "What Is It about an Elephant's Tusks that Make Them So Valuable?" *The Atlantic,* 6 Sept. 2012. http://www.theatlantic.com/business/archive/2012/09/what-is-it-about-an-elephants-tusks-that-make-them-so-valuable/262021/. Accessed 22 Feb. 2014.

Rousseau, Jean-Jacques. *Emile, or On Education.* Trans. Allan Bloom. New York: Basic Books, 1979.

Rushin, Steve. "Antarctica with Kate Upton." *Sports Illustrated,* 15 Feb. 2013, pp. 51–56, 200–7. http://sportsillustrated.cnn.com/vault/article/magazine/MAG1206858/index.htm.

Saad, Lydia, and Jeffrey M. Jones. "U.S. Concern about Global Warming at Eight-Year High." *Gallup,* 16 March 2016. http://www.gallup.com/poll/190010/concern-global-warming-eight-year-high.aspx. Accessed 13 April 2016.

Sagan, Carl. *The Demon-Haunted World: Science as a Candle in the Dark.* New York: Ballantine Books, 1996.

Sapolsky, Robert M. *A Primate's Memoir: A Neuroscientist's Unconventional Life among the Baboons.* New York: Scribner, 2001.

SA-Venues.com. "KwaZulu Natal Nature and Game Reserves." http://www.sa-venues.com/accommodation/kzn_game_lodges.htm. Accessed 13 April 2014.

Save the Rhino. "Rhino Population Figures." 19 March 2014. http://www.savetherhino.org/rhino_info/rhino_population_figures. Accessed 13 April 2014.

"Saving the Parrots: Texas A&M Team Sequences Genome of Endangered Macaw Birds." *PR Newswire*, 8 May 2013.

Schellenberg, Michael, and Ted Nordhaus. "The Death of Environmentalism: Global Warming Politics in a Post-Environmental World." Essay delivered at annual meeting of Environmental Grantmakers Association, Oct. 2004.

Schlosser, Eric. *Fast Food Nation: The Dark Side of the All-American Meal.* Boston: Houghton Mifflin Company, 2001.

Schumacher, E. F. *Small Is Beautiful: Economics as If People Mattered.* London: Blond & Briggs, Ltd., 1973.

Shabecoff, Philip. "Global Warming Has Begun, Expert Tells Senate." *New York Times*, 24 June 1988. http://www.nytimes.com/1988/06/24/us/global-warming-has-begun-expert-tells-senate.html. Accessed 3 Dec. 2013.

Shoumatoff, Alex. *The World Is Burning: Murder in the Rain Forest.* Boston: Little, Brown and Company, 1990.

Sinclair, Anthony R. E. *Serengeti Story: Life and Science in the World's Greatest Wildlife Region.* Oxford, UK: Oxford University Press, 2012.

Smith, Miranda, director. *The Shaman's Apprentice.* Documentary DVD. Susan Sarandon, narrator. Miranda Productions, Inc., 2001.

Snitch, Thomas. "Poachers Kill Three Elephants an Hour. Here's How to Stop Them." *The Telegraph*, 13 Feb. 2014. http://www.telegraph.co.uk/earth/environment/conservation/10634747/Poachers-kill-three-elephants-an-hour.-Heres-how-to-stop-them.html. Accessed 17 March 2014.

Snyder, J. M., and B. Stonehouse, eds. *Prospects for Polar Tourism.* Cambridge, MA: CAB International, 2007.

Solano, Pedro. "Legal Framework for Protected Areas: Peru." IUCN-EPLP No. 81, May 2009. http://cmsdata.iucn.org/downloads/peru_en.pdf. Accessed 13 April 2014.

Spotila, James R. *Saving Sea Turtles: Extraordinary Stories from the Battle against Extinction.* Baltimore, MD: The Johns Hopkins University Press, 2011.

Spotts, Pete. "Greenland's Ice Sheet: Climate Change Outlook Gets a Little

More Dire." *Christian Science Monitor*, 13 March 2012. http://www.csmonitor.com/Environment/2012/0313/Greenland-s-ice-sheet-Climate-change-outlook-gets-a-little-more-dire. Accessed 1 Dec. 2013.

Steig, Eric, et al. "Warming of the Antarctic Ice-sheet Surface Since the 1957 International Geophysical Year." *Nature* 457 (2009), pp. 459–62.

Stern, Nicholas. *The Economics of Climate Change: The Stern Review*. Cambridge, UK: Cambridge University Press, 2007.

Steves, Rick. "The Value of Travel," TEDxRainer. 12 Nov. 2011. http://tedx-talks.ted.com/video/TEDxRainier-Rick-Steves-The-Val. Accessed 26 Aug. 2015.

Stoknes, Per Espen. *What We Think About When We Try Not to Think About Global Warming: Toward a New Psychology of Climate Action*. White River Junction, VT: Chelsea Green Publishing, 2015.

Strasdas, Wolfgang. "Voluntary Offsetting of Flight Emissions: An Effective Way to Mitigate the Environmental Impacts on Long-Haul Tourism." Feb. 2007. www.ecotourismcesd.org Accessed 20 Aug. 2015.

Strauch, Dore. *Satan Comes to Eden*. Harper and Brothers, 1935.

Streever, Bill. *Cold: Adventures in the World's Frozen Places*. New York: Little, Brown and Company, 2009.

Stronza, Amanda. "Learning Both Ways: Lessons from a Corporate and Community Ecotourism Collaboration." *Cultural Survival Quarterly* 23.2 (Summer 1999). http://www.culturalsurvival.org/publications/cultural-survival-quarterly/peru/learning-both-ways-lessons-corporate-and-community-eco.

Sullivan, Tim. "In Awe of the Macaw." *The Oregonian*, 19 April 2004.

Sutherland, J. J. "Bugs Bunny: The Trickster, American Style." NPR, 6 Jan. 2008. http://www.npr.org/templates/story/story.php?storyId=17874931. Accessed 21 Sept. 2013.

Swan, Robert. *Antarctica 2041: My Quest to Save the Earth's Last Wilderness*. New York: Broadway Books, 2009.

Synnott, Mark. "Amid Hunt for Malaysian Plane, Ocean Swims with Missing Vessels." *National Geographic*, 19 March 2014. http://news.nationalgeographic.com/news/2014/03/140319-ghost-ship-malaysia-airliner-atlantic-ocean/.

Terborgh, John. *Five New World Primates: A Study in Comparative Ecology*. Princeton, NJ: Princeton University Press, 1983.

——. *Requiem for Nature*. Washington, DC: Island Press, 1999.

Thompson, Andrea. "First Half of 2016 Blows Away Temp Records." *Climate Central*, 19 July 2016. http://www.climatecentral.org/news/first-half-of-2016-record-hot-by-far-20540?utm_content=buffer571cc. Accessed 1 Aug. 2016.

Thompson, Leonard. *A History of South Africa*. New Haven, CT: Yale University Press, 1995.

Thoreau, Henry David. "Walking." *The Atlantic Monthly* 9.56 (June 1862), pp. 657–74.

"Tracking Poached Ivory: Research Overview." Center for Conservation Biology, University of Washington. 15 April 2014. http://conservationbiology.uw.edu/research-programs/tracking-poached-ivory/. Accessed 28 April 2014.

Treherne, John. *The Galápagos Affair*. New York: Random House, 1983.

Trinkle, M., N. Ferguson, A. Reid, C. Reid, M. Somers, L. Turelli, J. Graf, M. Szykman, D. Cooper, P. Haverman, G. Kastberger, C. Packer, and R. Slotow. "Translocating Lions into an Inbred Lion Population in the Hluhluwe-iMfolozi Park, South Africa." *Animal Conservation* 11 (2008), pp. 138–43.

Tveten, John L. "Tropical Forests of Peru's Tambopata Reserve Hold Treasure-Trove of Life." *Houston Chronicle*, 7 Feb. 1987.

Twain, Mark. *The Innocents Abroad*. Hartford, CT: American Publishing Company, 1869.

UK Energy Research Center. *Low Carbon Jobs: The Evidence for New Job Creation from Policy Support for Energy Efficiency and Renewable Energy*. 10 Nov. 2014. http://www.edie.net/.

UNEP. *Green Jobs*. Washington, D.C.: Worldwatch Institute, 2008.

UNFCCC. "Paris Agreement." 12 Dec. 2015. http://unfccc.int/files/meetings/paris_nov_2015/application/pdf/paris_agreement_english_.pdf. Accessed 28 May 2015.

Union of Concerned Scientists. "Clean Vehicles." http://www.ucsusa.org/clean_vehicles/why-clean-cars/global-warming/. Accessed 21 Sept. 2013.

United Nations Framework Convention on Climate Change. "Kyoto Protocol." http://unfccc.int/kyoto_protocol/items/2830.php. Accessed 8 July 2015.

U.S. Chamber of Commerce. *NAFTA Triumphant: Assessing Two Decades of Growth in Trade, Growth, and Jobs*. https://www.uschamber.com/sites/

default/files/legacy/reports/1112_INTL_NAFTA_20Years.pdf Accessed 8 July 2015.

U.S. Coast Guard Navigation Center. "How Much of an Iceberg Is Under Water." 17 Nov. 2015. http://www.navcen.uscg.gov/?pageName =iipHowMuchOfAnIcebergIsBelowTheWater.

U.S. Defense Department. "2010 Quadrennial Defense Review Report." 2010.

U.S. Energy Information Association. "Coal Explained: How Much Coal Is Left." http://www.eia.gov/energyexplained/index.cfm?page=coal_ reserves. Accessed 1 July 2015.

U.S. Environmental Protection Agency. "Greenhouse Gas Data Inventory Explorer." http://www.epa.gov/climatechange/ghgemissions/inven-toryexplorer/#allsectors/allgas/econsect/current. Accessed 8 July 2015.

U.S. Global Change Research Program. *The National Climate Assessment*. Washington, D.C. May 2014. http://nca2014.globalchange.gov/ report. Accessed 14 July 2015.

Uthicke, S., P. Momigliano, K. E. Fabricius. "Early Victims of Ocean Acidification Could Go Extinct this Century." *Scientific Reports* 3.1769 (3 May 2013).

Vanderbilt, Tom. *Traffic*. London: Allen Lane, 2008.

Vandermeer, John, and Ivette Perfecto. *Breakfast of Biodiversity: The Truth about Rain Forest Destruction*. Monroe, OR: Institute for Food and Development Policy, 1995.

Victor, David. G. *Global Warming Gridlock: Creating More Effective Strategies for Protecting the Planet*. Cambridge, UK: Cambridge University Press, 2011.

Vigo, Gabriela, Martha Williams, and Donald Brightsmith. "Growth of Scarlet Macaw (*Ara macao*) Chicks in Southeastern Peru." *Ornitologia Neotropical* 22 (2011), pp. 143–53.

Vince, Gai. *Adventures in the Anthropocene: A Journey to the Heart of the Planet We Made*. London: Chatto & Windus, 2014.

Vonnegut, Kurt. *Galápagos*. New York: Laurel, 1985.

Walker, Clive. *Signs of the Wild*. Cape Town, South Africa: Struik Publishers, 1991.

Wallace, Scott. "Last of the Amazon." *National Geographic* 211.1 (Jan. 2007), pp. 40–70.

Wapner, Paul. "Climate Suffering." *Global Environmental Politics* 14.2 (May 2014), pp. 1–6.

Watson, Paul. *Sea Shepherd: My Fight for Whales & Seals.* New York: W.W. Norton & Company, 1982.

Weiner, Jonathan. *The Beak of the Finch: A Story of Evolution in Our Time.* New York: Alfred A. Knopf, 1994.

Wheeler, Sara. *Terra Incognita: Travels in Antarctica.* New York: Random House, 1996.

The White House Office of the Press Secretary. "U.S.-China Joint Announcement on Climate Change." Beijing, China. 12 Nov. 2014. https://www.whitehouse.gov/the-press-office/2014/11/11/us-china-joint-announcement-climate-change. Accessed 24 Nov. 2014.

Wilder, Robert Jay. *Listening to the Sea: The Politics of Improving Environmental Protection.* Pittsburgh: University of Pittsburgh Press, 1998.

Wildlife Translocation Association. Heidelberg, South Africa. http://www.wtass.org/. Accessed 16 April 2014.

Wittmer, Margaret. *Florena.* Shropshire, UK: Anthony Nelson, 1989.

Wohlforth, Charles. *The Whale and the Supercomputer: On the Northern Front of Climate Change.* New York: North Point Press, 2004.

Woodford, James. *The Great Barrier Reef.* Rev. ed. Sydney, Australia: Macmillan, 2011.

"Woody Allen Interview—Vicky Cristina Barcelona," *Collider.com.* 15 Aug. 2008, http://collider.com/entertainment/interviews/article.asp/aid/8878/tcid/1/pg/2. Accessed 4 Jan. 2014.

The World Bank. "CO2 Emissions (Metric Tons per Capita)." Carbon Dioxide Information Analysis Center, Environmental Sciences Division, Oak Ridge National Laboratory, TN, United States. 2016. http://data.worldbank.org/indicator/EN.ATM.CO2E.PC. Accessed 24 Aug. 2016.

The World Bank. "Energy—The Facts." Aug. 2016. http://web.worldbank.org/WBSITE/EXTERNAL/TOPICS/EXTENERGY2/0,,contentMDK:22855502~pagePK:210058~piPK:210062~theSitePK:4114200,00.html.Accessed 20 Aug. 2016.

World Meteorological Organization. *WMO Sea-ice Nomenclature, Terminology, Codes and Illustrated Glossary.* Geneva, Switzerland: World Meteorological Organization, 1970.

Wyler, Liana Sun, and Pervaze A. Sheikh. "International Illegal Trade in Wildlife: Threats and U.S. Policy." Congressional Research Service, 23 July 2013. http://www.fas.org/sgp/crs/misc/RL34395.pdf.

Yago, Glenn. *The Decline of Transit: Urban Transformation in German and US Cities, 1900–1970*. New York: Cambridge University Press, 1984.

Yanarella, Ernest J., and Richard S. Levine. "Don't Pick the Low Lying Fruit." *Sustainability* 1.4 (August 2008). http://pages.ramapo.edu/~vasishth/Articles/Yanarella+Aim_High_for_Sustainability.pdf.

Yardley, Jim. "Illegal Districts Dot New Delhi as City Swells." *New York Times*, 27 April 2013. http://www.nytimes.com/2013/04/28/world/asia/unauthorized-colonies-dot-new-delhi-seeking-legal-status.html?_r=0. Accessed 26 Aug. 2015.

Yetiv, Steve. A. *Myths of the Oil Boom: American National Security in a Global Energy Market*. Oxford, UK: Oxford University Press, 2015.

Zolfagharifard, Ellie. "Carbon Emissions Reach 40 Billion Ton High." *Daily Mail*, 21 Sept. 2014. http://www.dailymail.co.uk/sciencetech/article-2764323/China-US-India-push-world-carbon-emissions-up.html. Accessed 1 June 2015.

INDEX

Note: Page numbers in italics indicate illustrations.